Sharon Rya

INTERVENTION, TERRORISM, AND TORTURE

AMINTAPHIL:
THE PHILOSOPHICAL FOUNDATIONS OF LAW AND JUSTICE

VOLUME 1

Series Editor:
Mortimer Sellers

INTERVENTION, TERRORISM, AND TORTURE

Contemporary Challenges to Just War Theory

Edited by

STEVEN P. LEE

*Hobart and William Smith Colleges,
Geneva, NY, U.S.A.*

A C.I.P. Catalogue record for this book is available from the Library of Congress.

ISBN-10 1-4020-4677-4 (HB)
ISBN-13 978-1-4020-4677-3 (HB)
ISBN-10 1-4020-4678-2 (e-book)
ISBN-13 978-1-4020-4678-0 (e-book)

Published by Springer,
P.O. Box 17, 3300 AA Dordrecht, The Netherlands.

www.springer.com

Printed on acid-free paper

All Rights Reserved
© 2007 Springer
No part of this work may be reproduced, stored in a retrieval system, or transmitted in any form or by any means, electronic, mechanical, photocopying, microfilming, recording or otherwise, without written permission from the Publisher, with the exception of any material supplied specifically for the purpose of being entered and executed on a computer system, for exclusive use by the purchaser of the work.

In memory of my sister
Sarah Jane Lee
(1951–2002)
who was taken before her time
from a life lived with quiet courage.

CONTENTS

Preface ix
Notes on Contributors xi

I. Introduction 1
   Just War Theory and the Challenges It Faces 3

II. Some Theoretical Background 21
   1. A Postmodern View of Just War 23
      William E. Murnion

   2. From Rights to Realism: Incoherence in Walzer's
      Conception of *Jus in Bello* 41
      David Duquette

   3. A Realist Response to Walzer's *Just and Unjust Wars* 59
      Patrick Hubbard

III. Intervention 73
   4. Walzer and Rawls on Just Wars and Humanitarian
      Interventions 75
      Rex Martin

   5. Humanitarian Intervention and Relational Sovereignty 89
      Helen Stacy

   6. Just War Theory Post 9/11: Perfect Terrorism
      and Superpower Defense 105
      Eugene E. Dais

   7. Preventive Intervention 119
      Steven P. Lee

IV. Terrorism 135
   8. Law, Just War, and the International Fight
      Against Terrorism: Is It War? 137
      Allen S. Weiner

9. Determining Moral Rectitude in Thwarting Suicide
Terrorist Attacks: Moral *Terra Incognita* 155
Jonathan Schonsheck

10. Terrorism and the Ethics of War 171
Stephen Nathanson

11. The War Against Terrorism and the "War"
Against Terrorism 187
Alistair M. Macleod

12. Terrorism and Universal Jurisdiction 203
Win-chiat Lee

V. Torture 219

13. Humanity, Prisoners of War, and Torture 221
Larry May

14. Assessing the Prohibition Against Torture 235
Kenneth Einar Himma

15. Liberalism, Torture, and the Ticking Bomb 249
David Luban

16. Torture and Self-Defense 263
Deirdre Golash

17. War Rape's Challenge to Just War Theory 273
Sally J. Scholz

18. Prisons, POW Camps, and Interrogation Centers:
Reflections on the Juridic Status of Detainees 289
Ken Kipnis

VI. The Impact of Technology 299

19. Non-Combatant Immunity in an Age of
High Tech Warfare 301
Richard T. De George

Index 315

PREFACE

This collection of essays is the first volume in a series entitled *AMINTAPHIL: The Philosophical Foundations of Law and Justice*, published by Springer under the general editorship of Mortimer Sellers of the University of Baltimore School of Law.

AMINTAPHIL, the American section of the International Association for Philosophy of Law and Social Philosophy (IVR), is an interdisciplinary professional organization that holds biennial meetings on issues of law, social ethics, and political theory. Its members include political philosophers, law professors, and political scientists.

The essays in this volume are based on papers originally presented at the 2004 meeting held at Stanford University in Palo Alto, California. The theme was Just War Theory: Contemporary Challenges. AMINTAPHIL has produced a number of earlier volumes of essays as well, and a list of these may be found at http://www.philosophy.utah.edu/AMINTAPHIL/publications.htm.

I would like to thank those who attended the 2004 meeting for some lively and insightful conversations, and the authors of the essays for the intellectual stimulation of working with them and their willingness to accept my comments and suggestions for revisions.

Steven P. Lee
Geneva, New York

NOTES ON CONTRIBUTORS

Eugene E. Dais is professor of law at the University of Calgary. He is editor or co-editor of three books and author of numerous articles in jurisprudence and constitutional law. His recent research focuses on political legitimacy and the use of force in the post 9/11 era.

Richard T. De George is University Distinguished Professor of Philosophy, and Co-Director of the International Center for Ethics in Business at the University of Kansas. He is the author or editor of 20 books, including *The Ethics of Information Technology and Business* (2003), and *Business Ethics* (2005), and past president of the American Philosophical Association.

David Duquette is professor of philosophy at St. Norbert College, De Pere, Wisconsin. He has published essays and articles in social and political thought and is also the editor of *Hegel's History of Philosophy: New Interpretations* (SUNY Press, 2003).

Deirdre Golash is associate professor in the interdisciplinary Department of Justice, Law and Society at American University. She is the author of *The Case Against Punishment* (NYU Press, 2005).

Kenneth Einar Himma is an associate professor of philosophy at Seattle Pacific University and formerly taught in the philosophy department, information school, and law school at the University of Washington. He specializes in legal philosophy, applied ethics, and information ethics.

Patrick Hubbard is the Ronald Motley Distinguished Professor of Law at the University of South Carolina School of Law.

Kenneth Kipnis is a professor in the department of philosophy at the University of Hawaii at Manoa. He is currently working on ethics in medical research.

Steven P. Lee is professor of philosophy at Hobart and William Smith Colleges. He writes on issues in moral and political philosophy, especially just war theory. Among his books is *Morality, Prudence, and Nuclear Weapons* (Cambridge, 1993, 1996).

Win-chiat Lee is associate professor of philosophy at Wake Forest University, where he also served as the chair of the philosophy department from 1993 to 2001.

David Luban is Frederick Haas Professor of Law and Philosophy at Georgetown University Law Center, Washington, DC. His interests include just war theory, legal ethics, and international criminal law, and his latest book, *Lawyers, Ethics, and Justice*, will be published in 2006 by Cambridge University Press.

Alistair M. Macleod teaches moral and political philosophy at Queen's University (Canada). In addition to a short book, *Social Justice, Progressive Politics, and Taxes* (2004), his recent publications include papers on free markets and democracy, the right to vote, the economic freedom ideal, and Rawls's narrow doctrine of human rights in *The Law of Peoples*.

Rex Martin has held university appointments in both the United States and the United Kingdom. Currently he is professor of philosophy at the University of Kansas and honorary professor at Cardiff University. His most recent book is *Rawls's Law of Peoples: A Realistic Utopia?* (co-editor) (Oxford: Blackwell, forthcoming 2006).

Larry May is professor of philosophy at Washington University in St. Louis. He has published 16 books, most recently *Crimes Against Humanity* (Cambridge, 2005), *War Crimes and Just Wars* (Cambridge, forthcoming), and an anthology, *The Morality of War* (Prentice-Hall, 2006).

William E. Murnion (dba PhilosophyWorks) is an independent scholar, lecturer, and counselor. His research interests, besides social and political philosophy, are philosophy of mind, methodology, Aquinas, and Lonergan.

Stephen Nathanson is professor of philosophy at Northeastern University in Boston. He is the author of several books including *Patriotism, Morality, and Peace* (Rowman and Littlefield, 1993) and *Economic Justice* (Prentice Hall, 1998), as well as papers on terrorism and the ethics of war.

Sally J. Scholz is associate professor of philosophy at Villanova University. Her research is in social and political philosophy, and her books include *On de Beauvoir* (2000), *On Rousseau* (2001), and the co-edited *Peacemaking: Lessons from the Past, Vision for the Future* (2001) (with Judith Presler).

Jonathan Schonsheck is professor of philosophy at Le Moyne College in Syracuse, New York. He has published widely on an array of issues in applied moral philosophy, including social and political philosophy, philosophy of law, and business ethics – which he teaches in Le Moyne's MBA Program.

Helen Stacy is a professor at Stanford Law School and the Freeman Spogli Institute for International Studies. She works in the areas of international law, jurisprudence, and human rights. She was in the Faculty of Law at Queensland University of Technology in Australia and practiced law with Shell Oil Company and as a senior crown prosecutor in the United Kingdom.

Allen S. Weiner is the Warren Christopher Professor of the Practice of International Law and Diplomacy and Associate Professor of Law (Teaching) at Stanford Law School and the Freeman Spogli Institute for International Studies at Stanford. Before joining the Stanford faculty, he served in the Legal Adviser's Office of the United States Department of State.

I. INTRODUCTION

JUST WAR THEORY AND THE CHALLENGES IT FACES

The extent to which the world changed on 9/11, with the terrorist attacks on New York and Washington, is a matter of debate. But, even if the attacks did not themselves introduce significant changes, it is clear that they highlighted and accelerated changes that were already underway in the role of military violence. This volume is an examination of the moral implications of those changes. The chapters consider how these changes should be understood in moral terms.

Traditionally, matters of the morality of military violence have been understood and assessed in terms of Just War Theory (JWT). This volume examines the extent to which recent changes in the role of military violence pose challenges to JWT. How has the role of military violence changed, and what are the moral implications? There are different ways in which this question might be approached. In this introduction, I will approach it by asking whether JWT is adequate to handle the challenges, or whether instead it needs to be revised or abandoned in favor of a different approach. What does it mean to ask whether JWT is adequate to the contemporary challenges? JWT has always been understood not as an abstract moral theory, but as a practical guide for political leaders and military personnel in their decisions about the employment of military violence. The adequacy of JWT is bound up with its continuing ability to serve this practical function. If the contemporary changes have left the theory unable to provide practical guidance, the theory is now inadequate.

JWT consists of a set of rules and norms that seek to control military violence, to limit or restrict its exercise. It is a theory of limited war. Unlike doctrines of pacifism, it does not seek to outlaw all war; it assumes that some military violence is morally justified. It accepts the assumption that in a world of sovereign states without an overarching governing authority, military violence must be available to states, at least to protect themselves from aggression. At the same time, unlike doctrines of realism, JWT does not assume that any use of military violence that furthers a belligerent's national interests is justified; it seeks to impose moral limits on military violence. It assumes that even in a world of sovereign states, states have some mutual moral obligations not to interfere with each other. As a theory of limited war, JWT is in a middle position, so to speak, between pacifism and realism, allowing some uses of military violence and disallowing others. Its adequacy is tied to its ability to maintain that sometimes precarious middle position, not to move too close to, or collapse into, either realism or pacifism. If JWT moves too close to realism, it is not serving its moral function. If it moves too far from realism, it is not serving its practical action-guiding function because military decision-makers will simply ignore rules that require too great a sacrifice of national self-interest.

The just war rules have been developed over time in response to given social, political, and technological realities, and, as these realities change, the question arises whether the rules remain adequate, whether they retain their action-guiding function. The concern is that the nature of current changes in military violence will deprive the theory of its practical import, relegating it to the status of an abstract moral theory without practical applicability, a classroom exercise, lacking relevance to those making decisions on the use of military violence. Or, perhaps the theory, in the face of the changes, continues to provide practical moral guidance to military decision-makers, proving adequate to the changes.

The rules of JWT are rules of moral permissibility. They indicate to military leaders and combatants (as well as to those observing their behavior) when military violence is allowed and when not. One part of JWT, *jus ad bellum*, consists of conditions that must be satisfied for a war to be initiated or joined. The conditions are that the war have a just cause; that it be declared by legitimate authority; that it be fought with the right intention; that the harm reasonably expected to be done by the war be proportionate to (i.e., not exceed) the good the war can be reasonably expected to achieve; and that the war be a last resort. The other part of the theory, *jus in bello*, involves principles that must be satisfied by the way violence is used to achieve the military objectives of a war. The two chief principles of *jus in bello* are discrimination, which requires that attacks not be made against civilians and civilian targets, and proportionality, which requires that particular military actions contribute to winning the war (i.e., cause no gratuitous harm) and contribute sufficiently to that end to outweigh the harm they are likely to do.

What are the contemporary changes to which JWT is called upon to respond? Perhaps the most important change is the accelerating pace of globalization, the growing economic and informational interconnectedness of nations. Globalization is affecting what parties are engaging in military violence, how that violence is organized and used, and the weapons available for its use. Other important changes are part of, or are reinforced by, globalization. One is the decline in state sovereignty; sovereignty is the idea that each state has exclusive authority over its own internal affairs and should not be subject to interference by other states. A second is the burgeoning international human rights movement, which is creating practical global standards for how states should treat their citizens. A third is the rise of international, nonstate terrorism. Another is the diffusion, through proliferation, and the resulting wider availability, of especially destructive military technologies, such as weapons of mass destruction. A related change is the Revolution in Military Affairs, the way the uses of military violence have been affected by the development of advanced forms of military technology, such as precision-guided munitions.

All these have led to changes in the use of military violence, and these pose challenges to JWT. Three of these challenges receive extended discussion in Parts III, IV, and V – intervention, terrorism, and torture. A fourth challenge is the development and use of high-tech weaponry discussed in Part VI. Part II addresses in a general way JWT and the challenges it faces.

1. THE RESOURCES OF JUST WAR THEORY

To begin to address the question whether JWT is adequate to the contemporary challenges, it is necessary first to have a better understanding of the theory itself and its resources. The history of the theory suggests that its capacity to encompass new forms of military violence is extensive. From the time that JWT was systematically formulated in the Middle Ages, there have been a series of revolutions in the nature of warfare. Through these, the theory has proved surprisingly flexible; it has survived and retained its practical relevance, though not without modifications. But is its flexibility sufficient to the changes of our own era?

The adaptability of JWT is strongly argued for by William Murnion in Chapter 1. He takes a perspective on the nature of the just war theory different from that presented above. In his view, the just war approach is not strictly a theory or a tradition yielding univocal judgments about the morality of particular wars or methods of fighting. It is rather a heuristic construct, a way of considering and talking about the morality of war. The just war perspective contrasts with four alternative approaches: realism, pacifism (as mentioned earlier), militarism, and idealism. These alternative approaches can be distinguished by different epistemological and ontological assumptions they make, and each can be found historically in both religious and secular forms. Part of the adaptability of the just war approach is its ability to take on characteristics of one or another of these alternatives. Murnion sketches the history of just war thinking, portraying it as a series of four paradigm shifts, from the divine law approach of Augustine, to the natural law approach of Aquinas, to the law of nations approach of Vitoria and Grotius, to the contemporary international law approach. It is the lability of the just war heuristic that makes it "the last best hope for meeting the contemporary challenges to the ethics of warfare."

Chapters 2 and 3 provide a more pessimistic read on the adequacy of JWT. Both David Duquette and Patrick Hubbard see the resources of JWT as more limited and currently under significant strain. The chapters concern the relationship between JWT and realism, and each criticizes the views on this relationship of Michael Walzer, the most prominent contemporary expositor of JWT.[1] Duquette faults Walzer for presenting a form of JWT that moves too close to realism, while Hubbard faults Walzer for not moving far enough toward realism. Despite their coming at the issue from opposite directions, each author would probably endorse the point that for JWT to be adequate, it must move much closer to realism. Hubbard endorses this move, finding in it the only way for the theory to retain its relevance, while Duquette condemns the move, seeing it as an abandonment of the theory as a coherent moral perspective.

Duquette sees the moral heart of JWT in the principle of discrimination, which expresses a respect for human rights. But the action-guiding capacity of this principle is always under pressure because the principle can interfere with the ability of a state to achieve its military goals. Duquette argues that Walzer's treatment of the issue of civilian deaths through "collateral damage" shows that he has moved the theory too far in an accommodation to realism. This is also the case with Walzer's doctrine of "supreme emergency," under which states are allowed to directly attack civilians if the attacking community faces utter destruction. When JWT is under pressure from realism to weaken its commitment to human rights, it must stand its ground, so to speak. Walzer's version of JWT tilts too far toward realism. The theory gains in adequacy, but its coherence as a moral theory is undermined.

Hubbard, on the other hand, reproaches Walzer for presenting a theory that cannot adequately guide action. Walzer argues that his version of JWT is action-guiding because the moral language it deploys can constrain policy choices before the fact and serve to hold leaders and combatants responsible after the fact. But it does neither. The moral language of the theory does not constrain policy choices because of the nature of the political process and the way that moral language is used to rationalize decisions made on other grounds. Moreover, leaders often regard their rule-violating actions as morally required because they are acting on their moral role responsibility to protect their nations. Nor does the moral language effectively hold leaders and combatants responsible after the fact. Walzer introduces supreme emergency as an attempt to deal with this problem, but it does not go far enough. Leaders regard all wars as emergencies, and tend to violate the constraints of the theory across the board.

Duquette calls for a less realist theory for the sake of moral coherence, while Hubbard calls for one closer to realism for the sake of practical effectiveness. In Hubbard's view, if the new forms of military violence are seen as necessary, they will be practiced whatever the theory prescribes. The opposing positions of Duquette and Hubbard represent one of the problems this volume addresses. To maintain its coherence and its integrity as a moral theory, JWT would have to prohibit the new forms of military violence. Because these new forms are seen as militarily necessary, this would weaken the theory as a practical guide to military action.

2. INTERVENTION

Intervention involves the first use or initiation of military force by one state against another in the absence of the latter's having committed aggression. Recently, two forms of intervention have come into prominence, humanitarian intervention, the use of military force to stop massive human rights violations in another state, and preventive intervention, the use of military force in response not to actual or imminent attack, but to an expected future attack. For example, the 1999 Kosovo War was a humanitarian intervention, while the 2003 Iraq War was a preventive intervention. Both of these forms of intervention have a long history, but recent changes have brought them to the fore. The changes fostering humanitarian intervention include the growth in the international human rights movement and an increase in the number and severity of intrastate ethnic conflicts, leading in some cases to genocide or ethnic cleansing. The changes fostering preventive intervention include the growth in international terrorism and the wider availability of destructive technologies. In addition, both forms of intervention have been given momentum by the decline of state sovereignty.

The main question is whether the reasons offered for humanitarian or preventive interventions provide a just cause under *jus ad bellum*. Intervention is often seen as morally problematic because the only just cause for going to war is thought to be self-defense, so that a state is prohibited from initiating war.[2] On this view, interventions are nondefensive wars and so forms of aggression. The prohibition of aggression is based on respect for national sovereignty. Does JWT have the resources to accommodate either humanitarian or preventive intervention?

Chapter 4 by Rex Martin is devoted largely to humanitarian intervention. He discusses the similar versions of JWT offered by Walzer and John Rawls.[3] Both Walzer and Rawls regard humanitarian intervention as justified, but it is unclear how this view fits into their overall theories. In general, humanitarian intervention is justified on the grounds of the defense of human rights, but, more specifically, we need to know what level of rights violations is required for intervention and what the theoretical justification for picking that level is. Martin finds that Walzer and Rawls answer the question of the required level of rights violations largely by pointing to shared judgments (intervention is justified when the rights violations "shock the conscience of mankind"), but do not provide theoretical underpinnings for their answers. Concerning the question of who should authorize intervention, which concerns the *jus ad bellum* condition of legitimate authority, Walzer and Rawls move away from regarding unilateral intervention as justified toward requiring some form of international authorization, though not necessarily by the United Nations.

Humanitarian intervention is also the subject of Chapter 5 by Helen Stacy. She argues that such intervention lacks an adequate foundation in international law, and, through appealing to what she calls relational sovereignty, she proposes legal revisions that would justify it. Relational sovereignty is a recognition that globalization has altered the conditions of sovereignty by blurring the distinction between domestic and international politics and making a government's claims of immunity from intervention conditional on its respecting its citizens' human rights. Stacy addresses the issue of the level of human rights violations needed to justify intervention by appealing to the legal doctrine of equity and to an analogy between intervention and individual rescue under tort law. This leads to the position that humanitarian intervention is justified when human rights violations are widespread and extreme, the victims support the intervention, and the intervention promises to do more good than harm. A fourth criterion is that the intervener be committed to helping the state to rebuild its institutions to avoid a recurrence of the humanitarian crisis.[4] Moreover, Stacy argues that intervention may be justified not only when victims are being killed, but when they are being starved.

Preventive intervention is taken up by Eugene Dais in Chapter 6. He argues that the world has seen the advent of "perfect terrorism," terrorism perpetrated by members of stateless organizations with potential access to weapons of mass destruction. Perfect terrorism justifies a form of preventive intervention. The goal of perfect terrorism has been the termination of the hegemonic role the United States plays in world affairs. Since the end of the cold war, the United States has become the single world superpower, and as such it has assumed a hegemonic role of policing the world to maintain the conditions of free trade and mutual prosperity. This has meant, for example, keeping the oil flowing, leading to its hegemonic interference in Middle Eastern politics. Islamic terrorists have attacked the United States to get it to abandon such interference. Given the extreme threat posed by perfect terrorism, it is necessary for the hegemon, in violation of the normal constraints of *jus ad bellum*, to have an exclusive right to engage in a form of preventive intervention, a "protective right of first strike." But this creates a problem of fairness, since the right is special to the hegemon. Partly in response to the fairness issue, Dais places a tight set of constraints upon the exercise of this right.

A different perspective on preventive intervention is offered by Steven Lee in Chapter 7. By focusing on the *jus ad bellum* criteria of just cause and proportionality, he argues that preventive intervention is not justified. He discusses just cause in terms of a domestic analogy between individual autonomy and state sovereignty. As it would be wrong to interfere with an individual based only on suspicions about his or her future malign actions, absent the initiation of such actions, so it would be wrong to attack a state based only on expectations of its future aggression. Preventive intervention fails also to satisfy proportionality because the consequences of such intervention are very likely to be negative, if we count not only the direct consequences of the particular intervention but also the indirect consequences on the international system, including an increase in the likelihood of war through the precedent of that intervention. But there remains the argument that the "new circumstances" of international terrorism require our rethinking this case against preventive intervention, but Lee concludes that the argument against preventive intervention holds nonetheless.

Martin's discussion suggests that just war theory may have some problems with humanitarian intervention, suggesting that changes in the theory may be needed. Stacy sees the need for changes in international law to accommodate such intervention, and since international law largely tracks JWT, this may support the need for changes in the theory as well. Dais endorses the need for changes in either JWT or international law to accommodate preventive intervention because such intervention is now necessary. Lee agrees that JWT would need to be changed to accommodate preventive intervention, but he does not endorse such changes.

Thus, it seems that Dais takes the Hubbard side of the more general argument, while Lee takes the Duquette side.

3. TERRORISM

The growth in the lethality and reach of international nonstate terrorism is perhaps the most prominent change in the use of military violence challenging the traditional understandings of the morality of war. One moral question for the states at risk from such terrorism is what their response to it should be. A question for us is whether JWT is adequate in providing an answer. This part addresses issues in addition to whether terrorism justifies preventive intervention. Is terrorism itself ever justified? Should the principle of discrimination be taken as a moral absolute? What should we say about the terrorism of state actors? Is a "war" against terrorism an appropriate, a morally justified, or even a coherent response? What about other, nonmilitary methods of fighting terrorism? Terrorism is an attempt to further political goals by using violence against civilians, and this definition applies to states as well as nonstate actors. Indeed, terrorism has been practiced by states that are the current victims of nonstate terrorists. It is interesting to note that terrorism has come in for special concern only since it has begun to be practiced by nonstate actors against states.

Approaching the question from international law, Allen Weiner in Chapter 8 asks whether the "war" against terrorism currently being waged by the United States is really a war. While it is not a war as defined by international law, it may be regarded as a war by a plausible "functional extrapolation" from international law. But there is an important caveat. Being in a state of war entails various legal restraints on the belligerents. The United States is not abiding by these restraints, as is evident, for example, in its claiming a right to attack individuals and states not part of al-Qaeda, ignoring the rights to which detainees in war are entitled, and not recognizing the reciprocity inherent in war. This undermines the claim that the United States could legitimately regard its activities as war under the functional extrapolation argument. The lack of proper restraints by the United States calls into question its being at war in a legal sense, and thus its right to take various actions to which it would be entitled were it at war.

The moral uniqueness of the threat posed by terrorism is emphasized by Jonathan Schonsheck in Chapter 9, and, like Dais, he argues that this may justify preventive intervention. But his argument for this is different and his conclusions more tentative. The moral uniqueness of the threat means that morality, including JWT, provides no guidance, but at the same time no basis for denying that preventive intervention is justified. The *sui generis* character of contemporary terrorism lies in the fact that suicide terrorists are neither combatants nor criminals and are undeterrable. Because defense cannot be sufficiently effective, the response to the threat must go beyond defense; it must be preventive. JWT does not provide guidance because the conflict between the United States and the terrorists is asymmetric, not only materially, but morally. The theory's assumption of moral universalism fails. Also failing to provide guidance is the Kantian argument that an action is morally permissible only if it is universalizable. The reason is that nations are not like individuals. We are in a moral *terra incognita*, and it is unclear where we go for guidance.

In his discussion of terrorism, Stephen Nathanson in Chapter 10 notes that, while the rhetoric of the war on terrorism condemns terrorism in the strongest moral terms, people often react cynically to this condemnation. This is due to the hypocrisy many sense on the part of those offering these condemnations, resulting from their failure to condemn terrorism practiced by states. What is needed for a credible condemnation of terrorism is a consistent and rigorous application of the principle of discrimination to all parties engaged in military violence, whether state or nonstate actor. This means condemning not only state actions such as the city bombings of World War II, but also much of the "collateral damage" killings of civilians. This is where JWT comes up short. If the theory includes Walzer's the doctrine of supreme emergency, it regards deliberate civilian killings as sometimes justified, and, even if it does not, it still accepts too many civilian deaths under the doctrine of double effect. In the indifference it shows to civilian lives, this doctrine is morally equivalent to terrorism. A credible condemnation of terrorism must endorse a moral theory that shows a greater respect for civilian lives. This is a theory that includes what he terms the "bend over backwards" principle of reducing the risk of civilian deaths.

In his discussion, Alistair Macleod in Chapter 11, distinguishes a literal (military) war against terrorism from a metaphorical one, where the means are nonmilitary, and explores reasons that the latter may be preferable to the former, both morally and prudentially. Even if military retaliation against terrorist attacks is deserved, it often ends up killing many innocent parties. This makes it both counterproductive and morally problematic. The best strategy for combating terrorism is a function of the best explanation for terrorism's emergence and persistence. In determining the best explanation, we must consider not only the motives of the terrorists, but also the motives of their supporters, without whom the terrorism could not continue. Also, we must recognize that in explaining terrorism, we are not justifying it, and in acting in the light of that explanation, we must not shrink from being willing to abandon sacrosanct foreign policies, so long as they are not obligatory. Also, we must not be scared off by a concern not to "give in to terrorists", for, if terrorists have adopted a demand in order to garner political support, refusing to give into that demand may play into the terrorists' hands.

Among nonmilitary alternatives to fighting terrorism, legal responses loom large. The legal response is explored by Win-chiat Lee in Chapter 12, who argues that terrorist crimes should be matters of universal jurisdiction, crimes that any state has a right to prosecute. Universal jurisdiction is jurisdiction independent of the two factors that have traditionally defined jurisdiction, territoriality and nationality. The need for terrorist crimes to be under universal jurisdiction is shown by the extradition dilemma: If a state receives an extradition request for a terrorist suspect, and the requesting state does not allow due process of law, the receiving state would face the dilemma of either handing over the suspect to an unjust procedure or allowing him or her to escape prosecution. If terrorist crimes were of universal jurisdiction, then the state could avoid the dilemma by trying the suspect itself. Genocide and other crimes against humanity have been viewed as subject to universal jurisdiction because they are heinous crimes that are likely to occur in states that are unlikely to prosecute them. Terrorist crimes create a related but opposite problem: they are likely to be prosecuted locally, but in a way not respectful of due process. In both cases, extradition-dilemma style arguments imply that universal jurisdiction is appropriate.

Weiner, from an international legal perspective, argues that the military war against terrorism is not justified. Nathanson, from a moral perspective, argues that a coherent struggle against terrorism requires that moral strictures on military violence not be weakened, but strengthened. His concern, like Duquette's, is not so much the practical adequacy of JWT but rather its intellectual adequacy, its ability to support a consistent language of condemnation, one that does not sustain a double standard between states and nonstate actors. Schonsheck is also concerned about a moral double standard, as in the Kantian requirement of universalizability, but he argues that preventive action against nonstate terrorism would not create a double standard because of the *sui generis* nature of such terrorism. The discussions of nonmilitary responses to terrorism by Macleod and W. Lee indirectly support the practical adequacy of JWT, in that they suggest that there are effective, nonmilitary approaches in responding to terrorism.

4. TORTURE

Torture, like terrorism, involves an abuse of fundamental human rights. Torture can be the imposition of gratuitous suffering, but it can also, like terrorism, be a means to an end, such as the extraction of information believed to be possessed by the victim. It is torture in the latter sense that is the main focus of discussion in this part. Torture has been practiced throughout history, but its prominence now is due to its being practiced as a matter of policy, despite denials, by the United States. Interestingly, while terrorism has our attention now that it is being practiced by the weak, torture has our attention now that it is being practiced by the strong. The moral challenge torture poses is the adequacy of the *jus in bello* rules that condemn it, given that it is believed to be militarily necessary. Given the nature of nonstate terrorism, proponents argue that the torture of detainees for information is a necessary means of defense. There are several moral questions about torture: What is the moral basis of the claim that torture is wrong? Are there any situations (such as in the so-called ticking time bomb example) where torture is justified? Given that torture is now practiced, should we seek to bring it under control or to end it, and how should we do this?

In his discussion of torture, Larry May in Chapter 13 begins by noting that, though torture is now being discussed as a live possibility, it has long been condemned by international law. Because our rejection of torture is based on the idea that it is an inhumane form of treatment, the question is how the notion of humanity condemns torture. Grotius provides some help, pointing out that humane treatment is especially required in the case of prisoners of war (POW) because of their defenseless and dependent position. While justice might not bar all forms of captive abuse, humanity does. Based on considerations of humanity, the dependent position of the captive creates either a fiduciary obligation, or at least a stewardship obligation, of captors toward their captives. But do these considerations apply in extreme cases of military necessity? Could the permissibility to torture in such cases be based on an analogue to Walzer's idea of supreme emergency? May admits that there may be such cases, but he argues that they would be so few that it would be better to adopt an absolute ban on torture.

But it is the perceived military necessity of torture in fighting terrorism that drives the contemporary case for torture. This argument is encapsulated in the hypothetical example of the "ticking time bomb," in which a person in custody knows the whereabouts of a bomb set shortly to explode, killing multitudes of innocent people, and can be got to reveal its location only under torture. The next three authors, assuming, like May, the general unjustifiability of torture, address especially this extreme case.

In Chapter 14, Kenneth Himma notes that the possibility of nuclear terrorism shows that the ticking time bomb example is not so far-fetched. Many regard torture as absolutely morally wrong, but that would make the anti-torture principle unique among general moral principles in being exceptionless. In fact, however, our recognition that torture may be justified in the ticking time bomb example shows the principle is not absolute. But, how broad is the exception? Conditions must be met for torture to be permissible, among which are that the threatened harm is grave, that the suspect is morally culpable, that torture is the only way to prevent the harm, and that the suspect can stop the torture by talking. In addition, the authorities must have proof beyond a reasonable doubt that these conditions hold. Torture does present culpable suspects with a forced choice, but a forced choice may be justified in such cases because the suspects' culpability implies that forcing the information from them would be forcing them only not to do wrong.

Chapter 15 by David Luban draws a different conclusion about the ticking time bomb example. The prevalence of this example results from the way that torture figures in the liberal imagination. Torture is a serious wrong for liberals because, by putting its victims under the will of the torturer and stripping them of their dignity, it is morally analogous to tyranny. At the same time, torture in the bomb example is meant to save many innocent lives, and this goal is part of the liberal project. The example bewitches liberals by appearing to allow torture as an exception to the general prohibition. The example is rhetorically powerful because it forces liberals away from an absolutist position and into a posture of haggling over the consequentialist price of torture. Luban sets out to disarm the example as "an intellectual fraud." First, the example is a fiction, in the sense that we cannot have the degree of certainty that the example stipulates. Second, the example looks at torture as an isolated case, when we live in a world of practices. To allow torture would be to allow a practice, and so a culture, of torture, and this is unacceptable.

The ticking time bomb example is also the starting point for Chapter 16 by Deirdre Golash, but her moral objections to torture run deeper than Luban's. While agreeing with him that the stipulations regarding the certainty of belief in the example cannot be satisfied, she argues that torture would not be justified even if they were. Part of the case for torture, as Himma argues, is that the suspect is known to be culpable, so the torture is not of an innocent person. But this does not, Golash argues, make a moral difference. The harm of torturing a culpable suspect is qualitatively different from, and worse than, the harm inflicted in punishment or even in self-defense. (Torture for information is morally worse than torture for punishment.) Retributive punishment requires respect for human dignity, but dignity is what torture for information denies. Torture requires that the victim betray herself or himself. The object of the torturer is to break or usurp the suspect's will. The moral issue of torture for information puts to us the question of what we value and who we are or what the bomber can force us to become. Torture in extremity is problematic not simply because it would require an institution, but because it is wrong apart from that.

Another form of torture in a military context is war rape, an issue discussed by Sally Scholz in Chapter 17. War rape is a form of torture when done gratuitously, with no military goal, as has generally been the case in the past, and it has long been recognized as a war crime. But contemporary war rape is mass rape, and, like torture for information, has become a means to an end. Mass rape may be intended to demoralize communities, achieve ethnic cleansing, or perpetrate genocide. It is genocidal when, for example, its purpose is to impregnate women whose children, with fathers from a different ethnic group, will not be accepted in the women's group, thereby helping to destroy that group. JWT may be adequate to our moral understanding of individual war rape, but not mass rape. A just-war individual rights approach cannot account for several features of mass rape, such as the bodily nature of the violation (which it shares in part with other torture), its cultural meaning, and the way mass rape can straddle the line between being a concern of *jus ad bellum* and a concern of *jus in bello*.

The main concern about torture has been its practice by the United States, post-9/11, as a means of obtaining information on the terrorist threat. Chapter 18 by Ken Kipnis addresses the institutional question of how these interrogation-by-torture practices are pursued. A global network of interrogation centers has been created, and these centers are neither POW camps nor prisons (echoing Schonsheck's claim that contemporary terrorists are neither combatants nor criminals.) The centers are designed to maximize the extraction of information with as little outside (domestic or international) legal interference as possible, a purpose different from that of prisons or POW camps. This lack of legal oversight has created a "jurisprudential *terra incognita*". What should the legal response to this reality be? How should these new legal institutions be regularized so as to bring them under some kind of legal constraints? These institutions may be here to stay; like the Japanese internment camps of World War II, the United States public has largely acquiesced in their existence. If the interrogation centers are here to stay, the job of social and legal philosophy is to think about how they can be brought under legal regulation.

Himma argues that the ticking time bomb example is a justified case of torture, showing that the moral prohibition against torture is not absolute. May and Luban seem to agree that the example may be a justified case in the abstract, but argue that the prohibition should be absolute nonetheless. Golash's moral understanding of torture does not recognize the possibility of a justified case. None of the four authors base his or her argument directly on JWT, but the conclusions of May, Luban, and Golash are in accord with the prohibition on torture implicit in the *jus in bello* principle of discrimination and conventions about prisoners. In contrast, Himma's argument supporting justified torture is in line with the claim that torture may be militarily necessary and that morality must accommodate this. Implicit in this claim is that just war theory and its implied absolute prohibition of torture is now inadequate as a practical guide. Scholz argues that JWT is inadequate in a different way, in its failure to conceptualize the harm of mass war rape.

5. TECHNOLOGY

The Revolution in Military Affairs is the transformation of the battlefield by technological developments such as accurate guidance systems, remote sensing, and computational power. Chapter 19 by Richard De George focuses on the moral implications. One fruit of the new technology is the "smart bomb," an explosive that can be delivered with much greater accuracy than in the past. Such weapons make states potentially more effective in adhering to the principle of discrimination because, with greater accuracy, the bombs have smaller explosive yields and do less collateral damage. As a result, the principle of discrimination has implications in peace as well as war. One new moral obligation is that states develop better smart bombs during peacetime, so as to be able to be more discriminatory when war comes, despite the counterintuitive implication of a morally prescribed arms race. A second obligation is that states assist their opponents by sharing with them the smart-bomb technology, thereby allowing them to be more discriminatory as well. Another obligation is that states have public debates on whether there should be international prohibitions on the development of certain forms of harmful technology such as directed energy weapons, which would kill many innocents indirectly by destroying the electronic systems on which urban life depends. Finally, computer technology now makes possible "private" wars fought over the internet by individual hackers against perceived foreign enemies, and there is a new obligation not to engage in such freelancing.

De George's proposal that these new obligations be considered implicit in JWT may show another way in which the theory is now at odds with military necessity. For example, if it is a matter of military necessity to keep one's military technology secret from one's opponent, then the first of De George's obligations would run counter to this.[5]

6. DOES JUST WAR THEORY MEET THE CHALLENGES?

Is JWT adequate to address the recent changes in the use of military violence?[6] Murnion argues that it is. The theory can accommodate great social, political, and technological change because it is a heuristic construct rather than a theory in a strict sense. In contrast, Duquette and Hubbard see a problem for JWT. To what extent can and should the theory resist a move toward realism? The concerns of realism are implicated in the recent changes in the use of military violence because some of these changes are seen as a matter of military necessity. Realism is, at minimum, the view that what is militarily necessary is permissible. Duquette argues, in effect, that just war theory should hold fast, resisting the call that these new forms of violence be regarded as morally permissible. This position risks the adequacy of JWT because, to the extent that the theory prohibits what is thought to be militarily necessary, its counsel will be ignored by military decision-makers. This is one of the main concerns of Hubbard, who argues that the theory must accommodate itself more fully to realism. Walzer's appeal to supreme emergency is, in their view, an accommodation to realism, but it goes too far for Duquette and not far enough for Hubbard.

The challenges to JWT may show the theory to be inadequate and thus indicate the need for it to be either revised or abandoned. But the inadequacies are of two kinds and would have to be addressed in different ways, one by revision and one by abandonment. The first kind, calling for theory revision, is seen, for example, in the challenge posed by humanitarian intervention. This may require, as Martin and Stacy suggest, that the rules of *jus ad bellum* be revised to permit the violation of sovereignty in the case of a great humanitarian crisis, but such a revision in JWT is consistent with the basic principles of the theory, namely, a concern for human rights. So to change the rules in the required way does not lead to a radical alternation in the theory; it is a matter of consistent development rather than radical change. The second kind of inadequacy, posed, for example, by preventive intervention may, as Dais suggests, require a radical change in the theory. This is because such intervention requires a violation of sovereignty that is not directly related to securing human rights. Changes in the theory in response to the second kind of inadequacy, because they seem at odds with its core moral values, bring the theory closer to realism. Here it is more appropriate to talk about an abandonment of the theory rather than a revision.

How would one argue for changing or abandoning the theory in this radical way? Consider that pacifism is sometimes criticized on the grounds that, since there will always be wars, it is better to adopt a moral theory, like JWT, that seeks to limit the violence of war, than to stick to a theory like pacifism that abandons the battlefield, so to speak, leaving military violence unrestrained. While the moral force of this criticism is unclear, because it may be pragmatic rather than moral, the same kind of criticism can be used against those, such as Duquette, who refuse to abandon just war theory in favor of a theory closer to realism. If there are going now to be preventive interventions, better to revise JWT to seek to bring them under limited control. The legal analogue of this criticism underlies the discussion of detention centers by Kipnis. Because the detention centers now exist, better to adopt the law in an effort to seek some kind of legal control over them than to treat them as outside the law and refuse to deal with them legally. But the claim that it is be morally appropriate to argue in this way for changes in an applied moral theory, such as JWT, is controversial.

Of course, in the face of the second kind of inadequacy, it is always open to defenders of JWT to argue against the assumptions about military necessity on which the arguments for the theory's inadequacy are based. This can be done conceptually or empirically. The conceptual approach is taken by Walzer, who argues that true military necessity, the necessity that can override the principle of discrimination, holds only in extremis, when the life of a community is at stake.[7] None of the new forms of military violence seem to rise to this standard.[8] The empirical approach is represented, for example, by Macleod, who suggests that nonmilitary responses to terrorism may be more effective, indeed, that military responses may be counterproductive.

We come in the end back to the idea that the change in circumstances chiefly driving the growth in the new forms of military violence is the decline in state sovereignty, the fact that states have less control over what happens to their citizens than used to be the case. This has been moving states toward accepting stronger forms of international governance, and a number of the chapters make reference to the ways in which developments in international law play or should play a role in controlling the new forms of military violence. This does not necessarily affect JWT, at least as long as these developments allow states to do what JWT allows them to do anyway. But when international law begins to take out of state's hands decisions about the use of military violence, just war theory may face a challenge of a different sort. That this kind of growth in international law may be an appropriate moral development is suggested by Walzer and Rawls, who, as Martin notes, see the need for an international organization, rather than single states, to authorize humanitarian intervention. This might be appropriate as well, contra Dais, in the case of preventive intervention. More generally, Murnion cites Yoram Dinstein and David Rodin, who argue that the world should move toward a cosmopolitan regime of collective security and law enforcement.[9] This may be morally desirable, but it seems to be an abandonment of JWT, which has always assumed the preeminence of the sovereign state. When all is police enforcement, there is no need for war or its rules.

NOTES

1. Michael Walzer, *Just and Unjust Wars*, 3rd edn (New York: Basic Books, 2000, 1977).
2. Unless an attack from the target state is imminent, in which case the initial strike is preemptive and not a case of intervention. The distinction between preemption and prevention is one of the controversial issues in this area.
3. Walzer, *Just and Unjust Wars*; John Rawls, *The Law of Peoples* (Cambridge, MA: Harvard University Press, 1999).
4. This kind of consideration is much discussed these days, often under the label of *jus post bellum*.
5. De George does address this, suggesting that the obligation could be crafted so as not to give away one's military advantage, but it seems doubtful that this is possible. A similar moral problem arose during the cold war when, for example, President Reagan argued that "star wars" missile defense technology would be shared with the Soviet Union.
6. It is the prejudice of an age to see its own changes as more revolutionary, more challenging to the status quo, than those of its predecessors. This suggests a note of caution in any easy assumption that the changes of our era are sufficient to nullify the practical relevance of the theory, when it has maintained its relevance through the changes of previous eras.
7. Walzer, *Just and Unjust Wars*; see, for example, pp. 251–255.
8. One might argue that nonstate terrorism does, if, for example, we imagine terrorists planting nuclear bombs in several of America's largest cities.
9. See Murnion, notes 26 and 27, and accompanying text.

II. SOME THEORETICAL BACKGROUND

WILLIAM E. MURNION

A POSTMODERN VIEW OF JUST WAR

From a postmodern perspective, just war – with its two components of *ius ad bellum* and *ius in bello* and their respective specifications – represents a heuristic construct, apt for delineating and considering the issues and aspects of the morality of war, rather than a theory, a doctrine, or even a tradition, according to which judgments can be made or conclusions drawn about the morality of particular wars or methods of warfare.[1] Historically, the development of just war has not been an organic evolution, but a series of paradigm shifts in response to a dialectic between transformations of values and technological, political, social, and cultural innovations. Concomitantly, just war has vied with alternative ethics of war – militarism, pacifism, realism, and idealism – each with its own metaethical foundation. No wonder, then, that contemporary proponents of a just war ethic have interpreted it in diverse senses while reaching contrary opinions both about the resort to and conduct of war and about the morality of particular wars and modes of warfare, with the consequence that just war, variously interpreted and applied, appears reducible to one or another of the alternative ethics of war. In today's global and multicultural world, it is also evident that just war is, like its alternatives, a Western ethic of war, rather than a self-evidently universal framework for the evaluation of war. Yet it can still be argued that just war, precisely because of its lability and adaptability, remains an irreplaceable framework for assessing both the prospect of engaging in war and the merits of various forms of warfare: the last best hope for meeting the contemporary challenges to the ethics of warfare from preemptive and preventive war; from insurgency, intrastate conflict, and nonstate guerilla aggression; from humanitarian and police intervention; from weapons of mass destruction; from torture, terrorism, and genocide.

1. RECONSTRUCTION OF THE HISTORY OF JUST WAR[2]

Four paradigms can conveniently be demarcated in the history of the development of the just war ethic. Each reflects a trade-off between the kind of law invoked to judge the morality of war and the available technology of warfare, as mediated by the political and social climate of the time. Each successive paradigm represents a deeper embedment of the just war ethic into political practice. And each, though a creature of its own environment, has become a model for a contemporary version of the just war ethic. Underlying this history from beginning to end is the assumption that, absent a superior authority capable of peaceably resolving disputes, a political entity may legitimately employ some measure of force, either in self-defense or for the protection of other (innocent) victims of (unjust) aggression.

1.1 The Late Hellenistic/Early Medieval Paradigm

The first paradigm is the prototype for the just war ethic to be found in the writings of St. Augustine.[3] A bishop in the western half of the Roman Empire, in which Christianity was the established religion, Augustine invoked divine law to authorize imperial forces to protect the church from heretical sects within the empire and to defend the empire itself against barbarians (generally also heretics) from without. He drew, to be sure, upon the Hebrew Bible/Old Testament, Roman law in the writings of Cicero, and St. Ambrose's sermons, but his brief remarks on the right (*ius*) to go to war became the conventional *auctoritas* for the medieval development of just war doctrine.[4] Citing Romans 13:4, Augustine invoked the command of God to punish idolaters and heretics or the demand of charity to recover the goods and punish the attackers of innocent his authorization of civil authorities to make war in order to restore peace. Clearly, a war for either reason was immediately offensive rather than defensive, and while Augustine admonished the prosecutors of war to prepare for peace by eschewing any feelings of hatred or revenge, he did not impose any restriction of weapons or tactics in the vindication of their cause. In this prototype of just war theory (JWT), therefore, there were virtually no *ius in bello* limitations and only the rudiments of a *ius ad bellum*, and these applied directly to offensive rather than to defensive wars.

Yet Augustine was the authority to whom in our time Paul Ramsey appealed for his version of just war as a forcible exercise of charity for the sake of restoring peace, a moral obligation he argued was faithful to Christ's commitment to peace and expressive of the Christian virtue of *agape*.[5] His students, the "Princeton" school, the most prominent of whom is James Turner Johnson, have amplified the Augustinian tradition of just war to argue that sovereign authority has a rational as well as a religious mandate to maintain order through war, without any presumption of a bias for peaceable over belligerent means.[6] Likewise, George Weigel invoked the Augustinian paradigm in his critique of the recent development within official Roman Catholic teaching – from John XXIII's encyclical *Pacem in Terris*, to Vatican II's constitution *Gaudium et Spes*, and the American Catholic bishops' pastoral letter *The Challenge of Peace* – of the interpretation that the just war ethic does indeed imply a presumption for peace and against war.[7]

1.2 The Medieval Paradigm

The second paradigm for just war was the medieval ideology of just war developed within the social and political context of Christendom.[8] This was an ideology in which natural law provided a rational armature for divine law, and it was designed to limit feudal conflicts within Christendom rather than to authorize crusades within or outside the (now Holy) Roman Empire.[9] St. Thomas Aquinas's theological codification of this ideology in his *Summa Theologiae* has come to be called the "classical statement" of JWT. And Aquinas's epitome of the tradition is indeed the crucial link in the chain by which the canon law strictures about the justification for war in Gratian's *Decretum* (1154), reinforced by the Decretists and Decretalists of the twelfth and thirteenth centuries, were converted into a purely rational ethic of war by Vitoria and Suarez in the fifteenth and sixteenth centuries, as well as by Grotius in the seventeenth century.[10]

Aquinas summarized the conditions for *ius ad bellum* as legitimate authority (*de facto* as well as *de iure*; that is, pertaining to kings and princes, in addition to the pope and the Holy Roman emperor); just cause (now implicitly self-defense, as well as the recovery of stolen goods and the punishment of malefactors); and right intent (including proportionate response, in addition to the pursuit of peace).[11] Although Aquinas concurred with Augustine's theological perspective in viewing war (apart from the stipulated conditions) as a sin against peace, a fruit of the supernatural virtue of charity, he underpinned this exposition in terms of divine law with an argument from natural law (with its rational endorsement of the love of God and neighbor) in which justice was the paramount virtue.[12]

Although Aquinas himself did not elaborate a *ius in bello*, his theory was, as James Turner Johnson has shown, but one ingredient, important as it was, in the medieval ideology of just war. This ideology derived from both religious and secular sources, on both theoretical and popular levels, and comprised elements of both *ius ad bellum* and *ius in bello*, eventually crystallizing at the turn of the fifteenth century into a consensus throughout Christendom about the justification and limitation of war.[13] After the failure of the Peace of God and the Truce of God movements, canon lawyers were concerned mainly about the *ius ad bellum* requirement of legitimate authority and the *ius in bello* prescription of discrimination. They attempted – futilely, as it turned out – to limit the incidence of war by restricting the authority to declare war to a sovereign, a lord with no superior: effectively the pope and the Holy Roman emperor. And they sought to exempt clerics and religious from the effects of war by defining them as *innocentes* (harmless ones) because of the canonical proscription against members of their status bearing arms.

This religious campaign to limit the incidence and the impact of war was aided and abetted by secular endeavors. A revival of Roman law tightened the restriction on the authority to declare war, while the chivalric code included peasants, along with clerics and religious, among the *innocentes* by exempting from warfare those who were unable as well as forbidden to bear arms. By the turn of the fifteenth century, therefore, the entire complex of religious and secular, theological and legal maneuvers coalesced, in the writings of Honoré Bonet and Christine de Pisan, into a consensus throughout Christendom about the recourse to and the conduct of war. This medieval paradigm remains the preeminent model for the contemporary Roman Catholic version of the just war ethic, whether in the official teachings of Pope John XXIII, Vatican II, and the American Catholic bishops or in the philosophical writings of John Finnis, Joseph Boyle, and Germain Grisez.[14]

1.3 The Early Modern Paradigm

In its own time, though, the medieval paradigm did not survive the disintegration of Christendom because of the Protestant and Catholic (or Counter-) Reformations and the concomitant emergence of the modern era, precipitated by the rise within Europe of the nation-state together with the Western exploration of Asia and Africa and discovery of the New World. The early modern paradigm of the just war ethic was a response to this set of events. It took two forms.

In the conflict spawned by the competing Protestant and Catholic Reformations, Protestant polemicists, and some Catholics as well, followed Luther in amending the just war ethic to make the defense of religion – and, once again, divine law – the primary if not the sole justification for war. They invoked the holy war ethic of the Hebrew Bible, combining it with Augustine's authorization of war against heretics and the precedent of the Crusades against Islam. In addition, they recalled that the medieval ideology of just war, designed to mitigate war between orthodox Christians, was never meant to prohibit Christian crusades against either heretics or infidels. For those who took this approach the justice of the cause – the repression of heresy – was usually supposed to vindicate a remorseless prosecution of the war.[15]

By contrast, the European conquest of the New World, accompanied by conflict among the emerging European nation-states over religious as well as political issues, led to a reconstitution of the just war ethic upon the foundation of right reason. Interpreted at first in terms of natural law, right reason came eventually to be construed in terms of *ius gentium*, a hypothetical law postulated to be common to all peoples by virtue of their very humanity. Francisco de Vitoria, who followed Aquinas in interpreting right reason in terms of natural law, thought right reason would provide a common ground for adjudicating the legitimacy of war both between Catholics and Protestants and between Christians and heathens. For Vitoria was as concerned about moderating imperial conflicts between Spain and England as about restraining the depredations by Spanish conquistadors of Indians in the New World. Not only did he attempt to avert religious wars between Protestants and Catholics by restricting the causes of war to reasons of state; he stipulated that, if only because of invincible ignorance, these reasons could give what Johnson has termed "simultaneous ostensible justification" to both parties to a conflict. Hence, Vitoria emphasized the necessity for both parties, in the absence of certitude about *ius ad bellum*, to adhere scrupulously to the prescriptions of *ius in bello*. Yet he qualified his own admonitions by allowing, in case of military necessity, for unintentional and indirect harm to noncombatants and, in the limit case of certitude about the justice of one's cause, for intentional though indirect harm to noncombatants.[16]

In the wake of the Peace of Westphalia (1648) ending the Thirty Years War, Vitoria's paradigm of just war based upon right reason was adopted by both Catholic and Protestant theologians. Grotius, the founder of international law, reinterpreted right reason, however, not as an innate natural law but as a hypothetical common law of all nations or peoples. He also codified the doctrine of just war into the now familiar diptych of *ius ad bellum* and *ius in bello*. *Ius ad bellum* he reduced, in an accommodation to the reality of modern nation-states, virtually to the possession of sovereignty, while he accordingly emphasized even more than had Vitoria the necessity for moderation in *ius in bello*, to limit the brutality of warfare. This paradigm of just war, reflected as well in the writings of Vattel and Locke, suited the "sovereigns wars" of the seventeenth and eighteenth centuries, limited as they were by the personal resources of sovereigns, the mercenary composition of armies, and the primitive technology of weaponry and transportation.[17] Yet this paradigm has also become the model for important contemporary versions of the just war ethic, in both Michael Walzer's *Just and Unjust Wars* and John

Rawls's *Law of Peoples*, with their common (albeit differently interpreted) assumption of a generally shared moral outlook about justice and rights among all, or at least all liberal, peoples.[18]

1.4 The Late Modern/Contemporary Paradigm

The late modern or contemporary paradigm of just war has arisen in response to the total wars of the nineteenth and twentieth centuries and is based upon positive law.[19] In 1832, Carl von Clausewitz defined total war as a prerogative of the sovereignty of nation-states, free to exercise politics by forcible as well as peaceable means and to prosecute war with their full resources, with the most devastating weaponry, and in the shortest period of time.[20] Total war became a possibility after (1) the French Revolution inflated national sovereignty to the ideology of nationalism as a defense of the "rights of man"; (2) the Napoleonic wars innovated the practice of universal male military conscription; and (3) the industrial revolution enhanced transportation on both land and sea and enabled the mass production of precision-made weaponry. The response of governments, with the endorsement of ethicists, was to attempt to limit through positive law the resort to war as well as the prosecution of war.

With *ius ad bellum* effectively reduced by the beginning of the nineteenth century to a nation-state's *competence de guerre*,[21] the first recourse for the limitation of war was to spell out *ius in bello* in official instructions. General Orders 100, the *Instructions for the Government of the Armies of the United States in the Field*, issued over Abraham Lincoln's signature on April 24, 1863, to guide Union armies in the Civil War, was the first official document to define the rights of both combatants and noncombatants and to specify the weaponry appropriate for combat.[22] This instrument of national law became a model for subsequent measures of international law. In the latter part of the nineteenth century and the early twentieth century, the Brussels and the Hague treaties defined the nature and extent of noncombatant immunity, while the Geneva conventions prohibited the use of unnecessarily cruel and entirely uncontrollable weapons.[23]

A parallel effort ensued to bolster *ius ad bellum*. In Article 10 of the Covenant of the League of Nations (1919) the members pledged in the abstract to respect and preserve one another's territorial integrity from external aggression. The Kellogg–Briand Pact (1928) attempted to enforce the Covenant by renouncing war as a lawful instrument of national policy, while giving tacit approval to war as a means of self-defense and preserving war under the aegis of the League of Nations as an instrument of international policy. In the aftermath of World War II, the Charter of the United Nations (1945) outlawed the threat or the use of wars of aggression, restricting the legality of war to individual nations acting in self-defense against aggression or to consortiums of nations engaging with UN authorization in humanitarian intervention.[24]

Together with the Brussels and Hague treaties and the Geneva conventions governing *ius in bello*, the measures adopted by the League of Nations and the United Nations to delimit *ius ad bellum* have institutionalized the just war ethic in international law.[25] Ethicists have given a philosophical endorsement to this late modern/contemporary paradigm of just war. Yoram Dinstein has espoused it in his brief for the advantages of progressing from the current international regime, in which nation-states may act with UN authorization in collective self-defense, to a cosmopolitan regime of collective security, to be maintained by an international police force.[26] It is likewise the direction in which David Rodin would take the just war ethic, denying the legitimacy of war as a means of national self-defense while restricting it in principle to an instrument of cosmopolitan law enforcement.[27] In fact, John Mueller has argued (even in the face of international guerilla warfare and the "war on terrorism") that the incorporation of the just war ethic into international law has already made war obsolescent, abandoned as a strategy among the developed nations and persisting only among developing nations, both in their internecine conflicts (hardly rising above criminality) and in the sporadic efforts of developed nations to police such conflicts.[28]

The history of just war reveals, therefore, four paradigms, each of them formulated in a specific social, political, and cultural context to meet the challenge of a particular form of armed conflict. The foundation of each paradigm has been a specific kind of law – divine law for the late Hellenistic/early medieval paradigm, natural law for the medieval paradigm, the law of nations or peoples for the early modern paradigm, and international law for the late modern/contemporary paradigm – but the intent in each case has been the same: to limit the incidence and constrain the conduct of war. Each of the three classical paradigms has been reformulated in contemporary terms, while the late modern/contemporary paradigm founded upon international law has been endorsed by philosophical arguments.

The logical result is four mutually exclusive paradigms, all contending for preeminence and often reaching opposing conclusions about the morality both of particular wars and of specific modes of warfare. The ethical effect is, however, of four mutually reinforcing paradigms, all evaluating the morality of both particular wars and specific modes of warfare in terms of principles intuitively plausible to their proponents.

Although the just war ethic has never, in any of its paradigms, succeeded in foreclosing the recourse to war or eliminating the brutality of warfare, proponents of the just war ethic may be forgiven for acclaiming its triumph, not just as the regnant academic theory for evaluating the morality of war and warfare, but as the at least implicit presupposition of political and military efforts to reduce the recourse to war and limit the brutality of warfare.[29]

2. DECONSTRUCTION OF THE ALTERNATIVE ETHICS OF WAR

Yet just war has not been, nor is it now, the only ethic of war. It has always vied, and continues to compete, with alternative ethics of war: militarism (or warism) and pacifism, realism and idealism. These alternatives have each had their own history and follow their own logic. Therefore, in order to assess the extent or validity of just war's putative triumph, it is necessary to compare and contrast it with these alternatives.

This is no simple task. For, from one perspective, just war can be argued to be the fundamental ethic of war because the alternative ethics of war can be delineated and differentiated in terms of the just war criteria of *jus ad bellum* and *ius in bello*. Yet from the perspective of their own epistemological and ontological presuppositions, the alternative ethics can be interpreted as the internally consistent theories into which the protean ethic of just war is prone to devolve. In assessing the aptitude of just war to meet the challenges of contemporary warfare, therefore, it is appropriate to match it with the alternative ethics of war from both perspectives.[30]

2.1 Summary Analysis of the Alternative Ethics of War

Before describing any of the alternative ethics in detail, it will be convenient first to characterize them summarily, both in terms of the just war criteria of the right to war (*ius ad bellum*) and the law of warfare (*ius in bello*) and in terms of their respective metaethical presuppositions.

Just war criteria first. Militarism presupposes a right to war and consequently denies any limitation from a putative law of warfare in the conduct of war. Pacifism, by contrast, denies there can be any legitimation for the conduct of war from a law of warfare and therefore denies there can be any right to war. Realism postulates a reciprocal necessity for the right to declare war and for the imposition of a law of warfare. Idealism denies any fundamental right to war, given the possibility of an authority capable of keeping the peace, but in the absence of such an authority, it demands a stringent law to mitigate the depredations of warfare.

The metaethical axes of the differentiation among the alternative ethics of war are epistemological and ontological. That is, ethicists differ in their advocacy of the ethics of war depending upon whether their epistemology is rationalist or pragmatist and whether their ontology is monist or dualist.[31] A rationalist epistemology presumes the possibility of a necessary and exhaustive identification between thought and reality, whereas a pragmatist epistemology takes such an identification to be only hypothetical, approximate, and progressive. A monist ontology assumes an underlying identity between the real and the ideal, whereas a dualist ontology postulates a fundamental dichotomy between the real and the ideal. The intersection of these two sets of metaethical commitments yields a complementary matrix to the one produced by just war criteria for the categorization of militarism and pacifism, realism and idealism.

Militarism is both rationalist and monist, presupposing no gap in knowledge between theory and practice, nor in actuality between the real and the ideal. That is, militarism presupposes no doubt about the justice of the cause for war and presumes any means may, indeed must, be employed in the prosecution of war. Pacifism shares the rationalist epistemology of militarism, but has a dualist ontology. That is, pacifism presupposes a certitude about the immorality of violence, but takes the goal of an end to war to be an ideal to be achieved either asymptotically or eschatalogically. Realism combines a pragmatist epistemology with a monist ontology. That is, realism takes this world as it finds it and decides the relative merits of peace and war and the permissible limits of warfare on a case-by-case basis, within a specifiable political and social context. Idealism concurs with realism in a pragmatist epistemology, but agrees with the dualist ontology of pacifism. That is, idealism takes peace to be an eventual and perhaps realizable goal, but in the meantime devotes its efforts to reducing the incidence and mitigating the horrors of war.

Now each of these alternative ethics of war has its own history. In fact, each has taken both a classical and a modern, a religious and a secular form. These are the forms into which the just war ethic has been prone to devolve.

2.2 *Historical Description of the Alternative Ethics of War*

Militarism in a religious context leads to the ideology of holy war. In the Hebrew Bible/Old Testament, holy war occurred as the Lord of hosts led the Chosen People in self-righteous and merciless wars against their foes.[32] In Christendom, the Crusades against infidel Muslims in the Holy Land and heretical Cathari in Provence expressly invoked this holy war ideology, while German princes in the Reformation employed the same ideology (in the guise of JWT) to rationalize their remorseless suppression of peasant uprisings and popular revolts.[33] In the secular setting of the modern era, militarism has become the ideology of total war or of terrorism. Total war has been an option for the nation-state: the complete mobilization of the nation for war, indiscriminate attack upon combatants and noncombatants alike, and the employment of weapons of mass destruction.[34] Terrorism is, on the other hand, the resort of nonstate agents, insurgents or guerilla warriors, on either a local or a global scale: the manifestation of a readiness to die for a cause, in random (perhaps suicidal) attacks on innocent civilians or horrific attacks on salient authorities or vulnerable political and economic facilities.[35] In either a religious or a secular form, the assumption behind militarism is that the ultimacy of the cause justifies any means to advance or defend it.

Pacifism shares with militarism an absolute conviction in the rightness of its cause, but is otherwise diametrically opposed to it, forswearing recourse to war because of an abhorrence of violence, even though its goal of universal peace remains an eschatological hope or an asymptotic goal. Pacifists expect to suffer persecution for their beliefs, either religious or secular, without succumbing to the temptation to return evil for evil, in the hope that their patience will eventually be the purity of their means evolves into the perfection of their end. In the religious context of primitive Christianity and the radical Reformation, pacifism entailed, if possible, a physical separation from the corruption of this world and, if necessary, a nonresistance to evil to the point of martyrdom, in the belief of an imminent apocalypse.[36] In a modern, often secular context, it has become nonviolent resistance to political violence and state terrorism – colonial oppression, slavery, apartheid, military occupation, institutional racism, fascism and totalitarianism, international war, nuclear weaponry – in the hope of absorbing their evils and, at the limit, of achieving a peaceful victory.[37] As the examples of Mohandas Gandhi, Martin Luther King, and Nelson Mandela, among others, have shown, both religious pacifism and secular pacifism remain vital movements, their proponents just as convinced as militarists are of the efficacy of their strategy and tactics.

Realism takes the tension and the alternation between peace and war as historically inevitable and seeks the most practicable defense of values under the circumstances. For a realist, the relative merits of peace and war and the permissible limits of warfare must both be evaluated on a case-by-case basis. In the religious context of Constantinian and medieval Christendom, realism was the approach that led to the reconstruction of the pacifism of early Christianity as JWT, particularly in setting the terms for a right to war (*ius ad bellum*).[38] In the modern and secular setting of the Peace of Westphalia and globalization, it has provided the motivation both for limiting the recourse to war and curtailing the savagery of warfare, erecting a bulwark of international law against *Realpolitik* and *Blitzkrieg*.[39] In religious as well as secular modes, realism has been an attempt both to make war a stratagem of last resort and to confine warfare to precision weaponry directed only at military targets, whether combatants or installations.[40]

Idealism rejects any right to war, sharing with pacifism a belief in the exclusive morality of peace, but it differs from pacifism in pursuing peace as much as practicable under historical circumstances. While it therefore differs from realism in its mooting of the morality of war, idealism joins realism in attempting, until peace is achieved, to limit the legality of both the recourse to war and the methods and the destructiveness of warfare. Thus it relies upon pragmatic arguments to advance the cause of peace and proposes institutional means to keep the peace.[41]

In a religious context, idealism was manifest in Dante's support for a Holy Roman Emperor to be sovereign in Christendom[42] and in Erasmus's advice to a Christian prince,[43] either of whom gave promise in his own time of becoming an appropriate authority for the peaceful resolution of political disputes. In a modern and more secular context, a similar approach is to be found in Kant's vision of attaining perpetual peace in a cosmopolitan order transcending international diversity.[44] Kant's vision has inspired Rawls's conception of a "realistic utopia" apt to render war pointless,[45] just as both Jürgen Habermas and Jacques Derrida (albeit from different presuppositions and with different emphases) now invoke it as the remedy for the contemporary phenomenon of global terrorism.[46] Although the contemporary movements of international law and world order do not share in Kant's ambition of transcending the regime of nation-states, they do, however, believe in the efficacy of eventually eliminating war through international politics.[47] Whether the motivation is religious or secular, idealism is an essentially political approach to the ethics of war, aiming to establish on a regional or global scale the conditions of law and order already achievable within a nation-state.

From both a just war and a metaethical perspective, therefore, it is clear that there are in Western culture – in both classical and modern, in both religious and secular contexts – four approaches to the ethics of war. It is, on the one hand, arguable that they are all versions of a just war ethic inasmuch as they can be interpreted as assessing the morality of war and warfare according to various combinations of the just war criteria of *ius ad bellum* and *ius in bello*. Yet, if they are examined according to their distinctive metaethical foundations and their independent evaluations of the morality of war and warfare, they appear rather to be the internally consistent theories into which the just war ethic can devolve in one or another pure form. This eventuality is not just a logical possibility; it has, in fact, occurred.

Luther, for one, gave just war a militaristic interpretation in his authorization of German princes to wage a holy war against rebellious peasants.[48] At the opposite extreme, Jenny Teichman, James Childress, and Richard Miller have all argued that just war has a common origin with pacifism in the Christian quest for peace, pacifism being but the more radical and just war the more pragmatic pursuit of human concord and nonviolence.[49] Certainly, both Protestant and Roman Catholic authorities and theologians have argued, to the chagrin of some just war theorists, that a just war ethic now warrants nuclear pacifism.[50] But realism remains the outlook, both in the explication of theory and in the assessment of particular wars and forms of warfare, of the just war school initiated by Paul Ramsey and developed by James Turner Johnson and George Weigel.[51] Likewise, Walzer's theory of just war, for all of its explicit opposition to political realism, bottoms out in ethical realism, given his acceptance of "supreme emergency" and "military necessity" as legitimate anomalies to the just war prescriptions of *ius ad bellum* and *ius in bello* respectively.[52] Yet idealism is the direction in which Pope John Paul II took Catholic just war theory with his persistent calls for the renunciation of violence, both within and between nations, in the resolution of political disputes and with his repeated advocacy of an international authority capable of keeping and restoring the peace.[53]

Hence, just as the history of the just war ethic reveals four distinctive paradigms, each with a classical and a contemporary analogue, so a theoretical analysis of the just war ethic in light of the alternative ethics of war discloses it to be both a fundamental heuristic for distinguishing them from one another and a protean construct capable of devolving into any of them.

3. SOME IMPLICATIONS OF THE RECONSTRUCTION OF THE HISTORY OF THE JUST WAR ETHIC AND DECONSTRUCTION OF THE ALTERNATIVE ETHICS OF WAR

Neither the historical mutability nor the theoretical lability of the just war ethic disqualifies it from serving as *an* appropriate and perhaps *the* fundamental perspective for evaluating the morality of war and warfare. In each of its historical paradigms, the just war ethic has provided an apposite prism for gauging the morality of a policy of war and modes of warfare, given the regnant values and the attendant circumstances of the time. The plasticity of the just war ethic is a tribute to its intellectual versatility as well as its functional adaptability. The current versions of the ethic are remarkable for both their classical precedents and their contemporary applications. Far from being a relic of a bygone era or the dogma of an ecclesiastical or academic magisterium, the just war ethic emerges from its tradition ready to meet the challenge of present-day problems. As it is applied according to prevailing values to address contemporary issues, it will, no doubt, once again undergo modifications, perhaps crystallizing into yet a new paradigm.[54]

Likewise, the ability of the just war ethic both to provide a framework for categorizing the alternative ethics of war and to devolve, in one pure form or another, into each of these types suggests that it is hardly possible to think of the morality of war and warfare in any but just war terms. The reason the just war ethic can provide a framework for categorizing the alternative ethics of war is that the two fundamental criteria of *ius ad bellum* and *ius in bello* (inclusive of their respective specifications) enunciate the two questions any ethic of war must answer: the question of what, if any, are the grounds for going to war, and the question of what, if any, are the procedures to be followed in combat. The complementary reason the just war ethic can devolve in a pure form into each of these ethics is that, being *a* (perhaps *the*) heuristic construct for assessing the morality of war and warfare, it can become a complete and consistent theory only when it is integrated into a set of metaethical foundations capable of producing logical and pertinent conclusions about the morality of undertaking and prosecuting war. Hence, even when ethicists differ, as they do, about the presuppositions or the implications of the just war ethic, either as a generic matrix or in its specific crystallizations, the ethic still supplies the context and delineates the issues for discussion.[55]

No wonder, then, just war adherents have had no hesitation about using the ethic to appraise nuclear warfare and nuclear deterrence,[56] as well as guerilla warfare and terrorism.[57] They have also applied it to the confrontation between the rights of insurgents or revolutionaries and the responsibilities of police forces, domestic or foreign.[58] Similarly, they have found it as adaptable to the question of and conditions for humanitarian intervention as to the provisions for individual self-defense, collective self-defense, and collective security.[59] They have found it equally helpful for pondering both the macro horrors of genocide and the micro atrocities of torture.[60] The just war ethic is as capable of surviving the reconstruction of its history and the deconstruction of its logic as it is of confronting the recurrent innovations in war and warfare.

NOTES

1. For conventional formulations of the just war criteria and their stipulations, see James F. Childress, "Just-War Criteria," in idem, *Moral Responsibility in Conflicts: Essays on Nonviolence, War, and Conscience* (Baton Rouge, LA: Louisiana State University Press, 1982), 63–94; Robert L. Phillips, *War and Justice* (Norman, OK: University of Oklahoma Press, 1984), 12–13; James Turner Johnson, *Can Modern War Be Just?* (New Haven, CT: Yale University Press, 1984), 18–29; idem., *Morality and Contemporary Warfare* (New Haven, CT: Yale University Press, 1999), 27–38.
2. The philosophy of history implicit in this reconstruction of the epistemes in which the four paradigms of just war were formulated is analogous to the one Michel Foucault supposed in his histories of the human sciences, in *The Order of Things: An Archaeology of the Human Sciences* (1970; New York: Random House/Vintage Books, 1973), see xxi–xxii, and *The Archaeology of Knowledge & Discourse on Language*, trans. A. M. Sheridan Smith (New York: Harper & Row/Harper Colophon Books, 1972), see 191. Philipp W. Rosemann adopted it for the history of medieval philosophy in *Understanding Scholastic Thought with Foucault* (New York: St. Martin's Press, 1999), see 11, 35–40.
3. John Langan, S.J., "The Elements of St. Augustine's Just War Theory," *Journal of Religious Ethics* 12/1 (1984): 28–37; William R. Stevenson, *Christian Love and Just War: Moral Paradox and Political Life in St. Augustine and His Modern Interpreters* (Macon, GA: Mercer University Press, 1987); see also Louis J. Swift, *The Early Fathers on War and Military Service* (Wilmington, DE: Michael Glazier, 1983), 110–149; Frederick H. Russell, *The Just War in the Middle Ages* (Cambridge: Cambridge University Press, 1975), 16–39; Roland H. Bainton, *Christian Attitudes toward War and Peace: A Historical Survey and Critical Re-Evaluation* (New York and Nashville: Abingdon, 1960), 91–100; Lisa Sowle Cahill, *Love Your Enemies: Discipleship, Pacifism, and Just War Theory* (Minneapolis, MN: Fortress, 1994), 55–80.
4. St. Augustine, *The City of God*, trans. Marcus Dods (New York: Modern Library, 1950), XIX, 12; XXII, 6.
5. Paul Ramsey, *War and the Christian Conscience: How Shall Modern War Be Conducted?* (Durham, NC: Duke University Press, 1961), esp. 10–41; idem., *The Just War: Force and Political Responsibility* (1968; Lanham, MD: University Press of America, 1983), esp. 7, 145–151, 204–06; see also Stevenson, *Christian Love*, 115–136.
6. James Turner Johnson, *Just War Tradition and the Restraint of War* (Princeton and Guildford, Surrey: Princeton University Press, 1981); id., *Can Modern War Be Just*, esp. 1–66; idem, *The Quest for Peace: Three Moral Traditions in Western Cultural History* (Princeton, NJ: Princeton University Press, 1987), 3–132; idem, *Morality and Contemporary Warfare*, esp. 41–70.
7. George Weigel, *Tranquillitas Ordinis: The Present Failure and Future Promise of American Catholic Thought on War and Peace* (Oxford: Oxford University Press, 1987), 25–45, 74–106, 257–313.
8. Russell, *Just War*, 213–257.

9. Alfred Vanderpol, *La doctrine scolastique du droit de guerre* (Paris: A. Pedone Editeur, 1925), 287–496; corrected in part by Robert Regout SJ, *La doctrine de la guerre juste de Saint Augustin a nos jours d'après les théologiens et les canonistes catholiques* (Paris: Editions A. Pedone, 1935), 79–93.
10. Joan D. Tooke, *The Just War in Aquinas and Grotius* (London: SPCK, 1965)
11. Aquinas, *Summa Theologiae* 2–2.40.1.
12. Aquinas, *Summa Theologiae*, 1–2.91.1,2,5; 93.2,6; 94.2,4; 2–2.44.1–8.
13. James Turner Johnson, *Ideology, Reason, and the Limitation of War: Religious and Secular Concepts 1200–1740* (Princeton, NJ: Princeton University Press, 1975), 1–80; M. H. Keen, *The Laws of War in the Late Middle Ages* (London: Routledge & Kegan Paul; Toronto: University of Toronto Press, 1965).
14. John Finnis, Joseph M. Boyle, Jr., and Germain Grisez, *Nuclear Deterrence, Morality and Realism* (Oxford: Clarendon Press, 1987).
15. See Bainton, *Christian Attitudes*, 136–151; Cahill, *Love Your Enemies*, 97–118; Johnson, *Ideology*, 81–203.
16. Francisco de Vitoria, *De Indis and De Iure Belli Relectiones* (Washington, DC: Carnegie Institution, 1917); see Johnson, *Ideology*, 154–203; James Brown Scott, *The Spanish Origin of International Law: Francisco de Vitoria and His Law of Nations* (Oxford: Clarendon Press, 1934), 68–172
17. Hugo Grotius, *On the Law of War and Peace*, trans. Francis W. Kelsey (Oxford: Clarendon Press, 1925); Johnson, *Ideology*, 208–255.
18. Michael Walzer, *Just and Unjust Wars: A Moral Argument with Historical Illustrations*, 3rd edn (1977; New York: Basic Books, 2000), xviii–xxiii, 3–20; John Rawls, *The Law of Peoples* (Cambridge, MA: Harvard University Press, 1999), 3, 89–105.
19. Johnson, *Just War Tradition*.
20. Carl von Clausewitz, *On War*, trans. Michael Howard and Peter Paret (Princeton, NJ: Princeton University Press, 1984), 75–77, 127–132, 190–209, 523–531, 577–605.
21. Yoram Dinstein, *War, Aggression and Self-Defence*, 3rd edn. (1988; Cambridge: Cambridge University Press, 2001), 69–72.
22. James F. Childress, "Francis Lieber's Interpretation of the Laws of War," in *Moral Responsibility*, 95–163.
23. Geoffrey Best, *Humanity in Warfare* (New York: Columbia University Press, 1980).
24. Dinstein, *War*, 73–86; Yehuda Melzer, *Concepts of Just War* (Leyden: A. W. Sijthoff, 1975).
25. Leslie C. Green, *The Contemporary Law of Armed Conflict*, 2nd edn (Manchester: Juris Publishing, 2000); Ingrid Detter, *The Law of War*, 2nd edn (1987; Cambridge: Cambridge University Press, 2000).
26. Dinstein, *War*, 222–282.
27. David Rodin, *War and Self-Defense* (2002; Oxford: Clarendon Press, 2004).
28. John Mueller, *The Remnants of War* (Ithaca, NY: Cornell University Press, 2004).
29. Michael Walzer, "The Triumph of Just War Theory (and the Dangers of Success)," *Social Research* 69/4 (Winter, 2002): 925–944; reprinted in idem., *Arguing about War* (New Haven, CT: Yale University Press, 2004), 3–22.
30. For two other typologies of the ethics of war, see Bainton, *Christian Attitudes*, who differentiates within Christian attitudes to war between crusade, just war, and pacifism; and Johnson, *Quest for Peace*, who divides moral traditions of the ethics of war into just war, sectarian pacifism, and utopian pacifism. Bainton's typology has the limitation of

being confined to Christian ethics. And while Johnson adds secular analogues of Christian types and revises Bainton's typology to include crusade under just war, his focus upon the quest for peace leads him to ignore militarism as a significant ethic of warfare.

31. This typology was suggested by William James, *Pragmatism: A New Name for Some Old Ways of Thinking* (1907) and *A Pluralistic Universe* (1909); reprinted in *William James Writings 1902–1910, The Library of America* (New York: Literary Classics of the United States, 1987), 496–498, 508–517, 625–820; Bainton, *Christian Attitudes*, 44–52, 101–121, 136–151; Johnson, *Ideology*, 81–133.
32. Michael Walzer, "The Idea of Holy War in Ancient Israel," *Journal of Religious Ethics* 20/2 (1992): 215–235.
33. Bainton, *Christian Attitudes*, 44–52, 101–121, 136–151; Cahill, *Love Your Enemies*, 119–148; Johnson, *Ideology*, 81–133.
34. See Clausewitz, *On War*; James Turner Johnson, *Just War Tradition*, 229–277; idem, *Can Modern War Be Just?* 30–66, 86–110; Robert L. Phillips, *War and Justice*. 71–100. For a study of war as the expression of a warrior ethos, see John Keegan, *A History of Warfare* (New York: Alfred A. Knopf, 1994); for a critique of the warrior ethos, see Chris Hedges, *War Is a Force That Gives Us Meaning* (New York: Random House/Anchor Books, 2002).
35. David C. Rapoport and Yonah Alexander (eds), *The Morality of Terrorism: Religious and Secular Justifications* (New York: Pergamon, 1982); J. Angelo Corlett, *Terrorism: A Philosophical Analysis* (Dordrecht, The Netherlands: Kluwer, 2003).
36. Jean-Michael Hornus, *It Is Not Lawful For Me To Fight: Early Christian Attitudes toward War, Violence and the State*, rev. edn., trans. Alan Kreider and Oliver Coburn (Scottsdale, PA/Kitchener, ONT.: Herald, 1980); James M. Stayer, *Anabaptists and the Sword* (Lawrence, KS: Coronado Press, 1972). See Bainton, *Christian Attitudes*, 53–84, 152–172; Cahill, *Love Your Enemies*, 15–54, 149–178; Johnson, *Quest for Peace*, 3–66, 91–132.
37. Peter Brock, *Pacifism in Europe to 1914* (Princeton, NJ: Princeton University Press, 1972); idem. *Pacifism in the United States* (Princeton, NJ: Princeton University Press, 1968); Ira Chernus, *American Nonviolence: The History of an Idea* (Maryknoll, NY: Orbis Books, 2004).
38. Bainton, *Christian Attitudes*, 33–43, 85–100; Cahill, *Love Your Enemies*, 55–118. See above, notes 1–14.
39. Bainton, *Christian Attitudes*, 173–229. See notes 15–28.
40. By "realism," I do not mean the kind of amoral political realism that acknowledges no criterion but reasons of state or national interest for policy decisions. For a review of that position, see Michael Joseph Smith, *Realist Thought from Weber to Kissinger* (Baton Rouge, LA: Louisiana University Press, 1986).
41. Johnson, *Quest for Peace*, 153–62, 173–207.
42. Dante Alighieri, *Monarchy and Three Political Letters*, trans. Donald Nichol (New York: Noonday, 1954), 66–94.
43. Desiderius Erasmus, *The Education of a Christian Prince*, trans. Lester K. Born (New York: Octagon Books, 1965), 248–257.
44. Immanuel Kant, *Perpetual Peace and Other Essays on Politics, History and Morals*, trans. Ted Humphrey (Indianapolis: Hackett, 1983).
45. Rawls, *Law of Peoples*, 4–12, 29–30, 44–45, 124–127.

46. Giovanna Borradori, *Philosophy in a Time of Terror: Dialogues with Jürgen Habermas and Jacques Derrida* (Chicago: University of Chicago Press, 2003), 52–55, 123–136, 162–169.
47. Richard A. Falk and Saul H. Mendlovitz (eds), *International Law, The Strategy of World Order*, vol. 3 (New York: World Law Fund, 1966); Jonathan Schell, *The Unconquerable World: Power, Nonviolence, and the Will of the People* (New York: Henry Holt/Metropolitan Books, 2003). See notes 22–28.
48. See notes 15 and 33.
49. Jenny Teichman, *Pacifism and the Just War: A Study in Applied Philosophy* (Oxford: Basil Blackwell, 1986), 5–9, 106–111; James F. Childress, "Just War Criteria," in *War or Peace? The Search for New Answers*, ed. Thomas S. Shannon (Maryknoll, NY: Orbis, 1980), 42; Richard Miller, "Christian Pacifism and Just-War Tenets,: How Do They Diverge?" *Theological Studies* 47/3 (1986): 448–472.
50. See notes 7 and 14.
51. See notes 1, 5, 6, and 7.
52. Walzer, *Just and Unjust* Wars, 251–268, 138–175. That just war theory is, at least in effect, reducible to realism is a claim Robert W. Tucker made some years ago in a series of writings: *The Just War: A Study in Contemporary American Doctrine* (Baltimore, MD: The Johns Hopkins University Press, 1960); *Just War and Vatican Council II: A Critique* (New York: The Council on Religion and International Affairs, 1967); "Morality and Deterrence," *Ethics* 95/3 (1985): 461–478.
53. John Paul II, Address in Drogheda, Ireland, *Origins* 9 (1979): 272–275; World Day of Peace Message, *Origins* 11 (1982): 473–478; Message to Youth on Nonviolence, *Origins* 18 (1988): 253–54; Letter to the Honorable George Bush, *Catholic News Service*, January 16, 1991. See Brian J. Hehir, "Just War Theory in a Post-Cold War World," *Journal of Religious Ethics* 20/2 (Fall, 1992): 248–252 (237–257).
54. Signs are that a new paradigm may indeed be emerging: Mark Douglas, in "Changing the Rules: Just War Theory in the Twenty-First Century," *Theology Today* 59/4 (January 2003), 529–545, suggests a number of changes in *ius ad bellum*, particularly a conversion of the specification of legitimate authority to shared authority, both intranationally and internationally. Brian Orend, in *"Ius Post Bellum," Journal of Social Philosophy* 31/1 (Spring 2000), 117–137, Walzer, in "Triumph of Just War Theory," 18–22, and Noah Feldman, in *What We Owe Iraq: War and the Ethics of Nation Building* (Princeton, NJ: Princeton University Press, 2004), all suggest adding a *ius post bellum* to the conventional criteria of *ius ad bellum* and *ius in bello*.
55. Walzer, "Triumph of Just War Theory."
56. See notes 6, 7, and 14.
57. John Dugard, "International Terrorism and the Just War," in Rapoport and Alexander, (eds), *The Morality of Terrorism*, 77–98; Jean Bethke Elshtain, *Just War against Terror: The Burden of American Power in a Violent World* (New York: Basic Books, 2003); Joseph Boyle, "Just War Doctrine and the Military Response to Terrorism," *The Journal of Political Philosophy* 11/2 (2003), 153–170; Walzer, *Arguing about War*, 51–66, 130–142.
58. William E. Murnion, "Aquinas on Revolution," in Werner Maihofer and Gerhard Sprenger, (eds)., *Revolution and Human Rights* (Stuttgart: Franz Steiner, 1990), 27–34.
59. Hehir, "Just War Theory," 254–256; idem, "Military Intervention and National Sovereignty: Recasting the Relationship," in Jonathan Moore (ed.), *Hard Choices:*

Moral Dilemmas in Humanitarian Intervention (Lanham, MD: Rowman & Littlefield, 1998); Mona Fixdal and Dan Smith, "Humanitarian Intervention and Just War," *Mershon International Studies Review* 42/2 (November, 1998): 283–312; Walzer, "The Argument about Humanitarian Intervention," *Dissent* 49/1 (Winter, 2002): 29–37; Gregory Reichberg and Henrik Syse, "Humanitarian Intervention: A Case of Offensive Force?" *Security Dialogue* 33/3 (2002): 309–322; Fabrice Weissman (ed.), *In the Shadow of 'Just Wars': Violence, Politics and Humanitarian Action* (Ithaca, NY: Cornell University Press, 2004).
60. Henry Shue, "Torture," and Elshtain, "Reflection on the Problem of 'Dirty Hands,'" in Sanford Levinson (ed.), *Torture*: A Collection (Oxford: Oxford University Press, 2004), 47–60, 77–89.

DAVID DUQUETTE

FROM RIGHTS TO REALISM: INCOHERENCE IN WALZER'S CONCEPTION OF *JUS IN BELLO*

1. INTRODUCTION

There is little doubt that Michael Walzer made a significant attempt in *Just and Unjust Wars*[1] to strengthen the moral rules of the war convention. He put forth two major considerations that effectively made the justification of killing in warfare significantly more difficult than had been generally thought. One is a sharpened distinction between *jus ad bellum* and *jus in bello* that allows each to be judged independently, so that the having of just cause does not in itself slant the judgment of whether war is being waged justly. The other is an amplification of the principle of discrimination between combatants and noncombatants and the making of noncombatant immunity a focal requirement. As a result, the moral bar is set rather high for just warfare, as evidenced in Walzer's survey of historical examples where we find an abundance of military decisions and actions that fail the moral tests.

Nonetheless, I will argue that there is a systematic tension in Walzer's conception of just warfare that allows for a significant compromising of his fundamental principle of noncombatant immunity. Moreover, I will suggest that, in particular areas where he attempts to provide moral justification for limiting or overriding this principle, he displays an incoherence in tilting toward realism, an ironic result to be sure given his explicit rejection of realism in the very first chapter of his book. It may be that moving into a realm of action that, so to speak, is beyond good and evil is necessary in order to avoid taking moral idealism to the point where the practical burdens of acting justly become unbearable. However, it is the conceptual and moral incoherence of this move within Walzer's conception of just war that I am interested in exploring, not the issue of whether realism itself is acceptable or inevitable.

In this chapter I will explore specifically Walzer's articulation of the principle of noncombatant immunity, his account of the moral obligations and their limits regarding collateral damage to noncombatants, and the justification for the lifting of immunity for noncombatants under a supreme emergency.

2. DISCRIMINATION AND NONCOMBATANT IMMUNITY

The focal principles for limiting how and when killing can occur in warfare so that it can be thought *just* (*jus in bello*) fall under the concept of discrimination. Combatants and noncombatants are distinguished according to the rights they possess in warfare. Soldiers have "war rights" that they possess equally, on both sides of a war, which means they can target each other for killing, although that should be limited and guided by strategic purpose, among other considerations, rather than being directed by emotions such as hatred, revenge, etc. (e.g., prisoners of war cannot be tortured, summarily executed, and the like). Civilians do not have these war rights but rather possess the full range of conventional moral rights, regardless of which side of the conflict they find themselves, and these rights cannot be altered for expediency sake: hence, the requirement of noncombatant immunity from undue harm and from being targeted. Walzer frames these principles in the following way. "The first principle of the war convention is that, once war has begun, soldiers are subject to attack at any time (unless they are wounded or captured)."[2] "The second principle of the war convention is that noncombatants cannot be attacked at any time. They can never be the objects or the targets of military activity."[3] However, because noncombatants are frequently put in danger because of their proximity to battle, care must be taken to avoid harming them. This doesn't mean stopping a battle because civilians in the vicinity might be harmed, but rather, based on the recognition of their rights and the reality of battle, appropriate effort be made not to harm them. "But what degree of care should be taken? And at what cost to the individual soldiers who are involved? The laws of war say nothing about such matters; they leave the cruelest decisions to be made by the men on the spot with reference only to their ordinary moral notions or the military traditions of the army in which they serve."[4] The fundamental question here is, if we ground the war convention on a conception of basic human rights, as opposed to a utilitarian view that makes all rights vulnerable to a cost/benefit judgment, what is the extent of the commitment required to noncombatant immunity when it comes into serious tension with waging war effectively?

In his book, Walzer clearly is committed to enhancing the protections afforded to noncombatants in traditional just war theory, with regard to both the principle of discrimination of combatants and noncombatants and the principle of double effect, which holds that one can only intend an acceptable effect (destroying military targets) and that the "evil effect," for example, harms inflicted on noncombatants, must not be the intention of military attacks.[5] Moreover, there is the proportionality rule, which states that "the good effect is sufficiently good to compensate for allowing the evil effect ...."[6] This principle allows soldiers to fight justly, for it allows good and evil effects to be weighed against each other such that evil effects can be justifiable, provided the proportion is right.

Also, Walzer enhances the principle of "double effect" by amplifying it with what he calls the principle of "double intention," which is that waging war justly means (a) intending only the good, thus not intentionally targeting or harming noncombatants and (b) actively considering the harms that can occur to noncombatants as a result of particular military strategies and seeking to either avoid them if possible, or at least minimize them.[7] According to Walzer, "subject only to the proportionality rule – a weak constraint – double effect provides blanket justification,"[8] that is, it not only will do little to limit unintended but foreseeable deaths but will actually provide a too easy justification of these evils in terms of military necessity. Leaving aside for the moment the issue of how to decide the right proportion, the principle, especially as understood in a utilitarian vein by Henry Sidgwick, effectively subordinates moral judgments to military considerations – the goal of military victory will tend to justify the means because excessiveness of means will be thought of functionally, as what is unnecessary to serve the goal, instead of by appeal to a strict moral constraint based on human rights, independent of what leads to victory.

Hence, for Walzer, double intention requires a positive commitment to save civilian lives over and above not intending to harm them.

> And if saving civilian lives means risking soldier's lives, the risk must be accepted. But there is a limit to the risks that we require. These are, after all, unintended deaths and legitimate military operations, and the absolute rule against attacking civilians does not apply. War necessarily places civilians in danger; that is another aspect of its hellishness. We can only ask soldiers to minimize the dangers they impose.[9]

How far must soldiers go to minimize the dangers and harms to noncombatants and at what cost to themselves? Walzer says this is difficult to determine and suggests that there is no formula for guidance, that the degree of risk to civilians that is permissible will vary with the circumstances. Generally, limiting harm to noncombatants means "that the foreseeable evil be reduced as far as possible ... aware of the evil involved, he [the actor] seeks to minimize it, accepting costs to himself."[10] But again, to what extent are harms minimized, at what cost? Given the variability of circumstances, Walzer declares it is best "to say simply that civilians have a right that 'due care' be taken."[11]

Despite his criticism of the way that the concept of "military necessity" or the "reason of war" is traditionally used, as if it carried some intrinsic moral weight when it is really about probability and risk assessment,[12] Walzer himself seems to appeal to the idea of military effectiveness to support his claim that there are limits on the constraints required by noncombatant immunity. "The limits of risk [in protecting civilians] are fixed, then, roughly at that point where any further risk-taking would almost certainly doom the military venture or make it so costly that it could not be repeated."[13] In a nutshell, soldiers must take risks so that civilians are not killed, but not to the point where soldiers cannot win battles in fighting the war – and the war must be waged and won.

3. JUSTIFYING COLLATERAL HARM TO CIVILIANS

Despite the significant thrust of the added requirement of double intention, and the number of examples used to illustrate the significant burdens it places on commanders and their soldiers, there are some places in his account where Walzer appears to be too willing to provide a somewhat questionable justification for lowering the limits of noncombatant immunity. In particular, there is the matter of whether and to what extent the coercive placing of civilians on the field of battle or in the line of fire by enemy soldiers or their commanders effectively relieves or reduces responsibility for harmful effects on those civilians caused by soldiers with good intention.

In discussing the British blockade of Germany in World War I, Walzer initially finds unacceptable the claim that the suffering of the civilian population, while the direct result of interdiction actions by the British, was "inflicted" upon them by the Germans themselves who "pushed civilians to the front line of the economic war" so that "the British could not help but kill them in the course of legitimate military operations."[14] However, in a footnote he appears somewhat supportive of the idea that the responsibility for unintended consequences of an army's actions can be lessened in light of the responsibility of the enemy for forcibly placing the civilians in harm's way. While a soldier "cannot kill civilians simply because he finds them between himself and his enemies," when it is no longer possible to get a "clear shot" at a legitimate military target because enemy soldiers have placed civilians in the way, responsibility for their deaths falls on the shoulders of those soldiers, even though the deaths were directly inflicted by the other side.[15] Here it seems that the responsibility of the attacking armies is limited by the responsibility that the enemy army has not to expose its own civilian population, in a sort of an inverse ratio of responsibility: the actions of the enemy army, in so far as they diminish the possibilities of avoiding harm to civilians, lowers the moral threshold of responsibility for the army that fires on civilians, unavoidably, in trying to fire at the enemy. So, if there is no feasible way of minimizing harm to civilians because of the tactics of the enemy, does this mean the civilian deaths inflicted by those firing are not thought to be morally wrong, or unjust? Even in a legitimate military operation, are not the rights of noncombatants unchanged regardless of the reasons for civilians being made vulnerable in the field of battle? The shifting of moral responsibility to the enemy for the harms inflicted upon civilians seems effectively to alter their rights, for justifying actions that can be seen ahead of time to directly cause civilian deaths seems to override the restriction on the direct killing of civilians, or at least to lessen the force of their claim of immunity against soldiers, especially when the soldiers have good intention.

Central to Walzer's position is the idea that "the structure of rights stands independently of political allegiance; it establishes obligations that are owed, so to speak, to humanity itself and to particular human beings and not merely to one's fellow citizens."[16] Of course, the obligation to minimize risks to civilians in the field of battle (fighting well) stands in tension with an obligation not to shift risks to soldiers to the extent that would jeopardize the war effort (winning), the responsibility to win the war resting on obligations soldiers have to their own country and fellow citizens. So the principle of noncombatant immunity is not absolute and some harms can be justified. Nonetheless, it is clear that the equality of the rights of all civilians is to some extent compromised both by political allegiance and by the circumstances in which some civilians find themselves.

But there is a further complication beyond determining whether soldiers are actually following or acting consistently with the ethical rules of war, and this involves circumstances under which those rules can be broken for the sake of a just cause. The level of the stakes, such as the continued existence of a political community, requires that the outcome of a war be considered in judging military decisions and that "the restraint on utilitarian calculation must be lifted" but without forgetting that "the rights violated for the sake of victory are genuine rights, deeply founded and in principle inviolable."[17]

4. OVERRIDING RIGHTS AND SUPREME EMERGENCY

Walzer considers two approaches to the justification of the overriding of rights. The one he calls the "sliding scale" expresses the "truth" about war rights as "the more justice, the more right," meaning "the greater the justice of my cause, the more rules I can violate for the sake of the cause – though some rules are always inviolable," or "put in terms of outcomes: the greater the injustice likely to result from my defeat, the more rules I can violate in order to avoid defeat," with some rules being inviolable.[18] The problem with this approach, according to Walzer, is not only that the war convention does not provide a "range of actions, over which the sliding scale might move, between legitimate combat and inadmissible violence" but also that "[t]he sliding scale makes way for those utilitarian calculations that rules and rights are intended to bar."[19] Moreover, the effect of the sliding scale is to erode war rights in a piecemeal fashion, enabling soldiers with just cause, or who believe their cause is just, "to do terrible things and to defend in their own consciences and among their associates and followers the terrible things they do."[20] However, according to Walzer, to respond to this position with a "moral absolutism," the claim that the rules of war provide prohibitions that can never be violated under any circumstances – "do justice even if the heavens fall" – is not a plausible moral doctrine for most people.[21]

Walzer's alternative doctrine that "stops just short of absolutism" is phrased as "do justice unless the heavens are (really) about to fall."[22] This "utilitarianism of extremity" allows that "in certain very special cases, though never as a matter of course even in just wars, the only restraints upon military action are those of usefulness and proportionality."[23] Although the rules of war do accommodate and make adjustments for the "everyday extremities of war" they cannot accommodate this larger idea of "extremity" which is about breaking the rules altogether. The argument from extremity, Walzer claims, "permits (or requires) a more sudden breach of the convention, but only after holding out for a long time against the process of erosion. The reasons for holding out have to do with the nature of the rights at issue and the status of the men and women who hold them."[24] Moreover, the rights at issue are not really eroded or undercut by "extremity" because "they are still standing at the very moment they are overridden: that is why they have to be *overridden*."[25]

According to Walzer, supreme emergency is defined by criteria relating to (a) the imminence of the danger and (b) the nature of the danger.[26] Contrary to the view that imminence of danger is in itself enough to warrant extreme measures, Walzer holds that the danger must also be of an "unusual and horrifying kind" that falls within a "region of desperation and disaster," involving a radical "threat to human values."[27] The paradigm example was the Nazi threat, a "threat to human values so radical that its imminence would surely constitute a supreme emergency."[28]

Assuming that this threat involved the likely enslavement or extermination of a people, even if restricted to a single nation like Britain, then one might argue that the rights of innocent people can be overridden for the sake of the safety and survival of this particular political community. Here we have the ultimate necessity in warfare, captured in the circumstance of an imminent catastrophe against which there is a moral urgency (necessity) to act (e.g., by the aerial bombardment of enemy civilian populations). As Walzer makes clear, this is not to be understood on analogy to an act of self-defense in domestic society, for an individual defending his or her life against an attacker is not morally permitted to attack innocent people – one can only attack those who attack you first. "But communities, in emergencies, seem to have different and larger prerogatives. . . . For the survival and freedom of political communities – whose members share a way of life, developed by their ancestors, to be passed on to their children – are the highest values of international society."[29] Moreover, according to Walzer, "Nazism challenged these values on a grand scale, but challenges more narrowly conceived, *if they are of the same kind*, have similar moral consequences. They bring us under the rule of necessity (and necessity knows no rules)."[30]

In an essay entitled "Emergency Ethics,"[31] Walzer acknowledges not only that "supreme emergencies put morality itself at risk" but that it is philosophically provocative and paradoxical to argue both that the constraints of morality always apply and that political leaders can do whatever must be done when collective survival is at stake.[32]

[M]oral limits are never suspended – the way we might, for example, suspend habeas corpus in time of civil war. But there are moments when the rules can be and perhaps have to be overridden. They have to be overridden precisely because they have not been suspended. And overriding the rules leaves guilt behind, as a recognition of the enormity of what we have done. . . .[33]

Walzer refers to his illustration provided in *Just and Unjust Wars* of the British decision to bomb German cities in the early 1940s and to intentionally aim at residential areas in order "to kill and terrorize the civilian population, to attack German morale rather than German military might."[34] It is clear, he admits, "that the intention was wrongful, the bombing criminal," but "if there was no other way of preventing a Nazi triumph, then the immorality – no less immoral, for what else can the killing of the innocent be? – was also, simultaneously, morally defensible. That is the provocation and the paradox."[35]

Walzer attempts to alleviate any skepticism that greets his account by explaining the paradox in terms of two opposing views of morality, the absolutism of the theory of rights versus the "radical flexibility" of utilitarian theory. According to the conception of rights, innocent human beings must never be targeted intentionally, while for utilitarianism "innocence is only one value that must be weighed against other values in the pursuit of the greatest good of the greatest number."[36] Because the claims of both moral conceptions are significant and important, such that claims on one side cannot totally defeat those on the other, "we must negotiate the middle ground."[37] On the one hand, moral absolutism cannot win out because consequences can have great moral significance and we cannot refuse to consider what it means to "do justice even if the heavens fall." On the other hand, utilitarianism, which puts great weight on attaining goals and allows this to excuse morally questionable goal promoting acts, tends to be "speculative and arbitrary" in assigning and measuring and particularizes cost/benefit analysis in a way that discriminates different constituencies – everyone's utilities do not count the same in situations of adversity and war. While this weakness in utilitarianism is what leads to an appeal to rights in order to properly establish the conventional constraints on warfare, the appeal to rights is itself based on certain "minimal fixed values" which when put at risk lessens these constraints such that utilitarianism reasserts itself as the "utilitarianism of extremity."[38] According to Walzer,

'Supreme emergency' describes those rare moments when the negative value that we assign – that we can't help assigning – to the disaster that looms before us devalues morality itself and leaves us free to do whatever is militarily necessary to avoid the disaster, so long as what we do does not produce an even worse disaster.[39]

Despite Walzer's casting of his paradox in terms of two opposed moralities that, in a sort of dialectical way, make competing demands upon us (which helps to shed light on a pervasive tension Walzer recognizes in *Just and Unjust Wars* between fighting well and winning), he seems here to arrive at a kind of realism (already hinted at in his treatment of collateral damage to human shields), despite his explicit rejection of realism in the first chapter of his book. Moreover, there are several important considerations that belie the notion that supreme emergency can be understood in the context of a kind of moral paradox or dilemma produced by equally relevant competing moralities.

First, as Walzer himself recognizes, the utilitarianism that overrides the constraints of rights in a supreme emergency is one that in war attaches only negative utilities to the enemy. It is difficult to see how this particularized utilitarianism can count in any commensurate way as a morality in opposition to rights claims if it gives up an equality of values. If we hold that morality applies universally to all people but then, due perhaps to extreme threats to our safety or existence, attach positive values only to our own utilities then the ultimate guiding consideration is not utilitarianism, but self-interest. A consistent utilitarian approach, if it is to be taken as a wide moral perspective, would allow the possibility that our safety and existence may not be required in order to satisfy the greatest good for the greatest number in a global context. Of course, in this context the calculations will be extraordinarily difficult to make because of the scope of knowledge required about the utilities of all other peoples. Moreover, there is the cultural difficulty of remaining impartial in these calculations regarding the value of one's own society versus the number of innocent lives taken in another.

Here is where we get to the center of the weakness in Walzer's principle of supreme emergency and indeed of his conception of the constraints that noncombatant immunity places on warfare generally. Rather than seeing supreme emergency in terms of a moral paradox created by competing moralities we should see it as a matter of partiality in the application of moral principles or rules to one's own. This is blurred somewhat by Walzer's claim that it is the threat to "our deepest values and collective survival" that triggers a supreme emergency. We have to be clear about *whose* values and survival are at stake. We may be convinced that our basic values are shared by the majority of peoples globally and that their survival depends upon ours but we will believe this primarily not because we have the best impartial and objective arguments for it but rather because of an acculturated disposition. When Walzer holds that the constraints that rights place on warfare can be lifted when the basic values underlying those rights are threatened – making it sound as if violating rights in a particular situation is for the sake of preserving rights in a more basic way – the underlying implication is that it is *our* rights that are most important and for which the rights of others can be sacrificed.[40] If we generalize this rationale to apply to any society or culture the existence of which is at stake in a war, then we have, in principle, realism in the appeal to the prerogatives of survival. Indeed, could not an aggressor nation-state make an appeal to supreme emergency when in the course of a war the existence of its political community is threatened by imminent defeat?

Second, Walzer's explanation of the lack of parallel between how moral constraints operate upon communities or leaders of communities and how they limit the behavior of human individuals in situations of self-defense also reveals a realist sort of appeal. While *individuals*, whether in domestic society or in warfare, cannot appeal to supreme emergency in order to have their own self defense override the rights of others, for example, by targeting innocent people ("A moral person will accept risk, will even accept death, rather than kill the innocent"),[41] political and military leaders are limited in the risks they can impose on their people, specifically those under their authority.

> [N]o government can put the life of the community itself and all of its members at risk, so long as there are actions available to it, even immoral actions, that would avoid or reduce the risks. It is for the sake of risk avoidance or risk reduction that governments are chosen. That is what political leaders are for; that is their first task.[42]

Underlying this "argument from representation" there is – in the spirit of Edmund Burke – an appeal to the "value of community," and a claim that commitment to continuity across generations, the *ongoingness* of a community, is a moral value so fundamental that when faced with extinction it can override the moral limits that normally govern behavior.

With this communitarian appeal, Walzer has moved not only beyond the fundamentality of universal moral rights but also beyond any globally contextualized utilitarianism. Moreover, the appeal to communitarianism as if it were a sort of moral principle in competition with individual rights is misleading, for it is actually either a sociological thesis about how social formations tend as a matter of course to prevail over individuals and/or it is an ideology that posits the value of community as having priority over the value of the individual, on the presumption that the individual can only have a meaningful existence within a community. Hence, while individuals can be put at risk, the community cannot, or will not. The ideological character of this position is evidenced in Walzer's comment that "[i]f the political community were nothing more than a neutral framework within which individuals pursued their own versions of the good life, as some liberal political philosophers suggest, the doctrine of supreme emergency would have no purchase."[43] This leads one to wonder whether such liberal societies are therefore morally expendable, in contrast to communitarian ones. Perhaps Walzer does not believe any liberal societies in the proper sense actually exist, but it would seem rather strange to suggest that the moral question of whether it is ever permissible to intentionally kill innocent civilians depends on whether it is a communitarian society directing the killing.

Again, apart from this ideological component, this stance implies realism in suggesting that certain social and cultural realities inevitably trump individual rights when the stakes are high enough. Given the power and influence of a communitarian social system over its members, how could it be otherwise? The "ought implies can" principle seems to indicate, in this context, that it is just not practical to expect that a political community can risk its existence for the sake of innocent individuals. Does this mean that the survival of a (or our) particular community can trump the survival of other communities, that have done no harm and are perhaps also struggling to survive under emergency conditions, should the existence of these communities for some reason be in mutual conflict? Moreover, what if the innocent lives to be sacrificed are not just those of a determinate number of individuals but of a whole ethnic or racial group? Can a political community that stands for justice make that sacrifice without contradiction?

Third, the very evaluative language Walzer uses to capture the moral tension that exists under a supreme emergency reveals his ambivalence as to whether the targeted killing of noncombatants can really be morally justified. On the one hand, moral rules always govern human behavior and can never be suspended, meaning they always have a hold on us no matter what the situation. On the other hand, the moral rules can be overridden in a situation of supreme emergency, for reasons already considered. When this happens, as when the British in 1940 killed and terrorized the German population in bombing their cities, Walzer says flatly "the intention was wrongful, the bombing criminal; its victims were innocent men, women, and children."[44] What the British did was *immoral* but simultaneously "morally defensible" because the consequences of not committing the immoral act were too great. Walzer claims that these are *moral* consequences that can be ignored at our physical and moral peril. However, we have seen that the weight of the term 'moral' here is a matter of the posited value of the *ongoingness* of a community, of the strength and depth of attachment to a community. But has not Walzer mixed together the moral and the psychological in such a way as to allow the latter to effectively determine "justification" of killing the innocent? This really is not rational moral justification but is, rather, a "justification" by appeal to collective egocentrism, to the privileging of what is ours.

"Do justice even if the heavens fall" may be impractical psychologically because of the extreme consequences, but it clearly is not immoral. Doing justice absolutely is implied in the fulfilling of moral duty, whether we think of it as fulfilling a moral maxim, as actualizing a virtue, or acting according to a utilitarian calculation or rule.[45] However, taking on the guilt of killing the innocent, thereby becoming a "moral criminal," can hardly be described as a moral act, no matter what the reason for doing it. The doctrine of "dirty hands" may explain why someone who adheres to certain moral rules will violate them and act immorally for the sake of a larger good, but this cannot make the violation morally permissible.[46]

Just as being moral can never be immoral, but in certain situations impractical, so being immoral can never be moral, but it can be practical given certain ends, such as survival. The idea that sometimes "it is permissible (or necessary) to get our hands dirty" is really just a way of saying that sometimes practicality wins out over morality. To say that this equates with moral permissibility is not just to state a formal paradox but to utter an incoherence. Even Machiavelli, who understood the value of dissembling in order to make immoral actions appear moral, was clear that things done in the service of "raison d'etat" could not seriously be captured in Walzer's claim that "moral communities make great immoralities morally possible."[47] The consummate realist understood that it wasn't a matter of the moral right of a state or community to exist but of its natural impetus to survive.

5. WALZER'S PRACTICAL MORALITY

My claim that Walzer falls into an incoherent tilt toward realism does not imply his embracing of realism in any full-blown manner. If realism means that in war anything goes and that we cannot make meaningful moral judgments about conduct in warfare, then clearly Walzer rejects realism in this sense. A fundamental premise of his work is that conduct in warfare can be judged and can either be given moral justification or moral criticism.[48] Moral argument regarding warfare is meaningful because "arguments and judgments shape . . . *the moral reality of war.*"[49]

> It is important to stress that the moral reality of war is not fixed by the actual activities of soldiers but by the opinions of mankind. That means, in part, that it is fixed by the activity of philosophers, lawyers, publicists of all sorts. But these people don't work in isolation from the experience of combat, and their views have value only insofar as they give shape and structure to that experience in ways that are plausible to the rest of us.[50]

Practical morality, therefore, is realistic in taking into account both the experience of war and the perceptions and judgments that are often made in relation to that experience. Of course, this involves not merely describing the judgments made and justifications commonly given.

> We can analyze these moral claims, seek out their coherence, lay bare the principles that they exemplify. We can reveal commitments that go deeper than partisan allegiance and the urgencies of battle. . . . And then we can expose the hypocrisy of soldiers and statesmen who publicly acknowledge these commitments while seeking in fact only their own advantage.[51]

How far can this method go in articulating a coherent conventional morality for *jus in bello*? Only so far as experience lends itself to a coherent moral treatment, which may be more limited than Walzer presumes. We arrive at the margins of coherence when confronted with moral dilemmas, such as situations of "forced choice," where there may be compelling considerations for departing from the moral rules of warfare. Walzer has attempted to capture such departures within the overall framework of his moral conception of rights and his practical method, perhaps at the expense of the overall coherence of his conception of rights (in the vein of Gödel's Proof, the system cannot both be complete and without contradiction). Are the parameters of just warfare better recognized by justifying exceptions to the moral rules of war and the constraints they impose, or is the coherence of morality better served by recognizing that certain exceptions, particularly those that fly squarely in the face of basic moral principles, cannot be morally justified? Moreover, if, as Walzer recognizes, necessity in warfare is never about inevitability but about probabilities and risks,[52] there always must be significant doubt as to whether a decision from supreme emergency is the right thing to do. Such a decision might be taken with even greater caution if it were understood to involve a transgression that cannot be given moral sanction.

At the end of the last chapter of his book, discussing war crimes by officers and their soldiers, Walzer recognizes that the necessities generated in the conflict between collective survival and human rights, in which we experience the "ultimate tyranny of war," result in "the ultimate incoherence of the theory of war."[53] We must, he admits, call those who in a supreme emergency override the rules of war and kill innocent people "murderers," albeit with a good cause. They have "dirty hands" in that, although they did what they had to do given their charge and responsibilities, they "must nonetheless bear a burden of responsibility and guilt. They have killed unjustly, let us say, for the sake of justice itself, but justice itself requires that unjust killing be condemned."[54] However, after presenting Thomas Nagel's conclusion, from his essay "War and Massacre," that "the world can present us with situations in which there is no honorable or moral course for a man to take, no course free of guilt and responsibility for evil," Walzer counters that we have more than moral indeterminacy, for political leaders must choose the "utilitarian side of the dilemma" and thus "must opt for collective survival and override those rights that have suddenly loomed as obstacles to survival."[55] They are not free of guilt but they are, apparently, justified. However, here moral justification must lack coherence, as the language Walzer uses suggests. If to target and kill innocent people is murder, then it cannot be morally right, and if it is morally right it cannot be murder but justified killing. One cannot give back with one hand what is taken away with the other.

This duality of judgments, where actions are decidedly both right and wrong, just and unjust, does not seem for Walzer to indicate an incoherence in his moral conception because, realistically, utilitarian or communitarian considerations ultimately win out, and given what is at stake this will perhaps be more right than wrong. This final stance certainly does not square easily with Walzer's rights-based conception of the rules of war where "[c]onsiderations of utility play into the structure at many points, but they cannot account for it as a whole. Their part is subsidiary to that of rights; it is constrained by rights."[56] If rights were the consistent guiding principle, then we would expect that in supreme emergencies the more morally correct thing to do would be not to sacrifice the rights of the innocent, even if it meant a grave threat of our collective defeat. We might still make this sacrifice and consider it somehow excusable given the costs of not doing so, but it would clearly lack moral justification on the basis of rights.

6. CONCLUSION

In this chapter, I have examined tensions and incoherence in Walzer's account of noncombatant immunity. While Walzer claims initially that the principle of noncombatant immunity holds absolutely and without exception with regard to risks that individual combatants must take to protect noncombatants (risks that may be very difficult for combatants to accept), when the risks endanger the political community that the campaign is intended to protect, then self-defense seems to have the final word regarding the killing of the innocent. To think of this decision as a *moral* one because, prior to resorting to the supreme emergency action, we have been guided by recognized moral rules that require us to resist such action unless and until there is no alternative, is to ignore the fact that fighting well morally is being subordinated to necessity. Despite Walzer's attempt to characterize this as a sort of higher moral necessity, based on the ultimate value of the existence of a particular community, at this point he actually has made a significant concession to the idea that in reality survival trumps moral behavior.

A coherent ethic of war does not absolutely prohibit that harm come to noncombatants, but it must articulate the limits of such harm with consistent adherence to the doctrine of noncombatant immunity, based on consistent adherence to the doctrine of rights, if that is its basis. Such a position will, however, recognize that (as Hume said regarding mitigated skepticism) despite the conceptual truth about the limits of what we can know and justify, instinct can prove too strong for principle. In the case of warfare, this may well mean that exceptional violations to the rules of war are practically too difficult to avoid and thus can be understandable, and perhaps at some level excusable, but never morally justified.

NOTES

1. Michael Walzer, *Just and Unjust Wars: A Moral Argument With Historical Illustrations*, 2nd edn. (New York: HarperCollins, 1992).
2. Walzer, *Just and Unjust Wars*, p. 138.
3. Walzer, *Just and Unjust Wars*, p. 151.
4. Walzer, *Just and Unjust Wars*, p. 152.
5. Walzer, *Just and Unjust Wars*, p. 153.
6. Walzer, *Just and Unjust Wars*, p. 153.
7. Walzer, *Just and Unjust Wars*, pp. 153–156.
8. Walzer, *Just and Unjust Wars*, p. 153.
9. Walzer, *Just and Unjust Wars*, p. 156. Further on the page, Walzer's analogy with the risks that occur in domestic society and how they can be relaxed in emergency situations seems weak. Military necessity does not, *pace* Walzer, work exactly like civil emergency, and not just because in war the standards are relaxed. War is a decision by the parties that enter into it, whereas a civil emergency is not, certainly not when the emergency is a result of accident, natural disaster, etc.
10. Walzer, *Just and Unjust Wars*, p. 155.
11. Walzer, *Just and Unjust Wars*, p. 156. As Brian Orend points out, "due care" seems to involve soldiers taking greater risks to themselves in order not to target civilians or harm them collaterally, meaning that "soldiers use only certain kinds of weapons . . ., move in more closely on targets . . ., gather and analyse intelligence on the precise nature of suspected targets, perhaps provide some kind of advance warning to nearby civilians, and certainly plan the tactic in advance with an eye towards minimizing civilian casualties." *Michael Walzer on War and Justice* (McGill-Queen's University Press, 2000), pp. 119–120.
12. Walzer, *Just and Unjust Wars*, pp. 144f.
13. Walzer, *Just and Unjust Wars*, p. 157.
14. Walzer, *Just and Unjust Wars*, p. 173.
15. Walzer, *Just and Unjust Wars*, p. 174.
16. Walzer, *Just and Unjust Wars*, p. 158.
17. Walzer, *Just and Unjust Wars*, p. 228.
18. Walzer, *Just and Unjust Wars*, p. 229.
19. Walzer, *Just and Unjust Wars*, pp. 229, 230.
20. Walzer, *Just and Unjust Wars*, p. 230.
21. Walzer, *Just and Unjust Wars*, p. 230. However, the idea of the moral equality of soldiers on each side of a war, as well as the moral equality of all citizens regardless of political allegiance, will not likely be plausible to most people either. In any case, plausibility should be a matter of the rational implication of a principle and not whether people are simply willing psychologically to follow it through in action, as Walzer seems to suggest. Appeal to this sense of plausibility goes against the thrust of Walzer's own tendency to challenge the overly permissive conventional wisdom on the justified killing of civilians.
22. Walzer, *Just and Unjust Wars*, pp. 230–231.

23. Walzer, *Just and Unjust Wars*, p. 231.
24. Walzer, *Just and Unjust Wars*, p. 231.
25. Walzer, *Just and Unjust Wars*, p. 231. It is interesting how the discussion of the more significant limits on noncombatant immunity as relates to collateral damage leads to a consideration of how rights can be overridden. Walzer does not provide a detailed conception of the overriding of rights but rather seems to presuppose that the idea is intuitively clear and noncontroversial.
26. Walzer, *Just and Unjust Wars*, p. 252.
27. Walzer, *Just and Unjust Wars*, p. 253.
28. Walzer, *Just and Unjust Wars*, p. 253.
29. Walzer, *Just and Unjust Wars*, p. 254.
30. Walzer, *Just and Unjust Wars*, p. 254. See his essay "World War II: Why Was This War Different" in *War and Moral Responsibility,* ed. Marshall Cohen, Thomas Nagel, and Thomas Scanlon (Princeton, NJ: Princeton University Press, 1974) where Walzer admits that the moral rules of war are not absolute but rather "establish very strong presumptions against certain sorts of actions, like the deliberate killing of noncombatants" (p. 103). However, "[t]hese are not irrebuttable presumptions. . . . It is possible to imagine situations where one would break the rules and accept the moral consequences of doing so" (ibid).
31. Included in his recent volume entitled *Arguing About War* (New Haven CT: Yale University Press, 2004).
32. Walzer, "Emergency Ethics," pp. 33–34.
33. Walzer, "Emergency Ethics," p. 34.
34. Walzer, "Emergency Ethics," p. 34.
35. Walzer, "Emergency Ethics," pp. 34–35.
36. Walzer, "Emergency Ethics," p. 35.
37. Walzer, "Emergency Ethics," p. 36.
38. Walzer, "Emergency Ethics," p. 40.
39. Walzer, "Emergency Ethics," p. 40.
40. See Michael Gelven's chapter "The We-they Principle," in *War and Existence: A Philosophical Enquiry* (University Park, PA: The Pennsylvania State University Press, 1994).
41. Walzer, "Emergency Ethics," p. 41.
42. Walzer, "Emergency Ethics," p. 42.
43. Walzer, "Emergency Ethics," p. 44.
44. Walzer, "Emergency Ethics," p. 34.
45. Thomas Nagel has an interesting response to the criticism that holding to moral absolutes reflects a narrow self-interest in preserving one's own moral purity: "Any theory which defines the right course of action in various circumstances and asserts that one should adopt that course, ipso facto asserts that one should do what will preserve one's moral purity, simply because the right course of action *is* what will preserve one's moral purity in those circumstances. Of course, utilitarianism does not assert that this is *why* one should adopt that course, but we have seen that the same is true of absolutism." "War and Massacre" in *Philosophy and Public Affairs* 1, no. 2 (Winter, 1972), p. 133.
46. See Walzer's essay "Political Action: The Problem of Dirty Hands" in Cohen et al., *War and Moral Responsibility*. The heroism that Walzer finds in Camus' "just assassins" does not seem to convey the sort of moral permissibility required for justification

of killing the innocent. The term "just" can apply only metaphorically to the actions of existential heroes whose actions are in a realm where everything is permitted, beyond good and evil.
47. Walzer, "Emergency Ethics," p. 50.
48. Indeed, Walzer suggests that appeals to realism often are a form of apologetics, a defense of conduct that may appear unjust, with implicit expression of moral anxiety (40–42).
49. Walzer, *Just and Unjust Wars*, p. 15.
50. Walzer, *Just and Unjust Wars*, p. 15.
51. Walzer, *Just and Unjust Wars*, p. xxix.
52. Walzer, *Just and Unjust Wars*, p. 8.
53. Walzer, *Just and Unjust Wars*, p. 325.
54. Walzer, *Just and Unjust Wars*, p. 323. Here Walzer seems to acknowledge the moral implication of having dirty hands, that the actions in question bring guilt and condemnation rather than justification.
55. Walzer, *Just and Unjust Wars*, p. 326. The quote from Nagel can be found in the essay in *Philosophy and Public Affairs* (cited above), p. 143.
56. Walzer, *Just and Unjust Wars*, p. xxx.

PATRICK HUBBARD

A REALIST RESPONSE TO WALZER'S *JUST AND UNJUST WARS*

> [T]he first war of the 21st century . . . is the war against terrorism and weapons of mass destruction in the hands of dictators.
> You are with us or you are against us in the fight against terror.
> There are no rules.
>
> George W. Bush[1]

Michael Walzer's *Just and Unjust Wars* is one of those rare books that more than deserves the glowing praise on the back of the paperback edition.[2] Because his thoughtful analysis is so thorough, readable, and well-grounded in numerous historical examples, it provides a broad basis for understanding the relationship between war and justice. Despite these strengths, however, Walzer's book has an important shortcoming: It does not satisfactorily address the lack of connection between his rights-based scheme of moral actions and actual conduct in the real world. One reason for this lack is the limited role that shared values play in constraining discourse and conduct in a modern nation. Another problem is that leaders believe they have a moral role-responsibility to protect the nation from the risk of catastrophic harm and often feel obligated thereby to engage in what they see as "justified" denials of rights. After a war, moral theory is sufficiently manipulable that it provides minimal guidance for assigning "responsibility." Moreover, a nation that has won a war is motivated to avoid imposing responsibility because of gratitude to leaders who satisfied their role-responsibility of protecting the nation, even if their success involved an unjust denial of rights. Given these problems, it is important to build on the strengths of Walzer's work by combining it with a more realistic approach that not only acknowledges the importance of rights and morality but also emphasizes prudential arguments and legal and political frameworks.

1. WALZER'S PRACTICAL MORALITY AND HIS ARGUMENT AGAINST REALISM

The lack of connection between moral theory and conduct is a fundamental problem with Walzer's theory because his goal is to write a "book of *practical* morality" based on "a doctrine of human rights" (xxi, xxii, emphasis added). This practical "moral realism" is designed to do two things: (1) provide "some guidance" for people "faced with hard choices," and (2) help control officials by exposing and condemning "the hypocrisy of soldiers and statesmen who publicly acknowledge these [moral] commitments while seeking in fact only their own advantage" (xxi, 20). If one has a concern for rights and morality, Walzer's practical morality provides "some guidance" on many difficult issues. However, the scheme is *im*practical in terms of controlling conduct and assigning responsibility for immoral actions because its moral "guidance" is widely manipulated, ignored, or reformulated into a less strict system. In short, there is a gap between reality and Walzer's moral scheme.

One of the strengths of Walzer's book is that he explicitly addresses such problems. The first chapter focuses on the issue of morality's influence on war by addressing the "realist argument" that moral judgments about war are simply a charade because, in fact, "anything goes" (3–4). The realist argument is initially addressed by considering Thucydides's account of the Melian dialogue in *The Peloponnesian War*. At issue is whether the island state of Melos can remain neutral and not be subject to Athens, which has developed an empire based on its naval power. The Athenians do not waste time with "fine words about justice," about what Athens "deserved," or about any "right" of Melos to be neutral as Athens struggles to maintain its empire (5). Instead, they say, "We will talk instead of what is feasible and what is necessary. For this is what war is really like: 'they that have odds of power exact as much as they can, and the weak yield to such conditions as they can get'" (5). "The neutrality of Melos 'will be an argument of our weakness' [and] will inspire rebellion throughout the islands . . ." (5). Even if the generals had talked in terms of justice, this talk would have been shaped by their interest in denying neutrality in order to maintain their empire. Consequently, "talk about justice cannot be anything more than talk" (10).

To Walzer, this realist position is *a*moral because it asserts that even if people engage in the "fair pretense" of moral talk, "we can understand what other people are saying only if we see through their 'fair pretenses' and translate moral talk into the harder currency of interest talk" (11). Thus, decisions concerning war and the survival of a particular conception of one's state (or tribe or culture) are "distinct and separate from the laws of moral life" (7). This separateness involves two interrelated aspects: (1) decision-makers lack the freedom to make moral decisions, and (2) talk about justice is just talk (10).

Walzer rejects both aspects of this realist position. He argues that moral freedom exists because choosing to deny rights is rarely necessary to further self-interest in the sense that the choice or the result to be avoided is inevitable (8). In virtually all cases, a particular war or military action is rarely essential to prevent a dire catastrophic result; the result may not really be catastrophic and no one can be sure of the future (8). For example, the Athenians cannot be certain that the goal of maintaining an empire based on "domination and subjugation" was essential to preventing the catastrophic "fall" of Athens (8). Even if maintaining the empire is essential, how can one be sure the destruction of Melos is necessary to do this? (8). Moral talk is meaningful because: (1) *it is limited* in the sense that it cannot be simply manipulated to justify any and all unjust conduct concerning war; and (2) *this limited moral talk can constrain conduct concerning war* because the ability to hold actors "responsible" for immoral actions offsets to some extent people's motivation to seek self-interest without concern for justice.

In addressing the nature of moral talk, Walzer recognizes that morality is, in part, a "world of ideology and verbal manipulation" (12). In this world, arguments based on morals can be manipulated to "justify" actions that are, in Walzer's scheme, unjust. However, he argues "the possibilities for manipulation are limited" because moral claims have "entailments" and involve underlying "principles" and "commitments" (xxi, 12). These claims are subject to analysis and canons of "coherence," and we can "hold such people to their own principles" (xxi). Therefore, persons making moral claims and using moral justifications are led into "a world of discourse where" they are "severely constrained" in what they say (12).

Even if moral talk can be limited, the realist argument is still valid if this talk does not, in fact, constrain behavior. "The moral theorist . . . must come to grips with the fact that his *rules are often violated or ignored* – and with the deeper realization that, to men at war, the *rules often don't seem relevant* to the extremity of their situation" (14–15, emphasis added). Walzer addresses this difficulty by arguing that, because his moral scheme is based on the shared values and meanings underlying justifications and judgments about war, officials can be held "responsible" for violating values they espouse to justify their conduct. In addressing the problem of unjust actions by officials, the theorist "does not surrender his sense of war as a human action, purposive and premeditated, for whose effects *someone is responsible*. . . . [H]e searches for human agents" (15, emphasis added). The theorist is not "alone in this task" because "*[a]ll of us are inclined to hold them responsible* for what they do ..." (15, emphasis added). "[T]he moral reality of war is not fixed by the actual activities of soldiers but by the *opinions of mankind*" (15, emphasis added). "The moral world of war is shared not because we arrive at the same conclusions ..., but because we acknowledge the same difficulties on the way to our conclusions, face the same problems, talk the same language" (xx–xxi).

The responsibility of those who wage war unjustly is the focus of Part Five, which opens with the assertion, "The assignment of responsibility is the critical test of the argument for justice" (287). "[T]he theory of justice should point us to the men and women from whom we can rightly demand an accounting" (287). "If there are recognizable war crimes, there must be recognizable criminals" (287). Despite the use of the terms "crimes" and "criminals," the task is to assign *moral* responsibility, not legal responsibility. "[W]e are concerned with the blameworthiness of individuals, not their legal guilt or innocence" (288). "What is crucial is that ... [the criminals] can be pointed at ..." (289).

2. A REALIST CRITIQUE OF WALZER'S PRACTICAL MORALITY

Walzer argues that his theory provides a *practical* morality of war because: (1) moral discourse will constrain the arguments that can be made to justify wars and the conduct of wars; and (2) "the opinions of mankind" will hold those who commit "crimes" "responsible for what they do" (14–15). These two assertions are interrelated because both assume that the "opinions of mankind" will in fact limit immoral conduct by constraining moral discourse and by assigning responsibility. As indicated below, Walzer himself seems to doubt the validity of this very questionable assumption.

2.1 Understanding Walzer's Argument in Terms of Western Democratic States

Walzer's reliance on discourse and the "opinions of mankind" has a dated feel to it today. The gender reference to *"man*kind" is jolting to some sensibilities. In addition, like Jefferson's reference in the Declaration of Independence to "a decent respect to the opinions of mankind," the phrase suggests unspoken qualifying adjectives, as in the qualified phrase: "opinions of *thoughtful, educated, right-thinking* mankind." Regardless of whether Walzer intended such qualifiers, the "opinions of mankind" are now viewed as fundamentally diverse, and it takes considerable optimism to think there will be worldwide consensus on anything about morality except generalities. Specifics, particularly where issues of the application of a general moral theory to a specific war are involved, will be matters of contention.

To the extent Walzer addresses specifics, he generally does so within the context of a modern Western nation-state. In this context, there is more basis for assertions like the following: "The Athenians shared a moral vocabulary, shared it with the people of . . . Melos; and allowing for cultural differences, *they share it with us too*" (11, emphasis added). Though this shift to "western culture" avoids the more extreme problems of global multiculturalism, the range of views in our culture still limits agreement to broad abstractions. In addition, this emphasis on western culture implicitly accepts the ways political and moral opinions are formed and operate within a modern Western state. Because this context limits and structures the role of popular opinions and moral discourse, theory can only provide, at best, "*some* guidance."

Walzer recognizes that debate about and the assignment of responsibility for injustice in war is difficult within a "realistic picture" of the state and politics, where "[t]he state that goes to war is, like our own, an enormous state, governed at a great distance from its ordinary citizens by powerful and often arrogant officials" (301). Recent events indicate this realistic picture sketched in the 1970s is still accurate. For example, regardless of one's moral or political views about American actions since 9/11, the *process* of forming opinions and making decisions about the Iraq war suggests a limited role for reasoned argument about morality.

One problem is that rhetoric like "war on terror" is used so widely. Unless radically redefined in some Orwellian manner, "war" is an activity where nations (or other identifiable groups) engage in violent, deadly actions directed toward one another. Where a broad social or political problem or a dispersed hidden "enemy" is involved, the violent techniques of war – armies, bombs, etc. – have limited effect and involve high collateral costs. Nevertheless, a metaphor like "war on terror" is used (like its predecessors "war on poverty" and "war on drugs") for a simple reason: "War" has a powerful rhetorical impact because the term conveys a sense of extreme urgency requiring unity and sacrifice and justifying denials of rights. Dissent and questioning are suspect, and liberties and moral rights tend to look like luxuries that should be sacrificed until the emergency passes. In "war," the world is divided into two worlds – us and the enemy. As with Melos, the third world of neutrality becomes suspect, dangerous, and subject to forceful conversion to "our" side. To the extent these wartime reactions are inappropriate for a metaphorical war, debate is distorted.

Distortion also results because debate about issues like the invasion of Iraq in 2003 "is mediated by a system which is partially controlled by . . . distant officials and which in any case allows for considerable distortions" (301). A sense of the impact of this *media*ting system is conveyed by the following description of press coverage of the invasion:

In Doha, the US built a $1.5 million press centre. 700 journalists were "embedded" with coalition forces. . . . John Donvan of ABC News [expressed the following "anxieties"]:
 [T]he networks were so enthusiastic about the prospect of covering the war in this excitingly close-up fashion that it coloured their entire attitude to the war itself. They *wanted* it to take place, because they knew how effective the reporting of it would be, and how large the audiences would be. And that meant . . . they largely ignored the anti-war protests in the United States and around the world as freakish and irrelevant.[3]

2.2 The Limits on Moral Theory in the Real World

2.2.1 Constraining Decisions as Wars are Declared or Fought: The Problem of Leaders' Role-responsibility
In contrast to the discussion of the assignment of responsibility, which is a backward-looking task, Walzer says little about the role of moral theory in constraining decisions about war as they are being made. To the extent he addresses this topic, his "realistic picture" of modern democracies causes him to recognize that moral theory imposes little, if any, constraint because "[w]e are not usually philosophical in moments of crisis . . ." (xvii).

War can present political leaders with the choice of risking the basic well-being or the existence of their nation, which are outcomes "that must be avoided at all costs," or avoiding such outcomes by denying the rights of others (325). Walzer argues a leader cannot choose the second alternative simply by using a "sliding scale" that devalues the rights of enemy citizens in order to further a "just cause" (231–232). Instead, that alternative can be taken only in "extreme cases" that satisfy two strict conditions. First, necessity provides a justification for denying rights, but only in the rare situation where there is "certainty" that: (1) the outcome to be avoided is an imminent, horrific result like a world ruled by Hitler's Nazis; and (2) the denial of these rights is essential to avoiding this outcome (8, 231–232). Second, because the decision to deny rights where the two requirements of necessity are satisfied should be "agonizing," leaders who decide to deny rights for this reason are not "free of guilt" (326). Walzer attempts to use these conditions to bridge the gap between the requirements of his moral theory and his candid appraisal of the conduct of the leaders within his realistic view of the state. However, this "bridge" does not work because it is based on an "ideal" view of leaders, not a realist view.

As to the first condition, Walzer concedes that this requirement does not limit leaders to the rare "extreme cases" where a denial would be appropriate. Instead, necessity arguments "are common enough in time of war," and "the case for breaking the rules and violating those rights is made . . . often, . . . by soldiers and statesmen who cannot always be called wicked . . ." (228, 253).

> It is not hard to understand why anyone *convinced of the moral urgency of victory* would be impatient with . . . [limits]. . . . Either fight all-out or not at all. This argument . . . is universal in the history of war. Once soldiers are actually engaged, and especially if they are engaged in a Righteous War or a just war, a steady pressure builds up. . . . And then, . . . the rules are broken *for the sake of the cause.* (227, emphasis added)

The conduct of political leaders is based on a different scheme from Walzer's for a basic moral reason: They have a role-responsibility to protect their citizens, who will suffer if the leaders' decisions result in a catastrophe for the nation. Satisfying this responsibility results in three important charges in Walzer's scheme. First, the requirement of "imminent" catastrophic is abandoned. Why is a catastrophe in five years any less catastrophic? Second, the certainty requirement is abandoned because realistic assessments of probabilities, much less certainties, concerning the risk of a catastrophe or the effectiveness of methods to address the risk are virtually impossible in war. In contrast to Walzer, leaders feel that their decisions must be based on "probabilities and risk" (*see* 8). Third, leaders address this risk and uncertainty by focusing on their concrete, specific obligation to protect their citizens and, in effect, placing less value on their more general duty to respect the rights of enemy citizens. These changes result in a more easily satisfied test: Deny rights where the denial may avoid a risk of some horrific impact on the national interest.

The generals who destroyed Melos adopted an approach that was not only different from Walzer's but also from the role-responsibility scheme sketched above. Does it matter whether the generals destroyed Melos simply out of a concern for power, feasibility, and the interests of Athens (5) or out of a concern to fulfill their role-based moral duty to Athenians to deny the rights of Melians in order to avoid risking the fall of Athens? Walzer argues there is an important difference because, if the Athenians claim to be doing what is morally right, their claims will be constrained by moral discourse. Such a claim of moral correctness "presumes on the moral understanding of the rest of us . . ." (20). "[T]he possibilities of manipulation are limited . . . [because] each . . . claim has its own entailments, leading into a world of discourse where . . . I am severely constrained in what

I can say" (12). "[T]hough it is not easy to judge [factual claims] . . ., it is important to make the effort" (20).

However, when Walzer addresses decisions within the context of his realist model of the modern state, he appears to think discourse does *not* impose constraints. In discussing ways "to get one's fellow citizens to think seriously" about the justice of a war or oppose an unjust war, Walzer notes: "It is not easy to know what course of action might serve these purposes. Politics is difficult at such a time" (303). One reason politics is "difficult at such a time" is the usual public reaction to war in the modern nation:

> When a state like this commits itself to a campaign of aggression, its citizens (or many of them) are likely to go along, as Americans did during the Vietnam war, arguing that the war may after all be just; that it is not possible for them to be sure whether it is just or not; that their leaders know best and tell them this or that, which sounds plausible enough; and that nothing they can do will make much difference anyway. (301)

Thus, Walzer appears pessimistic not only about whether discourse will constrain leaders to follow his moral scheme but also about whether it could constrain leaders acting under the more easily satisfied moral scheme based on role-responsibility.

As to the second condition, Walzer recognizes that there is a paradox in expecting leaders to feel guilty for properly acting on necessity even though they can hardly help but choose the "utilitarian side" because "[t]hat is what they are there for" (326). His sole defense of that paradox is that it reflects "the deeper complexity of our moral realism . . ." (326). Unfortunately, this "moral realism" is more conceptual than factual because Walzer provides little, if any, evidence in this book (or in other works[4]) to show that leaders, in fact, feel guilt or shame for denying rights in accordance with the leaders' role-responsibility to avoid a risk of catastrophic harm to the nation. Instead, even though he concludes that Truman engaged in the war crime of terrorism in using the atomic bomb and that Churchill was similarly guilty for intentionally bombing German civilian populations late in the war, he seems to adopt the position that both felt guiltless because they felt they had done the right thing (255–268, 325).

2.2.2 Assigning Responsibility and Blameworthiness After Wars: The Problem of Lack of Blame Walzer argues that "assignment of responsibility is . . . critical" because "[t]here can be no justice in war if there are not, ultimately, responsible men and women" (287–288). "If there are recognizable war crimes, there must be recognizable criminals." (287)

However, in Walzer's "realistic" model of the political world, it is not "easy to impose responsibility . . ." (301). Thus, it is not surprising that, with very few exceptions (virtually all of which involve losers in war), there has been little assignment of either moral or legal responsibility in accord with Walzer's theory. At times, Walzer himself tends to shrink from placing this label on specific actors. For example, after noting that many American "elites" were "morally complicitous in our Vietnam aggression," he states: I am not "interested in pointing at particular people or certain that I can do so" (302–303). Instead, he only wants "to insist that there are responsible people even when . . . moral accounting is difficult and imprecise" (303).

His discussion of "terrorist" action in World War II provides another example of this tendency to avoid assigning blame. In arguing that terrorism is a war crime, Walzer summarizes the purpose and methods of terrorism as follows:

> Its purpose is to destroy the morale of a nation or a class, to undercut its solidarity; its method is the random murder of innocent people. Randomness is the crucial feature of terrorist activity. If one wishes fear to spread and intensify over time, it is not desirable to kill specific people identified in some particular way with a regime, a party, or a policy. (197)

Because terrorism involves "the random murder of innocent people," it is unjust and morally criminal. Walzer labels two specific actions in World War II as criminal terrorist actions: intentionally bombing civilian populations in Germany after the initial extreme threat to Britain had passed and using the atomic bomb in Japan (261, 267–268, 323).

Because these actions "are recognizable war crimes, there must be recognizable criminals" (287). The "recognizable criminals" for the unjustified terror bombing should include Churchill, who had a central role in deciding to target German civilians later in the war, and Truman, who had the ultimate decision on the use of the atomic bomb (266–268, 324). However, the "opinions of mankind" have not labeled them "war criminals," and virtually no responsibility or blame for these terrorist actions has been placed on them.

Walzer's treatment of them is very similar. In describing the assignment of personal responsibility for the "terrorist" bombing of German cities, Walzer addresses blame in a conditional sense: "*if* blame is to be distributed for the bombing, Churchill deserves a full share" (324, emphasis added). To some extent, individual responsibility was assigned by the English after the war, but only to those who executed Churchill's orders. Arthur Harris, who directed the bombing campaign, "was slighted and snubbed . . . and not rewarded with a peerage . . . . The men he led were similarly treated" (324). Clearly, it was hypocritical to treat these people, who were implementing Churchill's orders, in this manner. Because exposing such hypocrisy is precisely what Walzer claims his practical morality will do, one would expect Walzer to give Churchill his "full share" of blame for the terror bombing and to denounce the hypocritical actions. However, Walzer neither blames Churchill for the bombing nor criticizes the hypocrisy.

Instead, he views the actions as those of an *im*personal actor doing what is necessary to achieve a greater goal – that is, the actions of "a *nation* fighting a just war . . . [that] *must* use unscrupulous or morally ignorant soldiers; and as soon as their usefulness is past, it *must* disown them" (325, emphasis added). In this way, the disowning of the men who executed Churchill's orders is separated from him and is praised, not criticized. The action is viewed as a positive, morally significant reaffirmation of the values defended in a just war. Though there may have been "some better way" to do this,

[t]he refusal to honor Harris at least went some small distance toward re-establishing a commitment to the rules of war and the rights they protect. And that, I think, is the deepest meaning of all assignments of responsibility. (325)

The hypocritical condemnation of men who executed orders may have affirmed values, but it is a questionable way of assigning responsibility, which Walzer asserts "is the critical test of the argument for justice" (287). From the perspective of theory, Walzer's treatment of the actions as that of the nation, rather than a person, contradicts his assertions that moral talk has meaning because the moral theorist "searches for human agents" when confronted with war crimes and because "[a]ll of us are inclined to hold . . . [these agents] responsible for what they do" (15). In addition, Walzer's approach to the British actions raises moral issues about making soldiers scapegoats for doing their duty to the nation and practical issues about how this method of assigning responsibility and affirming values will affect future leaders in Churchill's position.

2.2.3 The Conflict Between Walzer's Realist Account of Politics and his Rejection of Realism in his Practical Morality Walzer's "realist picture" of political decision-making conflicts with his rejection of realism in moral theory. At the beginning of the book, he rejects "amoral realism" and sketches out a scheme where hypocrisy will be exposed, the possibility of manipulating moral theory will be constrained, moral crimes can be identified, and personal blame for these crimes will be assigned. However, when Walzer addresses the actual exposure of hypocrisy and the assignment of responsibility, he does it within a realist view of the modern state. Morality does affect decision-making in this view, but it does so in ways that conflict with Walzer's scheme of morality. In particular, leaders feel justified in denying rights in order to satisfy their role-responsibility to avoid the risk of horrific consequences for the nation. In this context, rights are denied, responsibility is not assigned, and leaders are almost never blamed for actions that are immoral within Walzer's scheme.

Walzer recognizes that leaders tend to deny rights on the basis of a standard of necessity that is less strict than his standard of necessity measured by certainty of imminent catastrophe. He is also aware that his realistic assessment of leaders' conduct conflicts with his assertion that such improperly flexible "moral" arguments can be constrained by moral discourse. At times, when addressing specific events, Walzer resolves the conflict by accepting the less extreme situations as justifications. For example, even though he argues Churchill's decision to target civilians in German cities for bombing late in the war did not satisfy the strict requirements of necessity, he stops short of a serious assignment of blame to Churchill for this "crime." In addition, Walzer praises the hypocritical treatment of the soldiers executing Churchill's orders.

The tendency of leaders to do bad things for a good cause indicates a basic problem with Walzer's argument against realism. His argument is directed toward "the wicked and the simple," who attempt to "opt out" of the "shared" "moral world of war" in order to pursue their own self-interest or national self-interest by making the amoral claim that morality is irrelevant (xi–xxi). Regardless of whether Walzer's argument adequately addresses this selfish amoralism, the argument does not address the problem of leaders who sincerely believe they have a role-based moral obligation to protect the national interest by avoiding the risk of a national catastrophe. Because this is "what they are there for," they feel morally obligated to do wicked things which, absent their duty, would be clearly immoral. These leaders may be mistaken about their obligation, but they are not lying or engaging in hypocrisy. If they lie about the war in other ways, this is also viewed as required by their moral duty to the nation. Such leaders are both more common, and thus engage in more "unjust" conduct, than the amoral leaders addressed in Walzer's argument against realism.

3. CONCLUSION – A REALIST APPROACH TO MORALITY

Walzer's book provides an interesting and enlightening review of the moral issues involved in war and provides at least some "rules of thumb" for decision-making. These are important, substantial accomplishments. Is it fair to expect more from a philosophical discussion?

Apparently, Walzer expects more because he applies a very strict standard to international law:

> The UN Charter was supposed to be the constitution of a new world, but . . . [t]o dwell at length upon the precise meaning of the Charter is today a kind of utopian quibbling. And because the UN sometimes pretends that it already is what it has barely begun to be, its decrees do not command intellectual or moral respect – except among the positivist lawyers whose business it is to interpret them. The lawyers have constructed a *paper world, which fails at crucial points to correspond to the world the rest of us still live in.* (xvii–xix, emphasis added)

By this high standard, Walzer's "practical morality" is also deficient because it fails to constrain actions in the real world and thus fails "to correspond to the world."

On the other hand, when Walzer places moral philosophy within his "realistic picture" of the modern state, he adopts a more modest standard. After acknowledging the problems for his practical morality raised by his "realistic" model of the state, Walzer suggests that the following "intellectual work . . . is less difficult" to do:

> One must describe as graphically as one can the moral reality of war, talk about what it means to force people to fight, analyze the nature of democratic responsibilities. These, at least, are encompassable tasks, and they are morally required of the men and women who are trained to perform them. (303)

In this way, morality, though manipulable, can help structure and direct debate and help guide decisions because most people care about "being moral." Walzer notes,

> the *moral reality of war is not fixed by the actual activities of soldiers but by the opinions of mankind*. That means, in part, that it is fixed by the activity of philosophers, lawyers, publicists of all sorts. . . . [, whose] views have value only insofar as they give *shape and structure* to that experience in ways that are plausible to the rest of us. (14–15, emphasis added)

In the end, Walzer accepts the realist position that giving "shape and structure" is all that philosophy can do and that, to be effective, this "shape and structure" must be able to compete in the *mediat*ed world of the modern state. However, he paradoxically resists the conclusion that neither his "practical morality" nor "the opinions of mankind" are likely to have any substantial effect on official decisions about war. Perhaps this somewhat contradictory position helps us in trying to bridge (or at least to live with) the gap between moral theory and the reality of decision-making about war. However, we are likely to have more success in bridging the gap if we take a more realistic view of the problem. Such a view will provide a renewed appreciation of the need to use populist outlets for expressing the "shape and structure" of morality, to use prudential arguments that emphasize those areas where there is an overlap between a rights-based morality of law like Walzer's and a nation's self-interest, and to join in the efforts of "positivist lawyers" as they try to bind nations by international law, even if this rarely works unless the acceptance of law is in a nation's self-interest.

NOTES

1. Quoted in Dominic McGoldrick, *From '9-11' to the 'Iraq War 2003'* (Oxford: Hart, 2004), pp. 87, 161, 179.
2. Michael Walzer, *Just and Unjust Wars*, 3rd edn (New York: Basic Books, 2000). All parenthetical page references are to this work.
3. McGoldrick, *From '9-11'*, p. 41 (quoting from Randeep Ramesh (ed.), *The War We Could Not Stop* (New York: Thunder's Mouth Press, 2003), p. 286.)
4. In other works, Walzer develops his ideal of a political leader in terms of a concept of "dirty hands," which refers to the need for leaders to dirty their hands with immoral acts in order to avoid worse immorality or to accomplish more important goals. See Walzer, *Arguing About War* (New Haven, CT: Yale University Press, 2004), pp. 45–49; and Walzer, "Political Action: The Problem of Dirty Hands," *Philosophy & Public Affairs* 2 (1973), p. 160.

III. INTERVENTION

REX MARTIN

WALZER AND RAWLS ON JUST WARS AND HUMANITARIAN INTERVENTIONS

The continuing reflection on and incremental growth of the theory of just war has been an important feature of the post-World War II international order. In this chapter I want to compare two important contributions to this developing theory; my focus will be on John Rawls's theory of just war in his book *Law of Peoples* and on the theory of Michael Walzer.[1] Their theories are enough alike to warrant being treated together, as constituting something like a unified view of the subject. What makes them especially interesting is that each theory has made the notion of human rights central as the ground of justification (or justifiability) in just war theory (JWT). But the theories are sufficiently divergent to make fruitful an examination of their differences.

1. WALZER AND RAWLS ON JUST WARS

Both theorists argue that a country can justifiably go to war for two reasons: it can do so in self-defense or collective defense against aggression or it can do so in response to serious and unamendable human rights violations. In traditional JWT these two grounds are called "just cause." An important unifying idea undergirds these two grounds. For both Rawls and Walzer, the ultimate justification here is the defense of the human rights, of the inhabitants in a country, to life and liberty.

Accordingly, both urge that civilians (that is, noncombatants) can never be directly targeted and killed, certainly not as a matter of government or of military policy.

To this stringent doctrine of civilian immunity both Rawls and Walzer allow for one significant exception, that of "supreme emergency." Such an emergency would arise, and I cite Walzer on this, when a severe threat was both immediate and profound; here a deviation from the doctrine of civilian immunity is absolutely necessary in order to save a political community from annihilation, or its citizens from wholesale massacre or enslavement.[2] Even so, one main theme of Rawls's endorsement of the supreme emergency exemption is that it can be invoked only when doing so is absolutely necessary to the survival of a liberal constitutional democracy (or presumably of a decent nonliberal body politic), fighting in self-defense.³ Rawls's restriction of the exemption to such societies as these is one that we do not find in Walzer's account.

On the question of the moral status of combatants their positions are again similar. Each argues for the mutual vulnerability of combatants on *both* sides in time of war. Walzer tries to rationalize this mutual vulnerability with the idea that combatants temporarily forfeit their human rights to life and liberty and take on, in their place, certain "war rights."⁴ Rawls, to the contrary, emphasizes the idea of mutual self-defense against attack as the grounding justification for this mutual vulnerability. Here soldiers on each side are protecting themselves, in combat, from attacks by soldiers on the other side; and since the attacks from either side can be deadly, each side may use lethal force in self-defense.⁵

What I have said so far provides a very quick tour of the issues. Let us now take a second and closer look at traditional JWT. For the most part, traditional theory endorses the internationally established conventions on war, or some reasonable extension of those conventions. Walzer, for instance, treats most of these conventions as a given and tries to offer a rationale, a justification for them. But he does not endorse *all* the conventions; he does not endorse blockade or siege as valid instruments of war.⁶ And some of the extensions that he deems reasonable – the supreme emergency exemption or the assumption of risk by combatants to avoid or reduce the risk of serious injury or death to noncombatants – have not found favor with all theorists of just war.

One important, indeed, central, feature of the traditional theory is mutual combatant vulnerability. Walzer tries to rationalize this, as we saw, with his doctrine of forfeit. But there is something deeper in what he is doing than meets the eye. It is not merely that *all* soldiers, soldiers on both sides, are *equally* vulnerable; it is also the extensive scope, the radical extent of that vulnerability. So long as their nations are in a combat or belligerency situation, a soldier on either side can kill any soldier on the other side (providing, for example, that those on the other side are not soldiers lying wounded on the field of battle or in the act of surrendering). This means that active-duty soldiers can be killed not merely when they are in combat readiness or actually fighting on the field of battle or when they are so deploying, but also while they are dancing or dining in a nightclub, heading off for furlough, or taking a bath. The rules of war, as endorsed in traditional just war theory, seem to allow such an extensive range of killing as justifiable.⁷

Walzer's doctrine of forfeit constitutes a drastic measure, admittedly. But such a far-reaching move as this is required, he thought, in order to provide a rationale for the traditional just war doctrine of mutual combatant vulnerability, a norm which included *both* the idea that soldiers on each warring side are equally vulnerable (even if one side is the aggressor and the other a defender against aggression) *and* the idea that this vulnerability is quite extensive in times of warfare or belligerency.

Rawls's idea of emphasizing mutual self-defense against attack as the grounding justification would restrict the *extent* of vulnerability considerably (when contrasted with the case of forfeit just examined). In one plausible interpretation, the range of acceptable vulnerability might be restricted, under the standards of self-defense, to active deployment or readiness for combat on the field of battle or actual fighting. Whether it was Rawls's intention to do so or not, his notion of mutual self-defense would have a restrictive effect on the extent of vulnerability in traditional JWT and would prove, on this point as well as on others, to be distinctively different from the position Walzer has taken. Rawls's amendment (if we may call it that) to traditional JWT licenses a restriction on the *scope* or *extent* of the vulnerability of combatants but leaves intact the idea that combatants on both sides are *equally* vulnerable.

I have no doubt that a convention of war could be established, by international treaty, for example, that allowed for the *equal* vulnerability of combatants to lethal attack in time of war. And it is possible that this idea could win the assent of *conventional* morality. To a considerable extent it seems to have done so.

But I am not convinced that this endorsement would hold up, if we were to take seriously the *universality* of human rights – the idea that *all* people have them – and if we continue to insist on the importance of the aggressor/nonaggressor distinction (and on the attendant idea that one may forcibly defend one's human rights against aggression). I am not sure in such a case that we could justify the *equal* vulnerability of soldiers and other combatants as itself a general rule or norm. Justify it, that is, by reference to the standard of universal human rights and the propriety of defending such rights against violation by aggressors.

Consider. In World War II, the troops of Nazi Germany invaded France, the Netherlands, Denmark, Norway, and other countries and forcibly subjugated them. And they aimed to do the same with the Soviet Union (now Russia) and probably Britain. The Nazi troops were not defending the rights to life and liberties of people in those countries; they were violating those rights. These invasions and subjugations, and the violations that came in their train, were aggressive acts. From the perspective of human rights, as just described, those who defended against these invasions (assuming they stayed within the guidelines for conduct in warfare) were defending human rights, not violating them, and they were acting properly in doing so.

International law, the internationally established law and usages of nations, and a justificatory motif like human rights are two different things, and they may not come to the same conclusions. I have not denied that there may be a moral justification (a conventional moral justification) of traditional JWT on the score of the mutual vulnerability of combatants – or, at least, that of their equal vulnerability. I am simply saying that an argument framed exclusively or principally in terms of human rights cannot provide that justification since *mutual* vulnerability (*equal* vulnerability) would not be acceptable as a sound or defensible conclusion to draw in such an argument – in, for example, the circumstances we have just envisioned in World War II. It may be, then, that this particular notion or rationale, the mutual and equal vulnerability of combatants, one of the main staples of traditional JWT, could not be sustained within a theory of human rights.

Now we come to an even greater difficulty. We have relied, in the idea of defending human rights, on the notion that rights can be protected by (among other things) killing soldiers on the other side (the aggressor's side). But these very soldiers themselves have, by hypothesis, a right to life. It is a right that can be given a strong moral justification (by human rights norms), and it is a right that the soldier retains even on active duty, in time of war. It seems paradoxical to say that one can protect rights from violation by *violating* rights.[8]

Let me add here that any supposed analogy between justified individual self-defense in law and morals, on the one hand, and the forcible defense of human rights in war (using lethal countermeasures to stop extremely dangerous or harmful assaults on life or liberty by invading, aggressor troops), on the other, is unlikely to work in the present case. In war we have nothing like the careful calibrations and the judicial and procedural protections that exist in a typical system of law enforcement and are designed to prevent justifiable infringements on rights, in matters of justified defense or of punishment for wrongdoing, from becoming unjustifiable violations of rights.[9] Indeed, in war there would likely prove to be wholesale violations of important rights.

This brings us to the crux. The appeal to the defense of human rights as a basis for killing or severely wounding soldiers in time of war will work, within the existing tribunal of human rights, on some occasions. It will work, for example, in cases of defending against an all-out and deadly assault by an invading army fighting on the side of the aggressor nation. Here the aim of that invasion is subjugation, which will involve a drastic curtailment of the liberties of all the inhabitants of the country invaded, and that armed invasion will involve the loss of many civilian lives through "collateral damage," lack of due care, or intentional direct targeting.[10]

But no appeal to human rights will work, within that same tribunal, to justify the conduct of the *invading* troops when they violate the rights to life and liberty of the inhabitants there or even when they "defend" themselves by returning the fire of the troops on the other side who oppose them. This provides one salient way, then, in which an argument favoring the *equal* vulnerability of combatants would not satisfy the standards of a theory of human rights (and would not be acceptable there) even when it satisfies the standards of traditional JWT.

If these brief lines of argument have merit, there may well prove to be a fundamental incompatibility between the claims of human rights and their forcible defense, which informed the theory of just war of Walzer and Rawls, and the doctrine of the equal vulnerability of combatants, which both have endorsed. The idea of the equal vulnerability of combatants, taken as a supposed norm or reason for the conventions of war, a reason justified in turn by such notions as forfeit (Walzer) or mutual self-defense (Rawls), may turn out to be, then, one of the most problematic features of the just war doctrine we have been examining.

Let me be clear on the focal point of my claim to incompatibility here. Equal vulnerability (or, alternatively, the mutual vulnerability) of combatants can be taken to be an independent and overarching reason or rationale for the rules of war, and apparently was so taken by the two theorists we have been examining. It is this grounding *rationale* that I am saying is incompatible.

But the failure of mutual combatant vulnerability as a rationale does not tell against the actual conventional guidelines for warfare conduct, guidelines that are meant to be binding on both sides. Here soldiers on both sides are regarded as having been placed in harm's way by decisions that broke the peace (decisions made not by the soldiers, but by the leaders of nations), and the responsibility of soldiers is to fight in accordance with established guidelines for waging war.[11] These guidelines and adherence to them may be the best that humankind can accomplish in an imperfect, complicated, and confusing world where people again and again and in place after place have proven ready to go to war.

Nonetheless, there remains an incompatibility – a creative tension, if you will – between a theory of human rights and traditional JWT, specifically between a theory of human rights and the *rationale* of mutual combatant vulnerability offered by Rawls and Walzer. And, if we press hard the notion that soldiers fighting on the aggressor's side have a right to life, a right that is not to be violated, this tension may extend even so far as to include the pragmatically established guidelines for waging war.

2. HUMANITARIAN INTERVENTIONS

One of the most important new ideas in just war theory is the idea that governments and others can justifiably respond forcibly to serious and unamendable human rights violations that are wholly internal to another country. This idea, though it is not universally held today, represents a growing international consensus. As such it is another important feature of the post-World War II international order.

There are in my view three main points to consider under the heading of humanitarian interventions: First, the various kinds of humanitarian intervention and the level of human rights violation required to trigger forcible military interventions. Second, the justification of such interventions. Third, the appropriate agent(s) who might legitimately undertake a forcible military intervention. We will be returning to each of these points as the argument progresses.

One of the really difficult concerns about human rights emerges when we note that, of the many conceivable justifying arguments for human rights, none of them is currently accepted or put into practice at a suitable level by literally all peoples. Not even the justification provided by a bedrock standard like the general benefit, the mutually perceived benefit, of a vast number of human beings now alive is uniformly accepted. Even *it* is not accepted in the concrete. In some given "crux" cases (e.g., the case of freedom of conscience in matters of religion), it is not accepted everywhere, not by all peoples or all governments. It is a difficult question, then, whether any of these justifying arguments offer suitable grounds for intervention, in particular, forcible intervention, against societies (against peoples) that do not accept these justifications and, especially, against societies who engage regularly or unamendably in practices that are seriously unacceptable in the light of these arguments.

Consider here (as examples of severe or grave violations of human rights) genocide and "ethnic cleansing," slavery, and warlord-induced famine and starvation, all of them cases from our own day.[12] Such severe violations merit "forceful" intervention, in Rawls's view, by which he means intervention "by diplomatic and economic sanctions, or in grave cases by military force."[13]

Here we must take care. I would suggest that both Walzer and Rawls would endorse "forceful" diplomatic and cultural and economic measures against apartheid but *not* armed intervention.[14] And the same might be said as regards treatment of women and "hate" speech (speech much of which occurs under the heading of religious education). Rawls seems to reserve armed intervention solely for such matters as mass murder and slavery, where the offending state has not amended its ways under the pressure of diplomatic and economic and other measures.[15] And the same could be said of Walzer.

The kind of justification we are talking about in cases of *forcible* or armed intervention would have to rely on standards considerably stronger than a bedrock standard like mutual and general benefit or, for that matter, considerably stronger than the justifying standards Rawls himself invokes: that is, minimal protection against great evils, and protection of the necessary conditions of social cooperation.[16] We are talking here not merely about what justifies *any* given human right (or any right on a short list of quintessential human rights) but more especially about when, if ever, a particular human right should or could be enforced internationally by military action.[17]

I want to make a logical point here. If all the rights on a list of normatively justified human rights are justified by one and the same standard (e.g., mutual and general benefit) or a concurrent set of standards (e.g., by this standard *and* the two that Rawls invokes) and yet *some* rights on that list are *not* thought to be appropriately enforced by international military action, then a different standard for justifying forcible military intervention *other* than the one(s) already cited must necessarily be invoked.

Rawls clearly does think that some rights on that list are not appropriately enforced by international military action. Ending apartheid or the debased state of women, for example, would not be appropriately achieved by international military action in his view, nor should ending violations of due process of law in some societies be enforced in that way. Walzer is similarly cautious.[18]

So far as I can see, Rawls provides no standard for identifying specifically which violations of human rights, even when persisted in, rise to the level of making forcible military interventions suitable. In the end he seems to fall back on widely shared conventional judgments in this matter. And this is exhibited in Rawls's characteristic language in these cases: such violations as merit forcible intervention, he says, are "egregious" and "grave."[19] And the same could be said for Walzer when he speaks of acts that "shock the conscience of humankind."[20]

Rawls continues, "It may be asked by what right well-ordered liberal and decent [nonliberal] peoples are justified in interfering with an outlaw state on the grounds that this state has violated human rights." His answer is instructive: "[such] peoples simply do not tolerate outlaw states"; their "refusal to tolerate those states is a consequence of liberalism and decency." In short, Rawls argues, if the political conception of liberalism is sound and the resultant political conception of a law of peoples embracing both liberal and decent nonliberal peoples is sound, then "these peoples have the right, under the Law of Peoples, not to tolerate outlaw states."[21]

Or, to put his point somewhat differently: liberal and decent peoples have agreed to the same list of human rights and have agreed, in a rough way, about levels of enforceability, and this gives them the right to forcibly intervene in certain cases. I would reply: this might provide an *explanation* for the stance and conduct of liberal and decent peoples here but it still amounts to a conventionalist rationale, not the called-for *normative* justification.

However, one could still say a word in support of Rawls's approach. The list of human rights agreed to by liberal and decent peoples has a definite, and rather complex, normative foundation. The human rights on that list are justified by deep and accredited moral standards.[22] Accordingly, these rights are capable of giving normative direction to the conduct and understanding of individual persons; and when these human rights are violated, persons acting on their own or in concert with others are entitled to do *something*. This much is clear.

Now, we may not have clear norms for when forcible action, in particular, action arising to the level of military intervention, is allowed or enjoined, e.g., in dealing with the so-called ethnic cleansing. But a normative ground for taking action to stop or reverse severe violations of human rights is in place throughout. Even so, a decision to take forcible action is a difficult one. It will probably involve loss of life and grievous injury to some of the soldiers involved in the rescue; it will probably involve similar injuries to the civilian population in the area of military operation (and such civilians are the very group these soldiers are coming to aid). Clearly then, even when the intervention is well and justifiably motivated (and carefully thought through), "political will" is required to see it to conclusion. When coalitions of nations are involved (something that is often desirable in order to gain the benefits of consultation and shared judgment and of effective coordination of effort), questions of "political will" become even more pressing. Given all these factors, a reliance on widely shared conventional judgments and on the informed "conscience of humankind" is both highly appropriate and necessary.

I cannot fault Rawls and Walzer for emphasizing the importance of this point. But the express account they give of the normative background in *justification* of intervention is inadequate and undeveloped.

Sometimes forcible military intervention to prevent grave violations of human rights is justified. This is probably the *consensus* view today (one in which Rawls and Walzer share). But it is not a unanimous view: a few, usually from an international law background, would deny it outright.[23] Let us stick, though, with the consensus view.

This immediately takes us to another matter for deep concern. Clearly, one of the most pressing problems for the international protection of human rights is that the United Nations (UN) by and large lacks enforcement mechanisms of its own. Accordingly, the UN must rely on existing nation-states for the foreseeable future.

There is, however, a considerable variety of views as to who has legitimate authority, as it is called in traditional JWT, to authorize an armed military intervention to protect human rights from grave violations. Some say that only the UN can legitimately authorize such interventions. Others say that either the UN or some regional international political authority (e.g., the European Union (EU)) can legitimately so authorize.[24]

And some (most notably Walzer, in his earlier writings) have argued the virtues, in extreme cases, of unilateral intervention (of forcible intervention by *one* nation within the borders of another to prevent or stop grave violations of human rights). Examples usually cited (from the last 30 years or so) are India in East Pakistan (now Bangladesh), Vietnam in Cambodia, Tanzania in Uganda, and (most recently) Nigeria in Sierra Leone.[25]

Rawls's stance on the matter of legitimate authority is not altogether clear. He suggests that to cope with the problem of such interventions the "Society of Peoples needs to develop new institutions and practices under the Law of Peoples to constrain outlaw states when they appear."[26] It is clear that this Society of Peoples, as Rawls calls it, is not as extensive as today's UN. It is, rather, simply the liberal peoples or, for that matter, the decent peoples (both liberal and nonliberal) acting in concert.[27]

But Rawls adds that this concerted action *can* be done "within institutions such as the United Nations or by forming separate alliances of well-ordered societies." These alliances, and perhaps the UN itself, constitute what Rawls calls a "confederative center."[28]

It would seem that Rawls, were these new institutions and practices to begin to emerge, would side with those who say that either the UN or some regional international political authority (e.g., the EU) can legitimately authorize armed military interventions to protect human rights from grave violations. But there seems to be no insistence on his part that the UN, as currently constituted, *must* be involved; rather, "separate alliances of well-ordered societies" may do the job. It may well be, right now and for the foreseeable future, then, that Rawls thinks the problem of the international identification of the gravest threats to human rights, and the protection of human rights against these threats, can be most effectively dealt with by decent societies regionally, rather than globally.[29]

In sum, Rawls and Walzer have provided an answer to each of the main points concerning humanitarian interventions, raised at the beginning of the present section. Their first two answers (concerning the level of human rights violation required for military intervention and the justification of such interventions) are, perhaps, more conventionalist than many might have expected or hoped for. Rawls's third answer (concerned with legitimate authority) is not unexpectedly (given his Kantian proclivities) more confederative and regional than it is global and one-worldly. And Walzer's is more geared to the idea of a system of existing somewhat autonomous nation-states.

This summing up is, so far, merely a preliminary one, a summing up to date. I emphasize this because Walzer has amended his views on legitimate authority, and has taken a more internationalist direction in doing so.

In Walzer's recent book, *Arguing About War* (2004), he suggests, as an ideal, the value of what he calls "global pluralism." He conceives such pluralism as including a number of alternative centers (such as the UN and the EU), a dense web of social ties that cross state boundaries, and finally a number of institutions (such as the World Bank, the World Trade Organization, various nongovernmental organizations) that reflect these alternative centers and social ties. Global pluralism "maximizes the number of agents" who might engage in humanitarian interventions, but at the same time it identifies no single assigned agent that makes or must make the basic decision to intervene.[30]

Some have suggested, as we noted earlier, that the UN is the exclusive authorizing agency in matters of humanitarian intervention. But the UN charter has not explicitly assigned an authorizing role to the UN in this matter. More to the point, the UN as an institution has never unequivocally and categorically affirmed that it has the role of *exclusive* agent of authorization. And the UN has been notoriously reluctant to authorize or engage in such action. In sum, humanitarian intervention is not a role it has been conspicuous in supporting or performing, not even since the end of the Cold War. In light of these facts, it is difficult to make a case that the UN is or should be the *sole* legitimate authorizing agent for humanitarian intervention.[31]

Accordingly, an important idea lies behind the views of both Rawls and Walzer. It is the idea that there is a present and continuing need to *build* international and supranational agencies to affirm and protect human rights. And one goal here is to build up agencies that can, in the extreme case, forcibly intervene in the internal affairs of a country to prevent the government there or some group there from severe, shocking, massive violations of human rights. Such massive violations often take the form of "ethnic cleansing" – forced migrations of large numbers of people from their homes, migrations that are meant to be permanent, migrations that are typically accompanied by large-scale and horrific acts of murder, rape, and pillage. But the sorts of violations of concern to the international community are not limited to these forced migrations.

The theories of Rawls and Walzer are part of this project of the internationalization of relief and rescue that I have been describing, but they are not UN-centric. Rawls (with his pacific regional confederations or leagues) and Walzer (with his overlapping and decentered array of agencies, both national and international) provide important alternatives to the view that the UN is the exclusive authorizing agency in matters of humanitarian intervention. But they are, I would emphasize, *international* alternatives, as distinct from merely national (or solely national) options.

In the case of a pressing need for intervention, two issues need to be kept paramount: Can genuine rescue be effected without massive and ultimately self-defeating costs? Can that effort be conducted in such a way as to build international agencies and international support for justifiable humanitarian intervention? Rescue by one nation of the citizens of another may sometimes be the only viable option. But that fact should not preclude or blunt the significance of the second question. It must always be kept on the table.

One may well conclude, as did Rawls and Walzer, that the UN is not the exclusive authorizing agency in matters of humanitarian intervention, and conclude as well that, in a given case, an intervention by an individual nation or by a coalition of nations is both legitimate and justified. Even so, it does not follow that one should conclude that the UN has no appropriate role to play in those humanitarian interventions that it has not authorized. Indeed, given current views about the unchallenged legitimacy of the UN, both as an idea and as an institution, it may well be that nations or coalitions which engage in such interventions should report to the UN their reasons for any such intervention, and should be open to UN supervision and review of their action then and subsequently, and (perhaps most important) should involve the UN and its agencies in the postwar reconstruction of the society in which the grave human rights violations that triggered the intervention had originally occurred.

The answers by Walzer and Rawls to the issue of humanitarian intervention may not satisfy everyone, but they are clear cut and carefully considered. They merit close and critical attention. We must get beyond the point where we regard all rescues unauthorized by the UN as *illegal*.[32]

NOTES

1. See John Rawls, *The Law of Peoples with "The Idea of Public Reason Revisited"* (Cambridge, MA: Harvard University Press, 1999); and Michael Walzer, *Just and Unjust Wars: A Moral Argument with Historical Illustrations*, 3rd edn (New York: Basic Books, 2000; 1st edn, 1977; 2nd edn, 1992).
2. See Walzer, *Just and Unjust Wars*, Chap. 16, for the discussion of supreme emergency (esp. p. 254); also pp. 268 and 326. See also Walzer's paper, "Emergency Ethics," printed in *The Leader's Imperative: Ethics, Integrity, and Responsibility*, ed. J. Carl Ficarrotta (West Lafayette, IN: Purdue University Press, 2001), pp. 126–139, and reprinted in Walzer, *Arguing About War* (New Haven, CT: Yale University Press, 2004), pp. 33–50.
3. See Rawls, *Law of Peoples*, pp. 98–105, esp. pp. 99, 102, 104–105.
4. For Walzer's idea of forfeit (of a radical loss) here, see *Just and Unjust Wars*, pp. 193, 264–265; for the taking on of certain "war rights," as he calls them, see *Just and Unjust Wars*, pp. 135–136, 145n, 219.
5. See Rawls, *Law of Peoples*, pp. 95–96.
6. See Walzer, *Just and Unjust Wars*, Chap. 10.
7. Walzer develops this theme graphically in a section entitled "Naked Soldiers"; see *Just and Unjust Wars*, pp. 138–143.
8. "But in warfare the combatants cannot respect one another's human rights. . . . Hence, war as a means for securing respect for human rights has the drawback that it necessarily involves not respecting them." A.J.M. Milne, *Human Rights and Human Diversity: An Essay in the Philosophy of Human Rights* (Albany, NY: State University of New York Press, 1986), p. 171.
9. For discussion of this important point, as it bears on legal punishment, see R. Martin, *A System of Rights* (Oxford: Clarendon Press, 1993), Chap. 9, Sects. 3–5, esp. pp. 228–236.
10. David Rodin has criticized the moral justification of the claim that a state has the right of self-defense in his book *War and Self-Defense* (Oxford: Clarendon Press, 2002). The argument I have been developing is based on a somewhat different claim: that a forcible defense by government of the human rights to life and liberty of its own citizens (or those of another country) is licensed by contemporary human rights norms.
11. See Rawls, *Law of Peoples*, pp. 94–96, and Walzer, *Just and Unjust Wars*, Chap. 3.
12. Rawls in effect singles out items from this very list: "mass murder and genocide" (*Law of Peoples*, p.79 and n. 23 on p. 80), "slavery and serfdom" (p. 79); he also mentions "apartheid" (n. 23 on p. 80). Walzer's emphasis is similar; he cites a government's "massacre or enslavement of its own citizens or subjects" as grounds for intervention and later adds "mass expulsion" ("The Moral Standing of States: A Response to Four Critics," *Philosophy and Public Affairs*, 9.3 [1980], pp. 217, 218).
13. See *Law of Peoples*, p. 80; also p. 90n.
14. By "cultural" interventions I have in mind such things as refusals to engage in sports competition or invitations, in scholarly exchanges and invitations, in TV and movie and artistic exhibitions or performances, and the like. These proved significant in the

international campaign against South African apartheid policies (e.g., the widespread boycott of South African rugby football). And economic sanctions and private-company-enforced standards were important also. Some of these interventions were governmental or inspired by government; others were strictly private or associational interventions.

15. See *Law of Peoples*, p. 81, and Rawls's discussion of the Aztecs in n. 6 on pp. 93–94. Some extremely weak, marginalized societies might be excluded, the text suggests, from Rawls's rather blanket assertion here about justified military interventions.
16. For the point about a minimum, see *Law of Peoples*, p. 67 (and p. 79 for the urgency of attending to a minimal satisfaction of human interests); see pp. 65, 68 for the point about social cooperation.
17. It should be noted that the standard of mutually perceived benefit would probably hold in the three severe and urgent cases (genocide, slavery, etc.). All persons (including those in the affected country) could reflectively decide that the avoidance of these particular injuries was beneficial to them. It is not so clear that it could be met in the second-tier cases (treatment of women, soul-curdling religious intolerance and invective, etc.) in every single case. It might be, but again it might not be. It is the latter cases (cases where it is not met) that forcible international intervention becomes especially problematic and difficult.
18. Indirect evidence of Rawls's view in the matter of apartheid is provided by Walzer who says "The enforcement of a partial embargo against South African apartheid is a useful if unusual example. Collective condemnation, breaks in cultural exchange, and active propaganda can serve the purposes of humanitarian intolerance, though sanctions of this sort are rarely effective." In a footnote to this passage, Walzer says "These examples . . . were suggested to me by John Rawls." See Michael Walzer, *On Toleration* (New Haven, CT: Yale University Press, 1997), pp. 21–22, 115. For Walzer's own views on the matter of interventions in response to apartheid, see "The Moral Standing of States," pp. 216–219.
19. See *Law of Peoples*, p. 94n for the first of these terms, and pp. 37, 81 for the second.
20. See Walzer, "The Argument about Humanitarian Intervention," *Dissent* (Winter, 2002), pp. 29–37, at p. 29; see also *Just and Unjust Wars*, p. 107, and *Arguing About War*, p. 69. The paper from *Dissent*, just cited, is reprinted as "Arguing for Humanitarian Intervention," in Nicolaus Mills and Kira Brunner (eds), *The New Killing Fields* (New York: Basic Books, 2002), pp. 19–35; the passage cited can be found there at p. 20.
21. See *Law of Peoples*, p. 81.
22. For discussion of this important point, see David Reidy's paper, "Political Authority and Human Rights," in R. Martin and David Reidy (eds), *Rawls's Law of Peoples: A Realistic Utopia?* (Oxford: Blackwell, 2006), pp. 169–188 and my paper "Rawls on Human Rights: Liberal or Universal?" in B.A. Haddock, Peri Roberts, and Peter Sutch (eds), *Principles and Political Order: The Challenge of Political Diversity* (London: Routledge, 2006), pp. 192–212.
23. See Allen Buchanan, *Justice, Legitimacy, Self-Determination: Moral Foundations for International Law* (Oxford, Oxford University Press, 2004), Part 4 ("Reform"). And Bruno Coppieters and Nick Fotion (eds), *Moral Constraints on War: Principles and Cases* (Lanham, MD: Lexington Books, 2002), pp. 32, 43, 251, 253, 255.
24. For good overview discussions on the question of legitimate authority, see the chapter by Bruno Coppieters ("Legitimate Authority") in *Moral Constraints on War*,

Chap. 2, pp. 41–58, esp. p. 50, and the chapter by Shi Yinhong and Shen Zhixiong ("After Kosovo: Moral and Legal Constraints on Humanitarian Intervention") in *Moral Constraints on War*, Chap. 13, pp. 247–263.

The case for exclusive UN authorization is discussed in both these chapters (in Chap. 2 at pp. 49, 50; in Chap. 13 at p. 231). See also p. xvii. And the case for the suitability of either UN or regional political authorization is discussed, in each chapter, at pp. 50, 256 respectively.

Interestingly, two of the authors in *Moral Constraints on War* (in separate chapters on Kosovo), though they differ on the justifiability of the NATO intervention there in 1999, agree in thinking that NATO lacked legitimate authority to do so. (See Chap. 11 by Carl Ceulemans, pro-NATO, at p. 226, and Chap. 12 by Boris Kashnikov, anti-NATO, at p. 244.) The two authors in Chap. 13 also regard the intervention, said by NATO to have been undertaken on humanitarian grounds, as "illegal" (p. 257).

25. For the advocacy of unilateral intervention here see Walzer, *Just and Unjust Wars*, preface to the 3rd edition, esp. pp. xiii-xvi, and Chap. 6, esp. pp. 105–108; and Walzer, "The Argument about Humanitarian Intervention," esp. pp. 31–33 (in *New Killing Fields*, pp. 23–27). See also *Moral Constraints on War*, p. 50 and n. 27 on p. 262. Walzer is willing to treat both unilateral interventions and those "authorized by regional alliances" as being on roughly the same footing (see "Kosovo" [*Dissent*, 1999] as reprinted in *Arguing About War*, p. 103). For a more recent and somewhat different view by Walzer, see the concluding paragraphs of the present chapter.

26. *Law of Peoples*, p. 48.

27. The only extended discussion Rawls offers is that of a confederation of liberal peoples (see *Law of Peoples*, pp. 42–43 and the important note on p. 43).

28. See *Law of Peoples*, p. 93, for both these quotes; see also p. 111.

29. This seems to be confirmed by what Rawls says (in *Law of Peoples*, pp. 112–113) about the gradual growth of initially rather narrow confederations (he calls them "cooperative institutions") of "mutually caring peoples." Rawls (following along the lines of Kant's *Perpetual Peace* [1795]) seems to think that these confederations, at least initially, will be composed of "neighboring states," and hence will be regional in character (*Law of Peoples*, p. 36; see also p. 43n).

30. See Walzer's "Governing the Globe" (2000) as reprinted in *Arguing About War*, pp. 171–191, at pp. 186–187, 189. This particular piece originated as Walzer's Multatuli Lecture (of 1999) at Leuven.

31. For Walzer's strong critique of the UN record here, see *Arguing About War*, pp. 77–78, 128.

32. Various versions of the present chapter have been presented, most recently at the meeting of the American Section of the International Association for Philosophy of Law and Social Philosophy (familiarly known as AMINTAPHIL) in Palo Alto, CA, November 2004; at North Carolina State University, Raleigh, NC, January 2005; at the University of Richmond, Richmond, VA, March 2005; and at a special symposium organized by the School of European Studies, at Cardiff University (UK), June 2005. I am grateful for many helpful comments from the audience in each of these cases and for detailed written comments by two members of the symposium panel in Cardiff – Peter Sutch and Nick Wheeler. The present chapter is a reworking of an earlier and somewhat different paper of mine published in *Journal of Social Philosophy* 36 (4) (2005), pp. 439–456.

HELEN STACY

HUMANITARIAN INTERVENTION AND RELATIONAL SOVEREIGNTY

1. INTRODUCTION

Humanitarian intervention with military force has no firm theory under the international legal apparatus because sovereignty, the inviolate claim of a nation-state against all others, is a legal shield against outside intervention in a nation's internal affairs. The United Nations (UN) Charter under Article 2(4) prohibits the "threat or use of force" against another state, even when civil bloodshed is creating humanitarian disasters. The Charter allows only two exceptions to this prohibition: Article 51 in Chapter VII of the Charter allows a nation to use force in self-defense if an armed attack occurs against it or an allied country, and the United Nations Security Council (UNSC) is authorized to employ force to counter threats to breaches of international peace. Humanitarian intervention rests upon the unconvincing fiction of the danger that a civil conflict may spill over a nation's borders, at least if it is to be justified under the UN Charter.

A better account of the fate of national sovereignty in cases of international humanitarian intervention in human rights disasters derives from what I call a theory of "relational sovereignty." This theory arises under today's conditions of globalization and describes the role of the sovereign government as an obligation to meeting its citizens' civil, political, social, and economic needs, according to the government's capacity, and always working for its citizens' good. A government fails in its governance role when its murderous, corrupt, or persistently neglectful actions lead to serious human rights harms. Under the theory of relational sovereignty, widespread and extreme harm to citizens is evidence that sovereignty is no longer an absolute shield against international intervention. Put differently, relational sovereignty puts human rights at the heart of good governance.

A widespread and extreme humanitarian crisis alters sovereignty in two ways: First, citizens rather than the government are seen as the bearers of their national sovereignty. If their government no longer represents their best interest, the nation's sovereignty no longer coalesces in its government. Second, citizens rely on the international community to express their sovereign interest in good governance when they themselves are unable to depose a government that harms them. In other words, their national borders have metaphorically fractured, allowing other nations in the international community to step across to their assistance. When sovereignty is seen this way – as an obligation of attentive governance, which the international community can insist upon on behalf of a nation's citizens – it need not be breached when humanitarian intervention takes place.

This temporary dispersal of national sovereignty from a nation's citizens to the international community is easiest to map onto humanitarian crisis of murderous civil conflict. It is more difficult to map onto humanitarian crises of malnutrition and starvation. But I argue here that humanitarian intervention may also be justifiable for massive cases of letting-die, such as starvation and disease. In other words, national sovereignty cannot shield corrupt or neglectful governments that fail to distribute essential sustenance – food, medical care, and essential services – to their citizens in exigent circumstances. International morality is invoked not only for the commissions of nation-states, but also for their omissions. My argument is that widespread death by malnutrition or disease should make a government just as culpable as death by civil violence, where the government has the capacity to prevent starvation and disease and fails to do so. When a government *negligently* fails to prevent a national crisis that leads to widespread death, that government's claim to inviolate sovereignty *qua* other nations or the international community is invalid.

But expanding humanitarian intervention into a general license for war against repressive regimes is dangerous. The equitable principles of fairness show that humanitarian interventions should be restricted to very few situations. In what follows, I set out the problems with the legal apparatus of humanitarian interventions under Chapter VII of the UN Charter, and how this apparatus is out of step with an emerging notion of sovereignty. Using relational sovereignty as a theory for lowering the defense of sovereignty against the legitimacy of international humanitarian interventions, and using familiar principles of equity and individual rescue in tort, I set out three limiting principles for international humanitarian intervention and then briefly test these against the ongoing US invasion and occupation of Iraq.

2. THE PROBLEM WITH INTERVENTIONS UNDER CHAPTER VII OF THE UN CHARTER

The last decade of humanitarian intervention has been a patchwork of inconsistent justifications, too-often sluggish international responses, and varying degrees of efficacy in bringing assistance to failed states. On the face of Chapter VII of the UN Charter, intervention in purely civil unrest contravenes the principles of national sovereignty. There is no mention in the Charter for intervention on purely humanitarian grounds. And yet there have been several Chapter VII interventions in recent years. In each of the humanitarian crises of Somalia, Rwanda, Haiti, and Bosnia, the UN has authorized intervention across national borders. In each of these cases, internal national conflicts were incongruously reinterpreted as wars that could spill into other nations so that Chapter VII could be made to fit.

Not surprisingly, these awkward interpretations are contested. For example, in 1994, the UNSC passed Resolution 940 to justify an international military mission to Haiti under its Chapter VII powers, citing fears that the civil conflict in Haiti threatened the region's peace and security. In fact, Haiti's problems were specific to its own politics and history and were unlikely to cross its borders. The UN intervention was opposed by many Latin American countries and led to the charge that the real motive was not humanitarian but political – namely, to restore democracy and the rule of Jean-Baptiste Aristide.[1]

The fiction is that an internal human rights crisis may spill over a nation's borders and pose a threat to regional peace and security. But the "breach of regional peace" fiction does not easily apply to a human rights crisis in a remote part of island nation that has little impact on its neighboring nation-states. For example, when in 1999 rampaging Indonesian militiamen were slaughtering East Timorese by the hundreds, this human rights crisis did very little to threaten the peace or security of any other country in the region. In the absence of grounds for a Chapter VII intervention, even more creativity was called for. UN Secretary-General Kofi Annan issued a statement that senior Indonesian officials risked prosecution for crimes against humanity if they did not consent to the deployment of an available multinational force. Annan insisted that the Indonesian government either step in end stop the killing, or alternatively, consent to the deployment of international troops, failure to take one option or the other. Not surprisingly, Indonesian took the second option would result in Indonesians being held criminally liable for human rights violations.[2] The humanitarian intervention in East Timor has given rise to what has been termed the "Annan Doctrine": a loss of the traditional prerogatives of sovereignty in the face of crimes against humanity.[3]

Some scholars argue that Article 2(4) of the UN Charter prohibits *any* military intervention in other states on the grounds of purely internal violations of human rights. Others argue instead that the recent humanitarian interventions that have occurred with a UNSC resolution under Chapter

VII have created a de facto exception to Article 2(4). Still others argue that humanitarian intervention may be morally justified, albeit not legally justified, without a formal UNSC Resolution. In such cases, some other record of the UNSC's condemnation of the target country's human rights record is sufficient, and the lack of any formal UNSC Resolution simply reflects international politics rather than any lack of genuine humanitarian concern. This occurred in relation to the 1999 NATO attack on Serbia that successfully rescued the Albanian Kosovars from Serbian ethnic cleansing. NATO acted because the UN could not. Richard Goldstone, chair of the subsequent Independent International Commission on Kosovo, concluded that even though the Kosovo intervention did not have the backing of a UNSC resolution, it was never the less a *legitimate* intervention. NATO's actions had resolved a humanitarian crisis and had widespread support within the international community and civil society. Furthermore, the Commission argued that the gap between legal and legitimate humanitarian interventions is dangerous and needs to be removed by specifying the conditions for humanitarian intervention. In other words, what matters more than a legal permission to intervene is a moral permission to intervene. This moral permission legitimates the intervention, even though it cannot render the intervention fully legal under the terms of the UN Charter.

The legal constraints upon international humanitarian intervention are out of step with the moral urge to prevent loss of life in a nation with a humanitarian crisis. Efforts to fit humanitarian intervention into the existing international legal apparatus are fictions, crafted so that international action may follow international moral opprobrium. They are, more honestly, a simple judgment by the international community that a nation's government has failed its citizens. I want to suggest that the "Annan Doctrine" deployed in East Timor is the way ahead. It shows the sovereign – here, the Indonesian government – bargaining directly with the international community through the UN over human rights standards and trading some of the traditional prerogatives of sovereignty for freedom from international criminal prosecution. In this way, the sovereign answers not only to its own citizens for its failures of responsibility, but answers also to the international community. The stakes of the negotiation are sovereignty. Sovereignty is not only a duty of government to protect the human rights of its citizens, but a bargaining chip in international negotiation over humanitarian intervention, with the international community acting on behalf of a nation's citizens.

3. RELATIONAL SOVEREIGNTY

In the twentieth century the view was that national sovereignty applied universally to all nations with a seat at the UN table, but that it did not impose a practical requirement to assist people in need in other lands. It suggested that we need not be morally troubled that other people in other lands need our care. Under the twentieth century metric, international sovereignty was a "thin" responsibility – at heart, merely a duty or obligation each state owes to all others to observe national borders.[4]

Sovereignty today is best understood as vastly more complex. Economic interdependence between nation-states has grown, accelerating with the end of the Cold War, the expansion of the European Union (EU) and the growing influence of the World Trade Organization and the World Bank. More subtly, the proliferation of regional and international organizations has led to a diffusion of state influence beyond their sovereign borders. This distribution is uneven, and often unjust. Even so, globalization has blurred the distinction between domestic politics and international politics. What was once seen as a parochial national issue may now become a matter of regional or international concern.[5]

This growing transnational awareness of the plight of another nation's people has in part been the product of the last decade's expansion of human rights as an international rhetoric of demand aimed at governments by citizens and outsiders alike – a rhetoric that is simultaneously elaborated in international human rights treaties. Much of the human rights rhetoric, as well as the content of many international human rights treaties, is a "wish list" that goes far beyond a nation's capacity or political will to fulfill. Even so, new global and international communities are judging national compliance against international human rights standards. The UN, regional systems like the EU and the Inter-American systems, and myriad non-governmental organizations, have both direct and indirect input into human rights issues today. Claims that states have violated their citizens' human rights, either overtly or simply by maldistributing essential goods in exigent circumstances, come from sources both inside and outside the state. Ever-expanding economic, cultural, and intellectual interdependencies between states, and between the citizens of states, are forging tenuous bonds of interest and concern across national borders. Do these bonds – much more tenuous than the bonds of shared citizenship of a state, and contingent upon international communication – amount to a moral relationship that crosses state borders? And if it does, how should it influence the moral calculus about coercive interventions in a state's human rights abuses of its citizens?

Relational sovereignty proposes that sovereignty today is dependent on the measure of care by government for its citizens and that the international community may step in militarily to enforce this care. Sovereignty, in other words, carries a more expansive definition than it used to. Relational sovereignty describes sovereignty as an emerging set of obligations among citizens, governments, and the international community, with two dimensions. The first is a duty upon governments that correlates with the activities of their citizens, even if those activities extend beyond the nation's borders. For example, the activities of the US government extend beyond the borders of the United States not only because of US military and economic interests, but also because US citizens have myriad capital, corporate, professional, and recreational interests and activities beyond US borders. Second, relational sovereignty describes the interest that one country may have in the quality of governance in another country. For example, the nations of the EU have an interest in the quality of governance of nations applying to join the Union, and an improving human rights record is an important chunk of the EU accession process. In other words, sovereignty is a qualitative function rather than an unconditional status, and a function that may be assessed by citizens and the international community alike. A nation's claim to sovereignty – the sort of strong claim that under the traditional definition of sovereignty would have kept other nations at bay and beyond its borders – will not necessarily be recognized by other nations. This is especially so if a government is creating a human rights crisis. Relational sovereignty places such interactive judgments at the center rather than the periphery of responsible governance.

Relational sovereignty can be applied to humanitarian intervention. International peacekeeping activities of the last decade have emphasized the growing role of international human rights norms when considering the need to override sovereignty to protect a nation's citizens. In 1999, the UNSC's resolution authorizing the intervention of international peacekeeping in Kosovo referred to the resolution of "the grave humanitarian situation in Kosovo."[6] And more recently in 2004, Kofi Annan urged the UNSC to take action in the Darfur region of Sudan, citing "strong indications that war crimes and crimes against humanity have occurred ... on a large and systematic scale".[7] When national sovereignty is seen as a normative standard that is conditioned upon a government's good human rights performance, this decade's peacekeeping and humanitarian missions create a new principle for humanitarian intervention. National sovereignty will not deter the international community when a state is committing human rights abuses. National governments must discharge their duty of care towards their citizens, and the "court" of international opinion passes judgment. The international community acts as proxy for a state's citizens in judging its care for them. If the sovereign fails to treat its citizens within the bounds of human decency, the social contract between the ruler and the ruled collapses, and an assessment of that government's failings becomes a tripartite negotiation between sovereign, citizens, and the international community.

4. THREE PRINCIPLES LIMITING INTERNATIONAL HUMANITARIAN INTERVENTION

Widespread recognition exists that the UN Charter is out of step with contemporary international conditions. The 2004 UN Secretary-General's High Level Panel on Threats, Challenges, and Change[8] emphasized the interconnectedness of terrorism and civil wars, and extreme poverty. In welcoming the Panel's report, Annan enthused about the "opportunity to refashion and renew our institutions," including a more systematic and effective mechanism for intervention in humanitarian crises. In the meantime, while this reform process takes place, the gap between legal and legitimate justifications for interventions in humanitarian crises should be closed. In a world of complete justice, no government would ever seriously harm its citizens, either directly through violence or indirectly through incompetence, corruption, or maldistribution of social and economic goods. But there is no complete justice. At the same time, the extreme step of military intervention should meet an extremely high standard of clear need, even more so if intervention does not fit Chapter VII conditions of threatening regional peace and security. I want to offer the legal principle of equity as a way of justifying and containing the new global awareness of harm a state does to its citizens, pending full recognition of the legitimacy of humanitarian intervention under the theory of relational sovereignty. Equitable principles can balance the benefits and the dangers of humanitarian intervention.

Equity has its historical foundation in both morality and law. When, in the early days of modern courts, the letter of the law failed to provide a remedy for deserving plaintiffs, judges used their discretion to grant a remedy "in equity." Without a statute to guide them, judges have created the "common law" by articulating equitable principles that are so taken-for-granted that they do not need the authority of constitutions or legislation. The common law has in this way created fundamental legal principles that courts have elaborated over the years. These principles of equity have become the fail-safe of courts that ensure that justice is done. In these situations, "equity intervenes when there is no adequate remedy at law."[9] Courts fall back to equitable remedies in order to "provide fairness in a particular case of law."[10] In other words, equity allows a court to fill the gaps of formal laws so that justice and fairness may prevail.

Equitable principles are already part of international law, and have been applied in international judicial decision-making to ensure justice and fairness to the state parties. For example, the Statute of the International Court of Justice (ICJ) lists general principles of law recognized by civilized countries as one of the four sources of law, and the Court assumes that it is always entitled to have recourse to the use of equity. Equity, states the Court, is "implicit in the functions of a world tribunal."[11] One recent example is the Court's decision in the case about the Israel-Palestine wall. The Court directly cited equitable remedies, with all of the opinions referring to the "basic fairness" to the people of both territories, with Judge Owada stating:

Consideration of fairness in the administration of justice requires equitable treatment of the positions of both sides involved in the subject-matter in terms of the assessment both of facts and of law.

Equity should provide relief when the lives of innocent civilians are at risk:

Condemnation of the tragic circle of indiscriminate mutual violence perpetrated by both sides against innocent civilian population should be an important segment of the Opinion of the Court.[12]

My argument here is that equitable principles and equitable doctrines can be applied to sovereignty, describing the duties of government towards its citizens and constraining intervention by the international community. Using equity, together with principles of interpersonal rescue under traditional tort law, I suggest three threshold conditions for intervention.

The first condition is that the humanitarian crisis must be widespread and extreme for intervention to be justified. This test already de facto exists in international law and has been applied over the last decade to interventions in cases of genocide and widespread civil murder and mayhem.[13] I argue that this test ought also apply to interventions that seek to alleviate mass starvation and disease. The crucial element for both types of widespread harm is the culpability of the national government in either causing or allowing such harm. The second threshold condition is that intervention must be welcomed by a firm consensus of injured citizens within the ailing state. Of course, this test is difficult to establish because it requires an *ex ante* assessment of popular support for intervention. It is easy to assume popular support for intervention when there is some reliable institutional litmus of public sentiment, as when in 1999 the UN intervened in the East Timor mayhem after the overwhelming "yes" vote of the East Timorese referendum seeking secession from Indonesia. But such clear evidence is usually not available because oppressive governments rarely allow institutional expressions of unpopular sentiment about them. Finally, the third threshold test requires that international intervention do some good, and at very least, do no harm. This is also hard to establish: it requires excellent information about the politics, the capacity, and the popular preferences of the country where intervention might take place, and this information must point to the strong likelihood that intervention can improve conditions in the recipient country. If these three conditions are not in place, then intervention is unlikely to produce improved human rights. When they are, intervention can rightly be seen as an urgent expression of assistance to another nation's people in need. Improving respect for human rights is the raison d'être of humanitarian intervention.

4.1 Threshold Test 1: Conditions Must be Extreme and Widespread

International law holds that a nation's absolute sovereignty is sacrosanct and should be respected by other states. Despite this, military intervention, either multilateral or unilateral, has been justified under international law in the last decade where civil conflict was causing death or physical harm to innocents.[14] But whereas intervention has been a measure of last resort in halting civil conflict, military intervention has not been justified in other situations of widespread death to innocents, such as terrible malnutrition, starvation, and disease, even when those terrible circumstances have arisen from a government's culpable inaction. The international community typically intervenes in such cases by sending economic aid, both immediate aid with food and personnel, and longer-term economic aid for building a country's infrastructure. Yet corruptly governed countries, even those with very low internal revenues, still resist international economic incentives to prevent malnutrition and disease through better distribution of scarce social goods. Zimbabwe, for example, has high rates of government corruption and high rates of infant mortality and death from disease, including HIV-Aids. It has widespread poverty caused by its government. At the same time, Zimbabwe is resistant to international pressure to reform its politics. For countries that lie beyond indirect international influence, is there another way to incentivize their governments to distribute social goods more equally among their citizens? Where a Chapter VII intervention on the grounds or regional peace and security is not justified, and international economic incentives are not reducing the death toll, should there be an alternative rationale for forced intervention in a government's harm to its citizens?

One approach could be to revisit the justifications for military humanitarian intervention and ask: Is there a philosophical difference between intervention for genocide and intervention for mass malnutrition and starvation caused by corrupt or negligent governance? Why should a slow death through starvation be categorically different from a swift death by machete? The total numbers of deaths of citizens does not distinguish the cases, nor does the pain and anguish experienced by their victims. If it is accepted that the philosophical rationale for humanitarian intervention is the international community's interest in protecting the suffering citizens of a nation, surely this ought equally apply to death delivered by degrees over weeks and months. Equity looks to the moral culpability of a party for the harm of a victim. The test is justice and fairness, not just sovereignty. The key justification for international humanitarian intervention ought be a government's culpability in causing, or failing to prevent, the widespread death of innocents, rather than the method of causing those deaths.

The test of widespread harm has already emerged for international intervention in civil carnage. For example, after the civil and political crises in Rwanda and Kosovo, Annan stated that military intervention could be legitimate if there is an acute human rights crisis and if all diplomatic efforts have failed. Annan's test could be read to mean that military intervention may also be justified for widespread starvation through a government's negligent or intentional failure to distribute minimally necessary goods and essential sustenance. Governments that fail miserably in their duty to ensure their populations' well-being, either through bad intentions or through corruption or negligence, are surely failing in the obligations of the sovereign to care for its citizens.

States that have no capacity – commonly referred to as "failed states" – are outside this first threshold test because those governments are not the direct cause of the conditions causing the deaths of citizens. The crucial element here is a government's capacity to help its citizens. And surely there is no moral difference between deaths caused by a government's failure to keep the peace and deaths caused by a greedy government's failure to distribute social and economic goods among all its population. There is little practical difference either: recent studies have shown that the perception that intervention in civil war is straightforward is simply wrong. Instead, it is more realistic to acknowledge that intervention is always complicated, and its success or failure depends much more upon long-term support than it does on the initial justification for intervention. Death by civil violence and death by corruption or neglect ought to be treated equivalently, equally justifying military humanitarian intervention if the harms are as equally widespread.[15]

Applying this to the US invasion of Iraq, for example, a true humanitarian intervention would have depended upon more widespread harm. This threshold test would rule out humanitarian intervention in Iraq because human rights abuses there, though extreme in some cases, were not as widespread as either mass starvation or large-scale ethnic cleansing.

4.2 Threshold Test 2: Intervention Must be Welcomed by the Victims

The common law does not demand that an individual accept help from a bystander. The law of equity has applied this in the area of medical assistance, crafting the equitable doctrine of self-determination. This is defined as "one's ability to exert autonomy over one's own person, which includes the right to prevent unwanted bodily invasion and, therefore, the right to refuse unwanted medical treatment."[16] As long as a person has the rational ability of an adult, he may refuse medical treatment. Applying this principle to international military intervention, equity suggests that just as people may refuse medical intervention, citizens also may make a political choice not to be saved from their sovereign's tyranny. In other words, international intervention must only take place if the beleaguered citizens of a nation-state wish it. Using East Timor as an example, I want to suggest that this idea of consent is already forming de facto in the international system. From 1975 to 1999, there had been active resistance among the East Timorese people to Indonesian rule – resistance that was regularly reported in the international press and was a subject of heated diplomacy between Indonesia and other nations. When the 1999 referendum in East Timor voted overwhelmingly for independence from Indonesia, the UN's decision to send troops to stop civilian murder was easy. The East Timorese had expressed a clear mandate for the UN to step in on their behalf.

But in many cases of widespread civil unrest or widespread starvation and disease, there is no such unambiguous expression of the popular will as there was in East Timor. What information can the international community rely upon? Even more problematically, what are the moral obligations of the international community if it seems that a population consents to its own violation? Equity is a guide here. Sometimes, an individual's refusal of medical treatment may be overridden where there are other interests, such as the preservation of life, the prevention of suicide, the protection of innocent third parties, and the integrity of medical ethics. But the courts are extremely cautious about stepping over apparent consent to self-harm. For example, in *Gray v. Romeo*, 697 F. Supp. at 580, a 1988 decision of the US District Court of Rhode Island, the court stated:

Although Marcia Gray has a constitutional right to refuse life-sustaining medical treatment, no right is absolute . . . Accordingly, Marcia Gray's right must be balanced against competing governmental interests that include: the preservation of life, the prevention of suicide, the protection of innocent third parties, and the integrity of medical ethics... Upon examination, Marcia Gray's interest in self-determination outweighs all governmental interests.

Marcia Gray had the right to make a self-harming decision in refusing food and hydration. The same question needs to be asked about a nation's people who seem to be acquiescing in their own government's harm or neglect. The equitable doctrine of self-determination can either act as a brake on intervention by imputing to citizens their preference to suffer under a corrupt or violent government rather than have outsiders come in and impose solutions, or it might act as a justification for intervention by imputing that citizens could not possibly consent to the degree of extreme and widespread harm in their country.

The second threshold test will also be hard to satisfy in most cases, as most corrupt or authoritarian governments do not take the pulse of their citizens' feelings. Absent a referendum such as in East Timor, there must be clear evidence of such a groundswell of popular opinion that there is likely to be very little insurgent reaction against international intervention and very high levels of cooperation with those intervening forces in the days and weeks following invasion. Applying this to the US invasion of Iraq, for example, would have called for better empirical knowledge of the human rights conditions in Iraq, and would have meant taking seriously those provisions in the 1991 UNSC resolutions that referred to human rights by, for example, sending human rights monitors as well as weapons inspectors to Iraq. Anything less than East Timor's expressions of popular will must be viewed with extreme caution. Intervention must be informed by opinions of people currently living under a repressive government and not only the views of a vocal diaspora of past inhabitants.

4.3 Threshold Test 3: The Intervention Must Produce More Good than Harm

Finally, the third threshold test requires that international intervention ought only take place where it will do good, and at very least, do no overall harm. Returning to the individual rescue analogy, equity does not require a bystander to be a Good Samaritan and help another in distress. But if bystanders choose to intervene, two conditions apply: first, they must intend to help the victim; and second, at very least they must not do harm. If the bystander causes more harm to the victim, it raises the question of misfeasance or bad intent on the part of the bystander. Applying equity to international law, humanitarian intervention into another nation's human rights crisis ought to bring an improvement, and at the very least, must not make the human rights situation worse. If conditions worsen, the Good Samaritan has not been so good after all. Equity emphasizes two things: first, that humanitarian motivations must seek predominantly to help the people of another nation and not to pursue other geopolitical agendas; and second, intervention must improve, or at very least not worsen, conditions for the citizenry. Like Threshold Test 2, this makes intervention harder not easier, to justify. Improvement in conditions for citizens in the recipient country must be substantial, and not likely to be outweighed by harms that may come from insurgent resistance to the international forces. Improvements in living conditions must occur immediately, instantly providing relief from ghastly circumstances. And the intervention must also demonstrate the likelihood of long-term improvements, such as improved governance and better distributive mechanisms for social and economic goods.

How might this last threshold test operate? The United States' unilateral invasion of Iraq fails the Good Samaritan test because not only were weapons of mass destructions not found, but the invasion came at a huge cost of lives for the Iraqi people, with some 25,000 Iraqi civilians killed in the first two years. Given the relative size of the two countries, this number of civilian deaths would be the equivalent of roughly 300,000 American deaths. The application of an international Good Samaritan doctrine would seek to limit the harm within Iraq. An acceptable alternative might have been to deploy troops on the border to put pressure on the Iraqi regime to comply with the 1991 Security Council resolutions. The potential task of those troops would not have been invasion and regime change, but the protection of in the event that the government decided to crush an uprising, as happened, for example, in 1991. Under the equitable doctrine of the Good Samaritan, the US invasion could be seen as misfeasance – the sin of commission.

5. CONCLUSION

A couple of decades ago, neither the UNSC nor the governments of individual nations relied so heavily on issues like human rights, genocide, oppression, and torture when justifying intervention in civil conflicts. This is changing. There is today an unprecedented awareness of the plight of people in other nations. Globalization has accelerated this debate through its focus on the role of governments in responding to international pressures for expanded human rights. This awareness has altered the expectations of sovereignty: the international community places an affirmative duty upon national governments not only to keep the peace, but to distribute minimal material goods sufficient to prevent starvation. Military humanitarian interventions of the last decades are invoking a moral language of international interest in the competence of domestic governments. International humanitarian intervention has become one way of expressing compassion for citizens who are too silenced, too sick, too hungry, or simply too neglected, to demand more of their government.

While death by government violence or civil war may seem a more shocking failure of a government's duty of care to its peoples, in fact, widespread death through malnutrition or disease may render a negligent government equally culpable. The rationale for international intervention ought to apply to both active infliction of violence and passive ignoring of death and disease. In both cases, the sovereign government has failed in its role to protect its people. A murderous, corrupt, or neglectful government's failure to prevent the death or injury of its citizens amounts to a fracturing of sovereignty. This creates an opportunity – a moral permission rather than a legal obligation – for other nations to act as Good Samaritans. In these circumstances, the international community may provide a remedy to beleaguered citizens – a remedy that exists as a matter of equity rather than as a matter of law, and which may be the impetus for a Chapter VII intervention.

The test should be extreme and widespread harm, whether this comes from deadly civil mayhem or malnutrition and diseases. An equitable international right to intervene in the intentional harm inflicted by a government or its negligent failure to distribute public goods should come into play when national sovereignty has been overtaken by a government's action or inaction towards its people. It needs to be an overwhelmingly welcome intervention, with good *ex ante* evidence of internal support. And it must be an intervention that improves the lives of citizens, and certainly does not make their life harder. For, even when intervention is supported by a large majority of a population, history shows that some resistance and insurgency will likely cause further bloodshed and harm. For intervention to be justified, there must have been such extreme and widespread hardship in that country that the bloodshed of a forced international presence seems minor in comparison. Finally, humanitarian intervention is only justified if there is a long-term commitment to building something better in the place of what is destroyed.

NOTES

1. And yet another way of creating moral grounds for intervention arises when the UN is already participating in the settlement of a civil war or is somehow involved in the

region. Multilateral humanitarian action by a coalition of states without UNSC sanction in these conditions seems more plausible. There have been multilateral military interventions outside the UN Charter when, for example, the 1995 Serbian massacre of some 7,000 Muslim males in the supposed UN "safe haven" of Srebrenica gave rise to NATO's role in Bosnia. This led to Washington's coercive diplomacy that hammered out the Dayton agreement.
2. Annan warned that if Jakarta refused to accept the international community's assistance, it could not "escape the responsibility of what could amount . . . to crimes against humanity." See *Transcript of Press Conference of Secretary-General Kofi Annan, at Headquarters, 10 September,* United Nations Information Service UNIS/SG/2360, at: http://www.unis.unvienna.org/unis/pressrels/1999/sg2360.html?print. Or, in the words of the Geneva Conventions, Indonesian leaders would be left open to international prosecution because they had not taken "all feasible measures" to stop the violence. Geneva Convention Relative to the Protection of Civilian Persons in Time of War, August 12, 1949, art. 68, 6 UST 3516, TIAS No. 3365, 75 UNTS 287.
3. UN Secretary-General Kofi Annan, Speech to open the General Assembly on September 20, 1999.
4. This conception of sovereignty extended to both internal and external relations: a state exercises extensive control over its people within its territory, but at the same time it must respect the authority of other states within their territorial borders. This is a "thin" conception, as it concentrates on the state's right to govern its citizens, not on the state's responsibilities towards its citizens. For more on this see Jonathan H. Marks, "Mending the Web: Universal Jurisdiction, Humanitarian Intervention and the Abrogation of Immunity by the Security Council," 42 *Columbia Journal of Transnational Law* 445, 477 (2003).
5. An example for such occurrence can be found in the case of East Timor. East Timor declared its independence from Portuguese colonization on November 28, 1975. Nine days later it was invaded and occupied by Indonesian forces, killing 60,000 Timorese in the initial assault. At the time, the international community did not initiate any actions targeted at the protection of the Timorese people. More than 20 years later, on August 30, 1999, in a UN-supervised popular referendum, an overwhelming majority of the people of East Timor (78.5%) voted for independence from Indonesia. By this time, the region's aspirations for independence were the focus of the UNs, which agreed to send a multinational peacekeeping force to the region in the pre-referendum phase, at the request of Indonesia. Soon after the referendum, antiindependence Timorese militias – organized and supported by the Indonesian military – commenced a large-scale, scorched-earth campaign of retribution against the East Timorese. On September 20, 1999 the Australian-led peacekeeping troops of the International Force for East Timor (INTERFET) deployed to the country and brought the violence to an end. On May 20, 2002, East Timor was internationally recognized as an independent state.
6. See .SC Res. 1244, UN SCOR, 4011th mtg., UN Doc. S/RES/1244 (1999).
7. Emily Wax, "Sudanese getting little help U.N. estimates death toll has nearly doubled to 70,000 since Sept. 9," *The Washington Post*, November 17, 2004, A10.
8. The UN Secretary-General, Kofi Annan, established the High-Level Panel on Threats, Challenges and Change in November, 2003 in order to examine new dangers to international security and to recommend ways of strengthening institutions of collective security. See http://www.un-globalsecurity.org/panel.asp.

9. Thomas O. Main, "Traditional Equity and Contemporary Procedure," 78 *Washington Law Review* 429, at pp. 476–478.
10. Jack Moser, "The Secularization of Equity: Ancient Religious Origins, Feudal Christian Influences, and Medieval Authoritarian Impacts On the Evolution of Legal Equitable Remedies," 26 *Capitol University Law Review* 483 (1997), p. 484.
11. See General Information about ICJ: http://www.icj-cij.org/icjwww/igeneral information/ibbook/Bbookchapter7.HTM.
12. See ICJ website, http://www.icj-cij.org/icjwww/idocket/imwp/imwpframe.htm.
13. The requirement of an extreme and widespread humanitarian crisis, as a just condition for humanitarian intervention, has also appeared in the works of others. See Michael Walzer, *Just and Unjust Wars* (New York: Basic Books, 1977) and Fernando Teson, *Humanitarian Intervention: An Inquiry into Law and Morality* (Ardsley, NY: Transnational Publishers, 1997).
14. This threshold test would rule out humanitarian intervention in Iraq because human rights abuses there, though extreme in some cases, were not as widespread as either mass starvation or large-scale ethnic cleansing.
15. Here, I am utilizing the distinction between civil and political rights as they are expressed in the "International Covenant on Civil and Political Rights," and social and economic rights as they are expressed in the "International Covenant on Social, Economic and Cultural Rights."
16. See Kristin M. Lomond, 31 *University of Louisville Journal of Family Law* 665, 670 (1993).

EUGENE E. DAIS

JUST WAR THEORY POST-9/11: PERFECT TERRORISM AND SUPERPOWER DEFENSE

In its devastating surprise attack on the American homeland on September 11, 2001 (9/11), the global terrorist network al-Qaeda used suicide fighters to crash hijacked airliners into the Twin Towers of the World Trade Center, killing some 2800 noncombatants, and into the Pentagon, killing some 200 combatants. Since the Cold War ended a decade before, the United States reigned as the sole world superpower (SWS) in military and economic might. No rival great power state could seriously challenge American military force without suffering rapid, decisive defeat in retaliation. Despite this, however, with the terrorist attack, America's historic invulnerability to foreign aggression on its soil, enjoyed since the 1812 War with Britain, was gone in a matter of a few hours.

Moreover, the 9/11 terrorist attack did not seek the defeat and surrender of the United States. Instead, it aimed to punish America for taking on the hegemonic role Britain had performed during the nineteenth century. That century was known as Pax Britannica, the century Britain used its naval superiority to rule the oceans to protect international trade from the disruptions of great power wars and high seas piracy. States need one of their number to take the lead, if they are to overcome the mutual distrust of each others' intentions. To engage cooperatively in fair and honest trading, states must have the mutual assurance that they are not foolish to rely on what each other says. This mutual assurance is possible, so Hegemon Stability Theory holds, only when there is a single hegemon that holds both the economy and military rings, so to speak.[1] The deep worldwide depression of the 1930s, for example, resulted from the absence of a world hegemon. Britain was too weak in 1914 to stabilize the international free market economy and the United States was unwilling at the time to take on the role: hence, the two world wars.

The 9/11 attack by a terrorist network with global reach presented an unforeseen threat to the hegemonic role the United States had assumed. This attack, unlike the truck bombing of the Twin Towers in 1993, clearly revealed the network's potential to deliver by surprise and at will weapons of mass destruction (WMD) against the United States, something no state, with its territorial location, could do and hope to survive. This form of terrorism, whatever its content or purpose, I call *perfect terrorism,* perfect in the sense that, given its potential to involve WMD, even the SWS must fear its threat as a continuing clear and present danger.

The fact that the 9/11 attack hit the two most famous symbols of America's economic and military dominance clearly signaled al-Qaeda's intention to undermine the hegemonic role the United States reluctantly took on in 1945. Stability in the international economy for the last several decades has crucially depended on a reliable supply of oil, and most proven oil reserves are in Middle Eastern Muslim countries. The disruptive impact of modern secular culture and free markets on Muslim religious culture is intolerable to many of more than a billion Muslims, and not a few of them view the United States, because of its hegemonic role, as their real enemy. Hostile Muslims see 9/11 as dramatically initiating a cultural hot war that will be won only when the American hegemon withdraws from Muslim holy lands, especially from Saudi Arabia and other Muslim oil states.

With the world hegemon gone, extreme Islamic movements could more easily replace the existing moderate Islamic regimes. Extreme Islamic regimes could then significantly control the world oil supply and its wealth creation and use this wealth to empower Muslim minorities deeply embedded in Western states like Russia, France, Germany, Spain, and Britain, as well as, in particular, in the Muslim holy land of Israel. This limited victory over the SWS would be devastating. Not only would the international economy be seriously disrupted, harming most the people least able to bear it, but the military resources of all states would thereby be drastically weakened, thus facilitating the global spread of terrorist insurgencies.

Moreover, this limited victory is feasible because the American SWS is a liberal democracy. To realize its strategic aim, perfect terrorism has only to make the continued presence of the American hegemon in the Middle East more costly in American lives and fortune. Such costs are immediate and concrete, while the devastating economic consequences worldwide of the American withdrawal are remote and abstract. Americans tend to react more to immediate, concrete losses, particularly when the losses are on media display globally 24/7. The 9/11 attack may thus be seen as the first step in the al-Qaeda strategy of terrorism to intimidate the world hegemon for political purposes.

1. THE NECESSARY HEGEMON

Hegemonic dominance needs military supremacy to back its claim to deter states from unfair and dishonest trade practices and disruptive aggression. The only alternative is seeking peace through a balance of power under the anarchic Westphalian Paradigm of Positive International Law (WPIL). But this alternative fails in the face of the *security dilemma*. If the power to defeat other states is truly equal among all states, then it would be futile for any state to attack another state; for wars could not then be won for gain, but only negotiated for a zero-zero outcome. But, in fact, states are typically unequal in military and economic power. Weaker states tend to distrust stronger states and thus seek security by arming themselves to exercise more effectively their right to self-defense. But, stronger states see this as a threat, and thus arms races start. Arms races make it rational for the stronger state preventively to strike first while still in a stronger position. Preventive first strikes tend to start wars neither side really desires. Thus, balancing actual powers in fact leave all states less secure.

Nor does the purely normative force of the WPIL resolve the security dilemma. In the absence of a common sovereign, WPIL can work only by promulgating abstract norms grounded on state consent explicit in treaties and implicit in past state practices. The rules of WPIL may sometimes be enforced by multilateral institutions, like the International Monetary Fund and the World Bank, and by economic sanctions short of intervention into state sovereignty. But even when states consent to the promulgated norms, which is not always, the only sanction for violating the norms, besides shame, which not all states fear, is exclusion from the benefits of cooperating with other states. The perceived advantages of preventive strikes, however, often moves states to risk the costs of sanctions. Thus, while the norms of WPIL may rhetorically condemn preventive war, they cannot always prevent the worst outbreaks of armed conflict.

The WPIL, in operating through the multilateralism of equally sovereign states, fails to pay adequate attention to the key principle in effectively enforcing norms: when negotiations stalemate, inaction can be worse than unilateral action, and when all else fails, the buck must stop somewhere and clubs are trump. Multilateralism avoids this principle for the very good reason that respecting it is inconsistent with the practice of multilateralism and its ideal view that continuous negotiation is in itself effective enforcement. The point of having a hegemon is precisely to impart credibility to the threat of effective force, not only to deter violations of WPIL by aggression and unfair trade practices, but also to resolve the security dilemma by making arms races futile. Where the less coercive sanctions inherent in the WPIL may especially fail to work is when states tempted to cheat become rogue states, ready to attack the system itself by attacking the hegemon. Within WPIL constraints, rogue states in the guise of self-defense can often attack the hegemon with impunity, especially when they have a UNSC veto holder on their side. Rogue states may even seek to attack the hegemon by using nonstate surrogates practicing perfect terrorism.

But military force wielded unilaterally by a hegemon must be grounded in the co-opted consent of the other states in the system. Such consent is needed for the hegemon's legitimacy, and so for its effectiveness. The other states must recognize that a stable world economy is a public good from which all but the hegemon receive net benefit as free riders and without which all states would lose their opportunities for prosperity, thus endangering their domestic legitimacy. The world hegemon, in other words, is not a Hobbesian sovereign on the world stage with the power of coercive command to enforce obedience from the other states. But it must be a state with the credibility and political will to enforce rules equally against all sovereign states.

But the legitimacy of a world hegemon in the eyes of other states must be continuously earned and is never free from controversy and challenge. Its legitimacy is always at risk. First, the WPIL, even as modified by the United Nations Charter, denies the legitimacy of a hegemon and its protective role. From the UN perspective, hegemonic dominance subverts the peace sought multilaterally through the rules of the WPIL and the balancing of power among equally sovereign states. Second, the hegemon, when it acts unilaterally, creates it own peculiar dilemma, the *international legitimacy dilemma,* a dilemma inherent in the hegemonic role itself. The legitimacy of the hegemon in coercively enforcing the rules of fair trade and discouraging arms races comes mainly from the public good of a stable and protected international free market economy, as recognized by the free rider states that benefit from it. But the international legitimacy of the hegemon is at risk precisely because it performs its hegemonic duties. Other states may come to fear the power and the unilateral freedom of the hegemon, and they may become reluctant to grant it hegemonic status. Whenever the hegemon has to make good its deterrent threats by the actual use of lethal force, its legitimacy may be eroded by the other states' fear that the hegemon's unilateral action may endanger them. Thus, international legitimacy dilemma is the idea that the coercive actions the hegemon must take to protect and fulfill its stabilizing role simultaneously risk its legitimacy.

Another indication of the legitimacy problems of a hegemon is the way in which its actions place it is at odds with key aspects of just war theory (JWT), especially in terms of what counts as defense (self-defense or defense of another) to justify going to war (*jus ad bellum*).[2] The hegemon may need to take defensive action that would not be regarded as defensive by JWT. JWT seeks to limit wars to cases of defense against a direct attack, and it does this, in part, to avoid some wars. But a hegemon uses force, or its threat, to prevent all the wars it can, but for those it starts. Sometimes an appropriate use of force by a hegemon, especially when it seeks a necessary defense of its own hegemonic role, will not be in response to an actual attack, but will be anticipatory. The prospects of this have increased greatly in the age of perfect terrorism. The only anticipatory force allowed by JWT is preemption, a response to an imminent attack. But the hegemon may need to use anticipatory force in cases that go beyond preemption.[3]

For this reason I focus on two issues most relevant to this possibility: (1) Is it just or right for the SWS, simply because it has the hegemonic stabilizing role, to defend itself against perfect terrorism by exclusively exercising a right of first strike when in its own judgment this is necessary? (2) Can the SWS go beyond the preemptive right of first strike without abandoning the Westphalian paradigm of equal territorial sovereignty? I argue for a yes to the both questions. I argue that a hegemon has what I call *the protective right of first strike*, a strike that goes beyond preemptive, but stops short of being a preventive strike.

In Section 2, I sketch a model of the special threat perfect terrorism presents to the SWS (whichever state it may be) solely because it has taken on the hegemonic role. This unprecedented threat of perfect terrorism falls outside the moral scope of JWT as it informs WPIL. In the third section, JWT is examined more closely to identify which of its constraints obstruct an effective defense by a SWS, and I focus on the constraint that a SWS may only launch first strikes that are defensive in the traditional sense. I conclude that JWT and its reliance on WPIL must be rejected to the extent that it fails to provide in the post-9/11 world a coherent alternative in denying the hegemon a right of self-defense.

For this reason, in the final section, I argue for going beyond JWT to a morally constrained position that allows a SWS to protect itself and its hegemonic role from perfect terrorism by unilateral action, when necessary. Allowing a SWS to defend itself in this way, however, would grant it and it alone a special exemption privileging it to go to war without preemptive constraint when necessary in its own judgment. I propose that the hegemon be allowed a different right to go to war (*jus ad bellum*), the protective right of first strike, a right that as a last resort can be exercised to lead to regime change. This different right, because it is special and exclusive to the world hegemon, encounters serious objections, among them that it sets a double standard and allows the hegemon to be sole judge in its own case. I argue, however, that with appropriate constraints these objections can be avoided.

2. PERFECT TERRORISM

How is it possible, as happened on 9/11, for a few people organized in a terrorist network successfully to attack the United States, the reigning SWS, whose military and economic might has no recent parallel and suffices to deter any attack on it by another state or coalition of states? It is precisely this unprecedented capability of contemporary international terrorism that warrants calling it perfect terrorism. Perfect terrorists are perfect in the sense that they can do what no territorial state could risk, namely, to attack the SWS with WMD and survive. Perfect terrorists can accomplish what no rival state could do, to make it impossible for the SWS to resolve its own security dilemma by winning the arms race against all other states.

David Fromkin presented in 1975 the classic theory of "the strategy of terrorism,"[4] and this theory provides the background for the idea of perfect terrorism. In using lethal force terrorists aim not at a physical result that would defeat the enemy state, but at a psychological result, and this result is not their final goal but simply a means to it, the means of creating fear to induce the enemy state to act as the terrorists desire. Unlike assassins, revolutionaries, guerrilla fighters, and even soldiers, all of whom kill those they desire to conquer, terrorists are in the paradoxical position of killing those whom they may have no desire to kill. They may be completely indifferent. Killing is simply an efficient means to maximum fear in the expectation that the fear indirectly serves the terrorists' cause. Hence, for terrorists, constraints of justice during war (*jus in bello*), in particular, have no relevance. Fear is best maximized by indiscriminate and disproportionate killings of noncombatants.

Terrorism as a strategy works against the strongest states, and perhaps the stronger the state, the more successfully it works. While war is the strategy of the strong, terrorism is the strategy of the weak. The weak always lose in direct military confrontation with the strong. Thus, the weak must resort to terrorism, and terrorism by suicide fighters is by far the most effective. Terrorists cannot strike the military of the strong state, so they must strike its people. The strong state, however, is expected to protect its people not only from foreign violence, but also from the fear of it, a fear that can become so pervasive that it disorients and paralyzes normal everyday living. Once this happens, the state loses its domestic legitimacy to alienation and chaos, and the terrorists can claim victory.

This, however, is terrorism in general. Perfect terrorism differs in a crucial respect. It aims not to defeat or take over the SWS as a state, although its attacks could lead to delegitimating the SWS in the eyes of its people and so put its regime into question. Rather, the aim is to influence the foreign policy of the SWS by intimidating it into abandoning its hegemonic role. While perfect terrorism, like all terrorism, uses terror to instill fear, it uses the fear strategy on the world stage against the SWS and its allies. No state is immune from the attacks of perfect terrorism. But the SWS has to be the specific target for perfect terrorism to realize its overall goal: to undermine the hegemonic role of the SWS and thereby disrupt the international free market economy on which its political legitimacy depends.

When two states distrust each other, they face the security dilemma. The stronger state fears that the other may arm itself to overcome its relative weakness and thus prevail in a future war. The stronger state must then choose between unpleasant options, either engage in an arms race to seek to deter the rival state until they reach the point of mutually assured destruction and hence a cold war or quickly strike first in a preventive attack when a war against the rival state can more easily be won. While preventive war may make the stronger state secure for a time, the precedent invites other states to engage in an endless series of preventive wars. However, this security dilemma appears not to apply to the SWS. It is the SWS because it has won, at least for a time, the global arms race against all other states. But this dominance and security in relation to other states does not end the threat to the SWS from perfect terrorism.

When the SWS faces the asymmetrical threat from perfect terrorism, it confronts its own peculiar, legitimacy dilemma, both domestically and internationally. For the domestic part, there are two unpleasant options. First, the SWS may ignore the terrorist attacks on its people on the theory that if the terrorists cannot provoke the SWS to overreact, then the strategy of terrorism fails. But this threatens the domestic legitimacy of the SWS in the eyes of its people for failing to protect them. Second, the SWS may respond by homeland security measures to prevent further terrorist attacks. But it then jeopardizes its domestic legitimacy by imposing overly stringent police measures in seeking to capture terrorists who covertly infiltrate its population. Thus, perfect terrorism creates a domestic legitimacy dilemma for the SWS by creating the perception that it has done either too little or too much to protect its own people.

States historically have taken one or the other horn of the dilemma depending on their political judgment as to which alternative least risks their domestic legitimacy. Perfect terrorism, however, ups the stakes. First, its network not only infiltrates the target state, but it has global operations. Domestic police actions alone will not work for they leave perfect terrorists to operate freely from the outside. War has to be declared on the terrorist network itself and the states connected with it. Second, the network of perfect terrorism, through covert infiltration, may be more effective, for example, than missiles for delivering WMD without prior detection. A terrorist network with covert global operations and with potential access to WMD thus becomes the supreme threat to the SWS, which alone can respond to it globally.

The result is that perfect terrorism, unlike ordinary terrorism, creates a legitimacy dilemma with an international dimension. If the SWS takes what may seem the easy way out in the face of perfect terrorism and accepts the terrorist demands to abandon its hegemonic role, it would face loss of legitimacy not only from its own people, but more importantly and more quickly from the free rider states that count on its hegemonic role. For example, were the United States to withdraw from the Middle East, it could permit governments serving the terrorist cause to control over half the world's proven reserves of oil. The resulting instability from the terrorist disruption of a vital part of the international economy, possibly leading to extreme inflation and depression, would inflict economic hardship worldwide.

On the other hand, if the SWS reacts aggressively to the international dimension of the terrorist threat, it puts its legitimacy at risk beyond its borders. This is the other horn of the SWS's peculiar, double legitimacy dilemma. The difficulty with waging a counterwar on terrorism is that the war against the terrorist network has to be waged in states from whom no imminent armed attack would be observable or even forthcoming. Such use of force clearly goes beyond the preemptive self-defense that JWT and WPIL permit. But the unilateral use of force has the SWS claiming a special right to preventive action, acting on a double standard and serving as judge in its own case, thus creating fear among other states that they may be next. How is this international legitimacy dilemma to be avoided within the constraints of WPIL, as influenced by JWT, without undermining the underlying Westphalian paradigm of equally sovereign states on which the world hegemonic role depends?

3. JUST WAR THEORY

JWT limits the just cause for going to war to self-defense or defense of another state without regard to the security dilemma among states. Preventive war for the purpose of gaining or preserving greater advantage in the balance of power among sovereign states is absolutely prohibited because preventive war invites too much violence. In fact, however, the intention proper to going to war is often conceived in ways other than self-defense; for example, a war may be thought just because it has the intention of restoring the *status quo ante* to either the divine order or the order of secular international law that aggressive wars violate. But both of these alternative ideals of international justice are controversial. Mutually distrustful states engaging in arms races for their security always take their particular controversial view of divine order or international law as the right view, thus inviting the security dilemma sketched earlier. But, the mere presence of a SWS, which, in its self-interest, provides mutual assurance for all states, can block the temptation for arms races even by great powers because they perceive the disparity of military might as so great that attempts to match the SWS militarily would be futile.

The rule that only self-defensive wars are just, however, even when extended to include preemption, leaves the SWS without an effective defense for the resolution of its double legitimacy dilemma. Effectively proscribing preventive war requires a clear rule that avoids controversy in its application, and this is that a state is permitted to go to war only when it has suffered, or is about to suffer, an attack. The moral justification for the self-defense rule is that states are endangered only by territorial intervention, and there is no intervention until another state has, or is about to, intervene. But, while this rule may reduce the occasions for violence, it still leaves mutually distrustful states in their security dilemma waiting for an excuse to strike first.

Moreover, perfect terrorism makes the self-defense rule obsolete for the hegemon. Perfect terrorism endangers even the SWS by delivering WMD by covert infiltration into the target populations, making imminence largely undetectable. No state can tolerate even one strike with WMD, and no homeland defense can perfectly prevent all WMD strikes, especially when carried out by suicide fighters. Thus, the risk of a terrorist WMD strike would apparently justify first strikes against individual terrorists and their network wherever located. Consequently, a SWS needs a more flexible rule, one that gives greater latitude to the first use of force, than one that permits first strikes only when preemptive. The SWS should be allowed to strike against terrorist targets in states in conspiracy with the terrorists in recruitment, indoctrination, training, financing, and communication, even when those states are not an active part of the terrorist network. The SWS right of first strike, in other words, should extend to neutral states that merely tolerate the presence of perfect terrorists within their jurisdiction.

Terrorists must locate in the territory of some states, and invading state sovereignty in the absence of an actual or imminent attack undermines the principle of equal sovereignty. The rule that all states would equally have an extended right of first strike would violate JWT and WPIL, as well as undermine the legitimacy of the SWS. The SWS must claim the special and exclusive right of first strike beyond preemptive strikes. But that makes it vulnerable to the objections that it acts on double standards and as judge in its own case, thus eroding its legitimacy in the perception of the international community. Without the special right of first strike in its self-defense, however, not only the hegemonic role, but the sovereignty of the SWS, is jeopardized. What I propose in Section 4 for resolving the international legitimacy dilemma is a special unilateral right of first strike by the SWS that goes beyond the preemptive first strike allowed by JWT and WPIL, but stops short of the double standard and self-judging objections of the preventive first strike.

Before discussing this special right, however, let me say a brief word about moral constraints on the hegemon beyond those of *jus ad bellum*. The constraints of *jus in bello* – discrimination to avoid the loss of innocent lives and proportionality in the use of force – do apply to the hegemon, but not for the moral reasons of the modified pacifism advocated by JWT. A hegemon that uses violent force contrary to these constraints would quickly undermine its own international legitimacy. Moreover, JWT does not make explicit the stringent fiduciary-like obligation an attacking hegemon must undertake, to leave the target state and its people after war (*jus post bellum*) with a viable domestic order. The hegemon that leaves the target state in disorder, and thus vulnerable to perfect terrorist influence, becomes its own worst enemy.[5]

4. PROTECTIVE FIRST STRIKE

The special threat of perfect terrorism is directed at the SWS in its hegemonic role. The SWS cannot, like other states, afford to give in to terrorist demands. Its giving in would empower the terrorist conspiracy and undermine the legitimacy of the hegemonic role. That would have adverse worldwide economic and military consequences to be avoided if at all possible. Moreover, the perfect terrorist threat cannot be solved simply by the present hegemon "resigning" in favor of a new hegemon. For any successor hegemon would be faced with the same international legitimacy dilemma.

The threat of perfect terrorism depends on states that permit terrorists, for whatever reason, to locate within their borders. Any member of a perfect terrorist network, anyone tied to the network as a criminal conspiracy, should be captured and punished within states in which they are located. Part of the capture and punishment process would be extradition by request of the SWS. States willing to capture and punish terrorists on their territory, but lacking the capacity to do so, should be assisted by the SWS to acquire the capacity. If a state refuses to capture and punish the terrorists, or refuses the assistance of the SWS in doing so, then it would be classified as an unwilling state. Unwilling states would be proportionally subject to intervention by a protective first strike by the hegemon. If nothing less intrusive would be effective, the protective first strike could include regime change. The threat of perfect terrorism to instigate insurgencies globally should be a sufficient incentive for states in their self-interest to capture and punish network terrorists or cooperate with the SWS in doing so. If that incentive fails, the presumption must be that the regime of the unwilling state is itself a passive part of the conspiracy and thus as a last resort in the judgment of the SWS subject to regime change.

By its special right of protective first strike, the SWS aims to establish a minimum rule of law as the obligation of every state. A state may, of course, do more, but at a minimum it must be willing to capture and punish any person tied to the terrorist network as part of the criminal conspiracy. The special protective right of first strike is a necessary mechanism for making the minimum rule of law effective worldwide.

But the special right of protective first strike possessed by the hegemon would be subject to constraints. It is these constraints that would distinguish a protective right of first strike from a less restrictive right of preventive war. First and foremost, the protective right may be exercised only when justice after war is given priority over justice in going to war. In the case of regime change, for example, the SWS must be committed to an appropriate and feasible level of "nation building," assuring the defeated state a functioning order at least at the minimum level of the rule of law for capturing and punishing perfect terrorists. This constraint is compatible with leaving in place a stable despotic regime, provided it complies with the minimum rule of law. The basis of this constraint is that, however just the cause, the right to intervene forcibly for regime change is discredited unless the SWS can publicly convince relevant others that in a reasonable time the people of the state with the changed regime will come to see the invading troops not as conquerors, but as a legitimate policing force serving the public good of territorial security.

Second, the SWS must establish among its own citizens the domestic legitimacy of its interventionist policy. By reasoning in public with its citizens, through democratic processes, the government must convince them that the cost in their lives and fortune, a cost they alone may bear, is worth the gain in the security forced regime change (if necessary) would bring to the world and the role the hegemon plays in that world. The SWS must convince its citizens through processes that effectively check and balance the governmental decision to go to war. Such reasoning, fully open to world opinion, may not persuade the world immediately, but it is necessary that it persuade the citizens of the hegemon.

Third, a protective first strike designed to lead to regime change is permissible only as a last resort, and even then it must be conditioned by fair notice so that the target state has reasonable time to show that it is willing to capture and punish perfect terrorists within its territory. Target states would include not only states that aid perfect terrorists, but also states that merely tolerate their presence for whatever reason. Fourth, the protective right of first strike, as a special and exclusive right, has to be available over time to a future world hegemon in its performance of the stabilizing role. A present hegemon cannot simply claim its role as its own property.

Fifth, the SWS must show that its action, though illegal under the restrictions of JWT, WPIL, or the UN Charter, is well grounded in principled precedents that previous actions of the hegemon have set in which other states at least acquiesce. Specifically, each exercise of the protective right of first strike whose legality is in doubt must be publicly justified case by case as consistent with past exercises on principles no state which benefits from the security and prosperity made possible by the hegemonic role could reasonably reject. The SWS must establish the legitimacy of its illegality by the accepted procedure of customary international law: it must openly assert the illegality of its action, publicly present the rationale to justify it, act on the illegality then and consistently thereafter, and convince other states to accept that making the illegality legal is the better practice.

The need for this last condition is evident because even the most democratic processes for domestically legitimating a governmental decision to go to war are still open to the international danger of recreating the security dilemma: the effect of the hegemon's acting on a double standard and judging its own case has on the perceived security of other states. The double standard breeds the fear among states of which one is next, and the self-judging allows the SWS to seek its own self-advantage at the expense of all other states. Thus, the international legitimacy dilemma posed by perfect terrorism is not finally resolved even when SWS first strikes have the overwhelming support of its citizens. While world opinion should have no immediate veto, nor any major influence other than respectful consideration, world opinion over time is crucial. The fifth constraint is designed to bring world opinion along.

In the long run, the SWS must appear to be acting justly not only at home, but also before world. The SWS must be able to show through public reasoning that its exclusive final say does not promote its own national interests in disregard of the general security of all states. A process of principled precedents to constrain unilateral actions as the basis for making new international law in the customary way responds to these important concerns of world opinion.

Moreover, should the SWS fail to deliver to the world the expected economic stability while fighting perfect terrorism, another state could assume the special right for itself, but only if it complies with the same constraints. Thus, a significant constraint on a SWS abusing its special protective right for self-advantage is its awareness that a future world hegemon could rightly exercise the same special protective right of first strike against it in accord with the precedents it establishes. Before the hegemon sets a precedent for unilateral intervention, it must recognize that that precedent could make it subject to attack by a future hegemon.

There is, of course, the fear that a SWS by its very nature would seek to replace the Westphalian paradigm with an imperialist world order. But the legitimacy of the special right of first strike and the hegemonic role itself depends on furthering the minimum rule of law within the domestic jurisdiction of all territorial states. This goal would frustrate the imperialist ambitions of any SWS.

The overall purpose of the protective right of first strike is to make it possible for the SWS to resolve its double legitimacy dilemma, and hence the security dilemma among all states, by allowing it to do what it needs to do to create the public good of a world without any states unwilling to capture and punish perfect terrorists. In the end, the objections that such a right would allow the SWS to act on a double standard and to judge its own case are met by the SWS showing that exercising unilaterally this special right is not only rationally, but also necessarily, related to defeating the perfect terrorist threat, at least reducing the threat to the risk management of a criminal conspiracy.

In sum, because the SWS bears the final responsibility for performing the hegemonic role at its cost alone, if necessary, the SWS should have a protective right of first strike, once its citizens agree, as a unilateral right in relation to other states, when no other less interventionist, but equally effective, way to remove the perfect terrorist threat to it is feasible. It follows that the SWS, if it is to protect its hegemonic role effectively, cannot take the authority of JWT and WPIL, including the UN Charter, as the final word. Although those sources warrant respect, the final judgment on exercising the protective right of first strike must belong to the SWS, if only because its people must be ready to bear alone the total cost in lives and fortune.

NOTES

1. This idea is developed in Hegemonic Stability Theory. See Charles P. Kindleberger, *The World in Depression: 1929–1939* (Berkeley, CA: University of California Press, 1973).
2. JWT finds its classic modern exposition in Michael Walzer's, *Just and Unjust Wars* (New York: Basic Books, originally printed 1977, 3rd edn, 2000 with new Preface). Further discussion by Walzer is in *Arguing About War* (New Haven, CT: Yale University Press, 2004)
3. Despite its title, JWT provides no resources for considering the justice of the terrorists' goals. The possible justice of perfect terrorism's goals in challenging the world hegemon with deadly, suicidal force, however, should not be dismissed altogether. There may be a cosmic conception of justice inclusive of humanitarian values that would allow Muslim and other traditional communities to justifiably resist with force disruptions of their local culture and economy brought on by modernity. But JWT avoids the cosmic question of justice for good reason: cosmic justice has yet to find its intelligible, coherent expression.
4. David Fromkin, "The Strategy of Terrorism," *Foreign Affairs* 53 (4) (July 1975), 683, 686, 692–693.
5. In *Arguing about War*, p. 161, Walzer comments that the least developed part of JWT is the *jus post bellum* constraint. This constraint, post-9/11, would require the aspiration that everything possible is done to ensure that regime change leaves the people of the territory with self-government. This aspiration goes beyond the minimum rule of law for capturing and punishing perfect terrorists as a criminal conspiracy and would exclude despotic regimes willing to abide by the minimum rule of law even though the people democratically refuse to reject despotism.

STEVEN P. LEE

PREVENTIVE INTERVENTION

Intervention (short for military intervention) is the use of military force by one state (the intervener) against another (the target state) when the force is not in reaction to military aggression by the target state.[1] Intervention is not defense against an occurring military attack. This makes intervention morally problematic because *jus ad bellum* is usually understood to proscribe cross-border use of military force in cases other than defense against an occurring military attack. This chapter is about the moral status of *preventive* intervention, one form of intervention.[2]

In launching a preventive intervention, the intervener seeks to prevent an expected future aggression against it by the target state.[3] Preventive intervention is not a response to actual aggression, but to aggression expected at some indefinite time in the future.[4] Generally, the intervener expects future aggression because it perceives the target state as an opponent whose military power is on the rise relative to the intervener. According to Jack Levy, "The preventive motivation for war arises from the perception that one's military power and potential are declining relative to that of a rising adversary, and from the fear of the consequences of that decline."[5] Those consequences include, in the intervener's view, the opponent's future aggression. The aggression is expected because the intervener believes that the opponent will over time increase its relative military strength. The aggression is not expected immediately due to the time it will take the opponent to build its military strength. Preventive intervention is based on the intervener's calculation that it is better to fight now, when it has a military advantage, rather than later, when it does not. Better a small war in which it has the advantage now than a large war when it does not later.

Preventive intervention is often connected with the idea that states exist in a balance of power.[6] A state's expected rise in military power relative to an opponent would upset the balance and perhaps lead that state to aggress against the opponent when it has achieved a military advantage. Preventive intervention is a state's attempt to maintain an existing balance that an opponent's expected rise threatens to upset. Moreover, fear of such loss may be the spur for more acts of aggression than the desire for gain. In other words, most acts of aggression may be cases of preventive intervention, undertaken not for positive gain or conquest, but to avoid an expected loss.[7]

Preventive intervention may seem to be a form of self-defense, a kind of anticipatory or proactive self-defense, rather than aggression, given that it is undertaken to avoid aggression, albeit expected aggression. But the question is whether it is defensive in a morally relevant sense. To say that military action is defensive in this sense is to offer a prima facie moral justification for it, given the just cause criterion of *jus ad bellum*. It would be question begging at this point to regard preventive intervention as defense in this sense, because its moral status is precisely what is in question. One way to ask the question whether preventive intervention is ever morally justified is to ask whether it is sometimes an instance of defense in the morally relevant sense. David Luban points out that arguments for the moral justifiability of preventive intervention "in effect assimilate preventive war to the paradigm of self-defense."[8]

Any discussion of the moral justifiability of preventive intervention should begin by drawing the distinction between prevention and preemption. Preemption is acting militarily to thwart an attack that has, in some sense, already begun, but has not yet had its initial impact. A common way of glossing the distinction is to characterize preemption as a response to an *imminent* attack, one that is about to happen. The expected aggression to which prevention is a response is not yet imminent. But it is not immediately clear why this temporal difference makes a moral difference. If preemption is a response to an attack that has already begun, a better way to capture the difference between preemption and prevention would be to refer to the attack to which preemption is a response as *incipient*, as having already begun.[9] In contrast, the attack to which prevention is a response has yet to begin. Replacing the idea of imminence with that of incipience makes clear the moral basis of the distinction between preemption and prevention. The attacks to which both preemption and prevention are responses may both be intended, but only in the case of preemption has the attacker put its intention into action. There is normally thought to be an important moral distinction between merely intending to do some action in the future and beginning to perform an intended action.

The current relevance of the topic of preventive intervention is that the recently adopted US military policy is based on the view that some new international circumstances (revealed by the terrorist attacks of 9/11) have rendered preventive intervention sometimes morally justified. These new circumstances include the existence of international networks of terrorists independent of states and bent on civilian attacks in developed states, the fact that these terrorists may be able to get their hands on weapons of mass destruction (WMD) and would have no compunction against using them, and the reality that some states (so-called rogue states) may themselves be prepared to attack developed states with WMD or help terrorists acquire WMD. In response to these new circumstances, the Bush administration has adopted a strategy of preventive intervention: "As a matter of common sense and self-defense, America will act against such emerging threats before they are fully formed."[10] The Iraq War begun in 2003 was the first preventive intervention under the new strategy.[11] Under this strategy, other preventive interventions may be undertaken in the future, so moral clarity about this form of military action is important.

My discussion will focus on preventive intervention pursued unilaterally, undertaken by a single state on its own initiative without any formal international institutional sanction.[12] In addition, I will understand preventive intervention as having the goal of replacing the government of the target state ("regime change"). These features fits the traditional understanding of preventive intervention as well as the current US policy. But at the end, I will consider the implications of the discussion for alternative forms of preventive intervention, namely, those pursued in a formally multilateral way and those that may involve isolated military strikes rather than an effort to overthrow a regime.

1. JUST WAR THEORY AND PREVENTIVE INTERVENTION

To begin a consideration of the moral justifiability of preventive intervention, consider how it fares in terms of *jus ad bellum,* which consists of a set of criteria, each one of which must be satisfied for a war to be morally justified. I will focus on two of these criteria, just cause and proportionality. Because the *jus ad bellum* criteria are necessary conditions, if preventive intervention fails to satisfy either of these, it fails to be morally justified.[13] Just cause is usually understood to be largely a deontological matter, concerning whether a state has a right to use military force against another state. In contrast, proportionality is largely a consequentialist matter, concerning whether a proposed war would produce a balance of beneficial over harmful consequences. To put it roughly, preventive intervention will be justified only if a state has a right to use such military force and its use will produce more benefit than harm. I will argue that preventive intervention satisfies neither of these conditions.

2. JUST CAUSE: DEONTOLOGICAL CONSIDERATIONS

In *jus ad bellum*, deontological considerations of just cause are closely tied to the notion of sovereignty and to arguments based on a domestic analogy. States in international society are, it is argued, relevantly like individuals in domestic society in that the moral import of individual autonomy is mirrored by the moral import of national sovereignty. So, for example, as preventive "punishment" or detention of individuals in domestic society is contrary to their autonomy and morally wrong, preventive intervention is contrary to a state's sovereignty and morally wrong.[14] As it is morally wrong to use force against individuals based not on anything they have done, but on what they are expected to do, it is morally wrong to initiate war against a state based not on anything it has done, but on what it is expected to do. Preventive intervention is wrong because it interferes with activities that are within a state's proper jurisdiction,[15] as coercive interference with individuals is wrong when it impinges on activities that are within their sphere of free action. As individuals have rights that preventive coercion would violate, states have rights which preventive intervention would violate. Thus, intervening preventively cannot be a just cause for war.

The domestic legal world also provides an analogue showing that preemption is acceptable but prevention is not. Consider the crimes of conspiracy or attempt. While defendants can be liable for these because of what they intend, but have yet to do, making the crimes seem like analogues of prevention, liability in these cases requires that defendants have taken some action that puts the intention into motion. In the absence of this incipient action, there is no legal liability. Thus, in fact, such crimes analogically support the acceptability of preemption and the unacceptability of prevention. A critic of this argument might claim that the requirement for incipient action in the case of conspiracy or attempt is simply an evidentiary matter.[16] The intention is all that is necessary for legal liability, the action serving only the practical need for adequate evidence of the intention. *Actus reus* is merely evidence of *mens rea*, which alone is the source of the liability. If we could have reliable evidence of an intention in the absence of action, the intention alone would be sufficient. But intuitively, it seems that an *actus reus* is a necessary condition for legal liability and not simply a practical evidentiary requirement. Our aversion to punishing "thought crimes" seems to rest not simply on the practical difficulty of determining intent or the desire to avoid giving the state such sweeping power, but also on the importance of giving people a chance to conform their behavior to the law, based on a recognition that people can exercise self-control, can change their minds.

But a deeper objection to these arguments by analogy is that there is an important relevant difference between the two spheres, namely, that the international sphere is a state of nature, with no governing authority.[17] There is no international police to enforce the law. Can the analogical arguments survive this difference? Can claims about what legal authority is allowed to do to those under it imply anything about what states are allowed to do to each other? The answer is yes, if we assume that the law is based on moral considerations, that it is morally wrong to impose harm on someone, whatever his or her intentions, who has taken no action to harm others. If the law is based on independent moral considerations, then these same considerations can be applied in the international sphere, even though it is not under legal authority. Legal authority does not determine what is right, but, if it is legitimate, simply enforces what is right.

But the objection can be put in a different way. In the domestic case, it seems as wrong for an individual to use preventive coercion against another individual as it does for the state to do so. Perhaps the reason that person-on-person preventive coercion is wrong, however, is that the law has taken individuals out of a state of nature. Because aggressors risk being punished by the law, interpersonal aggression is not common (as it presumably would be in a state of nature). This leads to the idea that, if individuals were in a state of nature, as nations are, the greater reasonable expectation of aggression would make preventive coercion acceptable. Assuming that this is the case, and taking person-on-person preventive coercion as the domestic analogue of preventive intervention, the argument by analogy breaks down. Because the domestic sphere is in fact not in a state of nature, this is a relevant difference between the analogues, and the analogies are thus faulty. But the assumption itself seems faulty. Person-on-person preventive coercion is not wrong (or not wrong only) because the domestic sphere is not in a state of nature, but because individuals have moral rights against preventive coercion. The fact that nations are in a state of nature does not show that they do not also have such a right.

But there is a deontological argument against preventive intervention that does not rely on this domestic analogy because it originates at the *jus in bello* rather than the *jus ad bellum* level. Normally, these two levels are separate and independent, an idea referred to as the *independence thesis*.[18] According to this thesis, a just war can be fought unjustly, and an unjust war can be fought justly, so there is no room for appealing to *jus in bello* considerations when making a case at the *jus ad bellum* level, and vice versa. But the independence thesis seems to break down in one sort of instance at least: if a war cannot be fought justly, then it cannot be just to wage it. Jeff McMahan notes, "The absence of legitimate targets seems to imply the absence of a just cause."[19] The argument then is that a preventive intervention cannot be fought justly because those who would be the targets of the attack (the opponent's military forces) have taken no action to harm the intervener. Even if intention alone were sufficient for liability, the fact that the target state's leadership intended future aggression would not entail that the members of its military had such an intention. Michael Walzer notes that there is a "moral necessity of rejecting any attack that is merely preventive in character" because that attack would make "war upon soldiers who were themselves engaged in entirely legitimate (nonthreatening) activities."[20]

3. PROPORTIONALITY: CONSEQUENTIALIST CONSIDERATIONS

The proportionality criterion also poses problems for the justifiability of preventive intervention. Mary Ellen O'Connell notes: "Today states measure proportionality against attacks that have occurred or are planned. What measure can be used to assess proportionality against possible attack?"[21] McMahan offers a related point: "Because the magnitude of the threat has to be discounted for probability, it is also difficult to establish that the resort to war could be proportionate."[22] It is hard to know how large-scale the expected aggression would be, and it is hard to know its likelihood, probabilities that would have to figure as a discount into determining how much harm the attack would do. As a result it is difficult to show that the preventive intervention would satisfy the proportionality criterion.

But even if we knew the dimensions and likelihood of the expected aggression, and hence could calculate the requirement of proportionality with the appropriate discount, it is unlikely that an effective preventive intervention would be proportionate. To be effective, a preventive intervention is likely to require "regime change" because the danger of the expected aggression lies in the intentions of those in power. The leaders must be removed to remove the danger. The alternative of destroying the target state's capacity for aggression, while leaving the regime in place, may be very difficult, and, in any case, would likely be only a temporary measure since the capacity can be rebuilt. But, regime change entails the goal of unconditional surrender. Walzer argues that unconditional surrender is an illegitimate war aim, except with a morally horrendous regime like Nazi Germany.[23] When unconditional surrender is an illegitimate war aim, the harm imposed in achieving it would likely be disproportionate to the good of the intervention.

In addition, preventive intervention is very likely to violate another *jus ad bellum* criterion closely related to proportionality. The criterion of last resort requires that war be waged only if there are no alternative means of achieving the goals of the war. Last resort is related to proportionality because it is also based on a consequentialist concern to limit harm, given that an alternative means of achieving the goals would produce less overall harm. But it is unlikely that a preventive intervention would be a last resort. Because the expected aggression is in the future, there would usually be other resorts, alternatives to war such as negotiations, alliance formation, strengthening deterrence, and so forth. Given such alternatives, preventive intervention, it seems, could not be a matter of military necessity. A preventive intervention is always a war of choice.

With these initial difficulties with proportionality registered, let us look in more detail at the consequentialist case regarding preventive intervention. For the consequentialist case, the real evil of war is not the violation of sovereignty, as it is for the deontological case, but the suffering war imposes on individuals.[24] In examining the consequentialist case, I will consider, first, the consequences of preventive intervention on the belligerents (what I call the direct consequences) and, second, the consequences of preventive intervention on the international system as a whole (what I call the indirect consequences).

A preventive intervention occurs when the intervener believes that the opponent is growing in military power and will engage in aggression when it is stronger. If the intervener's beliefs are true, then preventive intervention now will likely lead to a smaller war than the one otherwise expected later because the target state is now weaker militarily. (It is also, of course, a war the intervener is more likely to win.) If the war is smaller, the overall suffering will be less. This argument, call it the *pro argument*, is the main consequentialist case for preventive intervention. Of course, what is foremost for the intervener is that the preventive intervention will be easier to win than a later war, and this may carry some consequentialist weight depending on the nature of the two regimes and the values they represent. But the principal consequentialist advantage alleged for preventive intervention is that it is, in terms of overall human suffering, the lesser of two evils. This is, however, at best a partial argument. It cannot by itself show that the preventive intervention satisfies the proportionality criterion because it considers only relative amounts of harm, ignoring whether the benefits exceed the harms.

In any case, in examining the pro argument, we must consider *expected* consequences, that is, possible consequences discounted by the likelihood of their occurrence. This leads to one of the strongest consequentialist arguments against war in general, namely, that in war, the harms are certain to occur, while the benefits are speculative. The benefits must be more or less discounted. This makes the weakness of the pro argument apparent. The expected benefit of a preventive intervention is the avoidance of a more destructive war, but it is less than certain that this war would occur in the absence of the intervention.[25] While the benefits of the intervention undiscounted may be greater than the harms, the benefits are generally subject to steep discounting. Potential interveners often speak of the "inevitability" of the opponent's future aggression, should they not intervene.[26] But this is a bald attempt to deny both the speculative nature of the prediction of future aggression and the resulting need to discount the alleged benefits of the intervention. Richard Betts notes: "It is almost never possible to know with enough certainty that war is inevitable . . . to warrant the certain costs and risks of starting it." He also notes that "briefs made for preventive war in the past have proved terribly wrong."[27]

There are clear reasons why interveners tend to overstate the likelihood of their opponent's future aggression. First, states have a tendency to assume malign intentions on the part of their opponents.[28] While there may be some prudential value in a tendency to plan on the basis of a worst-case scenario, doing so leads to an inflated perception of likelihoods of hostile action. Related to this is what Chris Brown calls the "chimera of absolute security." States tend to seek to eliminate all threats to their security, and this can lead states to frequent preventive interventions, "to an endless series of wars to end all wars."[29] Second, judgments of an opponent's future aggression tend, as Luban notes, to be burdened and infirm.[30] Judgments are burdened when they are about matters where there is reasonable disagreement and infirm when they are about matters on which the judges are seldom rational. A state's judgments of an opponent's future behavior toward it have both of these features.

Thus preventive interventions are less likely to be acceptable on consequentialist grounds than they appear to the intervener. A preventive intervention is likely to make things worse for the belligerents together and for each of them separately. So, we have Bismarck's quip that "preventive war is like suicide from fear of death."[31] This argument does not show that every preventive intervention is unjustified on consequentialist grounds. But the general consequentialist case against preventive interventions can be strengthened by considering their indirect consequences, their general effects on international order.

Preventive interventions have consequences not only for the belligerents, but also for the international system. Even if some particular preventive intervention were to have positive direct consequences, these would likely be outweighed by its negative indirect consequences. The principal indirect consequence is that preventive interventions lower the threshold for the use of force, increasing the frequency of war. Preventive interventions expand the conditions under which the use of force is seen as appropriate, leading to "innumerable and fruitless wars."[32] There are three overlapping mechanisms to explain this. Preventive interventions lead to an increase in the number of wars through (1) the precedent effect and (2) the use of the pretext argument, and this greater risk of war leads to (3) greater international instability, the source of a further increase in the risk of war.

The precedent effect is the tendency for one preventive intervention to lead to others. If state X can get away with it, thinks state Y, why can't I? But it is not simply a matter of states' copying each other or their believing that fairness allows them to do something other states have done, though this is important. A state's preventive intervention tends to reduce the costs of other states' following suit by reducing the severity of negative international reaction. States that want to engage in preventive intervention are sometimes held back by the expected negative reaction of the international community. But when other states have undertaken preventive interventions, the severity of this reaction is lessened, thereby decreasing the perceived costs. While preventive interventions by any state would have this effect, those by the United States, as the central international player, would have special potency in this regard. O'Connell argues that preventive intervention by the United States "would provide legal justification for Pakistan to attack India, for Iran to attack Iraq, for Russia to attack Georgia, for Azerbaijan to attack Armenia, for North Korea to attack South Korea, and so on."[33] There would be no moral problem with the precedent effect, if all or most preventive interventions had direct positive consequences. But the argument above implies that most, at least, do not.

The pretext argument is an additional, related mechanism by which precedents of preventive intervention tend to increase the number of such wars. States sometimes would like to engage in aggression for positive gain, not for preventive purposes, but are held back by the perceived costs of the negative reaction of the international community. This reaction is lessened to the extent that aggressive states can offer a rationale for their aggression that other states may accept as legitimate. With the precedent of preventive interventions, that rationale becomes available as a pretext for aggressions that are not preventive.

The precedent effect and the use of the pretext argument show how preventive interventions increase the risk of war. The greater the risk of war, the less stability the international system has, and, in a vicious cycle, this increases the risk of war further. The source of the instability is the undermining of deterrence. Deterrence is the main mechanism of restraint on war, and an increase in the risk of war undermines deterrence. Successful deterrence requires not only that states expect that their aggression would be met by retaliation, but also that their restraint or nonaggression would leave them free of attack. If aggression, whether or not preventive, is more frequent, the latter requirement is not satisfied. Why should states restrain themselves militarily if they may be attacked by their opponents whether they restrain themselves of not? Consider two military opponents. If neither is likely to aggress against the other, a state of deterrence exists between them and war is unlikely. But if aggression by one against the other becomes more likely, because preventive intervention is more common, each state may come to fear the other's aggression and so be tempted itself to engage in preventive intervention. There would exist between them "a reciprocal fear of surprise attack," which would make war more likely.[34] In short, preventive interventions create international instability by weakening deterrence, thereby increasing the likelihood of war.

Thus, there are two mutually supportive consequentialist arguments against preventive intervention. First, a focus on the direct consequences of preventive intervention shows that because states have difficulties predicting their opponents' future aggression and a tendency to overestimate the risk of that aggression, preventive interventions are unlikely to have the consequentialist advantages they are thought to have. Rather than try to determine if some particular preventive intervention, contrary to this tendency, is consequentially justified, it is better, as Walzer puts it, to "fall back upon" a rule not to intervene.[35] For, as Luban suggests, "everyone might be better off on consequentialist grounds if no one undertook the calculation" needed to justify preventive intervention in particular cases. This supports "the importance of a no-first-use-of-force rule for war prevention."[36] Instead of following a permissive rule allowing preventive intervention when certain conditions are satisfied, states should follow a prohibitory rule outlawing all preventive intervention. The second argument, relying on indirect consequences, supports the prohibitory rule because it strengthens the likelihood that the rule will be followed, and so increases its beneficial consequences. The more the rule is followed in the present, the more likely it is to be followed in the future.

Together, these considerations of the two criteria, just cause and proportionality, and the deontological and consequentialist factors they involve, provide a strong case that preventive intervention is seldom if ever justified, and that there should be an international rule or norm prohibiting it. Because, in just war theory, both criteria must be satisfied for a war to be justified, the argument against preventive intervention would still stand even if either of the two lines of argument were mistaken. But there is one kind of case where military action might be justified even if the just cause criterion were not satisfied. Some might argue that if the consequentialist stakes were high enough, deontological prohibitions may be ignored.[37] This brings us to what I referred to earlier as the new circumstances. Is the new kind of danger facing the United States and other developed nations of such a nature and magnitude that it implies that preventive intervention either may satisfy deontological constraints or may have a sufficient consequentialist advantage to override the deontological objections?

4. NEW CIRCUMSTANCES

Do our new circumstances, the risk of attack with WMD by terrorists or rogue states, alter the conclusion of the argument so far? The deontological argument against preventive intervention appears to remain intact. The inadequacy of mere intention for liability shows preventive intervention unjustified whether under the old or new circumstances. In the absence of an incipient action, military attack would still be undertaken without right.

But things may be different with the consequentialist argument. The new circumstances change the consequentialist calculations because, given the potential availability of WMDs, the potential targets of terrorists or rogue states aggression are now at greater risk of devastating attack. Their military inaction in the face of expected aggression now carries more of a risk, which strengthens the pro argument. But not, it seems, enough. The direct consequences of preventive intervention may now sometimes be more favorable than before, but it does not follow, given the earlier arguments, that they are likely to be overall positive.[38] Even less does it follow that the overall consequences of preventive intervention, including the indirect consequences, now favor the action. The tendency of preventive interventions to increase the number of wars by fostering a permissive international norm and creating greater international instability remains a powerful obstacle to any claim that preventive intervention would have overall consequentialist advantage. Even less does it follow that there could be sufficient consequentialist benefits from preventive intervention to override the deontological objections.

Finally, defenders of preventive intervention might respond that even if, under the new circumstances, preventive intervention, as traditionally understood, is not morally justified, there are alternative, nontraditional forms of preventive intervention that may avoid the moral objections. The traditional idea of preventive intervention, I have said, is unilateral and involves regime change. But preventive intervention need not have these features, and, as a result, may satisfy the just cause and proportionality criteria. First, there may be *preventive strikes*, which are forms of preventive intervention that do not have the goal of regime change. Preventive strikes are aimed at the capacity for aggression, rather than at the regime that embodies the intention of the expected aggression. An example would be the 1981 Israeli attack on the Iraqi nuclear reactor at Osirak. Second, there may be genuinely multilateral preventive interventions, which are those undertaken and/or formally authorized by a recognized international organization. The United States sought to make its attack on Iraq multilateral in this sense by seeking UN approval, but in the face of UN refusal, it went ahead unilaterally.

How to these alternatives fare morally?[39] Preventive strikes may be justified deontologically because the right to territorial integrity they violate is less significant than the right of a state to a regime of its own, which is violated in a war for regime change. In addition, preventive strikes may be justified in terms of direct consequences because the harm they directly cause would be less than a war for regime change. The key question is whether preventive strikes are justified when indirect consequences are considered. This would depend on whether they would serve as a precedent for traditional forms of preventive intervention. If so, their contributions to international instability, and so their negative indirect consequences, may be as great as those of traditional forms of preventive intervention. A case needs to be made by supporters of preventive strikes that they would not be such negative consequences.

What about multilateral, internationally authorized preventive interventions? A positive deontological case for such interventions depends on the claim that an intervention under international authorization does not violate the rights of the target state the way that a unilateral intervention does. There may be something to this claim, but on the surface it does not overcome the analogical arguments considered earlier. The UN authorizing preventive intervention against a member state, for example, would be analogous to the law authorizing preventive detention against an individual. The former seems as morally problematic as the latter. The consequentialist case for multilateral intervention depends on the argument that the sanctioning process of the international authority could involve, through creative institution building, various safeguards that would lessen the likelihood of harmful consequences. The international decision procedures for multilateral interventions could contain restrictions that militate against some of the harmful consequences to which unilateral interventions are prone. One imaginative example is a proposal by Allen Buchanan and Robert Keohane that an internationally authorized preventive intervention would involve the potential intervener receiving approval of an appropriate international body both before and after a proposed intervention.[40]

There is something to be said for from a consequentialist perspective for the positive effects of the international authorizing of interventions, though it is another question whether authorized interventions could yield a great enough level of consequentialist advantage to override the problems that seem to remain for such interventions from the deontological perspective. But let me raise one consequentialist problem for multilateral intervention. The matter, again, comes down to indirect consequences. Would multilateral interventions increase international instability, as unilateral intervention would? Would the existence of the institutional procedures for multilateral intervention act to stop such interventions being taken as precedents for unilateral interventions? The answer seems to depend on the extent to which international authority in general is respected by states. If the general level of respect were high, the precedent effect likely not be a significant factor because states would be constrained from intervening without authorization. But if the general level of respect were low, the precedent effect would likely remain significant. (In addition, if the level of respect were low, it might be infeasible to establish the institutions themselves, given the expected lack of compliance.) At any point in history, the level of respect is a given, something that could be changed only over the long term. It would not, for example, be greatly influenced by efforts to establish the authorizing institutions. The level of respect for international authority seems now to be fairly low, which implies that multilateral interventions would still carry the burden of negative indirect consequences. All things considered, the moral case for preventive intervention has yet to be made.[41]

NOTES

1. The general category of intervention refers to coercive interference by one state in the affairs of another, so that there are other forms of intervention besides military intervention, for example, economic pressures or sanctions.

2. Humanitarian intervention is another kind. Humanitarian and preventive intervention, while both forms of military intervention, have quite different moral characteristics, and should not be lumped together. In particular, it may be that humanitarian intervention is an exception to the claim that all justified use military force is defensive, though preventive intervention is not.
3. The expectation to which the preventive intervention is a response can also be of a future nonmilitary form of harm at the hands of the target state, such as economic decline or loss of great-power standing. David Luban suggests that the attack at Pearl Harbor was a preventive intervention launched mainly out of Japan's fear that the United States would in the future increasingly interfere with its economic well-being; see his "Preventive War," *Philosophy & Public Affairs* 32 (3) (Summer, 2004), 235. But I will restrict my discussion of preventive intervention to cases where the intervener's primary motivation is to avoid expected aggression. If any form of preventive intervention is morally justified, it would be this one.
4. Once a preventive intervention meets military resistance, it becomes a preventive war. I will use the terms "prevention" and "preventive intervention" interchangeably.
5. Jack Levy, "Declining Power and the Preventive Motivation for War," *World Politics* 40, no. 1 (October, 1987), pp. 82–107, quotation from p. 87.
6. See Michael Walzer, *Just and Unjust Wars* (New York: Basic Books, 1977), pp. 76–80.
7. See Levy, "Declining Power," pp. 82, 84. Using a domestic analogy, this would be consonant with the psychological observation that individuals value a given amount of utility more if it is something they stand to lose rather than something they stand to gain.
8. Luban, "Preventive War," p. 221.
9. This term is proposed by Yoram Dinstein, *War, Aggression and Self Defense*, 3rd edn (Cambridge: Cambridge University Press, 2001), p. 172.
10. Quotation from the 2002 *National Security Strategy of the United States of America* (http://www.whitehouse.gov/nsc/pdf), p. 6. The new policy has been referred to as a strategy of "preemptive war," but it clearly is one of preventive intervention in the traditional sense, as it proposes attacks when the expected aggression is not incipient.
11. The Iraq War is a preventive war because it was begun to in an effort to avoid what was expected to be future aggression by Iraq. In saying the Iraq War is the first war under the new policy, I am treating the Afghanistan War as a case of defense.
12. The Iraq War is not strictly speaking unilateral because it has been undertaken by a "coalition of the willing." But I count it as unilateral because the coalition is informal, not sanctioned by an international organization.
13. Of course, it might be that some preventive interventions satisfy these two conditions while others do not, but, because I consider preventive interventions in general, I develop arguments that preventive intervention is never (or perhaps very seldom) justified.
14. Interestingly, a domestic policy of preventive detention is being advocated because of the new circumstances, just as an international policy of preventive intervention is.
15. See Luban, "Preventive War," p. 213.
16. This is argued by Jeff McMahan, "Preventive War and the Killing of the Innocent," in David Rodin and Richard Sorabji (eds), *The Ethics of War: Shared Problems in Different Traditions* (Aldershot, UK: Ashgate Publishing, 2006), pp. 169–190, esp. p. 184.
17. See, for example, McMahan, "Preventive War," p. 173.

18. Walzer, *Just and Unjust Wars*, p. 21.
19. McMahan, "Preventive War," p. 178.
20. Walzer, *Just and Unjust Wars*, p. 80.
21. Mary Ellen O'Connell, "The Myth of Preemptive Self-Defense," The American Society of International Law Task Force on Terrorism (August, 2002), p. 19.
22. McMahan, "Preventive War," p. 172.
23. Walzer, *Just and Unjust Wars*, pp. 111–117.
24. Luban, "Preventive War," p. 218.
25. This is especially the case given the other preventive measures the potential intervener can take, the other resorts that make preventive intervention not the last, as discussed earlier.
26. Levy, "Declining Power," p. 98.
27. Richard Betts, "Striking First – A History of Thankfully Lost Opportunities," *Ethics and International Affairs* 17 (1) (2003), p. 18, and Betts, "Suicide from Fear of Death," *Foreign Affairs* 82, no. 1 (January/February, 2003), p. 40.
28. Walzer, *Just and Unjust Wars*, p. 77.
29. Chris Brown, "Self Defense in an Imperfect World," *Ethics and International Affairs* 17 (1) (Winter, 2003), 5.
30. Luban, "Preventive War," p. 227.
31. Levy, "Declining Power," p. 103.
32. Walzer, *Just and Unjust Wars*, p. 77, using a phrase from Edmund Burke.
33. O'Connell, "The Myth of Preemptive Self-Defense," p. 19.
34. See Betts, "Striking First," p. 19, and Luban, "Preventive War," pp. 227–228.
35. Walzer, *Just and Unjust Wars*, p. 77.
36. Luban, "Preventive War," pp. 227, 209.
37. This idea is similar to Walzer's notion of supreme emergency, though his doctrine operates at the *jus in bello* level rather than the *jus ad bellum* level. See *Just and Unjust Wars*, pp. 251–268.
38. The outcome of the 2003 Iraq War anecdotally supports this.
39. I can here provide only the briefest account of the alternative forms of preventive intervention.
40. See Allan Buchanan and Robert Keohane, "Preventive Force: A Cosmopolitan Institutional Perspective," *Ethics and International Affairs* 18 (1) (2004), 1–22. I offer a critique of their proposal in "A Moral Critique of the Cosmopolitan Institutional Proposal," *Ethics and International Affairs* 19 (2) (2005), 99–107.
41. I would like to thank Win Chiat Lee and Fredrick Kaufman, along with two anonymous reviewers, for helpful comments on an earlier draft of this paper.

IV. TERRORISM

ALLEN S. WEINER

LAW, JUST WAR, AND THE INTERNATIONAL FIGHT AGAINST TERRORISM: IS IT WAR?

1. INTRODUCTION

September 11 was not the first time the United States was victimized by terrorist attacks. In 1983, a truck bombing at the Beirut Airport in Lebanon killed 241 American Marines. In 1988, a bomb planted by Libyan intelligence officers detonated aboard Pan Am flight 103 as it passed over Lockerbie, Scotland, killing all 259 persons aboard. Truck bombings at the United States Embassies in Kenya and Tanzania in 1998 killed 225 people and injured thousands more. And in October 2000, suicide bombers maneuvered a small boat alongside the warship USS *Cole* in the port of Aden, Yemen, and triggered an explosion that killed seventeen US sailors. Nor was September 11 the first major attack by foreign terrorists on American soil. In February 1993, a massive explosion in the parking garage of the World Trade Center in New York City killed six persons and wounded more than 1,000.

Yet the magnitude of the events of September 11 fundamentally changed the United States Government's approach towards international terrorism. After September 11, the Bush Administration rejected the previous American approach to counterterrorism, which had primarily employed the combined tools of diplomatic cooperation, economic sanctions, and internationally coordinated law enforcement measures. Instead, the President declared in the aftermath of September 11 that the United States was engaged in a *war* on terrorism.[1] Subsequent statements and actions have made clear that President Bush's declaration that the United States would wage war against terrorism was not simply a spontaneous utterance, but is rather a formulation of national policy. Indeed, only a few days after press reports in July 2005 announced that administration officials would cease describing the conflict as a "global war on terror,"[2] the President publicly overruled his top advisors, saying, "Make no mistake about it, we are at war."[3]

The characterization of the United States's response to terrorism as "war" – or, in the parlance of international lawyers, "armed conflict" – has enormous implications for measures the United States may, as a legal matter, permissibly take in the course of the conflict. And yet whether the response to terrorism may properly be treated as "war" is far from clear. In this chapter, I argue that although the fight against terrorism does not qualify as war as a matter of positive international law, there are justifiable functional reasons for extrapolating from positive law and treating the conflict – or at least part of it – as war. But this is not the end of the inquiry. For even in war, substantive legal restraints apply. Moreover, just war theory demands reciprocity in wartime, such that the belligerents face each other with equivalent belligerent rights. Accordingly, assessing whether the exercise of wartime legal powers by the United States in the struggle against terrorism is justifiable requires us to consider not only the *prima facie* functional basis for treating the conflict as war. We must also evaluate whether the United States has accepted the duties that apply in wartime and the related principle of reciprocity.

Because the conflict against terrorism does not satisfy the formal international law definition of war, the exercise of wartime legal authorities by the United States since September 11 is justifiable only on the basis of a functional extrapolation from positive law. By itself, this move is defensible. The United States, however, has been unwilling to accept important corresponding legal restraints that should flow from such a functional extrapolation. Nor has it been willing to confer upon its adversaries the rights to which they should be entitled as a matter of reciprocity under such an approach. This assertion of wartime rights without acceptance of corresponding wartime responsibilities undercuts the justification for the United States's effort to move beyond positive law in selecting a legal framework for the struggle against terrorism. In other words, the means by which the United States has conducted its campaign against terrorism undermines the justification for treating the conflict as "war."

2. IS IT REALLY WAR?

2.1 War as Metaphor

The United States's response to terrorism is not the first time American leaders have invoked the concept of "war" in the face of challenges to the well-being of the country. The metaphor of war has been employed in the past to inspire comprehensive collective responses to major national crises. And so President Nixon launched a national "war" against crime.[4] President Reagan initiated a "war on drugs."[5] And some years before that, of course, President Johnson declared "unconditional war on poverty in America."[6]

In these cases, however, the metaphor of war was employed as just that: a metaphor. Even though some of the enemies against which American leaders declared war presented genuine security threats to the United States – including violence, murders, even challenges to governmental authority – these were not wars in the legal sense. The United States did not, in the context of the war on crime or the war on poverty, publicly claim the right to exercise the extraordinary measures permissible in a legal state of armed conflict, such as the right to invade other states or to kill one's adversaries.

2.2 War as Legal Status

With respect to the war on terrorism, in contrast, the notion of war is not employed merely as a metaphor to mobilize the public. The United States characterizes the war against terrorism as a real war, a war in the legal sense, and it is exercising many of the extraordinary authorities that are available only during times of war.

First, in response to the September 11 attacks, the United States has claimed – and exercised – the right to use international armed force against both terrorist actors and governments that harbor them, notwithstanding the prohibition on the use of force that ordinarily applies in international relations. On October 7, 2001, the United States reported to the United Nations Security Council (UNSC) that it had initiated military action against the al-Qaeda terrorist organization and the de facto Taliban government in Afghanistan. It did so pursuant to Article 51 of the United Nations (UN) Charter, the provision that guarantees to states the right to use armed force in self-defense in the event of an armed attack.[7]

Second, the United States has exercised the right to kill persons outside Afghanistan as combatants in the war against terrorism. In November 2002, a missile launched from an unmanned American aircraft killed al-Qaeda leader Sinan al-Harethi and five associates traveling in a car in Yemen. Commenting on the killing, a United States official stated: "We're at war, and we've got to use the means at our disposal to protect the country."[8] Administration officials explained that the killing did not violate the longstanding Executive Branch order prohibiting assassination[9] because al-Qaeda operatives had been defined as "enemy combatants and thus legitimate targets for lethal force."[10]

Third, the Executive Branch has relied on the wartime right to detain enemy soldiers for the duration of an armed conflict, without a judicial determination that they have committed crimes against the United States. Such detentions, in war, serve the preventive function of ensuring that enemy soldiers do not rejoin the conflict and participate in further battlefield action. In its briefs before the Supreme Court in the cases of enemy combatants detained at the Guantanamo Naval Station in Cuba and at military facilities in the United States, the Executive Branch justified its detention practice with specific reference to wartime legal authorities: "[T]he President's war powers include the authority to capture and detain enemy combatants in wartime. . . ."[11] Such powers, the Bush Administration argued, include the right to detain such combatants, whether foreign or American, without trial, for the duration of the armed conflict.[12]

2.3 "War" and the War on Terrorism: A Positivist Assessment

The question of whether it is justifiable to exercise wartime powers in the struggle against terrorism – whether the conflict is truly war in the legal sense – is a contested issue. Because the conflict has taken place largely abroad, it is useful to analyze the question by looking to the meaning of war under international law.

The key problem with treating the fight against terrorism as war in the legal sense, of course, is that under positive international law, armed conflict is a relationship between *states*. Yoram Dinstein explains that war, as a matter of customary international law, is "a hostile interaction *between two or more States*. . . ."[13] Similarly, as a matter of treaty law, the 1949 Geneva Conventions that govern international armed conflict stipulate that the legal regime of armed conflict – which I will refer to as the "war regime" – are triggered in the case of "declared war or of any other armed conflict which may arise *between two or more of the High Contracting Parties*" to the Conventions.[14] The war on terrorism falls outside these positive law definitions because the terrorist groups against which the conflict is being waged are neither states nor parties to the relevant treaties.[15]

2.4 "War" and the War on Terrorism: A Functional Assessment

Even if the war on terrorism does not qualify as war under positive international law definitions, however, is it nevertheless justifiable to extrapolate from those definitions and to treat the fight against terrorism as functionally equivalent to war? Is it justifiable, in other words, for the United States to exercise powers in the struggle against terrorism, such as the power to kill or indefinitely detain enemy combatants, that would not be legally permissible in non-wartime contexts?

On the face of it, the answer seems to be yes, at least with respect to the post-September 11 violence between the United States and the al-Qaeda organization. That struggle exhibits characteristics that strongly resemble traditional armed conflict between states, during which wartime legal powers may be exercised. On September 11, the United States sustained an assault that qualifies, in scale and effect, as an "armed attack" that would justify the use of force in self-defense under Article 51 of the UN Charter.[16] It suffered extensive casualties and severe economic losses, comparable to those sustained during the worst military confrontations that have taken place on United States territory in over a century. In addition, the events of September 11 were only part of a series of significant armed attacks committed by al-Qaeda that demonstrated its willingness and capacity to inflict substantial harm against the United States on an ongoing basis. In other words, al-Qaeda displayed the *capability* of inflicting on the United States the kind of harm that traditionally has been associated only with attacks by states.

Moreover, even though it is not a state, al-Qaeda arguably exhibits characteristics that, in the case of states, justify the application of the war regime – namely, the right to infringe the human and civil rights of enemy soldiers on a collective basis – during armed conflict. A state engaged in armed conflict need not establish that a given enemy solider has engaged in conduct harmful to it before it may detain or kill him. The soldier's association with the enemy state is sufficient; he is presumed to be an agent of a bureaucratically organized entity that is institutionally committed to committing violence against the first state to achieve some political goal.

Like a state, al-Qaeda seems to possess – or at least at the time of the September 11 attacks seemed to possess – clear, albeit decentralized, organizational and command structures.[17] In addition, al-Qaeda had declared its intention, as an organization, to engage in violence against the United States for the political purpose of altering United States foreign policy on key issues. In 1998, al-Qaeda leader Osama bin Laden issued a "declaration of war" that called on Muslims to "kill the Americans" and to "launch the raid on Satan's U.S. troops."[18] Unlike organized crime bosses in New York or drug lords in Cali, Colombia, the injury al-Qaeda seeks to inflict on the United States is direct and intentional, not merely incidental to some other activity like accumulating wealth or power through criminal activities.

Thus, although the United States's war on terrorism does not meet the definition of war under positive international law, the nature of the violence that has been inflicted on the United States, the character and goals of the al-Qaeda organization responsible for that violence, and the presence of an ongoing threat, together provided justifiable *prima facie* functional grounds for the United States to extend the war regime to the conflict with al-Qaeda.

3. THE REJECTION OF THE RESTRAINTS OF THE LAW OF WAR

The existence of a state of war does not imply only the applicability of belligerent rights, however. International law also imposes substantive legal *restraints* on the conduct of war. The restrictions of *jus ad bellum* regulate when a state may resort to international armed force and, as a consequence, claim the right to avail itself of those extraordinary powers that apply during war. The restraints of *jus in bello* restrict the means by which war is conducted and provide certain basic humanitarian protections to those who find themselves in the theater of war, whether as innocent civilians or as combatants. As such, both the right to conduct war and the means by which it is prosecuted are subject to important substantive restraints.

In prosecuting the war on terrorism, however, the United States has been willing to apply its functional extension of the war regime only with respect to the assertion of belligerent *rights*. In several highly prominent instances, the United States has taken a vastly different approach with respect to accepting the *restraints* that bind parties to armed conflict. This inconsistency undermines the justification for the United States's claim that the struggle against terrorism should be treated, in legal terms, as war.

3.1 Targets in the War on Terrorism

The first manner in which the United States has ignored the restraints of the law of war concerns the issue of the targets against which force may permissibly be used. Even if there are defensible *prima facie* functional reasons for treating the conflict with al-Qaeda as war, the United States has asserted the right to extend the war regime to all terrorist organizations. "Our war on terror," President Bush stated shortly after September 11, "begins with Al Qaida, but it does not end there. It will not end until every terrorist group of global reach has been found, stopped and defeated."[19]

The justification for extending the war regime to the conflict with al-Qaeda, as noted above, turns on the nature and goals of that organization, the character of the attacks it had committed against the United States, and the ongoing threat it presented. These characteristics justify engaging in war against al-Qaeda as if it were a state. Beyond this context, however, the general threat presented by terrorism does not obviate the substantive restraints governing the use of force, under which a state may use force only in self-defense or where authorized by the UNSC acting under its Chapter VII collective security powers. The existence of a justifiable basis for extending the war regime to the fight against al-Qaeda does not justify the use of force against persons or terrorist groups that are not part of that organization.

In addition, the Bush Administration has claimed a right to use force not only against terrorist groups themselves, but against states that support terrorists. According to President Bush:

> Every nation, in every region, now has a decision to make: Either you are with us, or you are with the terrorists. From this day forward, any nation that continues to harbor or support terrorism will be regarded by the United States as a hostile regime.[20]

There can be no question that governments that harbor terrorists act in violation of international law. Nevertheless, unless terrorists engage in forcible acts that are legally attributable to the supporting state under principles of state responsibility – that is, unless the terrorists are acting on the instructions or under the control of the supporting state – such violations do not justify the use of force against the supporting state.[21] The international community has for this reason generally condemned as unlawful unilateral uses of force against terrorist targets in states allegedly harboring them, largely because of concerns about the territorial integrity of the state where attack occurs.[22]

As such, the United States has not accepted the limits on the use of force that would apply even under an approach that treats al-Qaeda as the functional equivalent of a state against which war may justifiably be waged. The Bush Administration's position is analogous to an assertion by a state, in the context of traditional armed conflict, of a right to use force not only against the state that had attacked it, but also against other unfriendly states that had not yet engaged in belligerent acts. In this way, the United States has claimed wartime rights that go well beyond what would be justified even by a functional extrapolation of the war regime to the conflict with al-Qaeda. The undefined nature and scope of the conflict creates a too-tempting invitation to swallow up the limits on the use of force, and to allow the use of force against all would-be adversaries of the United States as part of a single war.

3.2 The Detention of Enemy Combatants

Beyond the issue of the legally permissible range of targets against which force may be used, the United States has also disregarded legal restraints that should govern the *means* by which it conducts war, even under a view that justifies the extension of the war regime in the struggle against terrorism on functional grounds. Of particular concern in this regard is the treatment by United States authorities of persons detained in Afghanistan (and elsewhere) and held at the Guantanamo Naval Station in Cuba (and elsewhere) as enemy combatants in the war on terror.

In non-wartime circumstances, both international law and domestic law strictly limit the capacity of the government to deprive persons of their liberty. Under the International Covenant on Civil and Political Rights, the United States has agreed, as a matter of international law, that no person in the United States or subject to United States jurisdiction may be "deprived of his liberty except on such grounds and in accordance with such procedures as are established by law."[23] It further agreed that "[a]nyone who is deprived of his liberty by arrest or detention shall be entitled to take proceedings before a court, in order that that court may decide without delay on the lawfulness of his detention and order his release if the detention is not lawful."[24] Such protections were long enshrined, as a matter of domestic law, in our own Due Process Clause, which permits imprisonment only on the basis of a judicial order – not merely an Executive Branch determination – following proceedings with formal allegations of wrongdoing, a hearing before an impartial tribunal, and ultimately conviction and judgment.[25]

In wartime, of course, states may free themselves from these restraints, at least with respect to the detention of enemy soldiers and, in some cases, enemy aliens. If the war on terror may justifiably be deemed war, the Executive Branch is right that it may detain members of the enemy force not because they have been convicted by a court of having committed criminal acts, but merely to remove them from the field of battle so as to prevent them from further combat against the United States. It was on this basis that the United States transferred over 700 persons detained during the combat in Afghanistan to Guantanamo, where approximately 480 persons – none of whom has been convicted of a criminal offense – remain in United States custody as of May 2006.

Even as it has claimed the right to detain those held at Guantanamo by invoking the war regime, however, the United States has been unwilling to apply the legal restraints regulating the treatment of detainees that apply in armed conflict. Ordinarily, opposing soldiers captured during international armed conflict must be treated as prisoners of war, in accordance with the Third 1949 Geneva Convention Relative to the Treatment of Prisoners of War. Under the Third Geneva Convention, a prisoner of war is defined as any "[m]ember[] of the armed forces of a Party to the conflict" who has "fallen into the power of the enemy."[26] The United States, however, has concluded categorically that none of the detainees captured during combat against the Taliban and al-Qaeda in

Afghanistan are entitled to be treated as prisoners of war. With regard to members of al-Qaeda, the United States eschewed the functional approach it has taken in asserting wartime powers in the fight against terrorism. It has instead relied on a positivist interpretation of the law to conclude that al-Qaeda fighters are not covered by the Third Geneva Convention because al-Qaeda is not a state. As for Taliban fighters, the White House concluded that they did not meet certain requirements for prisoner of war status under Article 4(A)(2) of the Third Geneva Convention because they: (1) were not part of a military hierarchy; (2) did not wear uniforms or other distinctive signs; (3) did not carry their arms openly; and (4) did not conduct operations in accordance with the law of war.[27] As such, the United States has concluded that both the al-Qaeda and Taliban fighters, although they are combatants in what the United States characterizes as war, may not claim the protections that ordinarily apply to captured enemy fighters in wartime. They have been treated as unprivileged, or unlawful, combatants.

There are several fundamental difficulties with the United States's conclusion that all the combatants in Afghanistan were unprivileged belligerents with no entitlement to prisoner of war status. First, the Third Geneva Convention specifically contemplates the possibility of disputes as to whether an individual combatant is entitled to prisoner of war status; in such cases, Article 5 of the Convention requires that there be an individualized hearing before a tribunal to make a status determination.[28] Such hearings could enable a detainee to establish that he had not taken part in armed conflict in Afghanistan, that is, that he was not, in fact, a combatant at all. It is notable in this regard that many of those in custody at Guantanamo were detained not by US forces, but by our Northern Alliance allies, on grounds that may have been unclear when they were transferred to US custody. Alternatively, a hearing could explore whether a detainee in fact failed to meet the requirements of Article 4(A)(2) of the Third Geneva Convention, as the United States has asserted is the case for Taliban fighters.

Despite the requirements of Article 5 of the Third Geneva Convention, which requires a hearing whenever there is "any doubt" about the status of a detainee, the United States refused, for over two and one half years, to conduct such proceedings. Eventually, in July 2004, the Defense Department announced that the United States would establish a "Combatant Status Review Tribunal" to enable detainees to contest their status as enemy combatants.[29] According to the order establishing the Tribunal, however, an individual will be deemed an "enemy combatant" if he "was part of or supporting Taliban or al-Qaeda forces, or associated forces that are engaged in hostilities against the United States or its coalition partners."[30] It is significant that the Combatant Status Review Panels do not entitle detainees to argue that they were *lawful* combatants entitled to prisoner of war status, either on the theory, in the case of Taliban fighters, that they complied with the Geneva Convention Article 4(A)(2) requirements or, in the case of al-Qaeda fighters, that they should be deemed lawful combatants under the functional extension of the war regime that the United States has embraced to justify waging war against them. In short, the United States continues categorically to reject the possibility of treating the detainees at Guantanamo as prisoners of war, even though their indefinite detention is justified solely by the United States's claim to be at war with them.

There is a second major problem with the Administration's selective application of the law of war with respect to the Guantanamo detainees. Even if the Administration is right that the detainees are not prisoners of war within the meaning of the Third Geneva Convention, it is not the case that they are entitled to no more than being treated "humanely"[31] and are otherwise exempt from protection under the laws of war. For even if these individuals are not prisoners of war within the meaning of the Third Geneva Convention, then they are persons protected by the Fourth 1949 Geneva Convention Relative to the Protection of Civilians in Time of War, which applies generally to all persons who "at a given moment and in any manner whatsoever, find themselves, in the case of a conflict . . . in the hands of a Party to the conflict . . . of which they are not nationals."[32] The protections of the Fourth Geneva Convention are admittedly limited; the treaty grants states considerable discretion to exercise measures of control over protected persons on security grounds, including internment. But it prohibits at a minimum subjecting protected persons to "physical or moral coercion . . . to obtain information from them."[33] It also ensures that even interned persons may communicate with the outside world. The United States has not accepted any obligation to comply with these provisions, or the obligation to grant review by a court or administrative board, at least twice a year, of the original decision to intern a person protected by the Convention.[34]

A third difficulty with the Administration's selective application of the war regime in the case of the Guantanamo detainees concerns the question of when such persons must, under the law of war, be released. Although the United States initiated an international armed conflict against Afghanistan in October 2001, that conflict is no longer an international armed conflict within the meaning of Geneva Conventions. Once the government of President Karzai was established, either as the Interim

Government in December 2001 or as the Transitional Government in June 2002, the United States and Afghanistan were no longer at war. Since then, the government of Afghanistan, with United States assistance, has been seeking to suppress an internal rebellion of residual Taliban and al-Qaeda forces.

Under the Third Geneva Convention, prisoners of war must be released and repatriated "without delay" after the cessation of active hostilities.[35] Although hostilities continue in Afghanistan, the legal character of those hostilities has changed. Consequently, the United States may no longer assert rights with respect to detainees from Afghanistan derived from the existence of a state of international armed conflict. A state may of course charge a prisoner of war with a crime committed before he was detained, and it may require him to serve a prison sentence even after the conflict has ended. (In the case of Guantanamo, even though many detainees have been held there for over four years, as of May 2006 criminal trials have been initiated before military commissions against only ten persons, and none of these has moved beyond the pre-trial stage, much less resulted in a conviction.) But once the international armed conflict has ended, the *preventive* justification for the United States to detain combatants from Afghanistan disappears.

The Administration would presumably respond to this critique by arguing that the international armed conflict has not in fact ended, because the international war against terrorism continues. Focusing on the conflict in Afghanistan, the Administration might continue, is the wrong frame of reference. Here, however, it is important to stress the limits beyond which the extension of the war regime to the conflict against terrorism cannot be justified. Even if we accept the possibility of a state of war against some terrorist groups, a substantial number of those held at Guantanamo appear *not* to be combatants in that war. Press reports based on interviews with officials familiar with the Guantanamo facility have revealed that military investigators "have struggled to find more than a dozen [detainees] they can tie directly to significant terrorist acts."[36] One United States officer, a member of the original military legal team assigned to work on the prosecutions, observed: "It became obvious to us as we reviewed the evidence that, in many cases, we had simply gotten the slowest guys on the battlefield."[37] More recent press accounts suggest, based on reviews conducted by the United States military, that "40 percent of those penned up at Guantanamo never belonged there in the first place."[38]

Indeed, the very definition of "enemy combatant" in the Defense Department order establishing the Combatant Status Review Panels as a person who was part of forces associated with al-Qaeda or the Taliban that were "engaged in hostilities against the United States" reinforces the likelihood that many of those at Guantanamo are being detained not by virtue of their involvement in the war on terrorism, but simply for their role in the battle for Afghanistan. They engaged in a conventional, ultimately unsuccessful, campaign against United States efforts to topple the Taliban regime on behalf of which they fought. To the extent these detainees were combatants in a conventional international armed conflict, and not the broader war on terror, their war is over. Under a proper application of the Geneva Conventions, they should be repatriated to Afghanistan, where the national government would be empowered to apply provisions of Afghan law to prevent or punish insurrectionary acts.

4. THE REJECTION OF THE RECIPROCITY OF WAR

Substantive legal rules do not represent the only means by which the law constrains the conduct of war. A second constraint, arising from just war theory, is the notion of *reciprocity*. Each party to an armed conflict is ordinarily aware and accepts that once it invokes its authority to wage war against an adversary, its adversary has the right to wage war back. Thus, a state whose soldiers claim the combatant's privilege to kill enemy soldiers, to destroy enemy property, and to capture and detain prisoners of war, ordinarily accepts that soldiers on the opposing front are entitled to exercise comparable wartime authorities. Once war begins, the reciprocal status of belligerents applies, without regard to the lawfulness or morality of the initial resort to force.[39]

Such reciprocity serves not only the moral requirements of just war theory. It also serves as an important disincentive for states to engage in war in the first place. Leaders know that the price of invoking wartime powers is to subject their own state's soldiers, citizens, and property to the wartime powers of the other side. Preserving the moral equivalence of warring parties, once a state of armed conflict exists, thus serves to deter the descent into barbarism that accompanies war.

In its war on terrorism, however, the United States has been unwilling to recognize reciprocal belligerent rights on the part of those we have identified as our adversaries. Although United States forces have claimed the combatant's privilege to kill both al-Qaeda and Taliban combatants in Afghanistan, we have rejected the notion that members of those groups may claim their own combatant's privilege, even when they engage in traditional, nonterrorist forms of armed combat. And so Guantanamo detainee David Matthew Hicks has been charged before a

US Military Commission with, among other offenses, "attempted murder by an unprivileged belligerent." The charge specifically alleges that Hicks attempted to murder American and other coalition "forces," through conventional military means and in the context of armed conflict, "while he did not enjoy combatant immunity."[40] Similarly, the indictment against American John Walker Lindh, which charges him with conspiracy to murder United States nationals, states that it was "part of the conspiracy that members and associates of al-Qaeda and the Taliban would violently oppose and kill American military personnel and other United States Government employees serving in Afghanistan after the September 11 attacks."[41]

The refusal to accord reciprocal combatant rights to our adversaries in the war on terrorism is not limited to Afghanistan. For instance, press accounts indicate that Ziyad Hassan, an insurgent in Iraq, was charged with the crime of terrorism, and ultimately convicted of murder, for killing an American soldier by means of a roadside bomb.[42] Despite having invoked the war regime in the struggle against terrorism, the United States treats violence by our adversaries – even when directed against what would be permissible military targets in wartime – not as acts of war, but as simple criminal acts, unprivileged by the existence of a state of armed conflict.

I should stress that I am in no way suggesting that acts of terrorism, as such, would be privileged if belligerent rights were applied reciprocally in the context of a justifiable extension of the war regime to the struggle against terrorism. To the contrary, acts of terrorism – the intentional killing of civilians by substate groups for political purposes – are prohibited means of conducting war. Recognizing belligerent rights under the law of war for terrorist groups against which the United States might justifiably wage war does not enable such groups to kill the very noncombatants the law of war is meant to protect. Combatants who intentionally target civilians violate international humanitarian law and are subject to prosecution as war criminals. Detainees at Guantanamo, if they in fact committed terrorist acts prior to their detention by the United States, are perfectly susceptible to prosecution, even if they are recognized as combatants entitled to belligerent rights under the war regime.

5. CONCLUSION

A time of "war" is an exceptional state, one in which barbarism and the subordination of human rights are legally accepted. Soldiers in wartime may kill their adversaries, or they may detain them without trial simply by virtue of their membership in the opposing force. It is the emergence of an existential threat to a state or its citizens, emanating from an organized foe – and not some lesser state of emergency – that justifies such derogation from normal restraints of law.

The United States's claim that it is engaged in a state of war – war in a legal sense – in the struggle against terrorism does not comport with positive law conceptions of war. Justifying the assertion of war powers in the context of the war against terrorism accordingly requires a functional extrapolation of the law. This is defensible at least with respect to part of the struggle against terrorism, namely, the use of force against an organized political entity – the al-Qaeda terrorist network – that has launched armed attacks against the United States. But the United States has refused to engage in a comparable extrapolation in construing the restraints that apply in wartime. It has not accepted that the United States's right of self-defense extends only to the entity that attacked it, but asserts the right to use force against all entities we deem terrorist or all states that support them. The Administration has claimed that affiliation with a terrorist organization is sufficient to render a person a legitimate target for wartime killing, but not for such a person to claim status as a lawful combatant, even when he engages in conventional forms of armed conflict.

This one-sided approach – claiming the legal rights associated with a state of war but refusing to recognize the full range of associated restraints – undermines the justification for the United States's effort to move beyond positive international law and to extend the war regime to the struggle against terrorism. In the context of a conflict that does not satisfy a positivist definition of war, a state cannot justifiably invoke war powers and authorities unless it is prepared to recognize both the associated constraints and the reciprocal rights of its adversary.

NOTES

1. On October 25, 2001, President Bush stated categorically: "As you all know, our Nation is at war right now." Remarks at the Thurgood Marshall Extended Elementary School, Washington, D.C., 2 PUB. PAPERS 1301, 1301 (October 21, 2001), http://www.whitehouse.gov/news/releases/2001/10/20011025-2.html.
2. Eric Schmitt and Thom Shanker, "New Name for 'War on Terror' Reflects Wider US Campaign," *New York Times*, July 26, 2005, at A7.
3. Richard W. Stevenson, "President Makes it Clear: Phrase is 'War on Terror'," *New York Times*, August 4, 2005, at A12.
4. President Richard M. Nixon, Annual Message to the Congress on the State of the Union, PUB. PAPERS 8, 12 (January 22, 1970), http://www.presidency.ucsb.edu/ws/index.php?pid=2921#.

5. President Ronald Reagan, Radio Address to the Nation on Economic Growth and the War on Drugs, 2 PUB. PAPERS 1310, 1311 (October 8, 1988), http://www.reagan.utexas.edu/archives/speeches/1988/100888a.htm.
6. President Lyndon B. Johnson, Annual Message to the Congress on the State of the Union, 1 PUB. PAPERS 112, 114 (January 8, 1964), http://www.presidency.ucsb.edu/ws/index.php?pid=26787.
7. Letter dated October 7, 2001 from the Permanent Representative of the United States of America to the United Nations addressed to the President of the Security Council, UN Doc. S/2001/946, http://www.un.int/usa/s-2001-946.htm.
8. David Johnston and David E. Sanger, "Fatal Strike in Yemen was Based on Rules Set Out by Bush," *New York Times*, November 6, 2002, at A16.
9. Executive Order 12,333, 3 CFR 200, § 2.11 (1982), http://www.dod.mil/atsdio/documents/eo1233.html.
10. James Risen and David Johnston, "Bush Has Widened Authority of C.I.A. to Kill Terrorists," *New York Times*, December 15, 2002, at A1.
11. Brief for the Respondents at 14, Hamdi v. Rumsfeld, 542 U.S. 507 (2004) (No. 03-6996), http://www.abanet.org/publiced/preview/briefs/pdfs_03/03-6696Resp.pdf.
12. *See* Brief for the Petitioner at 9, Rumsfeld v. Padilla, 542 U.S. 426 (2004) (No. 03-1027) (arguing that the President's "wartime authority . . . to capture and detain enemy combatants" was "fully applicable" in the case of a US citizen allegedly engaged in terrorist activity in the United States), http://www.abanet.org/publiced/preview/briefs/pdfs_03/031027pet.pdf.
13. Yoram Dinstein, *War, Aggression and Self-Defence* 15 (3rd edn, 2001) (emphasis added).
14. *See, e.g.,* Geneva Convention III Relative to the Treatment of Prisoners of War, *adopted* August 12, 1949, art. 2, 6 UST 3316, 3318, 75 UNTS 135, 136 [hereinafter "Geneva Convention III"]. The three other Geneva Conventions of 1949 contain an identical provision ("Common Article 2") setting out when a state of international armed conflict triggering the substantive provisions of the Conventions exists.
15. Traditional international law does recognize the existence of armed conflict between states and substate entities, but only in the context of civil or internal wars. Thus, Article 3 common to the 1949 Geneva Conventions ("Common Article 3") provides certain minimal humanitarian law rules applicable in "the case of armed conflict not of an international character occurring *in the territory of one of the High Contracting Parties.*" Geneva Convention III, *supra* note 14, art. 3, 6 UST at 3318, 75 UNTS at 136 (emphasis added). The 1977 Protocol to the Geneva Conventions elaborating international humanitarian law norms applicable in such cases applies to "all armed conflicts . . . which take place *in the territory of a High Contracting Party* between its armed forces and dissident armed forces or other organized armed groups which, under responsible command, exercise such control over a part of its territory as to enable them to carry out sustained and concerted military operations and to implement this Protocol." Protocol Additional to the Geneva Conventions of August 12, 1949, and Relating to the Protection of Victims of Non-International Armed Conflicts (Protocol II), *adopted* June 8, 1977, art. 1, 1125 UNTS 609, 611 (emphasis added).
16. Sean D. Murphy, "Terrorism and the Concept of 'Armed Attack' in Article 51 of the UN Charter," 43 *Harvard International Law Journal* 41 (2002).
17. *See generally* Rohan Gunaratna, *Inside Al Qaeda: Global Network of Terror* (2002).

18. "Declaration of War by Osama bin Laden, together with the leaders of the World Islamic Front for the Jihad Against the Jews and the Crusaders" (February 23, 1998), quoted in Gunaratna, *supra* note 17.
19. President George W. Bush, Address Before a Joint Session of Congress on the United States Response to the Terrorist Attacks of September 11, 2 PUB. PAPERS 1140, 1141 (September 20, 2001), http://www.whitehouse.gov/news/releases/2001/09/20010920-8.html.
20. *Id.* at 1142.
21. *See* Draft Articles on Responsibility of States for Internationally Wrongful Acts, Art. 8 (adopted by the United Nations International Law Commission in 2001), reprinted in *Report of the International Law Commission, 53rd Session*, UN GAOR, 55th Session, Supp. No. 10, at 45, UN Doc A/56/10 (2001), http://untreaty.uk.org/ilc/texts/instruments/english/draft%20articles19_6_2001.pdf.
22. *See, e.g.,* UNSC Res. 262, UN Doc. S/RES/242 (1968) (condemning Israeli attacks against the Beirut Airport in response to Lebanon's harboring of Palestine Liberation Organization terrorist groups); UNSC Res. 509, UN Doc. S/RES/509 (1982) and UNSC Res. 517, UN Doc. S/RES/517 (1982) (demanding that Israel withdraw from Lebanon following its invasion aimed at destroying Palestinian terrorist organizations and "censur[ing]" Israel for its failure to do so); UNSC Res. 573, UN Doc. S/RES/573 (1985) ("condemn[ing]" Israel's bombing of the Palestine Liberation Organization headquarters in Tunis as "act of armed aggression . . . against Tunisian territory"); UNSC Res. 1234, UN Doc. S/RES/1234 (1999) and UNSC Res. 1304, UN Doc. S/RES/1304 (2000) (deploring the presence of foreign forces in the Democratic Republic of the Congo, including Rwandan forces that attacked refugee camps from which terrorist strikes against Rwanda were launched, and demanding the withdrawal of those forces); *Report of the 4836th Meeting of the UN Security Council*, UN SCOR, 58th Session, 4836th mtg., UN Doc. S/PV.4836 (October 5, 2003) (during which most states condemned Israel's bombing of alleged terrorist training camps in Syria).
23. International Covenant on Civil and Political Rights, *adopted* December 16, 1966, art. 9(1), 999 UNTS 171, 175, 6 I.L.M. 368, 371.
24. *Id.*, art. 9(4), 999 UNTS at 176, 6 I.L.M. at 371.
25. *See* Hamdi v. Rumsfeld, 507 U.S. 507, 556 (Scalia, J., dissenting).
26. Geneva Convention III, *supra* note 14, art. 4, 6 UST at 3320, 75 UNTS at 138.
27. *Id.*, art. 4(A)(2), 6 UST at 3320, 75 UNTS at 138.
28. "Should any doubt arise as to whether persons, having committed a belligerent act and having fallen into the hands of the enemy, belong to any of the categories enumerated in Article 4, such persons shall enjoys the protection of the present Convention until such time as their status has been determined by a competent tribunal." Geneva Convention III, *supra* note 14, art. 5, 6 UST at 3324, 75 UNTS at 142.
29. News Release No. 651-04, US Department of Defense, Combatant Status Review Tribunal Order Issued (July 7, 2004), http://www.defenselink.mil/releases/2004/nr20040707-0992.html.
30. Memorandum from the Deputy Secretary of Defense for the Secretary of the Navy, Order Establishing Combatant Status Review Tribunal (July 7, 2004), http://www.defenselink.mil/news/Jul2004/d20040707review.pdf.
31. White House Fact Sheet, Status of Detainees at Guantanamo (February 7, 2002), http://www.whitehouse.gov/news/releases/2002/02/20020207-13.html.

32. Geneva Convention IV Relative to the Protection of Civilian Persons in Time of War, *adopted* August 12, 1949, art. 4, 6 UST 3516, 3520, 75 UNTS 287, 290.
33. *Id.*, art. 31. 6 UST at 3338, 75 UNTS at 308.
34. *Id.*, art. 43. 6 UST at 3544, 75 UNTS at 314.
35. Geneva Convention III, *supra* note 14, art. 118, 6 UST at 3406, 75 UNTS at 224.
36. Tim Golden and Don Van Natta, Jr., "After Terror, a Secret Rewriting of Military Law," *New York Times*, October 24, 2004, at A1.
37. Tim Golden, "Administration Officials Split Over Stalled Military Tribunals," *New York Times*, October 25, 2004, at A1. *See also* Tim Golden and Don Van Natta, Jr., "U.S. Said to Overstate Value of Guantanamo Detainees," *New York Times*, June 21, 2004, at A1 (suggesting that none of the detainees at Guantanamo "ranked as leaders or senior operatives of Al Qaeda" and that "only a relative handful – some put the number at about a dozen, others more than two dozen – were sworn Qaeda members or other militants able to elucidate the organization's inner workings").
38. Joseph Lelyveld, "Interrogating Ourselves," *New York Times,* June 12, 2005, § 6 (Magazine), at 36.
39. Michael Walzer, *Just and Unjust Wars* 127 (2nd edn, 1992) (noting that in wartime, opposing soldiers "face one another as moral equals" regardless of the justice of their cause); *see also id.* at 137 (the "war convention," i.e., the moral regime governing the means by which war is fought, "stipulates [combatants'] battlefield equality").
40. United States v. Hicks (US Military Commission) ("Charge Sheet" approved June 10, 2004), para. 21, at 5, http://www.defense.gov/news/Jun2004/d20040610cs.pdf.
41. United States v. Walker Lindh, Crim. No. 02-37A (E.D. Va.) (grand jury indictment issued February 5, 2002), Count One, para. 4, http://www.usdoj.gov/ag/2ndindictment.htm.
42. Jonathan Finer and Andy Mosher, "For Soldier, a Posthumous Day in Iraqi Court," *Washington Post*, June 28, 2005, at A11.

JONATHAN SCHONSHECK

DETERMINING MORAL RECTITUDE IN THWARTING SUICIDE TERRORIST ATTACKS: MORAL *TERRA INCOGNITA*

It can be asserted without controversy that one of the principal concerns of the US government must be endeavoring to thwart suicide terrorist attacks – to actually prevent their happening, and not just to clean up the carnage, and prosecute any surviving perpetrators. It can also be asserted, and also without controversy, that in endeavoring to thwart suicide terrorist attacks, the United States could act in ways that are morally upright – or, alternatively, it could act in ways that are morally wrong.[1] However: distinguishing morally permissible endeavors from morally *im*permissible endeavors is no easy matter; *that* is *not* without controversy. For as a moment's reflection will reveal, to (genuinely) *thwart* an attack by suicide terrorists is, quite inevitably, to engage in *preventive* actions. And preventive actions are, notoriously morally problematical. How, then, is the determination to be made; how can the morally permissible endeavors be distinguished from the morally impermissible?

The most general thesis of this chapter is that we are entering uncharted moral territory. I attempt to secure that thesis by arguing that the threat posed by suicide terrorists is *sui generis*; in consequence, it does not comfortably "fit" extant moral models. In an earlier paper,[2] I argued that suicide terrorists are neither "common criminals," nor soldiers; I synopsize those arguments in Section 1. In Section 2, I sketch a response to the *sui generis* threat posed by suicide terrorists that seems, intuitively, morally permissible. I then look for more solid moral grounding: in the distinction between prevention and preemption (Section 3), in just war theory (Section 4), and in a Kantian argument (Section 5). None of these seem to apply to this *sui generis* threat; there is much work here to be done by moral philosophers.

1. SUICIDE TERRORISTS AND SOLDIERS; SUICIDE TERRORISTS AND CRIMINALS

1.1 Suicide Terrorists

There are, to be sure, many different sorts of suicide terrorists: individuals willing to die for some cause or another, killing people in the process. In a chapter of this length, we need to focus on an exemplar. As the perpetrators of 9/11 (and other attacks), and as constituting the gravest threat to the United States, let us focus on al-Qaeda. And when we need to place al-Qaeda in a philosophical – religious context, let us consider the version of Islamic extremism espoused by their (recent) Afghani hosts, the Taliban. I believe that the arguments constructed will be applicable to other organizations and causes *mutatis mutandis*.

1.2 Suicide Terrorists and Soldiers

Suicide terrorists are like soldiers in some respects. They operate across international borders, and they use an array of military weaponry – including "weapons of mass destruction" (WMD), if they can obtain them. Furthermore, like soldiers, they are not motivated by personal gain, but by some (alleged) "higher cause."

But suicide terrorists are *un*like soldiers in crucial respects.

First – and quite apparently – they do not wear any sort of uniform or other "fixed insignia," as do members of a military.

Second, suicide terrorists quite intentionally target noncombatants. The deliberate killing of civilians – especially children, the elderly, etc. who decidedly cannot defend themselves – enhances the terror spawned by the attack, and thus is tactically preferred. Soldiers do not intentionally target noncombatants – or if they do, their actions constitute war crimes.[3]

Third, suicide terrorists are not the "army" of a nation-state; they are not under the command and control structure of any government. Consequently, they are under no authority that can formally declare war. Similarly, they are under no authority that can enter a treaty or sue for peace – to formally bring hostilities to an end.

Fourth, suicide terrorists are *undeterrable* adversaries. In this absolutely crucial respect, they differ from both soldiers and ordinary criminals; it makes sense, then, to turn to the ways in which suicide terrorists are like and unlike criminals – and then unite the argument on the issue of undeterrability.

1.3 Suicide Terrorists and Criminals

There is no denying the fact that suicide terrorists are criminals – at least, in the profoundly literal sense that they are persons who violate criminal statutes. Additionally, they engage in criminal conspiracies. In the aftermath, their "crimes" are investigated by (various elements of) police forces, especially forensics units. And they are mass murderers.

But suicide terrorists are *un*like ordinary criminals in crucial respects.

Criminals do not target civilians – that is, innocent bystanders. To be sure, innocents can be caught in the crossfire – especially, for example, in conflicts between rival gangs. Such a lack of concern for innocent bystanders is surely reprehensible – but just as surely, this unconcern is distinguishable from the intentional *targeting* of innocents.

1.4 Undeterrability

The fervent hope, the firmest intention of both soldiers and criminals, is to *survive*. Typically, soldiers are committed to the geopolitical objectives of their (respective) governments; they believe that their (respective) nation's interests justify their being put in harm's way. Whether the objective of the war is securing essential resources, vanquishing a threatening adversary, or establishing secure borders, the soldier undertakes the perils of combat in order to secure, and then to enjoy, those benefits. Typically, criminals want to survive their illegal actions in order to enjoy their ill-gotten gains.

A necessary condition for both soldiers and criminals, of course, is to *live*. Suicide terrorists, *un*like soldiers and criminals, intend to die.[4] And that – to paraphrase Robert Frost – makes all the difference.

The fact that soldiers and criminals want, hope, intend to *survive* their respective activities means that both are, in principle, deterrable. Both crooks and soldiers (by themselves or by means of the decisions of their governments) may be dissuaded from pursuing a particular course of conduct by means of credible deterrent threats: unless they do differently, the outcome will be worse for them, not better. They will be killed, or defeated, or even annihilated – *not* the outcomes they intended to bring about when initiating their actions. A credible deterrent threat provides compelling reason to *stop* – to reconsider, to do otherwise.

Consider now potential suicide terrorists and ask: What deterrent threat could we make, what could we threaten to do to them, that would dissuade them from their determined course of action? The answer is, of course: nothing. They are intending to die; they welcome death – and its promised rewards (in the afterlife). Unlike the deterrable criminal, who seeks to live lavishly; unlike the deterrable soldier, who seeks to survive the conflict; unlike the deterrable nation-state, which seeks to survive and prosper *as* a nation-state: suicide terrorists intend to *not* survive. Thus, the terrorist threat to be thwarted is posed by "un-deterrable" individuals. They cannot be dissuaded by threats; nothing we could plausibly threaten to do to them could be worse than what they intend to do to themselves – and while doing it, of course, also inflicting great evils upon us. Thus, the threat posed by suicide terrorists is quite distinct from the threat of the soldier or the criminal.[5] Indeed the threat is *sui generis*.

2. ENDEAVORING TO THWART SUICIDE TERRORIST ATTACKS

How can we, how ought we respond to this threat? Well, we can be *re*active; we can take various "defensive" measures, attempting to interdict the terrorists at the presumed *sites* of attack. Quite obviously, however, there are too many targets, too many modes of destruction, too few ways of interception. So these defensive measures, while important, simply will not suffice. In addition to being reactive, we must be *pro*active.

I propose the following set of intuitively acceptable initiatives. We must enhance, deploy, and coordinate a full range of intelligence-gathering assets: satellites, aircraft, the interception of all modes of electronic communication, the infiltration of terrorist groups – all to learn precisely who poses a threat. And then we must take actions to *prevent* those individuals from actually launching an attack. When we discover individuals whom we reasonably believe to be suicide terrorists, who thus pose a clear and present danger to the United States, or US interests abroad, or to allies and their interests, these individuals must be *incapacitated*. This has *got* to be the goal. And the harsh new reality is that "incapacitation" means killing, or incarcerating for as long as they constitute a threat.[6]

Furthermore, I propose the following standard for an individual's posing a threat: that responsible officials have a *bona fide* and reasonable belief that a person harbors ill will towards US interests, plus that that person commits (at least) one overt act that can reasonably be understood as preparation for an attack: an attack of one's own, or an attack by one's cohorts.[7] My proposal is that, if you chant "Death to America" and secure forged travel documents, or train at an al-Qaeda camp, or purchase explosives, or surveil targets, and so on – you have thereby signed your own arrest warrant. Or perhaps you have signed your own death warrant.

I introduced these measures with the claim that I found them "intuitively acceptable." Can they withstand moral scrutiny? How are these initiatives to be morally assessed?

3. PREVENTION AND PREEMPTION

Philosophers who write on these issues draw a distinction between preemption and prevention. Roughly, a preemptive first strike is intended to interrupt an adversary's attack "already in progress;" a preventive first strike is intended to disable an adversary prior to its initiation of an attack. Generally, preemptive first strikes are thought justified in certain specifiable circumstances; generally, preventive first strikes are thought not justified – or at least, are (far) more morally problematical. But while this distinction is crystal clear when "preemption" and "prevention" are considered as Platonic Forms, applying the distinction to armed conflict is considerably more cloudy. Even more challenging is its application to thwarting terrorists.

Consider a hypothetical. Imagine that your geopolitical adversary embarks upon a decade-long military buildup. You witness an escalating percentage of its GNP devoted to weapons research and development, with production following successful testing. You witness an escalation in espionage – military, political, and industrial. You witness an escalation in troop strength: both combat troops, and support personnel. You witness an escalating rate of computer and network incursions: the theft and corruption of data, and the launch of destructive viruses and worms. All this culminates in general mobilization, and a repositioning of entire armies. In the media, there are belligerent references to past borders, and past conflicts. And then comes the invasion.

Intuitively, a justified (preemptive) first strike could be launched sometime before the tanks can be seen from the border guardhouses. Intuitively, an attack on the economic infrastructure ten years earlier, to preclude the buildup, would be an unjustified preventive attack. Quite quickly, matters get murkier. Let us call the various actions taken by one's adversary that seem to be a buildup towards armed aggression "provocative acts" (in a mostly descriptive sense). Now any of the provocative acts in this sequence might instigate a "first strike." Logically, there must be a pair of provocative acts that have this property: a first strike in response to the first of the pair would be a *preventive* strike and therefore likely unjustified (or at least morally problematical); a first strike in response to the second provocative act of the pair would be a *preemptive* strike, and therefore likely justified (or at least less morally problematical). In point of fact, there may be a span of time between these two provocative acts; given the lethargy of all the logistics involved, there will be a wide "window of opportunity" for determining whether a contemplated first strike would be preventive or preemptive.

But the same cannot be said about a suicide terrorist attack. Consider now another hypothetical, a person whose activities seem aimed at a suicide attack on a subway. This person builds a bomb in an apartment. One day, he straps it to his body, walks to a subway station, boards a train, and detonates the bomb in the first tunnel. How are we to distinguish between preventive and preemptive interdiction in *this* case? The total elapsed time, from departing the apartment to departing this life, may well be a matter of mere minutes. Is there a corresponding "pair of events," between which we can plausibly distinguish prevention from preemption? Is there a "window of opportunity" at all, given that there likely will be no "security checkpoints" along the road to perdition? Or are interdictions which *appear* to be problematical preventions really unproblematical preemptions?

In *Just and Unjust Wars*, Michael Walzer asks and answers our question as regards nation-states:

> Now, what acts are to count, what acts do count as threats sufficiently serious to justify war? . . . The line between legitimate and illegitimate first strikes is not going to be drawn at the point of imminent attack but at the point of sufficient threat. That phrase is necessarily vague. I mean it to cover three things: a manifest intent to injure, a degree of active preparation that makes that intent a positive danger, and a general situation in which waiting, or doing anything other than fighting, greatly magnifies the risk.[8]

Well, as regards suicide terrorists, all three conditions for "sufficient threat" seem clearly to be met by the "intuitively acceptable" initiatives I sketched above. Chanting "Death to America!", for example, or reacting with approval to calls for violence by an Imam, is evidence of a "manifest intent." Overt acts of training, forging, gathering components, etc., could constitute "active preparation that makes that intent a positive danger." We could set a standard: either one unambiguous component (C4 explosive, detonators), or two ambiguous components (bomb ingredients, pocketed undergarments) will suffice. And the practical impossibility of defending the vast array of purely civilian (i.e., noncombatant) targets "greatly magnifies the risk"; I submit that the third condition is continuously met.

If the prevention/preemption distinction bears on thwarting suicide terrorists at all, it certainly seems that many thwarting interdictions are indeed morally permissible. Nonetheless, we lack specificity as regards permissible and impermissible first strikes.

My conclusion here takes the form of a disjunction. Either the prevention/preemption distinction is not relevant to the endeavor of thwarting suicide terrorists (there being no contiguous pair of provocative events to sustain the distinction), or a wide range of "first strikes" that might *seem* to be preventive are really preemptive. But in either case, little moral guidance is offered by the distinction.

We are indeed entering moral *terra incognita*.

4. JUST WAR THEORY: INAPPLICABLE

The Bush Administration and the media invariably refer to our endeavors to thwart suicide terrorists as the "War on Terrorism," or more recently the "Global War on Terror." This could lead the unwary to look to the venerable tradition known as Just War Theory (JWT) when seeking to distinguish permissible from impermissible courses of conduct. However, endeavoring to thwart suicide terrorists is not the prosecuting of a war; neither the perpetrators (as we have seen), nor the conflict itself, "fit" the conditions of JWT.

Reflect for a moment on the US invasion of Iraq in 2003, and (especially) the subsequent "insurgency." This is a perfect exemplar of what has come to be called "asymmetrical warfare" – a concept most easily understood through its contrastive, "symmetrical warfare." In symmetrical warfare, we find adversaries of (roughly) comparable military strength, with (roughly) comparable weaponry and technology, fighting on a (relatively) well-defined battlefield. World War II in Europe, from D-Day to the German surrender, would be an instance of symmetrical warfare. But when the United States invaded Iraq, it relied upon an array of high-tech weaponry – fighters and bombers employing stealth technology, missiles guided by Global Positioning Devices, unmanned aircraft (Predators) used for surveillance, and later for armed attack. That fraction of the Iraqi military which did not melt into the civilian population simply was no match – an asymmetry of force.

The endeavor to thwart suicide terrorist attacks is not a "war" per se, but it *is* an asymmetrical struggle: wildly unequal forces, Boeings as weapons of mass destruction, Manhattan and Washington as "battlefields."

JWT is, I contend, designed for the strategy and tactics of symmetrical warfare – and not the asymmetrical endeavor of terrorist-thwarting. Furthermore, I believe that JWT *presupposes* two distinguishable sorts of what we can call "moral symmetries" between the warring adversaries, a symmetry of their moral understanding of war and a symmetry of their fundamental political theory. Our conflict with al-Qaeda is morally asymmetrical in the moral understanding of war: Just War versus Jihad. In addition, it is morally asymmetrical in terms of the political theory: Liberal Democracy versus Wahabist Islam. So let us consider now the key provisions of JWT. Initially, my goal is to (briefly) explicate them and to show the morally symmetry, the moral universalism, that those provisions presuppose. After doing that, I examine the Taliban's interpretation of Islam and the tactics of al-Qaeda. What will become clear, I submit, is that the Islamic fundamentalists' repudiation of moral universalism, conjoined with al-Qaeda's wholesale dismissal of just war provisions, move this asymmetrical conflict (well) outside the domain of JWT. In consequence, we really cannot look to JWT for moral guidance.

For a contemporary account of JWT, I shall rely upon William V. O'Brien.[9] As is traditional, O'Brien distinguishes the conditions that make going to war morally permissible (*jus ad bellum*) from the conditions that govern the prosecution of a war (*jus in bello*).

As regards *jus ad bellum*, the first condition is "competent authority:" war "must be waged on the order of public authorities for public purposes." The second condition is that the war must be waged for a "just cause." The third is that the war must be waged with the "right intention."

There are two main conditions for *jus in bello*. The first is "proportionality" which requires that the good produced in going to war must exceed the evil. The second is "discrimination," which "prohibits direct intentional attacks on noncombatants and nonmilitary targets."[10]

As their further development makes clear, the broader context of these conditions is the meta-ethical position of universalism: all human beings are members of a single moral "universe;" each has the same moral status, or moral standing. There is a single, unified "moral law" applicable to all, and to all equally.

Of the set of *jus ad bellum* conditions taken together, O'Brien writes:

> The taking of human life is not permitted to man unless there are exceptional justifications. Just-war doctrine provides those justifications, but they are in the nature of special pleadings to overcome the presumption against killing.[11]

The phrase "is not permitted to man" is a clear indication that O'Brien considers the whole of humanity to constitute a single moral universe. And two further specifications of "right intention" are on point. "[R]ight intention requires that the just belligerent have always in mind as the ultimate object of the war a just and lasting peace. There is an implicit requirement to prepare for reconciliation even as one wages war." And more deeply, more metaethically telling: "[U]*nderlying the other requirements*, right intention insists that charity and love exist even among enemies. Enemies must be treated as human beings with rights."[12]

Moral universalism has implications throughout the just war doctrine; for example, in performing the calculations for proportionality, one is to "count" the deaths of one's enemies precisely the same as one counts the deaths of one's own. A war is unjust if the evil – including the *total* of the fatalities, one's adversary's as well as one's own – is disproportionate to the good to be achieved by the war.

In prosecuting a just war, each side continues to regard the citizens of the other nation as human beings, with rights equal to one's own. And they will respect each other in the morning – that is, after the war. Indeed, the goal of the just war must be a just peace.

The most perspicuous place to begin, I think, is at the end: with the competing conceptions of the "just peace" that is to follow the conflict. One party, the United States, seeks to continue its pre-9/11 pursuit of a liberal democracy (however fitful that pursuit sometimes seems). The ultimate goal sought by al-Qaeda, the other party, is a pan-Arabic Caliphate: Afghanistan under the Taliban, writ large. In such a society, there is no separation of church and state, most assuredly not a liberal democratic concept of religious tolerance. Furthermore, such a society is founded upon thoroughgoing gender inequality. One's moral, religious, and legal status – and these are essentially the same – is a function of one's gender. The US Department of State has issued a document with a telling title: "Report on the Taliban's War Against Women."[13] With a combination of anecdotes and discursive prose, it details the lives (and deaths) of women under the Taliban. Its summary: "[T]he Taliban's discriminatory policies violate many of the basic principles of international human rights law. These rights include the right to freedom of expression, association and assembly, the right to work, the right to education, freedom of movement, and the right to health care."

What we have here is not two discrete populations of a single moral universe – everyone subject to, and known to be subject to, an overarching moral law – but two discrete "moral communities," which subscribe to deeply incompatible core beliefs and values. And they are locked in mortal conflict.

And how is this conflict being carried out? Asymmetrically. At the theoretical level, it is a clash between Just War and Jihad. The conflict is not a war per se, as it is not a conflict between nations. Neither Osama bin Laden nor Ayman Al Zawahiri can be considered "competent authorities." To say that they aim at a "public good" would be to countenance the Caliphate and to renounce virtually every value constitutive of liberal democracy. The Taliban's interpretation of Islam, and within it Jihad, rejects universalism's moral equality; infidels have a (much) lower status than believers. In consequence, there are special rewards for killing infidels, or dying in the attempt.[14] The calculations of the just war principle of proportionality, which presuppose equality, are thereby rendered incoherent. JWT anticipates an end to the hostilities, and the subsequent repatriation of captured combatants – not unlike the Criminal Justice Model anticipates the release of a convict, after serving one's sentence. But in the effort to thwart suicide terrorists, there is no competent authority to end the hostilities, and – as was argued above – there can be no sane thought of releasing suicide terrorists still intending to attack. Finally – and most obviously – al-Qaeda quite intentionally transgresses the principle of discrimination, hoping thereby to enhance the terror aroused by its attacks.

More narrowly, I want to claim this: the struggle between al-Qaeda and the United States does not fit the conditions, nor the moral presuppositions, of JWT. And no amount of stretching or chopping by Procrustes could make it fit.

More broadly, all of this makes it more difficult to think about the moral constraints *on us* as we endeavor to thwart suicide terrorists. How constrained can we morally be, against an implacable and undeterrable adversary intending the destruction of our moral community itself?[15]

5. KANTIAN CONSTRAINTS: FOUNDED ON A FALLACY

Is the United States, in taking preventive measures, committed – on pain of inconsistency – to countenancing "similar" preventive actions by other nation-states? This argument begins with the concern that a "relationship" will develop – and here it is difficult to be precise – between the United States's acting preventively to thwart suicide terrorist attacks, and actions that will "come to be taken" by other nation-states. Those other nations will take note of US actions, and then – well, be *emboldened*, or *inspired*, or somehow *instigated* to elect allegedly "similar" actions, or at least to think themselves "justified" in taking allegedly "similar" actions.

Former Vice President Al Gore, in a major policy statement, expressed concerns about a *general* doctrine of preemption. And while the position I am defending is quite narrow – thwarting suicide terrorist attacks and not a general military doctrine of preemption – the argument's format is noteworthy.[16]

> President Bush now asserts that we will take pre-emptive action even if we take the threat we perceive is not imminent. If other nations assert the same right then the rule of law will quickly be replaced by the reign of fear–any nation that perceives circumstances that could eventually lead to an imminent threat would be justified under this approach in taking military action against another nation.[17]

In North Korea's campaign of escalating rhetoric, Ri Pyong Gap, a Foreign Ministry deputy director, claimed that "Preemptive attacks are not the exclusive right of the U.S."[18] And the usually thoughtful Michael Kinsley, towards the end of a critique of Bush Administration "diplomacy" – a critique with which I am in essential agreement – wrote: "[T]he president can start a war against anyone at any time, and no one has the right to stop him. And presumably other nations . . . have that same right."[19]

Now it is not clear just what to make of these "positions," just what is being alleged. They might be mere empirical predictions – in acting preventively, the United States will make *more likely* preventive actions by other nations. As such, they are predictions of (yet more) confirming instances of that mighty maxim, "Monkey see, monkey do." But the fear of inspiring "copycats" cannot be a guiding principle of US policy regarding suicide terrorists; that would yield paralysis, rather than a morally superior policy.

This "position" is *most* interesting, in my judgment, if it is construed to rely upon a particular formulation of Immanuel Kant's categorical imperative. In the *Grounding for the Metaphysics of Morals*, Kant writes: "Act as if the maxim of your action were to become through your will a universal law of nature."[20] What we are to imagine is this: When we act in morally significant ways, maxims "effervesce" from those actions; in performing those actions, we thereby *endorse* those maxims.[21] As a matter of universalizability, we thereby countenance relevantly similar actions by others. Put another way: it is inconsistent to act under a particular maxim, while claiming that others, if similarly situated, may *not* act under that selfsame maxim. So the United States – it is alleged – in acting preventively against suicide terrorists, effervesces a maxim; other countries are thereby "authorized" to act under that maxim. It would be inconsistent of the United States to so act, and then to claim that others may *not*, or to criticize them for so acting.

Now there is a superficial credibility to this argument – but it cannot withstand philosophical scrutiny. Let us turn to the task of abrading its patina of plausibility.

I have no interest in denying the obvious – that in thinking about and speaking about "nation-states," in praising them and criticizing them, we treat them as "agents," as if they are individual, unitary "beings." We speak of a nation-state as "acting" in various ways: as pursuing its objectives (narrowly), its policies (more broadly), or its destiny. And when a nation "acts," we may speak of it as acting clumsily or adroitly; intelligently or stupidly; with or without foresight, etc. In doing all of this, we are employing a (very) convenient shorthand,[22] but we are *not* taking a metaphysical stand. Nation-states are not individuals; when we think and talk in these ways, what we are really saying is that the decision-makers of the nation-state – whether an (actual) individual, or a small cadre, or a ruling elite, or the executive branch (whether checked and balanced, or not) have made decisions and implemented them (or attempted to implement them, or failed to implement them): have ordered, enacted, or declared, etc. It would be awkward and tedious to say all of this on every occasion. So I am not calling for linguistic reform here. But I do want to issue a (rather stern) reminder that this sort of talk is purely *metaphorical*, and that we must not be "captured" by a metaphor, coming to take seriously the notion that nation-states are agents per se.[23] In particular, nation-states are not *moral* agents. To mistake the *convenience* of speaking of them as if they were agents, for their *being moral* agents, is to commit the informal fallacy of "composition" on rather grand a scale.

The formulation of the categorical imperative cited above is intended to state succinctly two fundamental axioms of morality: to assert that every rational being is a moral agent, and to assert the moral *equality* of all the moral agents who comprise a "moral community." My thesis is that, despite the convenient shorthand, nation-states are not moral agents as required by this formulation of the categorical imperative, and the set of nation-states does not constitute a moral community of equal moral agents. Showing these is sufficient to dismantle the Kantian obstacle to the United States's acting preventively against suicide terrorists.

That individual human beings[24] are moral agents is philosophical bedrock.[25] So too is the moral equality of individuals constitutive of a moral community.[26] The Kantian argument we are scrutinizing depends upon a strong *isomorphism* between individual and nation-state; to the contrary, I believe that it is a weak analogy at best, and more aptly considered a mere metaphor. Consider a number of metaphysically important differences.

Historians and political scientists date the origin of the modern nation-state to the Peace of Westphalia (1648). Obviously, individual *homo sapiens sapiens* as moral agents predate the emergence of the nation-state.

Individual human beings are readily distinguishable; aside from obvious or arcane "exceptions," their "boundaries" are pretty well-defined.[27] The "boundaries" of *some* nation-states are indeed well-defined. The boundaries of others, however, are the creations of cartographers: some conscientious, some capricious or whimsical, some with a knowledge of local realities, some ignorant of local realities.[28] Indeed: if we were to take the person/country isomorphism seriously, some contemporary nation-states are profoundly and incurably schizophrenic.

Although some nation-states are relatively homogenous, there is no fundamental, "internal unity" as there is in a human body – any analogies between hearts/lungs/central nervous system, and classes/castes/towns and farms, are fanciful at best.

The modern political philosophers Hobbes, Locke, and Rousseau took note of the fact that human beings are remarkably similar in size, strength, and capabilities; this similarity was both a cause of, and justification of, mores – and, eventually, morality. To be sure, humans do vary in size. But the ranges of size, strength, and capabilities of contemporary nation-states are vastly greater. Consider some comparisons among the 192 members of the United Nations. The Gross Domestic Product of the United States is 74,514 times that of Palau. The population of China (1,284,972,000) is 116,816 times that of Palau (11,000). The landmass of the Russian Federation is 813,114 times that of Nauru. Add to these the disparities in natural resources, in the education and technological skills of the populace, and military capabilities – there is no (rough) equality among nation-states, as there is among human beings. So while we can – and should – speak poetically of the "community of nations," we must avoid getting carried away. And when we consider all nations as "equals" under international law,[29] we are invoking a legal fiction; we are not discovering the fundamental metaphysics of morality. We must resist the temptation to think of nation-states as moral agents per se. And we must resist the temptation to think of the "community of nations" as a *moral* community of presumed equality among its members.

Finally, we must resist the temptation to think of nation-states as effervescing Kantian maxims, and endorsing them by acting, such that every state – regardless of size, population, GDP, military strength, etc. has the moral authorization to act under the maxims effervesced by any other nation-state. Surely the specification of the moral role of the world's nations is more complex, more subtle, more textured than that. In particular, the sole superpower has *unique* permissions, and unique responsibilities. When under attack by those who would destroy it as a moral community, as the guarantor of essential rights – it need not seek the "consent" of other nations before acting.

But let us *now* consider the position that the individual/nation-state analogy *is* in fact a moral isomorphism, and, in consequence, that the relevant formulation of the Kantian categorical imperative is indeed applicable to the United States and all other nation-states. When the United States acts, any other nation-state, *similarly situated*, may act under *that maxim* – carefully specifying what it means to be "similarly situated," and the maxim that effervesces from US actions.[30]

We are to conceive, then, a nation-state constitutionally committed and conscientiously attempting to establish and maintain the liberal democratic "meta-values" of toleration and mutual respect: freedom of conscience, freedom of speech, freedom of religion, freedom of assembly, freedom of the press, the rule of law, and due process of law.[31] We are to conceive that nation-state under attack by suicide terrorists, that is, undeterrable individuals quite deliberately targeting civilians and the social and economic structure necessary for maintaining just institutions.³² The suicide terrorists have a (long-range) goal of *repudiating* tolerance and mutual respect and imposing an antithetical ideology. The nation-state under attack has acceptably competent intelligence agencies for detecting suicide terrorists; it has an acceptably competent military for incapacitating those whom it finds. In using its military, it has no designs to expand territorially or impose any particular ideology. (Indeed, it is willing to devote considerable resources to assisting other nation-states in developing the institutions which guarantee tolerance and mutual respect.) Furthermore, the maxim which effervesces from its actions to thwart suicide terrorists contains essential constraining qualifications regarding the nature of the threat. If there were such a state, thus "similarly situated," I would find it *quite* unobjectionable that it would act under the precisely qualified maxim. Indeed, I would *welcome* its so acting.

6. CONCLUSION

If the United States is to successfully thwart suicide terrorist attacks, it must engage in *preventive* measures. But what preventive measures are morally permissible? Where shall we turn for moral guidance? If my arguments are essentially sound, the threat posed by suicide terrorists is *sui generis*. The distinction between preventive and preemptive action is either inapplicable, or unsustainable; it provides little guidance. This asymmetrical struggle does not fit JWT; we do not find our guidance there. The Kantian Constraints proposed by some are based upon a fallacy; to speak of nations as moral individuals, as members of a moral community of nations, is to employ a convenient figure of speech, or to speak metaphorically. It is not a statement of moral metaphysics. To conclude: much work remains to be done by moral philosophers.

NOTES

1. Intuitively, for example, it would be wrong to suspend the civil rights of all Muslims, or to herd them into interment camps, or to deport them.
2. "Thwarting Suicide Terrorists: The Locus of Moral Constraints and the (Ir)relevance of Human Rights," in *Universal Human Rights: Moral Order in a Divided World*, ed. David A. Reidy and Mortimer N.S. Sellers (Lanham, MD: Rowman & Littlefield, 2005), pp. 209–228.
3. To be sure, various militaries are sometimes more scrupulous, and sometimes less scrupulous about preserving the safety of noncombatants – and the same must be said about criminals. But it is not the *intention* of either soldiers or criminals to injure "bystanders."

4. They may well intend to prosper – but in the next life, not in this (foreshortened) life.
5. The deep difficulty with considering suicide terrorists as criminals is that the institutions of the criminal justice system look backwards rather than forwards: they are designed principally to investigate crimes that have already been committed, and then to arrest and prosecute those who have committed them. But it is the *thwarting* of suicide terrorists, the (actual) preventing their attacking, that is the task at hand.
6. This constitutes yet another reason for *not* considering suicide terrorists as criminals, within the confines of the Criminal Law Model. A central element of the criminal law is the concept of proportionate sentences. But what is the "proportionate" sentence for an attempted (but unsuccessful) terrorist attack? Here we encounter a conflict in intuitions. A life sentence, without the possibility of parole, may well seem too harsh, disproportionately long – after all, the individual is not guilty of a successful attack. However, setting free an individual who is still bent on a suicide attack is as heinous as it is surreal. What follows is not that we ought to amend the CLM to accommodate it, but that suicide terrorists do not fit the Model. They, and the threat they pose, are indeed *sui generis*.
7. In actual practice, I suspect, we will often have less information than we would like to have. As will become clear, however, we cannot afford to err on the side of inaction, of restraint.
8. Michael Walzer, *Just and Unjust Wars* (New York: Basic Books, 1977), pp. 80, 81.
9. I use a selection from O'Brien's *The Conduct of Just and Limited War* (1981), Praeger Publishers, that appears in James P. Sterba, *The Ethics of War and Nuclear Deterrence* (Belmont, CA: Wadsworth Publishing Company, 1985).
10. O'Brien in Sterba, pp. 31, 39.
11. O'Brien in Sterba, p. 31.
12. O'Brien in Sterba, p. 36, italics added in second quotation.
13. US Department of State, "Report on the Taliban's War Against Women," Released by the Bureau of Democracy, Human Rights and Labor, November 17, 2001. file://E:I_%20The%Taliban's%War%Against%20Women.htm
14. *The Holy Qur'an*, translated by A. Yusuf Ali (Brentwood, MD: Amana Corp., 1983). See especially Sect. 9: 20–3, and n. 1270, and n. 1271.
15. On this point, see Jonathan Schonsheck, "Geopolitical Realism, Morality, and the War in the Gulf," *From the Eye of the Storm*, ed. Laurence F. Bove and Laura Duhan Kaplan (The Netherlands: Rodopi, 1995), pp. 162–163.
16. The contexts do not make clear whether Al Gore and Ri Pyong Gap are respecting the distinction between preemption and prevention (as typically drawn by philosophers and discussed above). If my rejection of the Kantian Constraints is successful, then neither preemption nor prevention is constrained.
17. The passage continues, "An unspoken part of this new doctrine appears to be that we claim this right for ourselves – and only for ourselves." I address this portion of the position below. Al Gore, "Iraq and the War on Terrorism," www.gwu.edu/~action/2004/gore/gore092302sp.html
18. "N. Korea warns of pre-emptive strike," MSNBC News Services, February 6, 2003. I suspect that the Deputy Foreign Minister is not an analytic philosopher – for a clear implication of the claim that such attacks are not the "exclusive" right of the United States, is that such attacks are indeed *a* right of the United States. www.msnbc.com/news/850567.asp?0cv=CB10

19. Michael Kinsley, "Sovereign authority," slate.com, March 20, 2003. One does want to ask: why ever would we make such a "presumption?"
20. Immanuel Kant, *Grounding for the Metaphysics of Morals*, trans. James W. Ellington (Indianapolis, IN: Hackett, 1981), p. 30.
21. I am grateful to my colleague Dana Radcliffe for illuminating conversations about this formulation of the categorical imperative.
22. As I have done, at various points, in this chapter.
23. Neither does the fact that they are "legal fictions" in International Law change the fundamental metaphysics. Consider an analogy with business corporations – which can be large collectives of individuals too, which are "individuals" as legal fictions, which we speak about as if they were agents – but which are not agents, strictly speaking (i.e., metaphysically).
24. At least, mature and nondefective ones. (Other qualifications may be necessary.)
25. At least in the Western, liberal moral tradition. I readily acknowledge that, in other traditions, the family or group or clan might be the "smallest" unit of moral significance, rather than the individual. But that's quite some philosophical distance from the claim that the nation-state, which can be composed of a billion (or more) individuals, is the fundamental unit of morality, and not just an analogue in a scheme of analogical thinking.
26. This raises the issue of the scope, or extent, of "universalizability": whether all rational agents are included in a "global" moral community (as Kant seems to have thought), or all sentient creatures are included in such a moral community (as John Stuart Mill seems to have thought; cf. *Utilitarianism*). I have argued at some length for some time that this latter position is untenable. See, for example, "Constraints on *The Expanding Circle*: A Critique of Singer," *Inquiries into Values: The Inaugural Session of the International Society for Value Inquiry*, ed. Sander Lee, (Lewiston, NY: The Edwin Mellen Press, 1988), pp. 695–707. If international conflicts are considered clashes between moral communities, and not as clashes between nation-states within some moral community, the argument for my thesis here is vastly strengthened.
27. Some exceptions are conjoined twins and dead skin cells that slough off.
28. On this point, see Winston S. Churchill, "My Grandfather Invented Iraq." One version appeared in *The Wall Street Journal*, March 2003; a version is available at www.warroom.com/iraqiwar/churchill.htm
29. Corporations are "equal" legal individuals – but corporations are not roughly equal in size and wealth and power.
30. Kantian moral assessment depends crucially, of course, upon precisely formulated maxims.
31. Schonsheck, "Rudeness, Rasp and Repudiation." *Civility and its Discontents*, ed. Christine Sistare (University Press of Kansas, 2004), pp. 182–202.
32. See John Rawls, *A Theory of Justice* (Cambridge, MA: Harvard University Press, 1971), pp. 274ff.

STEPHEN NATHANSON

TERRORISM AND THE ETHICS OF WAR

Although terrorism has been around for a long time, I, like most Americans, first began to take it seriously on the morning of September 11, 2001. On that day of stunned grief and horror, I, like others, was appalled at the death and destruction created by the attacks and worried about the possibility of more attacks. But from very early on, I also worried about what American leaders would do in response. At some level, I sensed that while all of us were condemning terrorism in the strongest moral terms, the temptation to commit or support comparable acts of violence is actually very great. Victims of wrongdoing often feel justified in doing what they would see as wrong if done by others. Although President Bush described the 9/11 terrorists as "flat evil," I suspected that they may have seen themselves as heroic soldiers fighting and dying for a good cause.[1]

One result of the 9/11 attacks has been that the belief that terrorism is morally wrong has become a kind of moral axiom within American public morality. The whole idea of a war on terrorism seems to rest on the belief that terrorism is always wrong and should be warred against.

While I share the belief that terrorist acts are always wrong, I do not see it as axiomatic or self-evident. In fact, I believe that given many people's beliefs, it will be hard for them to justify a categorical condemnation of terrorism. So, I want to begin by asking why terrorism is wrong. What are the features that make terrorist acts always immoral?

I also want to discuss a puzzling fact about moral criticisms of terrorism. If terrorism is so obviously immoral, why is it that moral condemnations of terrorism often provoke cynical responses? Indeed, there is even a kind of sympathy that flows from the view that terrorists are unfairly maligned by criticisms of their deeds. Some of the flavor of these responses is captured by Connor Cruise O'Brien, who writes:

Those who are described as terrorists, and who reject the title for themselves, make the uncomfortable point that national armed forces, fully supported by democratic opinion, have in fact employed violence and terror on a far vaster scale than what liberation movements have as yet been able to attain. The 'freedom fighters' see themselves as fighting a just war. Why should they not be entitled to kill, burn and destroy as national armies, navies and air forces do, and why should the label 'terrorist' be applied to them and not the national militaries?[2]

In order to respond effectively to this sort of challenge and make moral criticisms of terrorism more credible, we need to be clear about just what terrorism is and what makes it wrong.

In what follows, I will focus first on questions about what makes terrorism wrong and then turn to the problem of giving credibility to moral criticisms of terrorism. While much of the credibility problem arises from inconsistencies in the ways that public officials label and judge terrorism and other acts of violence, it may come as a surprise that it is hard to find a prominent theory of the ethics of war that condemns terrorism in all cases. Far from being axiomatic and self-evident, the absolute wrongness of terrorism is hard to square with widely held views. If this is the case, then we face a difficult choice: either we must admit that terrorism can be morally justified, or we must reject widely accepted views because they condone some terrorist acts. My own view is that terrorism is always wrong and that ethical theories that fail to yield that result are defective.

1. WHAT IS TERRORISM?

Although there has been considerable controversy about how to define terrorism, I will give – but cannot defend here – a definition that I believe identifies the features that characterize a terrorist act. With the definition in hand, I can both support my claim about what makes terrorism wrong and show why certain ways of condemning terrorism are not available to most people. The definition makes clear that what distinguishes terrorism from legitimate forms of violence is the means that terrorists use rather than the ends that they seek. The key objectionable feature is that terrorist attacks kill and injure people who are civilians rather than members of the military or government officials who control the practices that terrorists reject.

In my view, terrorist acts have the following four features.

1. They are acts of serious violence.
2. They are committed in order to advance a political goal.
3. They generally target limited numbers of people in order to influence a wider audience of ordinary people and/or public decision-makers.
4. They intentionally kill and injure innocent people.[3]

2. WHY IS TERRORISM WRONG?

If these are the key features of terrorism, then we can use this list to identify which features make terrorist acts immoral.

Feature 1, being an act of serious violence, cannot account for the wrongness of terrorism because many acts with this feature are not wrong. Killing in self-defense, for example, is an act of serious violence, but it is widely viewed as morally justified. If that is so, then terrorism cannot be wrong simply because it has this feature.

The same is true of feature 2, violence committed to advance a political goal. Anyone who believes that war can sometimes be justified, as most people do, must accept that some acts of serious violence that are done to advance a political goal can be morally justified. Given that they hold this belief, they could not consistently criticize terrorists on the grounds that they commit serious acts of violence in order to promote political goals.

Feature 3 also fails to distinguish terrorism from other practices that are sometimes permissible. In war, people seek to kill and injure some people so as to convince others to surrender. Likewise, the legal system imposes punishments on some people in order to deter a wider public from committing illegal acts.[4] If wars and punishments are justifiable, then it cannot be that terrorism is wrong simply because it harms some people in order to influence others.

Feature 4 gives the most plausible answer: *terrorism is wrong because it intentionally kills and injures innocent people*. Most people feel comfortable condemning acts that kill innocent people. While they accept that soldiers will be killed in war, the killing of civilians seems different. This also creates the "terror" associated with terrorism since more people are made to feel vulnerable by attacks on civilians.

The idea that this feature is central to the wrongness of terrorism gains further support from the fact that killing innocent civilians is prohibited by a central principle in the ethics of war, the *principle of noncombatant immunity*. It says that *while it permissible to kill enemy soldiers in war, it is not permissible to kill noncombatants or innocent civilians*. If terrorism always violates this principle and war does not necessarily do so, that provides a basis for distinguishing acts of terrorism from morally permissible acts of war.

3. "ONE MAN'S TERRORIST. . . ."

According to the definition I have given, the goal of a terrorist act must be in some sense political. Beyond this broad characterization, the nature of the goal is left open. What the definition stresses is that terrorism is essentially a means or tactic for achieving political goals. Terrorists use violence against innocent persons to accomplish political goals. Beyond that, whether something is a terrorist act does not depend on specifics about the goal.

Defining terrorism as the name of a means or tactic helps us to see what is the matter with the slogan "one man's terrorist is another man's freedom fighter." This slogan suggests that terrorists are distinguished from freedom fighters by their goals, and it assumes that people cannot be both terrorists and freedom fighters. Both of these ideas are mistaken. Calling someone a "freedom fighter" identifies his or her goal but says nothing about the means used to pursue it. These means can range from nonviolent protest to civil war. If freedom fighters try to achieve their goals through nonviolent tactics or attacks on military personnel, then they are not using terrorist means to fight for freedom, but if they commit serious acts of violence against innocent people, they are using terrorist tactics. It is their means and not their ends that determine whether they are terrorists or not. For this reason, being a freedom fighter and being a terrorist are not mutually exclusive. Since someone can use terrorist means to achieve the goal of freedom, calling someone a freedom fighter does not show that the terrorist label does not apply to them as well.

Although the slogan rests on a confusion about goals and means, it nonetheless expresses a valid protest against inconsistent and hypocritical criticisms of terrorism. The slogan is a complaint about the fact that critics only brand people whom they oppose with the "terrorist" label; when people whom the critics support commit the very same kinds of acts, they are called "freedom fighters" or some other honorific name.

It is clear that no one can make morally credible judgments of terrorist acts if they use language and evaluations in this way. The definition I have given requires that we apply the word "terrorism" to all acts that have certain features. If they have these features, then they are acts of terrorism. It does not matter whether they are done by friends or foes, by government officials or nongovernmental groups, for lofty goals or for evil ones. Impartiality in labeling must be matched by impartiality in moral judgments. Anyone who is genuinely against terrorist acts must be against them no matter who commits them or what their goals and purposes might be. Consistency in both labeling and judging is the first prerequisite for moral credibility.

4. FURTHER CONDITIONS FOR MORAL CREDIBILITY

Consistency, however, is not enough to sustain the view that terrorism is always wrong. The moral principles that people use must be true, or at least extremely plausible, as well as strong enough to support a negative judgment of all terrorist acts. The best candidate for this role is a rigorous form of the principle of noncombatant immunity, one that prohibits all intentional attacks on civilians and is highly restrictive in permitting acts that injure or kill civilians as collateral damage. Though some collateral damage killings may be justified, many show the same kind of callous disregard for human life that is exhibited by terrorism.[5]

A credible, antiterrorist morality also requires the acknowledgment that terrorist acts have been carried out by governments and officials who are generally regarded as respectable. Examples of such acts include the Allied conventional bombings of German and Japanese cities in World War II and the atomic bombings of Hiroshima and Nagasaki. Their explicit purpose was to attack civilians so as to destroy the morale of the people and make their leaders surrender.[6]

These historical acknowledgments are important for moral credibility. They also deepen our understanding of terrorism by helping us understand the strong temptations to violate noncombatant immunity during stressful times of war and conflict. There is a tendency to think that terrorism is only committed by barbaric or inherently evil people. History shows that when enough is at stake and attacking civilians appears to be an effective means of achieving victory, terrorism has proved hard to resist, both by people we view as evil and barbaric and by others who are respected in our society.[7]

5. FOUR VERSIONS OF THE ETHICS OF WAR AND THEIR IMPLICATIONS FOR TERRORISM

Terrorism has been hard to resist in theory as well as practice. To show this, I will explain how four prominent theories of the ethics of war permit terrorist acts or their moral equivalents. The views I will discuss are political realism, moral commonsense, the theory of Michael Walzer, and traditional just war theory. Because these views approve some acts of terrorism, people holding any of them cannot make morally credible condemnations of all terrorist acts. They face a dilemma. If they want to condemn all terrorism in a credible way, they must reject all of these views. Or, if they want to hold one of these views, they must reject the idea that terrorist acts are always wrong.[8]

5.1 *Political Realism*

Political realism has been influential in much thinking about war and foreign policy. Although realist thinkers are often ambiguous, their primary point is often taken to be that the conduct of war and international relations should be determined by a nation's interests rather than by morality.[9] It is useful to distinguish an "amoral" version of realism from a "moralized" version. The amoral version completely rejects the application of moral principles to war and international affairs. It seems to be asserted in George Kennan's statement, "there are no internationally accepted standards of morality to which the U.S. government could appeal if it wished to act in the name of moral principles."[10] The moralized version says that political leaders have only one moral duty: to promote the interests of their own nation or group. Kennan asserts this view when he writes: "Government is an agent, not a principle. Its primary obligation is to the interests of the national society it represents, not to the moral impulses that individual elements of that society may experience."[11]

In practice, both views lead to the same actions. Both versions express a *realpolitik* perspective that opposes the application of universal moral judgments; both affirm that the national interest is the basic value that applies to war and international relations; both reject any direct concern for the citizens of other countries or opponents in war.

Since both forms of realism endorse a version of the slogan "all's fair in love and war," realists have no moral basis for condemning terrorism. If terrorist attacks benefit a nation or group, that group will have good political realist reasons for engaging in them. The principle of noncombatant immunity, since it forbids attacks on enemy civilians, has no force as a constraint for realists except when respecting it happens to advance the interests of the nation itself. Since direct concern for enemy noncombatants is inappropriate, it follows that if the national interest can be promoted by terrorist tactics or indiscriminate collateral damage attacks, then these tactics are permissible.

If realism is adopted as a perspective for one's own nation or group, then others cannot credibly be condemned for adopting the same perspective. Though often espoused by respectable thinkers and by political leaders, realism's inability to support any condemnations of terrorism is an embarrassment in our post-9/11 world. No one will take moral denunciations of terrorism seriously when they emerge from people who espouse realism and make the national interest their supreme goal.

5.2 Commonsense Morality

By commonsense morality, I mean the set of moral beliefs on which there is a fairly stable, widespread consensus. In *Just and Unjust Wars*, Michael Walzer claims that commonsense morality contains "a comprehensive view of war as a human activity and a more or less systematic moral doctrine"; in later works, he suggests that we can resolve moral problems by interpreting the "shared understandings" that prevail in a society.[12] I believe that the shared views that make up the commonsense ethic of war lack this sort of unity. The commonsense ethic of war, I believe, is a hodge podge of deeply conflicting beliefs, ideals, and principles. Although one strand of commonsense morality is humanitarian and supports efforts to avoid civilian deaths in wartime, this concern for enemy civilians often gives way to a more nationalist perspective, especially during wartime. When the chips are down, if attacks that produce civilian casualties are necessary for victory or significantly diminish casualties to one's own soldiers, then such attacks and the civilian damages they produce will generally be seen as morally acceptable by the public.

This nationalist strand of moral common sense is reflected in a prominent defense of the 1945 atomic bombings of Japan by Henry Stimson, Secretary of War under Roosevelt and Truman. Writing in 1947, Stimson explained his decision to support these attacks as follows:

> My chief purpose was to end the war in victory with the least possible cost in the lives of the men in the armies which I had helped to raise.... I believe that no man, in our position and subject to our responsibilities, holding in his hands a weapon of such possibilities for accomplishing this purpose and saving those lives, could have failed to use it and afterwards looked his countrymen in the face.[13]

Stimson's statement is illuminating in several ways: first, it explicitly attempts to justify a massive attack on civilians by appealing to the goals of attaining victory and minimizing American military casualties; second, it shows that Stimson saw it as his moral duty to authorize the attacks; finally, it expresses his belief that not using these weapons would have been strongly condemned by the American people.

Stimson's interpretation of the commonsense ethic of war seems to have been correct. His defense was widely accepted and remains widely accepted now, even though the atomic bombings were direct attacks on cities and produced hundreds of thousands of civilian casualties. Harry Truman, who authorized the bombings and remains a much admired President, said that he never lost a night's sleep over the bombings and felt great contempt for the physicist Robert J. Oppenheimer because Oppenheimer felt guilt about his role in developing the atomic bomb.

Yet, according to the definition I gave earlier, the atomic bombings were acts of terrorism – direct attacks on civilians for the sake of achieving a political goal (the defeat of Japan). Because commonsense morality approves these acts, it accepts the view that terrorist attacks are justified under some circumstances and thus fails to provide a sound basis for condemning all acts of terrorism.

5.3   Walzer's Theory

Michael Walzer's *Just and Unjust Wars* is widely regarded as a modern classic on the ethics of war. One of Walzer's main aims in the book is to defend the central place of the principle of noncombatant immunity in the ethics of war. According to him, the most basic ethical requirement in the fighting of war is that while military personnel are permissible targets of attack, civilians may not be attacked. Walzer grounds this prohibition in a view about human rights. "A legitimate act of war," he writes,

> is one that does not violate the rights of the people against whom it is directed. . . . [N]o one can be threatened with war or warred against, unless through some act of his own he has surrendered or lost his rights. This fundamental principle underlies and shapes the judgments we make of wartime conduct.[14]

While soldiers have forfeited their immunity to attack, civilians have not and thus may not be attacked. Appealing to this principle, Walzer supports many demanding restrictions on how wars may be fought and argues that soldiers must strive to avoid unintended harm to civilians, even when this requires them to increase risks to themselves.[15] Moreover, he harshly criticizes most of the Allied bombings of German and Japanese cities during World War II.[16]

Nonetheless, because Walzer believes that the British bombings of German cities early in World War II were justified, he argues that the principle of noncombatant immunity is not always binding on parties to a war. In the kind of circumstance that he calls a "supreme emergency," Walzer claims that the principle of noncombatant immunity no longer applies.[17] While noncombatant immunity generally applies in wars fought against ordinary enemies, it gave way in this case, he claims, because of the extraordinary nature of the threat posed by Nazi Germany. He writes:

> Nazism was an ultimate threat to everything decent in our lives, an ideology and a practice of domination so murderous, so degrading even to those who might survive, that the consequences of its final victory were literally beyond calculation, immeasurably awful. . . . Here was a threat to human values so radical that its imminence would surely constitute a supreme emergency.[18]

According to Walzer, if one's enemy is evil enough, if the threat it poses is imminent, and if there are no other effective means of military resistance against that enemy, then direct attacks on civilians are permissible. While noncombatant immunity holds in ordinary warfare, in a supreme emergency, he writes, "one might well be required to override the rights of innocent people and shatter the war convention."[19]

Although Walzer categorically condemns terrorism in his book and in later writings, the supreme emergency permits terrorist attacks if they occur in response to a supreme emergency. His condemnation of all terrorism is inconsistent with his allowing exceptions for supreme emergencies. If he allows these exceptions, then he must accept at least the possibility of justified terrorism.[20]

More fundamentally, the supreme emergency exception severely weakens the principle of noncombatant immunity. Because the concept of "supreme emergency" is vague, it sets no clear boundary to demarcate when noncombatant immunity applies and when it does not. We can see this in Walzer's own examples. While he plausibly classifies Nazism as an extraordinary threat, he does not count the threat posed by Japan as a supreme emergency. Japan, he says, "never posed such a threat to peace and freedom as the Nazis had."[21] In a criticism of Walzer, Tony Coady's response is "Tell that to the Chinese!" and, he adds,

> In the Japanese invasion of China in the 1930s it is soberly estimated that more than 300,000 Chinese civilians were massacred in Nanking alone in a racist rampage of raping, beheading, and bayoneting that lasted six weeks.[22]

The Japanese killed hundreds of thousands of Chinese and were notorious for their brutal treatment of prisoners of war. Yet Walzer does not see the fight against Japan as a supreme emergency. Why not? Surely, this requires some explanation.

Coady's sharply critical response reveals both the vagueness of the term and the resulting arbitrariness and subjectivity of its application. While Walzer wants to use the concept of a supreme emergency to create a narrow set of exceptions to noncombatant immunity, he lacks clear criteria for distinguishing ordinary and extraordinary threats. Without such criteria, Walzer's distinction between ordinary and supreme emergencies cannot do the work of safeguarding noncombatant immunity. Supreme emergencies end up being emergencies that people feel are supreme, and given the understandable tendency of people to see all serious threats to themselves or people they identify with as very great, applications of the supreme emergency exception are likely to be more extensive than Walzer intended. As a result, his theory as a whole no longer supports a strong constraint on attacks against civilians. Rather, it provides the language for justifying departures from the constraints of noncombatant immunity.

Recent terrorists – most prominently members of al-Qaeda and Palestinians – appear to believe that their highest political and religious values cannot be defended without resorting to the killing of innocent people.[23] They probably see their situation as a supreme emergency, even if others do not. Closer to home, think of the sense of emergency in the

United States since the September 11 attacks. It has been used to justify detention without trial, torture of prisoners, preventive war, and bombings in Afghanistan and Iraq that have killed many civilians. American leaders have defended these actions on the grounds that our way of life is jeopardized by the threat of terrorists. Whenever large numbers of people are killed or a way of life is threatened, people may well think they are in an emergency that justifies departures from both noncombatant immunity and other important rules of civility.[24]

For these reasons, the "supreme emergency" exception severely weakens the status of noncombatant immunity and undermines Walzer's criticisms of terrorism. At a minimum, Walzer's view justifies terrorist acts in very extreme circumstances. More broadly, because those circumstances are so vaguely defined, Walzer's overall theory undermines the strong version of noncombatant immunity that he tried to defend. The bottom line is that Walzer's view permits violations of noncombatant immunity and leaves open the possibility of justified terrorist acts.

5.4 Traditional Just War Theory

Traditional just war theory appears to be in a strong position to support credible condemnations of terrorist acts because one of its central components, the principle of discrimination, explicitly prohibits direct attacks on civilians. In their 1983 restatement of just war theory, the National Council of Catholic Bishops affirmed the principle of discrimination in these words:

[T]he lives of innocent persons may never be taken directly, regardless of the purpose alleged for doing so. . . . Just response to aggression must be discriminate; it must be directed against unjust aggressors, not against innocent people caught up in a war not of their making.[25]

A naive reading of this statement might take it to forbid any actions that kill innocent people. Read in that way, however, the principle of discrimination might forbid not only terrorism but any form of modern warfare. The reason is that the power of modern weapons makes it virtually certain that civilians will be killed in any modern war. If this is true, then one possibility is that modern warfare cannot be morally justified.[26] While this is the conclusion reached by antiwar pacifists, just war theorists reject a sweeping rejection of war. Instead, they interpret the principle of discrimination to permit some acts that kill innocent people.

This more permissive view makes use of the "principle of double effect," which gives great weight to the distinction between the intended results of actions and their unintended side effects. "Double effect" evaluates actions based on their intended results only. This idea is signaled in the Bishops' statement by the word "directly"; the principle of discrimination is understood to forbid the taking of innocent lives "directly" (i.e., intentionally) but not "indirectly" (i.e., unintentionally).

The principle of double effect tells us that morality permits war so long as innocent people are not intentionally killed or injured. It permits an attack on a military target if, as a side effect, it will kill civilians whom one has no intention or desire to harm. It prohibits only those attacks that deliberately aim to kill innocent people.[27] Thus, attacks that cause civilian deaths and injuries as collateral damage may be justified or at least excusable. Both traditional just war theory and commonsense morality are rather permissive about these unintended deaths and generally accept expressions of regret as a sufficient response to them.

I want to show that the principle of double effect undermines just war theory as a credible basis for condemning all terrorist acts. It does this because it permits actions that are either terrorist acts or are morally equivalent to them. Anyone who wants to make credible criticisms of terrorism must reject both the principle of double effect and the watered-down version of noncombatant immunity that it gives rise to.

To see why, consider first the September 11 attacks, which killed about 3000 civilians. While the attackers probably intended these deaths, what would be the implications if they had not? Suppose the September 11 attackers' had only intended to damage or destroy the World Trade Center and the Pentagon buildings. Suppose that they knew that innocent people would be killed but that these deaths were not part of their goal. In this imagined scenario, these deaths would have been "collateral damage" – the unintended but foreseen effects of an attack.

The key point here is that virtually no one would view the September 11 attacks as less wrong if they fit this description. If tapes of Osama bin Laden had shown him saying that he had only wanted to attack the buildings and regretted the collateral damage deaths of innocent people, I very much doubt that this would diminish our condemnation of these attacks. Even if innocent people had not been the intended targets, the attacks would have shown such a high degree of callous disregard for the lives of innocent people that we would still judge them to be morally indefensible. Nonetheless, these imaginary attacks appear to comply with the principle of double effect and its prohibition of intentionally killing civilians.[28] This shows that the principle of double effect is too weak to condemn acts that are morally indistinguishable from terrorism. It rules out intended killings but not reckless or negligent acts that people commit even though it is clear that what they are doing seriously endangers people.[29] By failing to distinguish different kinds of unintended consequences, the principle of double effect leads to an overly permissive view of the duty to discriminate. As a result, it undermines protection of innocent human life in wartime.

Indiscriminate killings of civilians are quite common, even in wars that many consider to be justified. Often, they result from the use of indiscriminate weapons and tactics like cluster bombs, land mines, and high-altitude bombing. Thousands of Afghans and Iraqis have been killed in the "war on terrorism" fought by the United States since 9/11.[30] In Iraq, the US military claims that it does not even count civilian casualties, thus reinforcing the message that civilian lives do not count. These killings make a mockery of our condemnations of terrorism and our expressed commitment to the value of innocent human life.[31] Since the traditional just war theory's principle of discrimination permits these collateral damage killings, it, too, fails to provide a strong basis for condemning terrorism.

6. TOWARD A CREDIBLE ETHIC OF WAR

If we are both to explain why terrorism is wrong and make morally credible criticisms of terrorist acts, we need an ethic of war that provides a principled condemnation of both intentional attacks on civilians and of many collateral damage killings that are generally accepted as regrettable but necessary. The principle of discrimination contained in traditional just war theory fails to distinguish different kinds of collateral damage killings, some of which are permissible and others not.

Many collateral damage killings are wrong for the same reasons that terrorism is wrong. They show a callous indifference to human life. This is evident in cases where civilian deaths are both foreseeable and avoidable. Yet in other cases, collateral damage killings and injuries can be reasonably judged to be permissible or excusable. If, for example, these deaths and injuries are not foreseeable or if they occur in spite of strenuous efforts to avoid them, then the attacks may be legitimate. Walzer calls the principle that requires serious efforts to avoid civilian casualties the principle of "double intention"; I call it the "bend over backwards" principle to suggest more vividly the idea that serious efforts must be made to avoid harming civilians.[32] It requires that combatants try to foresee whether civilian casualties will result from an attack, and, when they are likely, to look for other means of fighting that avoid civilian damage as much as possible. This may require avoiding weapons such as cluster bombs and land mines and using ground troops or low flying planes rather than high-altitude bombing that makes discriminating between military and civilian targets difficult or impossible.

A country that implemented rules of this sort would be in a better position to condemn terrorist attacks on innocent civilians. As we all know, practicing what we preach enhances moral credibility while failure to live by the principles we apply to others undermines it. What I have tried to show here is that it is not merely the hypocrisy of public officials that undermines condemnations of terrorism. Rather it is the lack of a well articulated ethic of war that shows due regard for the value of human life. The standard theories in this area fail to do this.

7. CONCLUSION

If we want to condemn terrorism in a morally credible way, this requires several things: (1) greater consistency in the use of the term "terrorism," (2) consistent, impartial application of moral principles to acts of political violence, (3) an absolute ban on targeting civilians, (4) and a restrictive approach to collateral damage killings and injuries.

In addition, it requires rejecting central features of several prominent views in the ethics of war. Unlike realism, a credible view must make moral judgments based on factors other than the national interest. Unlike moral common sense, it must prohibit attacks on civilians even when such attacks will lead to victory and minimize military losses on one's own side. Unlike Walzer's view, it must not permit a supreme emergency exception to noncombatant immunity. And, unlike traditional just war theory, it must not permit collateral damage deaths and injuries simply because they are not intended.

Terrorist acts are, in my view, grave evils. But I hope to have shown that it is not enough simply to say or think this. Our views only have credibility when they are part of a consistent set of principles and beliefs. Unfortunately, many people who categorically condemn terrorism have an overall ethic of war that permits some terrorist acts. This is unfortunate for many reasons. But the most important reason is that when moral judgments are seen as hypocritical and self-serving, we lose the power of moral ideals to help us communicate and cooperate across serious disagreements and group boundaries. The undermining of moral ideas makes it even harder to create the conditions for a shared and civilized form of human life.

NOTES

1. For Bush's remarks, see "'We're going to get Justice'," *Boston Globe*, 9/26/01, A8.
2. Connor Cruise O'Brien, "Liberty and Terrorism," *International Security* 2 (1977), 56–57.

3. I discuss this definition in "Prerequisites for Morally Credible Condemnations of Terrorism," in William Crotty (ed.), *The Politics of Terror: The U.S. Response to 9/11* (Boston, MA: Northeastern University Press, 2004), pp. 3–34. For similar definitions, see C. A. J. (Tony) Coady, "Defining Terrorism" and Igor Primoratz, "What is Terrorism?", both in Igor Primoratz, ed., *Terrorism: The Philosophical Issues* (Palgrave Macmillan, 2004). For discussions of the definition issue by social scientists, see Bruce Hoffman, *Inside Terrorism* (New York: Columbia University Press, 1998), Chap. 1; and Alex P. Schmid and Albert J. Longman, *Political Terrorism* (New Brunswick, NJ: Transaction Books, 2005), 1–38.
4. On terrorism and punishment, see Walter Sinnott-Armstrong, "On Primoratz's Definition of Terrorism," *Journal of Applied Philosophy*, 8 (1991), 115–120.
5. David Rodin includes certain collateral damage killings and injuries within the definition of terrorism in "Terrorism Without Intention," *Ethics*, 114 (2004), 752–771.
6. On the World War II bombings, see C. A. J. Coady, "Terrorism, Morality, and Supreme Emergency" and Stephen A. Garrett, "Terror Bombing of German Cities in World War II," both in Primoratz, *Terrorism*, and Ronald Schaffer, *Wings of Judgment: American Bombing in World War II* (Oxford, 1985).
7. On the history of attacks on civilians, see Caleb Carr, *The Lessons of Terror* (New York: Random House, 2002).
8. I omit utilitarianism because it is so widely assumed that utilitarianism permits terrorist acts when their good effects outweigh their harms. For a utilitarian defense of terrorism, see Burleigh T. Wilkins, *Terrorism and Collective Responsibility* (Routledge, 1992). Douglas Lackey gives a utilitarian argument against noncombatant immunity in *The Ethics of War and Peace* (Englewood Cliffs, NJ: Prentice-Hall, 1989), 64–65.
9. For a useful analysis of realism, see Jack Donnelly, "Twentieth-Century Realism," in T. Nardin and D. Mapel, eds., *Traditions of International Ethics* Cambridge: (Cambridge University Press, 1992), 85–111.
10. George Kennan, "Morality and Foreign Policy," *Foreign Affairs*, 64 (Winter, 1985/86), reprinted in *Morality and Foreign Policy* (US Institute of Peace, 1991), 61.
11. Kennan, "Morality and Foreign Policy," 60.
12. Michael Walzer, *Just and Unjust Wars* (New York: Basic Books, 1977), xiii. The phrase "shared understandings" appears in Walzer's *Spheres of Justice* (New York: Basic Books, 1983); Walzer defends his interpretive methodology in *Interpretation and Social Criticism* (Cambridge, MA: Harvard University Press, 1987).
13. Henry Stimson, "The Decision to Use the Atomic Bomb," *Harper's Magazine* 194 (February, 1947), 106–107. Quoted in Schaffer, *Wings of Judgment*, 169.
14. Walzer, *Just and Unjust Wars*, 135.
15. Walzer, *Just and Unjust Wars*, 151–156.
16. Walzer, *Just and Unjust Wars*, 263–268.
17. Walzer, *Just and Unjust Wars*, 251–262.
18. Walzer, *Just and Unjust Wars*, 253.
19. Walzer, *Just and Unjust Wars*, 259.
20. Walzer concedes the possibility of justifiable terrorism in a parenthetical addition to an earlier essay in *Arguing About War* (New Haven, CT: Yale University Press, 2004), p. 54. See also "Emergency Ethics" in the same volume, pp. 33–50. For further discussion of Walzer's views, see my "Terrorism, Supreme Emergency, and Noncombatant Immunity: A Critique of Michael Walzer's Ethics of War," *Iyyun: The Jerusalem Philosophical Quarterly* 55 (January 2006), 3–25.

21. Walzer, *Just and Unjust Wars*, 263.
22. C. A. J. (Tony) Coady, "Terrorism, Just War and Supreme Emergency," in T. Coady and M. O'Keefe (eds), *Terrorism and Justice* (University of Melbourne, 2002), 17. On the Japanese treatment of the Chinese, Cody cites Iris Chang, *The Rape of Nanking: The Forgotten Holocaust of World War II* (Penguin, 1998), 4–6. See also, Coady's "Terrorism, Morality, and Supreme Emergency," *Ethics* 114 (2004), 772–789.
23. On the motivations for the 9/11 attack, see Michael Scott Doran, "Somebody Else's Civil War: Ideology, Rage, and the Assault on America," in J. Hoge, Jr. and G. Rose (eds), *How Did This Happen?* (Public Affairs, 2001), 31–52.
24. This type of reasoning appears in James Sterba, "Terrorism and International Justice," in James Sterba, ed., *Terrorism and International Justice* (Oxford, 2003), pp. 206–228.; and in Robert Young, "Political Terrorism as a Weapon of the Politically Powerless" and Uwe Steinhoff, "How Can Terrorism Be Justified?", both in Primoratz, *Terrorism*.
25. National Conference of Catholic Bishops, *The Challenge of Peace* (US Catholic Conference, 1983), Sect. 104, p. 33.
26. Robert Holmes argues that modern warfare cannot be just in *On War and Morality* (Princeton, NJ: Princeton University Press, 1989).
27. The principle of double effect often includes other conditions such as proportionality, but I find it best to keep these criteria separate. For an account that criticizes readings like mine as oversimplifications, see A. J. Coates, *The Ethics of War* (Manchester University Press, 1997), 239–246. For discussions of double effect, see P. A. Woodward (ed.), *The Doctrine of Double Effect* (Notre Dame, 2001).
28. Timothy McVeigh apparently sought to destroy the federal building in Oklahoma City and saw the hundreds of victims as "collateral damage." We do not regard this as justifying or excusing his act.
29. On collateral damage, see David Rodin, "Terrorism Without Intention," pp. 752–771; as well as other works cited in n. 33.
30. On civilian casualties in Iraq, see Peter Ford, "Surveys pointing to high civilian death toll in Iraq," *The Christian Science Monitor*, May 22, 2003; Brad Knickerbocker, "Who counts the civilian casualties?," T*he Christian Science Monitor* March 31, 2004; and Elisabeth Rosenthal, "Study Puts Iraqi Deaths of Civilians at 100,000," *International Herald Tribune*, October 29, 2004. On Afghanistan, see http://www.cursor.org/stories/civilian_deaths.htm for Marc W. Herold, "A Dossier on Civilian Victims of United States' Aerial Bombing of Afghanistan: A Comprehensive Accounting." Herold attributes the over 3000 civilian casualties to "the apparent willingness of U.S. military strategists to fire missiles into and drop bombs upon, heavily populated areas of Afghanistan."
31. Peter Singer documents the hypocrisy of claims made by President George W. Bush about the ethics of killing in *The President of Good and Evil: The Ethics of George W. Bush* (Dutton, 2004), Chap. 3, especially pp. 49–58.
32. On "double intention," see Walzer, *Just and Unjust Wars*, p. 155. For the "bend over backwards" principle, see my "Is the War on Terrorism a Defense of Civilization," *Concerned Philosophers for Peace Newsletter*, 22 (Spring/Fall, 2002), 19–27; and my "Is Terrorism Ever Morally Permissible? An Inquiry into the Right to Life," in M. Sellers and D. Reidy (eds.), *Universal Human Rights: Moral Order in a Divided World* (Lanham, MD: Rowman & Littlefield, 2005).

ALISTAIR M. MACLEOD

THE WAR AGAINST TERRORISM AND THE "WAR" AGAINST TERRORISM

Whether the appropriate response to a terrorist attack is to declare (literal) war on terrorism or to conduct a (metaphorical) "war" against terrorism – or both – depends in large measure on the nature of the terrorist threat. The question is potentially controversial because views can differ dramatically both about the sources of the kinds of terrorism that pose a threat and about the kinds of strategy that may be called for to neutralize the threat. Despite such differences, however, it ought to be a matter of agreement that ideally the grand objective to be served both by military and by nonmilitary strategies for combating terrorism is the prevention of terrorism. Advocates of a (literal) war against terrorism, no less than those who stress the need for a (metaphorical) "war" against terrorism, would be in no position to claim victory in the fight against terrorism if they had to concede, at the end of the day, that, despite their best efforts to anticipate or respond to particular terrorist attacks, they had been unable to reduce to reasonably manageable proportions the more serious forms of the long-term threat of terrorism. It may of course be unrealistic to hope that the threat can be wholly eliminated. Nevertheless, not even to aim at the prevention of terrorism is to be indefensibly unambitious.

But if the grander objective – prevention of terrorism; elimination of the terrorist threat – is to be kept alive, importance obviously attaches to serious efforts to understand the sources of terrorism. Defensible strategies both in the war against terrorism and in the "war" against terrorism must be informed by the best available information about the causes of terrorism. If this is to be achieved, it is important not only for the search for the best explanations to take fully seriously the myriad forms terrorism either does or could assume but also for recognition to be given to the potentially very diverse conditions that can facilitate the emergence (and persistence) of terrorism.

To ask how the threat of terrorism is to be combated defensibly and effectively (whether by military or by nonmilitary means, or by both) – that is, to ask how defensible and effective strategies are to be identified for the prevention of terrorism – is different from asking (merely) about what the response ought to be to particular acts of terrorism. It is different, in part, because the latter question arises only in the wake of terrorist attacks, whereas it is possible to raise the former question even when no terrorist attack has yet taken place. But even when the asking of the question about strategies for the prevention of terrorism is triggered by the fact that a terrorist attack has already occurred, it is one thing to ask what response would be appropriate while assuming that the preferred response will be one that contributes to the prevention of terrorism and another thing to ask about the appropriate response without making this assumption. The two questions are different because asking how future terrorist attacks are to be prevented need not be what is emphasized by those who are trying to decide how to respond to a particular terrorist attack. Instead, the emphasis may simply be on ensuring that there is a retaliatory strike at the terrorists. Even if this kind of retaliatory response could be justified on strictly retributive grounds – and it is plausible to think that a measured retributive response is bound to be even more difficult to achieve in this kind of context than it is when penalties are being meted out in a court of law – to assign too much importance to trying to ensure that the perpetrators of terrorist acts get what they deserve is to divert attention from a more urgent task, the task of trying to reduce the threat of terrorism. Of course those whose priority it is to retaliate may suppose that a primarily retributive response is also an effective way of deterring further attacks. However, this further claim is subject to challenge.[1] Not only is there a real possibility that focusing on retaliation will mean that potentially more effective preventive strategies are overlooked, but the retaliatory strategy may itself increase the risk of further terrorist attacks: a fundamentally retaliatory response often generates a spiraling cycle of violence that merely heightens, instead of diminishing, the threat of terrorism. And if, as is often the case, the retaliatory response is, at least in part, wrongly targeted – with those who are not themselves terrorists (or terrorist supporters) being among the principal victims of the response – the retaliatory response may have to be characterized both as counterproductive from the standpoint of prevention of terrorism and as itself morally indefensible.

A merely (or principally) retaliatory response to a terrorist attack is thus perilous. Even if the retaliation could be represented, fairly, as the sort of measured and well-targeted response against the perpetrators of the terrorist act that they might be said to deserve – an extremely demanding condition (in part, because of its obscurity) – the fit may in any case be poor between such a response and one that is carefully calculated to prevent the recurrence of such acts. When decision-makers are trying to respond in a way that will prevent terrorist acts in the future, not only will they find that the strategies they must consider are not limited to those that might be thought to give the terrorists what they deserve; they may also find that maximally effective preventive strategies are actually in conflict with those suggested by retributive considerations.

1. THE WAR AGAINST TERRORISM AND THE TARGETING PROBLEM

Whatever the putative rationale for going after the perpetrators of terrorist acts – retribution, deterrence, prevention, or some combination of these – if going after them is thought to require resort to war, one of the trickiest questions that has to be faced (from the standpoint of identifying both effective and morally defensible strategies) has to do with selecting the target for military action. It is a notorious feature of many terrorist attacks that little may be known, initially certainly and often in the long run too, about both the precise identity and the precise whereabouts of the perpetrators. And even when these problems are thought to be resolvable, targeting the terrorists without also inflicting grievous harm on nonterrorists in the general vicinity can be expected to present a formidable challenge. Wrongly targeted military action is obviously open to objection both on effectiveness and on moral grounds: on effectiveness grounds, because (and so far as) the actual perpetrators (and their supporters) survive the attack; on moral grounds, because the right uninvolved third parties have not to be gratuitously harmed is being breached. The problem here is a rather special case of the problem that is apt to arise in any war when, in the course of a military campaign, the lives of noncombatants are either taken or seriously disrupted. What makes the problem special, in a sense, is that, when military action is taken against terrorists whose identity and whereabouts are largely unknown, the risk of adverse impact on persons other than the terrorists themselves may be much greater than it is in more conventional wars.

2. MILITARY VS. NONMILITARY STRATEGIES FOR THE PREVENTION OF TERRORISM

Preventive military action against terrorism is obviously only one possible means of preventing terrorism. What the strategies are that need to be at least considered in connection with this broader question – the question how terrorism is to be prevented – depends, equally obviously, on what the best explanations are (1) for the emergence of terrorism and

(2) for the successful execution of terrorist campaigns. The effort to combat terrorism would collapse into the adoption of a military strategy for the prevention of terrorism – a strategy that involves, let it be supposed, the launching of preventive military strikes against terrorism – only if, given the best explanations of these two kinds, it turned out (surprisingly) that resort to military action against terrorists and their supporters is either the only or the most effective way, in all situations in which the threat of terrorism has to be coped with, of preventing terrorism.

This last supposition, however, seems obviously false – if only because the use of military force against terrorism is never seen as excluding (more or less simultaneous – and parallel) employment of nonmilitary strategies. If, for example, there are possible ways of putting economic pressure on terrorists and their backers, not even the most enthusiastic advocate of military action against them would contemplate vetoing such economic strategies.

Once it is noted that (a variety of) nonmilitary strategies for dealing with terrorists and the threat they pose are usefully complementary to strictly military strategies, the possibility has to be reckoned with that some of these nonmilitary strategies may sometimes be preferable to strictly military strategies. They may be preferable for a number of reasons. For example, they may be preferable because, in given historical circumstances, they are likely to be more effective: locating the terrorists with a view to using military force against them may be too difficult, or military action even when feasible may contribute indirectly to the strengthening of terrorist groups by making it easier for them to find new recruits. Again, nonmilitary strategies may be preferable because they would be less damaging not only to the nonterrorist members of targeted societies but also to those who would otherwise be taking military action against terrorists. And the case for concentrating on nonmilitary strategies becomes particularly compelling when – as may very well prove to be the case – conventional military responses have to be regarded not only as too ineffective or too costly, but also as morally problematic. Why morally problematic? Partly because, once preventive military strikes are distinguished – as arguably they must be – from military action for purely defensive purposes, their moral permissibility is very difficult to establish.[2] Partly also because, even if preventive military action against terrorism could in principle be exempted from an otherwise fairly general moral objection to preventive war, it may be difficult or impossible, under most of the conditions that are likely in practice to obtain, for such preventive military strategies to be resorted to without serious breaches of the requirements of *jus in bello*. On any plausible version of this branch of just war theory, those against whom military action is to be taken must be targeted without the infliction of significant damage on civilian populations. This condition is particularly difficult to satisfy when the target is an elusive enemy. Yet notoriously, one of the standard features of any (literal) war against terrorism is that terrorists and their supporters are often horrendously difficult to locate and isolate.

3. WAGING WAR AGAINST THE STATE SPONSORS OF TERRORISM

It may be argued, however, that the targeting problem has a ready solution when states can be identified that "sponsor" terrorists. Military action against terrorists and their supporters can then take the form of waging war against the sponsoring states. And certainly if – though it is a big "if" – the appropriate connections can be established between the states against which military action is taken and the terrorists they are allegedly "sponsoring", the war against terrorism raises issues that present no *special* difficulty for the requirements of *jus in bello* in just war theory. Although fighting terrorism is what provides the rationale for resort to war in such cases, the war that is actually waged must be viewed through much the same (*jus in bello*) lens as other wars, wars not triggered by the attempt to combat the threat of terrorism. However, even if all this is conceded, establishing that the targeted state can correctly be viewed as "sponsoring" terrorists is often a difficult task, partly because of differences of view about what ought to be allowed to count as "sponsorship" in this context, and partly because, in any case, the crucial evidence of sponsorship of the requisite sort(s) may be elusive. The war against Afghanistan after 9/11 may have to be viewed as something of a special case in this connection, partly because al-Qaeda had an ascertainable and geographically determinable base of operations within Afghanistan, partly because of the closeness of its ties to the Taliban regime, and partly because of the regime's determination to continue to offer it protection even after its role in the 9/11 terrorist attack on New York had been uncovered.

However, when it comes to cases, in a worldwide effort to combat terrorism, where either (1) the identity of the terrorists who pose a threat is very difficult to establish or (2) their connections with readily identifiable states cannot be confidently described in ways that make it possible for these states to be targeted as "sponsors" of the terrorists – the problem of targeting a military response to the threat of terrorism may admit of no such straightforward solution. As David Luban points out,[3] states that sponsor terrorists must be distinguished both from states that "tolerate" terrorists and from states that "negligently fail to repress terrorists." Once these distinctions are drawn, it becomes highly questionable whether a military response to the threat of terrorism can defensibly take the form of waging war against the states in which terrorists happen to have a base of operations.[4]

But whatever the reasons in detail are for its being difficult – indeed highly problematic – to mount a defensible military response to the threat of terrorism by waging war against the states in which terrorist organizations have, in some sense, a base of operations, it is clear that the existence of such reasons is a powerful argument for giving serious consideration to the nonmilitary strategies that might profitably be pursued in the effort to combat the threat of terrorism. The argument, in a nutshell, is this. If (and so far as) strictly military strategies in the war against terrorism prove to be unavailable – whether because the preventive use of force even against terrorists is morally problematic or because military targets cannot be identified that would permit military action against terrorists to be appropriately and effectively undertaken – then the search for nonmilitary strategies assumes correspondingly greater urgency and importance.

4. THE "ROOT CAUSES" OF TERRORISM AND THE "WAR" AGAINST TERRORISM

Just as it is obviously a mistake to suppose that combating terrorism is always (or only) a matter of devising military strategies for the prosecution of a war (a war in the literal sense of "war") against terrorism, so too it is a mistake, when the broader question is being tackled – namely, the question how to combat terrorism (how to conduct an effective and morally defensible war against terrorism even when "war" has to be given a merely metaphorical reading) – for too narrow a range of possible strategies to be canvassed. However, a crucial condition of getting clear about the full range of conceivably appropriate nonmilitary strategies for combating the terrorist threat is careful attention to the best explanations that can be developed for the emergence and persistence of terrorism as a complex sociopolitical phenomenon. Unless a rationally grounded account can be arrived at about the factors that generate the terrorist threat in the many forms it can assume, policymakers may be condemned to trying to respond to the threat not only in ways that prove to be ineffective or inappropriate but also in ways that fail to so much as consider options that a better understanding of the "root causes" of terrorism might point to. This type of failure is a familiar feature of two other "wars" that have been declared, and that are currently underway, in the United States. In the so-called "war" against crime as well as in the so-called "war" against drugs – in both of which it is (overwhelmingly) nonmilitary strategies of various sorts that need to be pursued – the identification of potentially fruitful strategies has been hobbled by failure (or refusal) to undertake suitably comprehensive inquiries into the "root-causes" of criminal behavior in the one case and of drug use in the other.[5]

When the "root causes" of the threat of terrorism are being explored in a suitably unprejudiced and comprehensive way, several mistakes must be avoided.

(1) First, and obviously, the quest for such explanations ought not to be artificially restricted by the fear that they are designed to exonerate the perpetrators of terrorist acts and perhaps even to shift the blame for their occurrence onto the victims. For one thing, what is at stake is the discovery of the explanations for the threat of terrorism in given historical circumstances, and the question what explains the threat is sharply distinguishable from the question whether the terrorists who pose the threat are themselves pursuing strategies that are either justifiable or excusable.[6] The questions that need to be asked are *empirical* questions. They may be questions, for example, about the actual motives, beliefs, objectives, assumptions, plans, etc., of terrorists and their supporters. Or they may be questions about the attitudes towards terrorists of the populations in which they have a base of operations and in which they enjoy at least some measure of tacit and indirect support from members of the community who share their political objectives while disapproving of their methods. Or they may be questions about the social, economic, cultural, religious, and political conditions that provide fertile ground for the development of terrorist organizations and for the cultivation of the kinds of (active and passive) support they need in order to survive and prosper. All these questions can (and should) be answered without reference to such expressly normative questions as whether the attitudes, motives, actions, etc., of terrorists and their supporters are morally defensible or indefensible. And the answers to the normative questions, when they are taken on, cannot be deduced, or even in some looser way "derived", from the answers to the empirical questions.

(2) A common misconception about the role played by explanations in terms of "root causes" in the fashioning of a rational response to the

threat of terrorism is that it is sufficient to focus attention on the motives, beliefs, plans, and assumptions of the terrorists themselves or of those who provide them with explicit backing.[7] It is uncontroversial, of course, that it is important to try to command a clear view of the actual motives (beliefs, assumptions, attitudes, etc.) of perpetrators of terrorist acts – for example, of Osama bin Laden and the members of the al-Qaeda organization – and of the motives (etc.) of those who help to organize, finance, and protect the terrorist campaigns they develop. However, an adequate explanation of both the emergence and the success of terrorist groups must also take into consideration the attitudes, beliefs, and grievances of those rank-and-file members of the societies in which they have their base on whose silent and tacit support they have to rely, even when this support takes the form of little more than sympathy with the political objectives they ostensibly seek and even when this sympathy is coupled with deep misgivings (or outright disapproval) of the methods to which they resort in pursuing the objectives. If terrorism is understood in many familiar sociopolitical contexts as a form of politically motivated violence, one marked (among other things) by a commitment on the part of terrorists to the achievement of political goals through the intimidation of civilian populations, the indirect role played by popular support for some of these goals in the development and execution over time of successful terrorist campaigns ought not to be underestimated.

It is of course a mistake to suppose that this support – indirect and heavily qualified though it is – suffices to make terrorists of all the members of such tacitly supportive populations. It is clear that most of the members of such societies are not "terrorists" – on any plausible (even "elastic") understanding of what counts as terrorism – and that despite this, their reluctance to actively oppose terrorist campaigns in pursuit of objectives they endorse may be an important factor in enabling these campaigns to be sustained. It is also a mistake to think that, even if they cannot strictly be counted as "terrorists", they ought automatically to be condemned for not actively opposing terrorist organizations when they support the objectives but not the methods of these organizations. In some cases the explanation for their reluctance to dissociate themselves from merely "tacit" supporters of a terrorist campaign may be traceable to the fact that the terrorists are prepared to use terrorist techniques against their own people, securing their silent acquiescence through intimidation. Important though these cases are, they are clearly not the only cases. The attitudes of the nonterrorist members of a society towards the terrorists in their midst are often driven, not by fear, but by support for the political objectives ostensibly being pursued by terrorist organizations. When this is the case, simple condemnation of their "complicity" is inconsistent with proper recognition of the complexity of the difficult circumstances in which they find themselves. For example, it may be certain, in these circumstances, that explicit opposition to the adoption of terrorist means of achieving agreed political objectives will be powerless to bring about any change in strategy. It may also be the case – relatedly – that viable opportunities for the adoption of alternative strategies for the achievement of the objectives in question do not so much as exist. And even if the members of societies that give various forms of tacit support to terrorist organizations are in some way and to some degree morally blameworthy for their failure to dissociate themselves expressly from – or for their failure actively to oppose – the terrorist organizations in their midst, the architects of sensible antiterrorism policies in other countries have nothing to gain from refusal to obtain an accurate reading of the special nature of the contribution silent acquiescence plays in facilitating terrorism. Indeed they have a great deal to lose if they fail to see that the adoption of policies that address the underlying grievances of those who provide silent support may go a long way towards reducing the effectiveness of terrorist campaigns by cutting off this important source of support.

(3) It may be true that greater attention to a suitably comprehensive account of the conditions that facilitate the emergence and the survival of terrorist organizations will point to the need to develop counterterrorism strategies in the light of a broader range of normative questions than might otherwise be raised – questions, for example, about the assessment of the attitudes of those whose passive support for (or even whose toleration of) terrorist campaigns makes an indirect (but easily overlooked) contribution to their success. And it may also be the case that some of the counterterrorism strategies that emerge for serious consideration in this way will be strategies that call for significant modifications to be effected in some of the policies (economic, diplomatic, military) to which the countries that are exposed to the threat posed by terrorists are currently committed, including policies of the sorts that help fuel the discontents of some of the passive supporters of terrorist organizations. However, neither the fact that a broader range of possible counterterrorism strategies than are normally envisaged may have to be given serious

consideration nor the fact that some of these call for hitherto sacrosanct policies to be modified can be regarded as reasons for disallowing, or devaluing, empirical research into the "root causes" of terrorism.

(4) Even when the enquiry does uncover a causal connection between policies that have been or are in place and the putative grievances that (at least indirectly) help to generate (effective) terrorist campaigns, the question what policy revisions – if any – ought to be contemplated is still a crucial normative question to which an answer must be returned that is logically independent of the fact that there are causal links between existing policy positions and the sense of grievance that helps to sustain terrorist campaigns. For example, the sense of grievance, once examined, may have to be dismissed as indefensible – connected though it no doubt is, causally, to the implementation of certain policies by the state that is the target of the terrorist threat. The policies in question may be perfectly defensible policies – in which case adjusting the policies in order to ward off a possible terrorist attack may, for good reason, be viewed as an entirely unacceptable option. Again, even if the sense of grievance that is widespread among the members of a society who can be depicted as more or less passive supporters of a terrorist campaign is, at some level, understandable (in that their circumstances really are wretched, and not only through no fault of their own but also *because* they are the victims of indefensible policies), the aggrieved may well be targeting their complaints inappropriately – through failure to trace their unhappy lot to, say, the reactionary policies of the authorities *in their own society*. (Contemporary Saudi Arabia provides a possible example here.) Where circumstances of this general sort obtain, the appropriate response to the threat of terrorism will be – though in part only, no doubt – not to change policy direction but to try to correct misconceptions about the *real* sources of miserable conditions in the society in which there is at least some measure of toleration for a terrorist campaign directed at foreigners.

(5) When the root causes of terrorism are being investigated, moreover, a suitably comprehensive view of these causes should be sought. Complex social attitudes – including ambivalent attitudes in unfortunately situated societies towards the terrorist organizations in their midst – can seldom be explained adequately if single-factor explanations are sought or accepted. (A possible example here is the not uncommon tendency to trace the terrorist threat posed by al-Qaeda – or by Palestinians who mount terrorist attacks against Israel – to a

narrow, and distorted, version of Islamic doctrine.) Most adequate explanations will be multifactor explanations and it will of course be incumbent on those whose research provides the empirical evidence on which these explanations are based to try to specify the role played by these many factors and to bring out not only their comparative importance but also the special conditions under which their importance may have to be accorded recognition.

(6) It is a big mistake to suppose that the threat of terrorism is a single, more or less unitary, threat. The truth of course is that it assumes a wide variety of forms under different sets of social, economic, political, and cultural circumstances. There may well be important respects in which these threats – and the sorts of terrorist organizations in which they originate – have certain common features. But there are bound also to be important differences. It is only to be expected, consequently, that any adequate explanation of the threat posed by terrorism to the members of a given society at a given time will be different from the explanations that careful investigators will come up with for the terrorist threats to which the members of other societies are exposed. And it is therefore to be expected that appropriate and potentially effective responses to the threat of terrorism will have to be different for different societies that face this threat – and different, too, for the same society at different junctures in its history.

(7) Yet another misconception – the last I shall say something about here – is that recognition of the role played by support for the political objectives of terrorist organizations will lead to the adoption of counterterrorism policies that give terrorists what they want, thereby violating a cardinal rule in the battle against terrorist threats – namely, the rule that forbids any capitulation to the demands terrorists make. This rule requires that terrorists who make demands under threat of violence to innocent civilians ought *never* to be rewarded.

It may not be at all clear, however, precisely how this rule is to be applied in some of the contexts in which policymakers have to decide how far to go towards modifying or abandoning policies that have generated some of the deep discontents in societies in which terrorists have a base of operations. Consider the following possible scenarios.

Suppose, for example, that the terrorists are demanding that certain policies of the targeted state be abandoned or modified, but not because of any real commitment they have to the alleviation of the discontents of the members of the society within which they are operating, but simply because it is useful for them to secure the support – the passive support, at any rate – of these members in the terrorist campaign they have launched against the state that is responsible for the policies. Under these circumstances, how should we view the determination of the targeted state to respond to these demands by adamantly sticking to the offending policies on the ground that not to do so would be tantamount to rewarding terrorism? Is this a case where adherence to the rule about not capitulating to the demands of terrorists requires the targeted state simply to reaffirm its commitment to the policies? Arguably not. The reason is that, in these circumstances, staunch refusal to modify or abandon the policies in question may have to be seen as playing into the hands of the terrorists. For one thing, the perpetuation of these policies makes it easier for the terrorists to continue to receive the tacit support of those who suffer under the policies – this support being a crucial condition of the success, over the long run, of the terrorist strategy they are pursuing. For another, it is a feature of the case under discussion that the terrorists are not themselves seriously committed to alleviating the discontents generated by the policies. There is consequently an important sense in which modification or abandonment of the policies ought not to be seen as a matter of doing, under threat, what the terrorists actually want.

Part of what a scenario of this sort underscores is the importance, in dealing with terrorist demands, of not underestimating either the deviousness or the cleverness of those who make the demands. What the terrorists really want to achieve, when they demand of the threatened state that it abandon certain policies that are viewed as objectionable by their tacit supporters, may well be very different from what, at first glance, it might be thought to be. Their principal aim (and hope) may be, not to have the hated policies abandoned, but rather to have the demand for their abandonment summarily rejected. In these circumstances, is the rule about not giving in to terrorists more likely to be breached by a response that gives them what they *say* they want or by a response that gives them what they *really* want? It is true, no doubt, that there is a sense in which what counts in these circumstances as "giving in" is at least as much a matter of perception as it is of reality – a point frequently emphasized by defenders of the rule forbidding concessions to terrorist demands. Even so, if the terrorists know that compliance with their surface demands is not what they really want to achieve, it is surely a nice question which response on the part of the threatened state ought to be viewed, in the circumstances supposed, as "appeasing the terrorists."

If it should be claimed, in support of the conventional answer to this question – the answer for which any move towards policy modification on the part of the targeted state is tantamount to capitulation to terrorist demands – that what the rule about not giving in to terrorists principally requires is the avoidance of any *appearance* of weakness, it ought to be asked whether what matters, in the struggle between terrorists and the targeted state, is how the response is perceived *by the terrorists* or how it is apt to be perceived by *supporters of the targeted state*. Since it is obviously the terrorists' perception of the significance of the response that has a bearing on whether they will be emboldened to escalate their demands, it should be clear that in the imagined case there is no basis for the fear that any modification of the hated policies by the targeted state will be seen as a sign of weakness. As for the concern that supporters of the targeted state are bound to perceive any policy modification as capitulation to terrorist demands, *it* can readily be allayed by frank public disclosure of the rationale for the response. It can be made clear, for example, that, contrary to their stated demand (and contrary, therefore, to appearances) the ulterior purpose of the terrorists was to goad the targeted state into reaffirming its support for the hated policies, thereby making it less difficult for them to pose as the true defenders of the communities whose support they need.

Consider another possible scenario. Suppose the state responsible for the alienating policies the terrorists are exploiting in their effort to get the members of their own societies to lend (at least tacit) support to their terrorist campaign has an interest, now, in abandoning the policies – perhaps (at least in part) because it has become apparent how damaging they are to many of those affected by them and also how cunningly the terrorists are exploiting this fact in order to secure the tacit support of those who have been adversely affected. Suppose, though, that it is a matter of agreement – as between the terrorists and rank-and-file members of the society – that the policies are objectionable, an important source of some of the miseries being endured by the members of the society. Would a decision on the part of the targeted state to abandon (or modify) the policies have to be seen as breaching the rule about not making concessions to terrorists? Would it have to be seen as appeasement? Again, arguably not. The reason is that, in these circumstances, modification or abandonment of the policies can readily be seen as a means of depriving the terrorists of the support they are otherwise able to enjoy from the alienated members of the society who are not terrorists. If loss of this sort of support would make it more difficult for the terrorists to continue with their terrorist campaign, why should not the state that is the target of this campaign seriously contemplate abandoning or modifying the offending policies?

What these examples show is that too crude an interpretation – or application – of the rule about not making concessions to terrorists can contribute, even if only indirectly, to the success of terrorist campaigns.[8] If there is reason to believe that terrorists are prepared to try to secure the tacit support of many of the ordinary members of their society who do not necessarily approve of their methods by representing themselves as committed to political objectives that have broad public support, it is arguably incumbent on smart counterterrorism strategists to try to deprive them of this sort of popular base. This can sometimes be done by the abandonment or modification of policies that have been a standing obstacle to achievement of the objectives, especially when (as is not infrequently the case) the policies are themselves misguided and the objectives quite reasonable.

5. CONCLUSION

I have argued, albeit briefly and schematically, that precisely because waging (literal) war against terrorism in a manner that is both morally permissible and reasonably effective requires the fulfillment of a number of difficult-to-satisfy conditions, a great deal of importance attaches to combating the threat of terrorism by conducting a (merely metaphorical) "war" against terrorism. Since the aim of this latter war – like the aim of the former – is, at least ideally, to prevent terrorism by eliminating so far as possible the threat of terrorism, importance obviously attaches to working, on a broad front, towards elimination of the many sources of the threat. And this, in turn, calls for serious investigation of the many factors – social, cultural, religious, economic, political, and so on – that play a role, direct or indirect, large or small, in facilitating the emergence and survival of terrorism in the various forms it can assume.

But although it is important for work on nonmilitary strategies to combat terrorism to be undertaken against the backdrop provided by a reasonably comprehensive account of the causes of terrorism in the many forms it can take in different kinds of historical circumstances, clearly not all the strategies for combating the threat of terrorism that are consistent with this set of explanations are going to be in principle acceptable strategies. Acceptable strategies have to satisfy (at least) two important sets of constraints: moral permissibility constraints and effectiveness constraints. On the one hand, they must be respectful of the fundamental human rights of all who are affected by them. On the other, they must make a positive contribution, directly or indirectly, to diminishing the threat of terrorism.

The review of nonmilitary strategies for the purpose of picking out those that are both morally permissible and potentially effective must be conducted with at least two dangers in mind. On the one hand, there is the danger – about which nothing has been said in this chapter – that strategies aimed at increasing domestic security in the face of terrorist threats may be adopted even when they violate fundamental human rights. A leading example of this sort is the authorization of coercive interrogation techniques in the hope that their use may help to extract valuable information in the fight against terrorism from uncommunicative detainees, despite the fact that these techniques violate the right not to be tortured. Another is the relaxation of freedom and privacy constraints on methods of intelligence-gathering, in disregard of the fact that the constraints are essential to the protection of fundamental human rights. The other danger – which it has been a major purpose of this chapter to underscore – is that strategies that might be highly effective means of diminishing the threat posed by terrorism may be overlooked or rejected because of undue or unwarranted attachment to existing legal arrangements or current policy commitments. For example, economically and politically motivated support for repressive regimes may have to be abandoned if the threat of terrorism posed by antigovernment movements in countries with repressive regimes is to be reduced or eliminated. Again, certain kinds of global "free market" policies may have to be modified if in their current form they are found to be counterproductive from the standpoint of the fight against terrorism, as they might well be if it could be shown that terrorist organizations are able to entrench themselves in economically underdeveloped societies because thoroughgoing "free market" investment and trade policies are insufficiently respectful of indigenous rights to fair conditions of economic development.

When nonmilitary strategies for combating the threat of terrorism conflict with the principles of justice that underpin doctrines of human rights, it is of course the strategies that must be abandoned. But when the conflict is between potentially effective strategies and current laws and policies, it is the laws and policies that must be modified.

NOTES

1. It is worth noting that while this claim presupposes that well-founded judgments about the deserts of terrorists can be made, it can make no contribution to the defense of those judgments. Even if a retributive response to terrorism could be shown to reduce the threat of terrorism, this could not be cited as part of what justifies the desert-ascribing judgments presupposed by the response.

2. Michael Walzer's verdict in *Just and Unjust Wars* (New York: Basic Books, 1977) is that preventive war, once its distinguishing features are accurately described, must be seen to be morally unacceptable. See also the recent discussions of the question by David Luban ("Preventive War", *Philosophy and Public Affairs* Vol 32 No 3, Summer, 2004) and Allen Buchanan and Robert Keohane ("The Preventive Use of Force: A Cosmopolitan Institutional Perspective", *Ethics and International Affairs*, 18 (1), 2004). While they do not endorse Walzer's blanket condemnation of preventive war, neither the (narrowly drawn) exceptions to a general ban on preventive war that Luban argues for nor the international institutional safeguards that Buchanan and Keohane recommend for the authorization of the preventive use of force would legitimize any general resort to military force as a means of combating the threat of terrorism.
3. Luban, "Preventive War."
4. It is even more obvious that a military response to the threat of terrorism cannot defensibly take the form of attacking states in which terrorist organizations have a base of operations when the states in question are themselves, in some sense and to some degree, "at war" with the terrorists in their midst. In these cases, it may be undeniable that the terrorists have a base in the territory over which the states have at least nominal jurisdiction, but it may be equally undeniable that the states cannot be regarded as in league with them.
5. Resistance to serious investigation of "root-causes" – whether of crime, or of drug use, or of terrorism – often goes hand-in-hand with the leveling of the charge that those who value such research are "soft" on crime (or drug use, or terrorism), or that they are pathologically predisposed to "coddle" criminals (or drug-users, or terrorists).
6. It is this latter question that figures prominently in the paper on terrorism that Walzer wrote in 1988, the paper that has been reprinted in *Arguing About War* (New Haven, CT: Yale University Press, 2004).
7. Something pretty close to this assumption pervades large parts of Jean Bethke Elshtain's *Just War Against Terror* (New York: Basic Books, 2003).
8. Actual examples of this kind of misguided "toughness" are not difficult to cite. For example, when the Israeli government has broken off (or indefinitely postponed) negotiations with the Palestinian authorities in response to terrorist attacks orchestrated by Palestinian factions opposed to the peace process, its response, despite its touted "toughness", has in fact given the terrorists precisely what they want.

WIN-CHIAT LEE

TERRORISM AND UNIVERSAL JURISDICTION

1. INTRODUCTION

Under international law, a nation may typically claim jurisdiction over a criminal case on the basis of two principles, namely, the principle of territoriality and the principle of nationality. The principle of territoriality is the principle by which a nation may claim jurisdiction over an alleged crime if it is committed within its territory. The principle of nationality, by contrast, allows a nation to extend its criminal jurisdiction beyond its borders. However, the extraterritorial jurisdiction allowed by the principle of nationality is rather limited; as it stands, this kind of extraterritorial jurisdiction is limited by the connection of a nation to a crime through either the nationality of the alleged perpetrator of the crime (active nationality) or that of the victim (passive nationality). The principle of nationality, active or passive, is the principal uncontroversial means by which a nation may assert extraterritorial jurisdiction.

In recent years, however, a highly controversial principle of criminal jurisdiction under international law has gained prominence, as well as significance, due to a number of high-profile cases. Though the use of this principle by nations to assert criminal jurisdiction is still rare, the frequency of its use has increased significantly in recent years. I am referring to the *principle of universal jurisdiction*. By this principle, a nation may claim jurisdiction over a criminal case without regard to where it is supposed to have taken place or the nationality of either the alleged perpetrator or the victim of the crime. Perhaps the proper way to state the principle of universal jurisdiction is that in its pure form, it allows a nation's claim of jurisdiction over an alleged crime to be "based solely on the *nature* of the crime."[1]

Clearly, the principle of universal jurisdiction expands the scope of a nation's extraterritorial criminal jurisdiction in a significant way. But this expansion is still rather limited. Even its most enthusiastic defenders would want to restrict the use of universal jurisdiction to a special class of serious crimes under international law, often known as "international crimes" – crimes such as torture, genocide, and crimes against humanity.

However, as a matter of international law, it is only fair to say that the list of crimes subject to universal jurisdiction is still evolving. Regardless, even with the clear restriction of its applicability to a very small number of serious crimes, universal jurisdiction is rightly considered problematic and controversial.

Universal jurisdiction has been used in a number of high-profile cases such as Israel's prosecution of Eichmann in 1961 and, more recently, beginning in 1995, Belgium's trial and eventual conviction of a number of Rwandans for war crimes committed against other Rwandans in Rwanda. In 1996, universal jurisdiction was also invoked when Spain considered the prosecution of the former Chilean dictator, General Augusto Pinochet, for crimes committed against Chilean citizens under his rule.[2] Later Spain even sought the extradition of General Pinochet from Britain when he was in Britain on a private visit.

While much has been said concerning the appeal, as well as the pitfalls, of the principle of universal jurisdiction in relation to genocide, torture, crimes against humanity, and other serious violations of human rights, the discussion of the use of universal jurisdiction in relation to terrorism is relatively rare.[3] The use of universal jurisdiction in relation to terrorism may not be without precedents. A crime that has a long history of association with the principle of universal jurisdiction is piracy. One can perhaps quite readily extend the justification for the use of universal jurisdiction in piracy cases to cases involving the hijacking of airplanes and ships. But it is important, especially in the current environment, to consider the use of universal jurisdiction to deal with terrorist crimes in general and not only in relation to those that are committed on the high seas, in international airspace, or with multiple claims of territorial jurisdiction.

The purpose of this chapter is to argue that terrorism in general should be included as such, and not merely incidentally, among the crimes subject to universal jurisdiction. There is much that is similar between terrorism and other crimes that are considered to be subject to universal jurisdiction. Like the perpetrators of genocide, torture, and crimes against humanity, terrorists typically inflict violent harms and/or death on innocent people, violate their fundamental human rights, and cause widespread fear and sense of insecurity within certain groups of people, often with the purpose of serving political ends. More importantly, as in most of these other crimes, the violence committed in terrorist acts involves the depersonalization of the victims. However, I do not wish to make a case for subjecting terrorism to universal jurisdiction solely on the basis of the family resemblances between terrorism and some of the other crimes considered to be subject to universal jurisdiction. After all, it is not clear in the first place why only certain serious crimes, but not others, are subject to universal jurisdiction, not to mention the fact that the controversial idea of universal jurisdiction itself needs justification.

While it would be impossible to give a detailed justificatory account of universal jurisdiction in this short chapter, in order to motivate the case for subjecting terrorism to universal jurisdiction, I will here attempt a relatively brief philosophical account of the moral basis of the principle of universal jurisdiction, as well as an account of what it is about certain crimes that make them justifiably the subject of universal jurisdiction.

The discussion in this chapter is focused more directly on international terrorism, that is, terrorist acts committed by the citizens of one nation against those of another. But on the argument I will present, it is not the international nature of these terrorist acts that would justify their being subject to universal jurisdiction. The argument should apply also to domestic terrorism. This way of thinking about terrorism and universal jurisdiction is consistent with the general idea of universal jurisdiction, in that the crimes that are typically considered to be subject to universal jurisdiction – crimes such as genocide, crimes against humanity, and torture – are not necessarily international in the relevant sense either.

2. THE EXTRADITION DILEMMA

Before I turn to the more general question about the justification for universal jurisdiction and the conditions that a crime must satisfy in order to qualify as subject to universal jurisdiction, I will begin by describing and discussing first the situation in which the international community finds itself as a result of the United States' legal response to the 9/11 terrorist attacks. This situation illustrates in a nutshell the sort of moral concern that motivates my view that the exercise of universal jurisdiction may be just the right moral response to certain terrorism cases.

Given that the terrorists the world confronts today and will continue to confront in the future often belong to international networks and seem to be mobile around the globe, an effective fight against terrorism will require international legal cooperation, especially in terms of the extradition of suspected terrorists to the territorial state (the state within whose territory the crime is committed) for prosecution. In my view, nothing would impede such cooperation more than for the territorial state (or any other state with jurisdiction) to deny terrorist suspects the due process of law or the rights they are entitled to under international law. Under such conditions, if such a state were to make an extradition request to another state in order to bring home for prosecution a suspected terrorist found within the latter's territory, it would put the latter in a very difficult moral position.

This is exactly what the United States has done to the rest of the world with its highly controversial procedures for detaining, prosecuting, and trying terrorist suspects after the 9/11 attacks. There are good reasons to believe that these procedures do not satisfy due process. Thus, if a nation refuses to honor a request from the United States to extradite someone found within its territory to the United States for prosecution for alleged terrorist crimes, one would think that it may indeed be morally justified in doing so. In fact, one could go further and argue that the refusal to extradite is not only permissible, but also morally required. Plausibly, one could claim that it is morally wrong for a nation to extradite knowingly someone to another nation it has good reason to believe will not afford the person the due process of law.

After the United States announced its legal procedures for terrorist crimes, Spain announced that it would refuse to honor extradition requests from the United States concerning some terrorism suspects.[4] But the moral problem Spain would face is more complicated if it were to find within its territory a non-Spanish national whose extradition was sought by United States for suspected terrorist crimes. Spain would be caught in a serious moral dilemma. Let us call this "the extradition dilemma." The two horns of the extradition dilemma as applied to our example are as follows. On the one hand, it would be unconscionable for Spain to honor the extradition request if the suspect in question would face serious charges (especially capital charges) in the United States without the due process of law. On the other hand, it would be equally unconscionable for Spain to let someone suspected of such heinous crimes go with impunity.

In this hypothetical scenario, Spain's most obvious escape from the extradition dilemma would be to prosecute and adjudicate the case itself. Under international law, some serious international crimes are governed by the principle, *aut dedere aut judicare*, which imposes on nations the obligation to either extradite or prosecute and adjudicate the cases involving these crimes themselves.[5] The principle, *aut dedere aut judicare* (extradite or prosecute), makes sense from the moral point of view. Our duty of justice would presumably require us to act to prevent the impunity for crimes, especially the serious ones, by subjecting someone whom one has good reason to suspect as a perpetrator of one of these crimes to the due process of law to determine her guilt or innocence. Thus, if a nation finds within its territory a person who allegedly has committed a serious crime, albeit outside its territory, the duty of justice would presumably require that nation to extradite the person to a place where she could be properly charged and tried. If such a place is not available or with good justifications the nation in possession of the suspect cannot extradite her, then the duty of justice would require that that nation itself proceed with the prosecution and trial of the suspect, *provided it can afford the accused a fair trial*. (I will say more about this important proviso shortly.)

If, as I have argued in the hypothetical case, Spain would be morally required to decline to extradite the suspect to the United States, it would then be under an obligation to prosecute, assuming that it can afford the accused a fair trial and that no other forum in a better position to give the accused a fair trial is available for extradition. In order to prosecute, however, Spain would need jurisdiction over the case. Unfortunately, in some of these cases, Spain – and indeed most other nations – would not be able to avail themselves of what I have mentioned earlier as the two standard principles of criminal jurisdiction under international law, namely, the principles of territoriality and nationality. This is when universal jurisdiction could come in very handy as a relief for the kind of moral dilemma we are discussing.[6]

In any case, even if it is under no obligation to do so, it would be bad policy for any nation to refuse to extradite alleged terrorists unless it is willing to prosecute the cases itself. It would make that nation a safe haven for terrorists and thus a victim of its own concern for justice and due process.[7] Indeed, generally speaking, it seems that universal jurisdiction would be a very useful tool for any nation which would deny certain extradition requests on grounds of justice or humanitarianism.

A nation's having jurisdiction over a certain case, however, does not mean that it is therefore reasonable for it to proceed with the prosecution and trial of that case.[8] But this is true not only of universal jurisdiction, but also of territorial jurisdiction. Discretion is needed in the exercise of any jurisdiction. In exercising universal jurisdiction, however, a nation has to determine first that there is not another nation with jurisdiction to which the subject could be extradited that would be in a better position to adjudicate the case justly. Earlier I mentioned that a nation asserting universal jurisdiction over a case should proceed with the prosecution of the case *provided* it can afford the accused a fair trial. To be sure, without the cooperation of the territorial state, any nation exercising universal jurisdiction (and indeed, for that matter, any extraterritorial jurisdiction over a criminal case) will have to contend with some practical problems, such as how to make available evidence and witnesses for both the prosecution and the defense. Such problems can seriously affect its ability to conduct a fair trial. But one should not overgeneralize this problem and reject the principle of universal jurisdiction entirely on these grounds. There may be cases in which witnesses and evidence for both the prosecution and defense are available outside the territorial state that are sufficient to support a fair trial. There may also be cases in which the territorial state is sufficiently willing to cooperate so that some of these practical problems concerning the availability of evidence and witnesses can be overcome.

3. THE PHILOSOPHICAL FOUNDATION OF UNIVERSAL JURISDICTION

I have argued in Section 2 that universal jurisdiction over terrorism comes in handy as a relief for the extradition dilemma and helps those nations caught in such a dilemma to discharge their duties of justice that would otherwise be in conflict. For some this is sufficient justification for universal jurisdiction over terrorism. For others, especially those who are skeptical about the justifiability of universal jurisdiction to begin with, this is begging the question. On their view, universal jurisdiction will be no help to those caught in the extradition dilemma, no matter how "morally convenient" it is, if it is not just to begin with. So as not to beg the question against the critics of universal jurisdiction, I would like to address in this section some of the fundamental issues in political philosophy that bear on the moral justifiability of universal jurisdiction. My account should also explain why terrorism, domestic or international, should be considered from the moral point of view a crime subject to universal jurisdiction.

It should be obvious why the idea of universal jurisdiction is troubling for many people. The principle of universal jurisdiction allows a state to assert jurisdiction over certain criminal cases even though it has no direct connection to them either through its territory or through the nationality of the parties involved. What makes this principle profoundly intriguing, as well as problematic, philosophically speaking, is precisely the fact that it seems to upset the traditional conception of sovereign political states as, in a manner of speaking, discrete social entities whose legitimate authority overlaps only minimally, if at all. According to this traditional conception of sovereignty, the legitimate exercise of a state's political power through its laws has boundaries, not only in the geographic/territorial sense, but also in the social sense, that is, in the sense that it is limited to a particular group of people, namely, the state's citizens. Others get included but only in a relatively temporary and specific way. The other side of the same coin is the idea that only the citizens of a state owe it political obligations, which presumably include the duty to obey its laws.⁹ It is clear that the two standard principles of jurisdiction, territoriality, and nationality, fit in better with this traditional conception of sovereign political states. The principle of universal jurisdiction, even if limited to certain classes of crimes, would require *some* rather fundamental revision of this conception.

The main moral interest behind the exercise of universal jurisdiction, in terrorism as well as a host of other cases of human rights violations, is, presumably, the concern about impunity for heinous crimes. By "impunity," I mean the state of affairs in which the perpetrator of a crime is not punished or otherwise held accountable for the crime. There is no denying that such a state of affairs is unjust and needs to be prevented or rectified, even if philosophers do dispute about why such a state of affairs is unjust. Universal jurisdiction, in my view, is clearly intended to address or, in any event, is justifiable only insofar as it addresses the problem of impunity as a concern of justice. Universal jurisdiction, by maximizing the number of forums in which a perpetrator of a crime can be prosecuted, minimizes the number of circumstances under which she would fail to be called to account for her act because of where she happens to be or some other reasons.

If justice is the main concern and what provides the justification for universal jurisdiction, what we need is an account for why on the one hand, there are certain crimes, such as murders and securities frauds, that should be subject to jurisdiction limited by the principles of territoriality and nationality, while others, such as genocide, torture, crimes against humanity, and (as I would argue) terrorism, should be subject to universal jurisdiction. Is it simply the heinousness or the atrociousness of the latter category of crimes that set them apart? That aspect probably has something to do with it. But I doubt that it can be the whole story.

The principles of justice the violation of which are subject to only territorial and national jurisdiction are close to what Jeremy Waldron calls "range-limited" principles of justice, principles whose range of application is limited to the territory or to the members of a particular state.¹⁰ These range-limited principles of justice are administered by the state whose members and territory constitute the "range" within which these principles are applicable. In the same article, Waldron also gives an account of why justice allows and requires multiple systems of range-limited principles that do not overlap in scope. Even though Waldron's main interest is to explain why justice allows for or even requires multiple states, each with its own legal system of range-limited principles, it is my contention that Waldron's account also leaves room for certain principles not to be range-limited, thus opening up the possibility of universal jurisdiction. In my view, Waldron's argument is necessary only because justice requires us not to make arbitrary distinctions between persons. Therefore, insofar as justice is concerned, there is a presumption in favor of having the same principles of justice applied to everyone and administered in the same way; it is the range-limited principles and the territorially based or nationality-based jurisdiction in their application that more clearly need to be accounted for.

Following Waldron, I will start with the Kantian argument that the natural duty of justice requires us to abandon the state of nature and enter into the state with those who live near us. On this argument, because the state of nature is an extremely miserable state of affairs, we have an urgent moral duty to get out of it and enter into a state with others as soon as we can, in order to establish a scheme to resolve conflicts and govern our interactions with one another justly. The establishment of such a just scheme may require some conventions and stipulations. But, on this argument, our duty in the first instance is only to enter into a state with those who live near us for two reasons. First, they are the ones with whom we come into conflict most frequently. A global approach to resolving conflicts justly might not be needed very often or add much to a more local approach in this first instance. Second, the task of leaving the state of nature behind and resolving conflicts justly is so urgent, morally speaking, that we are not only allowed, but also required to seek a more local approach when such an approach is clearly more feasible and easier to come by. This is what I take to be the argument in Waldron's account that provides the moral basis not only for establishing just political and legal institutions, but also for establishing a single set of them for a particular territory with principles of justice that are limited in their range of application to only the inhabitants of that territory.[11] We now have an argument to show why justice, at least on a pro tem basis, not only allows, but also requires multiple legal systems in the world, each with a limited and nonoverlapping scope of application and jurisdiction.

But our conflicts are not only with those who live adjacent to us. Indeed, as we, so to speak, globalize, we increase the number of occasions for conflicts with those who do not live adjacent to us. Terrorism is clearly the result of one such conflict that can originate from outside our locale. For the United States today, for example, the international terrorist organization al-Qaeda is at least as likely to be the source of the problem as a home-grown Timothy McVeigh. Therefore, following the same Kantian argument Waldron uses, it seems that we would be duty-bound to enter into an arrangement with one another on a global scale to handle terrorism cases and to forestall impunity in such cases.[12] Will this give us a set of range-unlimited principles of justice governing terrorism to be administered by all nations via universal jurisdiction? Not necessarily. This is because ranged-limited principles administered by each individual state through its territorial jurisdiction will still be sufficient to deal with the international nature of those terrorist acts that take place within a particular state's territory, assuming that arrangements have been set up for extradition from one territory to another for prosecution.

Indeed, our duty of justice would require us to engage in such extradition practices. The argument Waldron puts forward is intended to show that our natural duty of justice is compatible with there being multiple states in the world, each with its own system of law and its own set of range-limited principles of justice to apply that does not overlap with the others. As a result, it appears that our natural duty of justice would require us only to obey the law of the state (assuming that it is just) of which we are a citizen or on whose territory our action is to take place. But this is not the complete story. In addition to the duty to obey the range-limited principles of justice that apply to us, our natural duty of justice, on Waldron's account, also gives rise to an accompanying set of duties, including the duty not to interfere with or sabotage or impede other states' attempts to enforce their principles of justice even though strictly speaking, because of their limited range, these principles of justice do not apply to us.[13] Let us call these additional duties of justice, "international political obligations." In my view, such "international political obligations" should also include a state's duty to extradite in order to facilitate other states' attempt to enforce their range-limited principles of justice.

At any rate, assuming that a unified account is preferable, the appeal to the expansion of the scope of human interaction will not explain why certain other crimes, such as genocide, torture, and crimes against humanity are also subject to universal jurisdiction. Most of these crimes are still local in the sense that they are committed by one member of a state against another within the territory of that state.

According to a view prevalent in international law, a distinction can be drawn between two kinds of crimes. Some crimes set back only the interest of the particular communities where they take place while others affect negatively the common interest of all humankind regardless of where they take place. It is the involvement of the common interest of all humankind in the latter kind of crime that makes it appropriate to treat them as international crimes. On this view, it is claimed that while a murder committed by one person against another for monetary gains affects only the community in which it takes places, genocide, even if committed within a state, is taken to have implications for international peace and security – a common interest of all humankind – regardless of where it takes place.[14] Terrorism, especially international terrorism, is also taken to have implications for international peace and security.[15]

I do not think that this common interest argument and the distinction on which it is based, even if sound, will justify the application of universal jurisdiction to terrorism and, indeed, any other crimes that concern the common interest of all humankind. Nor will it require setting up range-unlimited principles to govern these crimes. The common interest argument in the case of terrorism is the appeal to the claim that we, that is, all of us in this world, have a common security interest in seeing terrorism suppressed everywhere in the world because terrorism anywhere in some ways affects the security of people everywhere else. The common interest argument would thus presumably require that terrorism be prohibited and punished everywhere in the world. But there is nothing about this requirement of universal suppression of terrorism that cannot be met by each nation having strong local range-limited laws against terrorism with the use of domestic territorial jurisdiction, plus good international cooperation for the extradition of terrorist suspects.

Thus, it is not the globalization of human interaction or the international or global nature of certain crimes that justifies the subjection of these crimes to universal jurisdiction. What, in my view, can justify the use of universal jurisdiction for a certain kind of crime is the concern about the failure or the expected failure of territorial jurisdiction to deliver justice for that kind of crime, together with the claim that such failure can be redressed by universal jurisdiction. Let us take for example the crimes that are typically considered to be subject to universal jurisdiction – crimes such as genocide, torture, and crimes against humanity. These are heinous crimes that the territorial state would often fail to prosecute because of the state's vested interest in not prosecuting them. These crimes are often committed by the officials or agents of the state or parties acting in a semi-official capacity. It may also be politically inexpedient to prosecute these cases. There may also be reconciliation efforts by the state that will be compromised by prosecution.[16] The list of possible reasons and excuses goes on. More importantly, some of these heinous crimes are committed often when the state is in the process of breaking down or no longer serving its essential functions properly. So impunity for these heinous crimes could be expected to be often the result, if we rely solely on territorial jurisdiction to deliver justice.

Terrorism, especially international terrorism, in my view, poses a different, but related kind of problem for territorial jurisdiction. The fear here is not that the territorial state will not prosecute, but rather that it will prosecute overenthusiastically, not only because of the vested political interest of the state, but also because of the pressure from the community to see terrorism dealt with swiftly and harshly. The concern here is whether the territorial state will be able to afford the accused a fair trial and safeguard the rights of the accused.[17] This may be instructively compared with that which motivates a change of venue for a criminal trial away from the community in which the crime takes place, due to the fact that the community may be too sensitized to make a fair trial possible. In terrorism as well as in the other kinds of cases, however, impunity is what is at stake. But in the terrorism cases, impunity is only indirectly at issue through the kind of extradition dilemma I have described earlier. Regardless, in my view, universal jurisdiction is intended to address these problems concerning impunity.

What we have established so far is that, as an extension of the kind of Kantian argument Waldron uses, our natural duty of justice would require us to enter into some kind of global arrangement that, under some conditions, may allow or even require that one state administer justice for another state for certain kinds of crimes that occur within the latter's territory. But in establishing this, we are only halfway toward justifying universal jurisdiction for these crimes. In order for a state (call this "the forum state") to prosecute and try a case that involves members of another state or takes place within another state's territory, the relevant principle of justice has to be unlimited in range in Waldron's sense because it has to be applicable to those outside the forum state. This is different from simply saying that the crime in question has to be universally regarded as crime. As I have noted earlier, a crime can be universally regarded as crime without involving range-unlimited principles of justice. We can have every nation in the world recognizing a certain crime as a crime, but as long as each nation's law in relation to that crime is intended only to be applicable to its citizens or its territory, all we have is many range-limited principles of justice governing that crime, none of which can be applied outside a nation's territory or against foreigners. In order for Spain to exercise universal jurisdiction and prosecute a terrorist act committed in the United States, for example, it is not enough that Spain have laws prohibiting that terrorist act in Spain (range-limited) or that the United States has similar laws prohibiting that same terrorist act in the United States (range-limited). It is also necessary that the law that is operative in Spain prohibits that terrorist act in Spain *and abroad* and *by anyone regardless of nationality* (range-unlimited).

Furthermore, there can be only one unique range-unlimited principle or set of such principles of justice governing a particular crime in order for that crime to be subject to universal jurisdiction. Otherwise, a forum state might recognize one principle or set of principles and the territorial state another, not to mention that other potential forum states might recognize yet others. Since each of these states could claim jurisdiction over the crime, the accused would be simultaneously subject to many different, even conflicting standards of justice, not to mention that she could not know in advance which principle of justice she would be judged by and thus which she needed to obey. That clearly would be a form of injustice. This means that not only is it the case that the principles of justice that are subject to universal jurisdiction cannot be limited in range, but also that they cannot contain any element that is a matter of choice or convention, which would make it possible for them to vary from community to community. Nor can they be considered just only within the context of certain other institutions and practices that may or may not exist in a community.[18] Or if these principles of justice involve conventions, it would have to be the case that our duty of justice would require us to settle on one set of conventions universally.

It seems to me that terrorism, as well as genocide, torture, crimes against humanity, and all of the other crimes typically considered to be subject to universal jurisdiction, involve the kind of principle of justice that does not contain conventional elements. Or if they do, one could readily make a case that the world has a moral duty to come together and set down one set of conventions governing it.

4. CONCLUSION

In this chapter, I have attempted to account for the moral legitimacy of the principle of universal jurisdiction. I hope this account, while brief, helps make a case for the view that universal jurisdiction is, from the moral point of view, a plausible idea that warrants further consideration. Given the kind of issues about justice that universal jurisdiction is supposed to address, I have also argued that terrorism should be included among the crimes that are subject to universal jurisdiction.

By way of conclusion, I would also like to address briefly the question concerning the jurisdiction of international judicial bodies, such as the International Criminal Court (ICC), over the kind of criminal cases covered by universal jurisdiction. There are many people who would find it more acceptable for an international court, such as the ICC, to adjudicate the kind of criminal case we have been discussing, rather than individual states exercising universal jurisdiction. For example, in the hypothetical extradition dilemma discussed earlier, many people would prefer that Spain hand over the terrorist suspect to an international judicial body, such as the ICC, rather than for Spain to exercise universal jurisdiction and prosecute and adjudicate the case itself.

If territorial states would voluntarily agree to subject such cases to an international court, the whole controversial issue of universal jurisdiction could indeed be avoided. The territorial state would then be handing its territorial jurisdiction over a certain case to another party for it to exercise. Unfortunately, such agreements, either in the form of a prior treaty or an ad hoc agreement, do not always exist. Without such agreements, the authority and jurisdiction of an international judicial body over such cases would need to be accounted for, no less than the universal jurisdiction claimed by another nation.

If criminal jurisdiction in international law remains based solely on either territoriality or nationality, then an international judicial body would lack jurisdiction over any criminal case except whatever such jurisdiction it acquires from the states through an agreement from them. This would mean that it lacks jurisdiction over cases that are committed within the territory and involve only the citizens of a nation that is not a party to the treaty that sets up the international judicial body. If, on the other hand, an international judicial body has jurisdiction over certain crimes regardless of where they occur and the nationality of the parties, then what it has is equivalent to universal jurisdiction over those crimes. Since the jurisdiction of such an international body cannot be presumed, questions can then be asked about what justifies its claim to universal jurisdiction over those crimes. If this claim is derived from the member states, then the member states will need to have universal jurisdiction over those crimes to begin with. If it is not derived from the member states, then we can ask more directly, why any political institution outside a territorial state can claim universal jurisdiction over a crime that is committed within the latter's territory. Either way, we have the same problem I have tried to address in this chapter.[19]

NOTES

1. As the Princeton Project on Universal Jurisdiction puts it, "[universal jurisdiction] is jurisdiction based solely on the nature of the crime." (*Princeton Principles on Universal Jurisdiction,* Program in Law and Public Affairs, Princeton University, Princeton, NJ, p. 23.) The Princeton Project is an international conference of international law scholars and jurists convened by Princeton University in 2000. The participants in this conference also contribute chapters to Stephen Macedo ed.,

Universal Jurisdiction: National Courts and the Prosecution of Serious Crimes Under International Law (Philadelphia, PA: University of Pennsylvania Press, 2004).
2. Spain's case against Pinochet included both Spanish as well as non-Spanish nationals as the victims of the crimes with which General Pinochet was charged. In fact, Spanish domestic law does not allow for the principle of passive nationality. Thus, even if Spain were to seek justice on behalf of Spanish nationals only, it would have to invoke universal jurisdiction. According to Reydams, non-Spanish nationals might have been added to the original complaint as victims so as to force the issue of universal jurisdiction allowed by Spanish law. See Luc Reydams, *Universal Jurisdiction: International and Municipal Law Perspectives* (New York: Oxford University Press, 2003), 184–185.
3. Terrorism is not one of the seven serious crimes under international law recognized by the Princeton Project for the purposes of the Princeton Principles on Universal Jurisdiction. (*Princeton Principles,* 29) The Princeton Project does consider terrorism as a candidate for inclusion, but it decides against it for reasons unexplained (48).
4. See the *New York Times* article, "New Code, New Power," October 24, 2004.
5. Reydams traces the formulation of this principle in the form of a maxim to the sixteen-century Spanish author D. Covarruvias who claims that the principle has a natural law origin. (See Reydams, *Universal Jurisdiction,* 29.) For the purposes of this essay, I am not taking this principle to be a jurisdictional principle, that is, a principle that *confers* jurisdiction on a nation that for one reason or another cannot extradite the accused sought by another nation.
6. Incidentally, Spanish domestic law does allow for universal jurisdiction over terrorism (Ley Organica del Poder Judicial, article 23.4). I am playing a bit fast and loose with the concept of "universal jurisdiction" here. In the kind of extradition dilemma we are discussing, the country facing the dilemma has the suspect in its possession. Therefore, one could argue that if it has jurisdiction over the case, such jurisdiction would not have to be based solely on the nature of the crime, and thus would not be a pure case of universal jurisdiction. What we need is something like "custodial state jurisdiction," or the jurisdiction of the *judex deprehensionis*. But custodial state jurisdiction is quite close to universal jurisdiction if the only connection that the custodial state has to the case is that the suspect happens to be found within its territory. Regardless, establishing universal jurisdiction over a certain crime certainly also establishes custodial state jurisdiction over that crime. The argument I will present later in the chapter will also establish universal jurisdiction, and not only custodial state jurisdiction over certain international crimes.
7. According to the *New York Times*, Britain has become home to some international terrorists in part because of its refusal to honor certain extradition requests made by other nations, including Morocco, Spain, and France. In some of these cases, Britain's reason for rejecting the extradition request clearly had something to do with the concern for due process and civil liberties. (*New York Times*, July 10, 2005.)
8. I am indebted to Leslie Francis for discussion in relation to this question.
9. This is the famous "particularity requirement" for political obligations – a term coined by John Simmons in *Moral Principles and Political Obligations* (Princeton, NJ: Princeton University Press, 1979), 31.
10. Jeremy Waldron, "Special Ties and Natural Duties," *Philosophy and Public Affairs,* 22 (1) (1993), 13.
11. I am clearly not doing justice to Waldron's argument in the short space here. See Waldron's own account of this argument in "Special Ties and Natural Duties," esp. pp. 14–15.

12. Waldron seems to think that his Kantian argument justifies the use of range-limited principles, but only in a "provisional" way. Waldron writes, "As the sphere of human interaction expands, further conflicts may arise, and the scope of the legal framework must be extended and if necessary re-thought, according to the same Kantian principle." ("Special Ties and Natural Duties," 15)
13. See Waldron, "Special Ties and Natural Duties," 9–11 and 17.
14. For a discussion of how this type of argument is used in the classification of international crimes in international law, see the chapter on "Peace and Security" in Nina H. B. Jørgenssen, *The Responsibility of States for International Crimes* (New York: Oxford University Press, 2000), 131–138.
15. This argument is used by the United Nations. See Security Council Resolutions 635 (December 14, 1973), 731 (January 21, 1992), and 748 (March 31, 1992).
16. A territorial state may decide not to pursue the accountability for heinous crimes committed under different political conditions that either no longer exist or are in the process of breaking down. Some of these decisions can be quite legitimate. But there is no denying that they also result in impunity for heinous crimes. It does not seem obvious to me that a territorial state's reconciliation interests, even if legitimate, should always override the concern for impunity for heinous crimes. Furthermore, in some cases a different nation pursuing justice outside of the territorial state by exercising universal jurisdiction might not be as disruptive to the community that is engaging in reconciliation. In other cases, as in the Pinochet case, the territorial state might be prompted by another nation's use of universal jurisdiction to reconsider whether it should prosecute these heinous crimes itself.
17. About the advantages of the principle of territoriality, the distinguished international jurist, Antonio Cassese, recently writes, "[the *locus delicti commissi* (the place where the offence has allegedly been committed)] normally is the place where the rights of the accused are best safeguarded . . ." (Cassese, *International Criminal Law* (New York: Oxford University Press, 2003), 278.) I doubt that that is true generally. But the current situation in the US with regard to terrorist suspects is certainly a counterexample to this claim.
18. This is Waldron's claim, following John Rawls, that justice is systematic in the sense that it involves interrelated institutions that have to be evaluated as a whole. See Waldron, "Special Ties and Natural Duties," 24. I do not think that all matters of justice are "systematic" in this sense.
19. In preparing the final draft for this volume, I am greatly indebted to Ralph Kennedy, for his extensive written comments and suggestions. I am also grateful to Tara Lee for her very helpful comments on an earlier draft.

V. TORTURE

LARRY MAY

HUMANITY, PRISONERS OF WAR, AND TORTURE[1]

Torture and other forms of cruel and degrading treatment have been condemned by all the relevant documents in international law for over a hundred years. Torture has been condemned so strongly that it is normally said that it is unacceptable even when seemingly required by military necessity.[2] I will here mention only the most significant of the documents. Common Article 3 of the 1949 Geneva Conventions states that torture "shall remain prohibited at any time and in any place whatsoever."[3] The 1966 International Covenant on Civil and Political Rights, in Article 7, states that "no one shall be subject to torture or to cruel, inhuman or degrading treatment or punishment."[4] The 1984 Convention Against Torture and Other Cruel, Inhuman and Degrading Treatment creates an absolute ban on torture.[5] And the 1998 Rome Statute of the International Criminal Court, in its own condemnation of torture as a crime against humanity as well as a war crime, refers to torture as one of the Grave Breaches of the Geneva Conventions.[6] Adam Roberts, summarizing these and other documents, says: "the laws of war . . . have helped to bring about a degree of acceptance and observance of certain valuable basic ideas: for example . . . that there can be no justification for torture."[7]

Despite the fact that torture of prisoners of war has been condemned by every major document in international law, it has seemed to some, especially those in the administration of George W. Bush, that terrorism creates a special case for how prisoners of war (POW) are to be treated.[8] The prisoner may belong to a "cell" of those who have committed themselves to the use of tactics that risk horrible consequences for many innocent people. The prisoner may have information about future attacks on civilian populations that could, if learned, be instrumental in the prevention of these attacks. In addition, in a "war" against terrorists, it seems clear that the terrorist side is not willing to play by the rules of war, and hence that the terrorist prisoners should not be afforded the privilege of humane treatment that they deny to others. Nonetheless, I will argue that POWs should be treated humanely in that they are not subject to torture when captured and imprisoned. Our humanity demands as much.

I will ask what it is about humanity that might restrict or prohibit the use of torture and other forms of physical coercion in the treatment of POWs. In Section 1, I draw on insights from Hugo Grotius to argue that it is the principle of humanity not justice that should be definitive of the rules of war, especially concerning torture of POWs. In Section 2, I consider how the circumstance of being captured and placed into confinement changes the rules of the game. In Section 3, I argue that there is a fiduciary or stewardship relationship between a captor and a POW that underlies the obligations of humanity of captors and dictates that POWs not be tortured.

1. GROTIUS ON SLAVES AND PRISONERS OF WAR

In the seventeenth century, Grotius begins the task of considering what can be done to prisoners in wartime by setting out what he thinks is true according to principles of natural justice and the current law of nations. He begins by pointing out that at his time it was thought that POWs were simply to be treated as slaves. Yet, "in the primitive condition of nature, no human beings are slaves."[9] No one can kill or limit the liberty of another person, as a matter of natural justice, "unless the latter has committed a capital crime."[10] Yet, many states have given to masters the absolute right over their slaves. According to the conventionally based law of nations, slaves may be justifiably killed or tortured; indeed "there is nothing which a master is not permitted to do to his slave."[11] Grotius puts the point starkly by saying: "even brutality on the part of masters towards persons of servile status is unpunishable," and then points out that "limits have been set to this power by the Roman law" nonetheless.[12]

Grotius also claims that most states treat POWs similarly to slaves. Indeed, "all without exception who have been captured in a formal public war become slaves from the time they are brought within the lines."[13] As a result, according to the law of nations, there is no limit, even concerning brutality, to what may be inflicted on prisoners of war with impunity. Grotius signals that he finds this to be disturbing, but at this point in the *De Jure Belli Ac Pacis* (Book III, Chapter VII) he does not disagree with the doctrine that POWs have no customary rights at all, just as is true of slaves. Although, he does say that giving captors the right to punish POWs may reduce the likelihood that they feel the need to kill their prisoners outright, there is no attempt to limit this right of captors by considerations of what the captives deserve. From the perspective of the law of nations in the seventeenth century, there are apparently no restrictions on what can be done to POWs.

Yet, Grotius argued that there should be severe restrictions placed on captors concerning POWs. In Chapter XI of Book III, Grotius begins by saying that there is "a limit to vengeance and to punishment." Grotius argues: "Even where justice does not demand the remission of punishment, this often conforms with goodness, with moderation, with high-mindedness."[14] It is shortly after this remark that Grotius makes his famous allusion to "humanitarian instincts" that should govern how we treat our enemies.[15] Nowhere is this more important, in my view, than in the treatment of those who are confined by one party, especially where the party in question has every reason to want to exact vengeance or retribution on those who have been killing members of one's armed forces. Indeed, Grotius says: "To spare prisoners is commanded by the nature of goodness and justice." Even when burdened by too many POWs, it is better to "release all rather than to kill them."[16]

According to Grotius, while prisoners should not be killed, they may in some cases be punished. But the punishment must be based on the specific crimes they have committed, that is there should be no "retaliation except against those who have done wrong." On grounds of justice, those who have done wrong deserve to be punished only according to the extent of their wrongful behavior.[17] This is the basis of the contemporary view that prisoners should only be punished proportionately to what each has specifically done, for to do otherwise is for the captors to enforce an unjustified "sharing of punishing" upon the prisoners.[18] In particular, contrary to what was believed at his time, Grotius argued that hostages should never be put to death, no matter what their leaders do, unless the hostages "have themselves done wrong."[19] Considerations of justice, plus the important idea of humanity, combine together to place severe restrictions on what can justifiably be done to POWs, even if the prisoners are the enemy and have taken the lives of the captors' troops.

Grotius thus presents a strong case for thinking that POWs, like slaves, should be treated humanely, and should only be punished, and to that extent, based on specific wrongs that they have done, not based on what others around them have done, or what their leaders have done. What Grotius objected to were reprisals taken against POWs for what their leaders, or perhaps fellow soldiers, have done. Grotius also objected even to treating confined prisoners as harshly as they may have deserved. For the principle of humanity required that to be honorable more restraint was needed based on seeing people as fellow humans rather than as enemies deserving of punishment. In the case of POWs, who have been confined, a Grotian position is even stronger in insisting that extreme restraint be exercised.

Grotius insists that on the battlefield there is no other moral option but to exact punishment only proportionate to wrongs that have been done. War is truly a state of nature, where no one has the authority to create judicial proceedings to determine whether a punishable offense has occurred and to what extent it should be punished. But after a soldier has been captured, or has surrendered, that soldier is now under an authority that can provide a proper judicial basis for determining whether, and how, that soldier should be punished. On the battlefield there is no authority to determine who is guilty and who is not, and quick decisions need to be made so that one's life is not jeopardized. In such situations, it is sometimes justifiable to punish someone who is not convicted of a crime. But once one is off the battlefield, and there is a civil authority that can determine guilt and innocence, it is no longer justifiable to punish those who have not been convicted of a crime.[20]

The laws of nations seem to allow for abuse of POWs as a kind of recognition that the conquering army could have simply killed these soldiers rather than sparing their lives. The conquering army gets to treat POWs as slaves for no other reason than as one of "so many advantages" from its victory over the captured soldiers.[21] Grotius is so focused on providing reasons for why prisoners of war should not be killed that he does not say much about other forms of treatment of these prisoners. But in a series of telling remarks in Chapter XIV of Book III, Grotius argues that severe punishment is not acceptable according to natural justice and "humane considerations."[22] Indeed, POWs should be treated with moderation, rather than with severity, as the title of this chapter ("Moderation in Regard to Prisoners of War") indicates, because in the end they should be treated "as second selves, since they are human beings no less than we are."[23]

Humanitarian considerations are most at play when we are discussing confined soldiers who have unjustly refused to disclose information that is of military importance, or soldiers who were fighting an unjust war. In both cases, justice-based considerations do not rule out abuse of these prisoners. If information is needed to save lives, and it is unjustly withheld, extracting that information by the use of torture does not seem to be clearly unjust. And justice-based considerations, having to do with what the prisoners deserve for fighting without just cause, actually tell against restraint. Yet the laws of war should counteract the strong possibility of abuse, perpetrated by those who have weapons against those who do not. This is especially true of POWs since there is also a strong tendency of armed captors to wish to act in unrestrained ways against those who have information that could save their comrades' lives or against those who were moments before captured plotting the destruction or injury of the capturing soldiers.

So we have several important lessons from an examination of Grotius' seventeenth century discussion of our topic. First, POWs are not to be treated in an unrestrained way. Most importantly, these prisoners are not to be subjected to reprisals for what their leaders or comrades have done. Second, POWs are not to be summarily dealt with, as might perhaps be justified on the battlefield, since these prisoners are now under the authority of the conquering army and subject to the same judicial adjudications of their cases as would be true of anyone else in society. Once off the battlefield, all parties are back in society and no longer in the state of nature. Third, captives are in a special moral situation since they are utterly dependent on their captors, and vulnerable in ways that soldiers on the battlefield are not. Fourth, considerations of humanity are especially apt in POW cases since the capturing army is virtually unrestrained otherwise. We must be scrupulous in insisting that these prisoners be treated humanely.

While justice-based considerations tell against some abuse of POWs, such considerations will not tell against all such abuse. A Grotian argument can be advanced that nonetheless humanitarian considerations, especially having to do with compassion and mercy, should rule out nearly all forms of abuse and torture of POWs. In section 2 I will advance that argument in more detail by considering the special status that POWs occupy and the moral relevance of that status. From this "humanitarian" perspective, POWs should be treated with moderation and not with the severity that might otherwise be deserved.

2. CONFINEMENT AND TORTURE

On the model of a two-person battle, or a duel (a model that has problems to be sure), certain kinds of advantage bestowed on one party but not the other is thought to be unfair. If each played by exactly the same rules, then war as a contest of strength would be an acceptable way to settle disputes. According to Walzer and contemporary defenders of Just War Theory, if the contest is fair then soldiers have a kind of moral license to kill and injure each other.[24] Once the battle has ceased, different considerations of fairness apply. In this section, I want to spend some more time analyzing the significance of the changed circumstances of the solider who is captured or who surrenders as far as the fairness of the contest is concerned.

Assume there is a convention in war as follows: if a soldier wishes to surrender, and to be spared from being killed in exchange for being removed from the battle, that soldier should throw down her weapons and raise a "white flag." Why would it be worse to kill her after she raised the white flag than before she did so? In wartime situations, the surrendering or captured soldier is no longer able to defend herself the way she was before since she is now unarmed and has foresworn the use of weapons. The soldier now needs certain protections and restraints that were not needed before. And after placing herself under the command of a previously belligerent force, other forms of restraint, than merely not being killed, are also called for.

Confinement, whether forced or voluntarily sought, makes a difference in how we are to treat a person. Imagine a boxing match in which one of the participants has had his hands shackled behind his back. The fight will not be considered to be a fair one, and any blows landed by the unshackled boxer will not be considered to be justified the way they would have been if his opponent was also unshackled. But what if one boxer voluntarily shackles himself and steps into the ring? That the act was voluntary would certainly make a difference, but it would still be considered inhumane for the unshackled boxer to land blows on the defenseless shackled boxer. Of course, when a soldier surrenders it is not merely as if he has shackled himself, since the soldier to whom he surrenders retains his or her arms and can take the surrendering person's life in a second. The soldier who surrenders is more like the boxer who resigns from the match but is still in the ring – he has taken himself out of the contest, and now we are back to a time when the rules are not that of a contest between adversaries who are roughly equal.

In life, as opposed to contests, people do not feel entitled to kill each other; indeed, in life intentionally killing someone is considered one of the worst things that one human can do to another human. So, after a soldier is captured or surrenders, there is a very serious question about whether the soldier is still a soldier, and hence still subject to the odd rules of contests, or not a soldier, perhaps some kind of a civilian. One way to answer this question is to realize that soldiers are taught to try to escape and return to battle. So, if the soldier has been captured, there are good reasons to think that he is still a soldier since he will try to return to the battle. If the soldier voluntarily surrenders, things are much more complicated, since it is unclear why he would have surrendered if he still intended to return to the battle. And yet, there certainly are situations where the soldier feels that surrender is the only hope, at the moment, of saving his life, but where the soldier also hopes, later, to be able to return to the battle under more favorable terms than when he surrendered. In both situations, as long as the soldier is indeed confined he is not in a contest with anyone.

In US criminal law, it is thought to be an aggravating condition if an assailant first binds his victim, or finds him incapacitated, and then kills him. The idea is supposed to be that not giving the victim a chance to try to save his or her life makes the act of violence much worse than it would have been otherwise. When a person is confined, and hence has little opportunity to defend herself, then injuries done to that person seem especially unjustified. It seems clear that one person takes advantage of another person's vulnerability.[25] Indeed, even if a person deserved to be injured, there is something especially nasty about preventing the person from properly defending himself or herself or even from striking back. It appears that one is taking advantage of another. At very least we would say that it is worse (an aggravation) to injure someone who one is controlling than to injure someone who is not under one's control.

Think of one of the most disturbing pictures from the Abu Ghraib Prison to have surfaced in the Iraq War in 2004. A prisoner huddles outside his cell. He is stripped naked and has no weapon with which to defend himself. His hands are tied. Two growling dogs are on long leashes snapping at him. Other prison guards, all fully clothed and with weapons, seem to be surrounding the prisoner, and generally encouraging the dogs to attack the prisoner. The prisoner cowers, bent almost into a fetal position, in expectation of the attack to come. This is so clearly an instance of inhumane treatment that when this picture was published and then broadcast it caused outrage around the world.

Things look especially bad if the person in question has voluntarily placed himself or herself under the captor's care, and the captor is now abusing the prisoner. One way to understand this is to see things as if there has been a kind of contract where the surrendering soldier offers to stop fighting in exchange for a guarantee not to be assaulted, and by accepting the prisoner's surrender, the capturing army seems to accept the terms of the surrender. On this analysis, abusing the surrendering prisoner is a violation of an agreement. And the soldier who is forced to put down his arms and who then cooperates with his captors, also seems tacitly to accept a similar contract where his or her cooperation is exchanged for a promise of good treatment while in captivity. But this does not fully capture the seriousness of the matter, for even if there was no contract it would still seem to be wrong for the confined soldier to be abused.

There is also a kind of fiduciary or at least stewardship duty that is quite independent of any explicit or implicit contract. Where one party has voluntarily assumed the role of protector and where that party is in control of another, an obligation of heightened care arises for the protector. If one surrenders, but also hopes to go back to the battle, or if one is forced into the dependent role by being captured, why should one be treated with restraint? At least in part, this is because one is forcibly placed under the care of another and that other then has a fiduciary or stewardship obligation to provide care for the one who is dependent. Of course, the capturing army can refuse to accept the surrender, or not attempt to capture enemy soldiers. But if it does accept them, it has placed them under its care and then members of the army must treat the prisoners with much more consideration than if the prisoners were still free to fight.

The fiduciary or stewardship obligation is clearest when the soldier has surrendered; but what of those who have been captured? While the captured soldier has not voluntarily placed himself in the care of the capturing soldier, this is in effect what has happened nonetheless. By capturing rather than merely killing an enemy soldier, the capturing soldier could be understood to be merely securing a slave, as Grotius said was the custom at his time in the early seventeenth century. But even slaves, or perhaps especially slaves, are owed humane treatment since their condition is so vulnerable. Indeed, it is the vulnerability rather than the voluntary act of the captured soldier that triggers the fiduciary or stewardship obligation. The fact of one's vulnerability, combined with the voluntary acceptance of the vulnerable one as dependent upon the capturing soldier that creates the obligations to act humanely.

The confinement of soldiers as prisoners, as I said above, changes the rules of the game so that the captor goes from being a competitor of the enemy soldier to having a kind of fiduciary or stewardship responsibility for the soldier. And with this change, the idea of proportionality of treatment takes on a much greater prominence. Before capture or surrender, the enemy soldier should not be killed or injured unless this was somehow necessary for one's own survival. But the traditional rules of war allowed for quite wide latitude in terms of what was acceptable behavior in this domain, since it was assumed that soldiers were all on the same level, at all times ready to kill or injure one another. After capture, even on this (mistaken) view, it could no longer be assumed that soldiers are all ready to kill or injure one another, for among other reasons the captured soldier no longer has the ready means to effect this killing or injuring.

So, while it seems to matter how it came to be that a soldier is currently in confinement, in all such circumstances, the rules of war have traditionally set severe limits on what can legitimately be done to a confined soldier. It is mainly the fact of confinement that changes the moral universe, as we will see in Section 3. The question then is whether this change is enough to warrant the claim, often made throughout the centuries, that prisoners must only be punished proportionately to what they deserved based on what they had done while incarcerated. Why can't prisoners be tortured, either to obtain needed information, or to set an example to others still fighting, or as representatives of those who unjustly tried to kill members of the capturing army?

3. HUMANITARIAN OBLIGATIONS AND PRISONERS OF WAR

The confinement of soldiers as POWs, changes the rules of the game so that the captured soldier goes from being a competitor of the enemy soldier to being the enemy soldier's fiduciary or stewardship responsibility. The key consideration, I think, is that once a soldier is under the control of an enemy army, that soldier cannot be seen as a combatant and must be treated as a ward of the capturing army, with the rights that would be associated with someone who is now being forcibly subjugated by another. Once confined, the duty of the detaining soldiers is to treat the detainees as their fiduciary or stewardship responsibilities, regardless of what they might have done or learned while on the battlefield. In light of our earlier discussion, it is interesting that one of the earliest English cases to discuss fiduciary obligations referred to the trust relationship as a "principle of humanity."[26] The status of the POW, as confined, dependent, and vulnerable is crucial. Humanity requires restraint in such situations.

Fiduciary duties, as framed by the principle of humanity discussed earlier, normally attach in situations when a person has placed into another's hands either his or her own life or a valuable piece of property that the fiduciary is trusted to take care of. It is the trust that one person expresses to another that generates the fiduciary duty. It is a violation of this trust to abuse the life or object that one has been entrusted to care for. Fiduciary duties can also arise when one person has been placed in a position of dependence vis-à-vis another person. Think of the guardian of a minor child. In general, it seems to me, the fiduciary duty originates in the dependence or vulnerability of one person toward another, either voluntarily or involuntarily caused. If this is right, or if there is a relationship somewhat like that of the fiduciary relationship that fits this bill, then I would argue that the prisoner/warden or detainee/confiner relationship is of this sort.

Stewardship relationships are slightly less stringent than fiduciary relationships, and I have said that I am not sure which of these models is best for understanding the relationship between POWs and their captors. Some see fiduciary relationships as incredibly stringent, where the one party must place the interests of the second party over everything else even the interests of the first party. As I will explain, I do not have this in mind when I talk of fiduciary relationships. For that reason it might be better to think of these relationships as stewardship relationships. Stewardship relationships are not as well defined as fiduciary ones but seem to call for extra care on the part of the steward. While I think that a bit more than this is required of captors toward POWs, I am willing to admit that this might be the best way to capture that relationship, if the only alternative is a very severe understanding of fiduciary relationships.

A fiduciary relationship is a "functional relationship . . . not a contractual one since the expectations of the parties are not based on mutual promises, consideration or consent, for one party owns and has custody of the other party."[27] These are the words of the authors of *American Jurisprudence*, (2nd edn), concerning the nature of the relationship between a parent and a subsidiary corporation. Interestingly, these authors then go on to say that this type of fiduciary relationship is "like the relationship between parent and child, warden and prisoner" which is also based on "the status of the parties."[28] While there are many forms of fiduciary relationships, they all have in common the idea that "a person in a fiduciary relationship is under a duty to act for the benefit of the other as to matters within the scope of the relationship."[29]

In a sense, it does seem appropriate to think of prisoners of war and their captors as existing in a fiduciary relationship since the captor certainly controls, and even could be said to own, the POW. If there are duties of the captor to the POW they are certainly not based on contract. And while it may seem to be too much of a stretch to think of the POW as a child or ward, this is not so important since there are many other forms of fiduciary relationships than those that are based on complete dependency. When one person is rendered vulnerable and the other person is assigned the care and protection of the vulnerable one, a fiduciary relationship can also arise. In the most dependent relationship the duties are extremely strict, where the dominant party is to sacrifice his or her interests for the sake of the dependent party, as in the case of parents and children. But when the dependency is not quite that great, then it makes sense to think that the duty is also less strict, perhaps where the dominant party must give slightly more weight to the dependant party's interests than to the dominant party's interests. And the idea here turns on status, as does the original Grotian idea of humane treatment that follows from the Seventeenth-century idea of the principle of humanity.

While soldiers may do various horrendous things on the battlefield, once they have been captured (or have surrendered) it does not matter what they have done on the battlefield (at least before trial), for as confined soldiers they are all roughly equal in terms of how they should be treated. At the very least, those who hold POWs must meet a minimum of morally acceptable conduct regardless of what the POWs have done on the battlefield. And the main reason for this is that confinement transforms these previously dangerous soldiers into people who are dependent on their captors for many of the essentials of life. Of course it might be necessary to place some prisoners into special cells because of a greater risk of escape, or of hurting the guards. But to torture POWs based on what they have done on the battlefield, or based on trying to obtain the information they attained on the battlefield, is not acceptable, as both the US Supreme Court and the Israeli Supreme Court recently held.[30]

The idea that all POWs are to be treated with restraint is the background assumption of the Third Geneva Convention when it declares that:

> Persons taking no active part in the hostilities . . . shall in all circumstances be treated humanely, without any adverse distinction founded on race, colour, religion, faith, sex, birth or wealth, or any other similar criteria.[31]

Thus, the Third Geneva Convention subscribed to the view that there is a minimum that all such POWs can demand, regardless of who they are or what they did on the battlefield. They are not to be subject to reprisals and, while they can be disciplined for what they do while in custody, punishment for what they did while on the battlefield must wait until there has been a proper judicial proceedings.

The moral argument for thinking that captors should not abuse POWs hinges on the relationship of dominance and dependency between them. Once a person is in such a relationship, then it is status rather than behavior that counts morally. The captor is to treat the POW humanely, and to follow the specific restraints that that entails, because of the vulnerable and dependent position of the prisoner of war. The POW is to be treated mer; regardless of what that person did on the battlefield, because of the current status of the prisoner of war. Remember Grotius' comment that if there are too many prisoners of war to be treated humanely in a camp, then the captors have a duty to let them all go free. The fiduciary or stewardship relationship means that the captor must look to the interest of the prisoner with slightly more importance than the captor's interests. The dependency status of the POW demands as much.

I wish to end this paper by addressing the question of whether it is justifiable to abuse prisoners in cases of extreme emergency. Here the classic case involves officials of George W. Bush's Administration who may have signed secret orders allowing for such prisoner abuse by the CIA in order to stop a future terrorist attack on the United States in 2004. If only these prisoners could be made to talk, they may be able to tell who was planning such an attack as well as where and when it was to occur. Isn't this indeed the classic case of extreme emergency, and hence a basis for thinking that the rules of war could be suspended so as to achieve this clearly worthwhile military objective, despite the moral and prudential equality of the prisoners?

I wish to argue that if there are such cases that are ever justified by the principles of proportionality and necessity, they are far fewer, and much harder to justify fully, than people like to think. I admit that there might be cases where torture appears to be justified. I am nonetheless inclined to support an absolute ban nonetheless. I accept absolutist or near-absolutist principles when they are very narrowly tailored, as is true of the prohibition on the torture of POWs. While abuse might be justified in extreme emergencies, given that these cases are themselves extremely rare, it will also thus be rare indeed that detaining soldiers might be justified in torturing or otherwise abusing POWs. And it is always bad policy to set rules on the basis of very rare exceptional cases. So, while it might indeed appear that there could be emergency cases of justified torture, since we do not want to be rule fetishists, nonetheless it could still make good sense to have rules, such as are enshrined in the Geneva Conventions common Article 3, that prohibit such practices

The rules of war constitute a system of norms for regulating the behavior of States and their agents, in the absence of a World State. And the system of norms is meant to apply to one of the most stressful of times, when war has broken out and both sides to a dispute not only call the other "enemy" but also can find no other way to resolve the dispute but to attempt to annihilate each other. In such times, to have any agreement about what are the rules of the game must be seen as a good thing. Humanitarian law is about just this attempt to reconfigure the way people think, so that it is possible that peace might be restored, and that in the mean time suffering is reduced. It is in this way that we can understand why the rules of war, especially concerning torture, are said to derive from the "laws of humanity and the dictates of public conscience."[32]

NOTES

1. This paper is cut from Chap. 7 of my booklength manuscript, "War Crimes and Just Wars," which is itself the second volume of a projected multivolume work on the normative foundations of international criminal law. The first volume, *Crimes Against Humanity: A Normative Account*, was published by Cambridge University Press in 2005.
2. *The Commentary on Geneva Convention (I)*, by Jean S. Pictet et al., Geneva: International Committee of the Red Cross, 1952, pp. 134–135, points out that the prohibition on torture was to be an unconditional requirement as one of the main ways to give specificity to the idea of humanity and humane treatment in the common core of the Geneva Conventions. This was understood to be an advance over earlier Geneva Conventions that did not clearly indicate that torture and other forms of inhumane treatment were to be prohibited even when seemingly required by military necessity.
3. Geneva Convention (III), Article 3.
4. The International Covenant on Civil and Political Rights, 999 UNTS 171 (December 9, 1966), Article 7.
5. Convention Against Torture and Other Cruel, Inhuman and Degrading Treatment, 23 ILM 1027 (1984).
6. Rome Statute of the International Criminal Court, Article 8.
7. Adam Roberts, "Introduction," *The Documents on the Laws of War*, 3rd edn (Oxford: Oxford University Press, 2001), p. 31.
8. See: "Memo for Alberto R. Gonzalez, Counsel to the President," prepared by the Justice Department Office of Legal Counsel, August 1, 2002. This and many other documents are collected in Karen J. Greenberg and Joshua L. Dratel (ed.), *The Torture Papers: The Road to Abu Ghraib*, (New York: Cambridge University Press, 2005).
9. Hugo Grotius, *De Jure Belli ac Pacis* (On the Law of War and Peace) (1625), translated by Francis W. Kelsey (Oxford: Oxford University Press, 1925), p. 690.
10. Grotius, *De Jure Belli*, p. 256.
11. Grotius, *De Jure Belli*, p. 691.
12. Grotius, *De Jure Belli*, p. 691.
13. Grotius, *De Jure Belli*, p. 690.
14. Grotius, *De Jure Belli*, p. 731.
15. Grotius, *De Jure Belli*, p. 733.
16. Grotius, *De Jure Belli*, p. 739.
17. Grotius, *De Jure Belli*, p. 741.
18. Grotius, *De Jure Belli*, p. 741
19. Grotius, *De Jure Belli*, p. 742.
20. Grotius, *De Jure Belli*, p. 59.
21. Grotius, *De Jure Belli*, p. 692.
22. Grotius, *De Jure Belli*, p. 764.
23. Grotius, *De Jure Belli*, p. 762.
24. See Michael Walzer, *Just and Unjust Wars* (New York: Basic Books, 1977, 2000).
25. See Robert Goodin, *Protecting the Vulnerable* (Cambridge: Cambridge University Press, 1984).
26. Hylton v. Hylton (1754) 28 Eng. Rep. 349, 2 Ves Sen 547, at 549.

27. 18A Am Jur 2d CORPORATIONS Sect. 773.
28. 18A Am Jur 2d CORPORATIONS Sect. 773.
29. Restatement of Trusts (3rd), Sect. 2.
30. Justice O'Connor, writing for the majority, stated: "Captivity is neither punishment nor an act of vengeance . . . A Prisoner of War is no convict; his imprisonment is a simple war measure . . . He is disarmed and from then on must be . . . treated humanely." Hamdi v. Rumsfeld, 2004, 72 USLW 4607.
31. Geneva Convention III, Article 3.
32. The so-called "Martins Clause" of the Preamble of Hague Convention (IV) Respecting the Laws and Customs of War on Land, 1907, declares that "Until a more complete code of the laws of war has been issued . . . the inhabitants and the belligerents remain under the protection and the rule of the principles of the law of nations, as they result from the usages established among civilized people, from the laws of humanity, and the dictates of the public conscience."

KENNETH EINAR HIMMA

ASSESSING THE PROHIBITION AGAINST TORTURE

There is something uniquely horrifying about torture. Our biggest fears in life are as much concerned with the experience of severe pain as they are with death; people commonly claim that what they fear most about the end of their lives is not death itself but rather the pain of dying. The prospect of experiencing pain severe enough to break a person's will and spirit cuts to the heart of our worst fears about life. The idea that anyone would ever be deliberately subjected to treatment intended to produce such pain repels most of us in a way that no other behavior does.

Our moral reactions to torture tend to track our emotional reactions. Deliberately subjecting a person to pain severe enough to break his or her will strikes most of us as wrong regardless of circumstances. On this common view, there is no possible situation in which torturing someone is morally permissible.[1] For most of us, then, the moral prohibition against torture is absolute in a strong sense: it is not just that torture is always wrong; it is rather that torture is necessarily wrong.

In this chapter, I reject this view. The centerpiece of the argument is a "ticking-time-bomb" example of the sort championed by Alan Dershowitz, a hypothetical situation in which torture appears to be morally permissible. Using this example, I argue that torture is not absolutely prohibited and attempt to extract principles that define the conditions under which torture is permissible.[2]

1. AN ABSOLUTE MORAL IMMUNITY AGAINST BEING DELIBERATELY CAUSED PAIN?

The claim that torture is absolutely wrong needs a theoretical foundation because there are very few other examples of principles admitting of no exceptions that are expressed at such a high level of generality. Though the idea that all moral principles are absolute might have once been common, this is no longer true. As far as ordinary views are concerned, the foundational prohibitions against lying, stealing, and killing are qualified by exceptions that permit such acts when necessary to avoid significantly greater evils.

One might think we can find a foundation for the claim that torture is absolutely wrong in the form of a general moral right not to be deliberately caused suffering, but this is difficult to reconcile with ordinary views on punishment. We believe that persons convicted of violent attacks against other persons are legitimately punished by means explicitly calculated to cause suffering. Incarceration in a maximum security prison, for example, is *supposed* to be an unpleasant experience. But if persons have an absolute right not to be deliberately caused suffering, then punishment would be wrong.

It is true that the ultimate purposes of punishment have nothing to do with making sure that the wrongdoer is suffering. According to retributivist theories, the legitimizing purpose of punishment is to restore the balance of justice by giving the wrongdoer what he or she deserves. According to utilitarian theories, the legitimizing purposes of punishment are (1) to deter other persons from committing similar wrongs; (2) to prevent the wrongdoer from committing further wrongs; and (3) to rehabilitate the wrongdoer. The moral respectability of some or all of these purposes is thought to justify the state in punishing criminal acts.

Nevertheless, these legitimizing objectives are brought about by means that are deliberately calculated to inflict a harm like incarceration or execution – harm that is quite severe from the recipient's perspective. It would not be unreasonable to prefer torture to being executed, or even to prefer being tortured for a short period of time (short enough not to do any lasting psychological damage) to a lengthy period of incarceration. These judgments say something about the comparative severity of the harm caused by torture and by such punishments as execution and lengthy incarceration: legitimate punishment sometimes involves harm and suffering that are worse, as far as our judgments are concerned, than torture.

What this suggests, however, is that there is no moral principle defining an absolute immunity against intentionally caused suffering. If our ordinary judgments regarding punishment of wrongdoing are any indication, it is false that persons enjoy an absolute immunity of this kind. Of course, one can always reject these ordinary judgments, but that is neither plausible nor practicable, as it would require a comprehensive reform of our criminal justice practice.

2. AN ABSOLUTE IMMUNITY AGAINST TORTURE?

The above analysis provides little, if any, reason to think torture might be permissible in some circumstances. Incarcerating, fining, or even executing a person is, after all, different in a host of ways from torturing a person.

Unlike torture, the kinds of punishment available in Western nations are not intended to cause *physical* pain or injury; indeed, measures intended to inflict physical pain for the purpose of punishment are universally considered unacceptable in Western nations. Moreover, while punishment is intended to inflict something unpleasant; punishment, unlike torture, is not intended to cause so much pain that it breaks the offender's will. Every Western nation seeks to ensure that prisoners get as much access to exercise, sunshine, social activities, and so on, as is compatible with the security interests of the public, prison employees, and other prisoners.

Most people reject the idea that convicted criminal defendants may legitimately be punished by being tortured. This is particularly telling because torture-as-punishment would promote some of the legitimate ends of punishment. First, violent crime would likely drop dramatically if convicted offenders were quickly and publicly tortured. Second, if the harm one deserves is directly proportionate to the harm one wrongly causes to other people, then a criminal who tortures her victims deserves to be tortured. Despite all this, most people regard torture as beyond the pale of legitimate punishment.

What accounts for this judgment is probably what makes torture uniquely horrifying: human beings performing acts intended to produce physical pain severe enough to break the will of other human beings. The idea is that it is never permissible for any one human being to deliberately attempt to bring about such intense pain in another person. On this view, then, people have an absolute immunity against acts that are, either singly or together with other acts of the same kind, reasonably calculated to bring about sufficient pain to break a reasonable person's will. Torture is not a morally permissible means of achieving any purpose.

At first glance, the idea that we have an absolute immunity against torture grounded in our dignity as moral persons should seem quite plausible. Punishment is an evil because it involves deliberately causing suffering to a person; but it is compatible with human dignity to the extent that it is deserved. Torture is necessarily incompatible with human dignity because it uses the threat of severe pain to neutralize the very capacity for free choice that confers this dignity upon us.

Nevertheless, the idea that we have an absolute immunity against torture is problematic. To see this, consider whether torture would be permissible in the following situation (hereinafter *TBE* for the "Time Bomb Example"). Suppose that US officials have as much evidence as anyone could have for believing that: (1) there are ten hydrogen bombs hidden in the ten most populous US cities; (2) the bombs are powerful enough to decimate each city leaving no survivors and extensive radioactive fallout;

(3) the bombs are set to go off in 24 hours; (4) it is not possible to evacuate any of the cities within 24 hours; (5) a conspirator in custody knows where each of the bombs is and will reveal this information quickly enough, if tortured, for officials to find and disarm each of the bombs; and (6) there is no other way to avoid having the bombs detonate.

There are a couple of observations worth making here. First, US officials are as certain about *each* of these propositions as any human being could be about *any* contingent empirical proposition – which includes scientific propositions describing laws of nature, but excludes mathematical truths like *2 + 2 = 4*. Second, these bombs will kill hundreds of millions of people. While the ten most populous cities have 23,899,236 inhabitants, their metropolitan areas are considerably larger. The bombs are powerful enough not only to kill the vast majority of inhabitants of these metropolitan areas, but also to produce clouds of radiation that would kill many millions of other people.

As far as I can tell, most people believe it would be morally permissible for officials to torture the conspirator. I have spoken to hundreds of people in a variety of different contexts about this unhappy example (university classrooms, continuing legal education courses for lawyers, etc.) and have never encountered a person who thought it wrong to torture the conspirator. Though torture even here would be a deeply regrettable choice to have to make, it seems, intuitively, to be morally permissible. If these intuitions are correct, torture is permissible in *TBE*.

This utterly changes the way we must think about torture. If the prohibition against torture were absolute, all one would have to do to show that, say, the US treatment of Iraqi prisoners at Abu Ghraib is wrong is to show that such treatment is "torture." Since anything that counts as "torture" is morally wrong if the prohibition against torture is absolute, merely showing that some act is "torture" is, by itself, sufficient to justify condemning that act. But if torture is permissible in *TBE*, we have to determine whether the circumstances in question are sufficiently similar to the circumstances of *TBE* that explain why it is permissible to torture the conspirator. Instead of simply rehearsing the syllogism "torture is wrong; this act is torture; therefore, this act is wrong," we must look more closely at the surrounding circumstances. This involves a radically different – and far more difficult – kind of reasoning.

3. EVALUATING TORTURE

There are a number of considerations that seem to explain the judgment that torture is permissible in *TBE*. First, the threatened harm is especially grave. Second, the person to be tortured is a conspirator and hence morally culpable for bringing the harmful situation about. Third, the catastrophic harm cannot be prevented without torturing the conspirator. Fourth, torturing the conspirator will enable officials to prevent the harm. Fifth, the officials have as much evidence for believing the first four propositions as there could be for any empirical proposition. Sixth, the conspirator can stop the torture at any time by producing the information.

3.1 How Much Evidence is Necessary?

Perhaps the most conspicuous feature of the example as so far sketched is the unusual epistemic situation of the officials: they *know* quite a bit about the conspiracy. They know, for example, that there are nuclear devices poised to go off in the ten most populous cities unless they are found and disarmed within 24 hours. They know the person in custody is a conspirator with the information needed to avoid the catastrophic outcome. They also know that they cannot find those devices without getting that information from the conspirator and that he or she will provide that information in enough time to avert disaster if and only if he or she is tortured. The fact that the officials are as justified in believing all these things as anyone could be in believing any empirical proposition plays a central role in explaining the judgment that torture is permissible in *TBE*.

This raises the question of how much evidence is necessary to justify torture. One possibility is that it is a necessary condition of justifiable torture that officials have sufficient evidence regarding each of the relevant factors to justify certainty beyond all doubt, but this is too strong. Even if we assume that the conspirator confessed to all this and that a voice thundering from the sky has informed us in a way that appears unmistakably miraculous that the conspirator is telling the truth, we would still not be justified beyond all doubt. Formal philosophical skepticism remains possible even here: we cannot rule out the possibility that we were hallucinating or that a powerful evil genius was deceiving us.

But these doubts are not important enough to think that officials are not justified in acting on the basis of what information they have. If these are the only doubts officials have about the situation, then the chances of making a mistake are so small as to be negligible. It is true, of course, that a mistake here would have very grave effects on the victim; an innocent person, after all, would have been tortured. But this is true in other contexts: though a mistaken conviction would have very grave effects on the person who is convicted, no one would argue that a criminal conviction ought to be reversed on the ground that a powerful evil genius might be deceiving us about the guilt of the defendant.

This suggests that no more than proof beyond a *reasonable* doubt is needed to justify torturing the conspirator in *TBE*. The concern that we are being deceived by a powerful evil genius might be a possible doubt, but it is not a reasonable doubt. A reasonable doubt is one supported by some other proposition we have adequate reason to believe is true; and there are no propositions we have adequate reason to believe that would support the claim that we are being deceived by an evil genius. The concern that we might be deceived by such a being arises not because we have reason to think it is true, but because our reasons for thinking it false are not conclusive. In the case of the conspirator, there is no reason whatsoever for thinking that the officials are mistaken about their beliefs.

Notice that the reasonable doubt standard is not sufficiently stringent to preclude the possibility of mistakes. There have been many instances in which innocent persons have spent years in prison – or even been executed – on the strength of a mistaken conviction. Sadly, sometimes the evidence overwhelmingly points to the guilt of the wrong person.

Even so, nearly everyone accepts that proof beyond reasonable doubt is enough to justify imposing harsh treatment on someone convicted of a serious offense under this standard, despite the fact that mistakes are sometimes made. No mainstream thinker believes that the possibility of a mistaken conviction precludes sentencing a convicted murderer to life imprisonment. Absolute certainty is simply not possible; and our survival depends upon making decisions about whom to punish for breaking laws prohibiting violent crimes. Given that our survival is likely also at issue in situations like *TBE*, it seems clear that no more than evidence beyond reasonable doubt can be required in the torture case.

3.2 How Much Harm is Needed?

Another feature of *TBE* that helps to explain the judgment that torture might be justified in such circumstances is the amount of harm that would be avoided: torturing the conspirator in *TBE* is the only way to save hundreds of millions of lives. If one believes that torturing the conspirator is permissible in *TBE*, this belief was undoubtedly grounded in a judgment that the evil involved in torturing the conspirator was less significant than the evil involved in allowing the conspiracy to succeed and letting the bombs go off.

This reasoning has a couple of implications with respect to thinking about when torture might be permissible in interrogation contexts. First, it tells us that torture is sometimes permissible when necessary to prevent harms of a certain magnitude. This, of course, is not surprising: once it becomes clear that the prohibition against torture is not absolute, the situations in which it is most likely that torture is permissible would be those where it is needed to prevent some terrible harm.

Second, it tells us that the permissibility of torture in any given situation in determined by a weighing process. Torturing some person P always involves an evil of some magnitude, which I will designate $EVIL(Tor)$. Assuming that we have sufficient evidence to eliminate the possibility of reasonable doubt on all the other elements necessary to be justified in torturing P, we have to determine whether $EVIL(\sim Tor)$, the magnitude of the moral evil we can prevent only by torturing P, outweighs $EVIL(Tor)$. If so, it is morally permissible to torture P; if not, it is not morally permissible to torture P.

$EVIL(Tor)$ might be equivalent to the amount of pain caused to P by torturing her, but it need not be. One might think that the act of torturing another human being involves evil far beyond the pain caused to the victim; torture involves an affront to human dignity that constitutes tremendous evil beyond the evil that results from the pain caused to the victim. On this line of thinking, then, the magnitude of the evil involved in torture is achieved by adding the magnitude of the affront to human dignity to the magnitude of the pain caused to the victim.

How much harm torture would have to prevent to outweigh $EVIL(Tor)$ depends on how this latter value is determined. If $EVIL(Tor)$ is equivalent to the pain inflicted on P, some torture might be permissible to save just one life; after all, most people would prefer being tortured for a short period of time to being killed – a reliable indication that death is a greater harm. If, however, $EVIL(Tor)$ includes the affront to human dignity, then the amount of harm it takes to outweigh $EVIL(Tor)$ will depend on the magnitude of the evil in the affront to human dignity. The larger the value, the more harm torture will have to prevent in order to offset it.[3]

Still, once we admit that torture is allowable to save innocent lives, it is implausible to think that millions of lives are needed to offset the evil involved in torture. If millions of lives suffice to offset $EVIL(Tor)$, however this is determined, surely thousands of lives would suffice to do so; it is hard to believe that the $EVIL(Tor)$ is so great (including the the affront to human dignity) that it cannot be offset by fewer than a hundred million saved lives.

Indeed, it would be an odd moral calculus that accords greater weight to the affront to human dignity than to the loss of even one innocent person's life.[4] There is no easy calculus for comparing the *affront* to human dignity caused by torture and the harm in being killed, but our own prudential preferences are probably reliable in determining the respective moral evils; what is a harm or evil to us is determined in part by our nature, and our shared preferences are a reliable indication of the relevant features of our nature. For my part, I care much more about the pain caused by torture than about the affront to my dignity; and I would prefer being tortured (for short periods of time) to death.

One might think that torture is justified only when necessary to save lives, but even this might not be true. Suppose officials are justified beyond reasonable doubt in believing that (1) John Doe has been kidnapped and will be tortured until found; (2) a conspirator in custody knows where Doe is and will reveal this information within a short period if tortured; and (3) it is not possible to find John Doe any other way.

It is not unreasonable to think that torture is justified here. Regardless of how *EVIL(Tor)* is determined, the balance of evils seems to favor torturing the conspirator because the evil in torturing the conspirator is offset by the evil that is prevented because the innocent person will be saved from torture; indeed, since we know that the conspirator will confess quickly and that the innocent person will be tortured indefinitely, torturing the conspirator will minimize the amount of moral evil in the world. If so, then torture might be justified in situations not involving loss of innocent lives.

3.3 *Culpability and Forced Choices*

In one sense, *TBE* is different from cases in which torture might be used as punishment against a known wrongdoer: the victim in *TBE* has it within his or her direct control to stop the torture; all he or she has to do is give the torturers the information they are seeking. If torture is permissible in *TBE* but not as punishment, this feature of the situation in *TBE* plays an important role in explaining why it is permissible in that case.

Of course, the fact that the victim can stop the torture by making a choice is not, by itself, sufficient to explain why torture is permissible in *TBE*. The victim's choice is clearly a "forced choice" in that torture is used to coerce him or her into making the desired decision by threatening a harm that greatly outweighs the benefits of choosing otherwise. In most instances, however, forced choices are impermissible because autonomous beings are generally immunized from deliberately coercive treatment. It is clearly wrong, for example, for me to threaten you with harm to induce you to withdraw your application for a job that I have applied for.

But *TBE* presents a forced choice that is different from threatening you to induce your withdrawal from a job search: the victim in *TBE* is being coerced to refrain from doing something that is a grave violation of clear moral requirements – namely, concealing the whereabouts of nuclear devices that will kill hundreds of millions of people. There is simply nothing like this in a case where you and I have applied for the same job: your claim to apply for the job is no less legitimate than mine. The torture victim in *TBE* has nothing that even remotely approximates a legitimate claim to conceal that information.

The point is not just that the victim in *TBE* is doing something wrong; it is rather that the victim in *TBE* is doing something that is *egregiously* wrong. Lying is clearly wrong, but it would also be wrong for the state to coercively prohibit lying in every circumstance – such as, say, a fine of some kind for such behavior. Moral persons are entitled to a sphere of autonomy against the state that includes a right to perform some immoral acts free of coercive interference.

But participation in a scheme to detonate nuclear devices does not fall within that sphere; and neither does concealing information about the location of those devices. Those behaviors involve such grave threats of harm that they fall far outside the protected sphere within which people may make moral mistakes without coercive pressure from the state. In this case, torture is regrettable, but the victim's behavior falls outside the sphere of autonomy protected against coercive pressure from the state.

Forced choices are sometimes permissible to prevent behaviors that involve egregious breaches of moral standards because they threaten grave harm to innocent persons. Laws that prescribe severe penalties for murder, such as execution or life imprisonment, present a choice that is forced in the same sense that the choice torture presents is forced: it attempts to coerce a desirable choice (e.g., refraining from murder) by threatening or inflicting a serious harm on the subject for making the undesirable choice.

Two factors, then, are working together to help explain why torture is permissible in *TBE*. First, the conspirator can stop the torture at any time by choosing to refrain from something that constitutes an egregious moral violation. Second, it is permissible to resort to coercive means to force a person to choose against committing an egregious moral violation – particularly one that involves tremendous harm to many innocent persons. While it might ordinarily be impermissible to present a forced choice, it is permissible for officials to do so because of the conspirator's culpability in an egregious scheme.

Together with the epistemic considerations discussed above, this suggests a very stringent condition that must be satisfied for torture to be justified: officials may resort to torturing a person P only if they are justified beyond reasonable doubt in believing that P is culpable for acting (or conspiring to act) in a way that involves an egregious moral violation.[5]

3.4 Efficacy of Torture

Another important issue in determining whether torture is permissible in some context is whether officials have adequate reason to think it will be efficacious in producing the desired information. In many instances, certain kinds of treatment can be ruled out because not likely to result in the production of legitimating information. For example, treatment intended to humiliate victims by subjecting them or their beliefs to ridicule, unlike treatment intended to inflict severe physical pain, is not reasonably calculated to produce information. Humiliating someone is more likely to strengthen her resolve not to cooperate with officials.

It is sometimes argued that torture can be ruled out in interrogation contexts as a matter of principle because there is no reliable way to determine in advance whether it will be efficacious in producing the desired information. If officials cannot know in any situation they will actually face that torture will induce the victim to provide accurate information, they will never be justified in resorting to torture.

There are two different sources of uncertainty with respect to the efficacy of torture – only one of which is of genuine moral significance in evaluating torture. The first involves uncertainty about whether some culpable person with enough information to otherwise legitimate the use of torture will respond to being tortured by disclosing that information. Not everyone breaks under the pressure of being tortured; and there is no reliable way to determine whether a person who has such information will reveal it in response to being tortured.

This kind of uncertainty is of little significance. To see this, consider a slightly modified version of *TBE*. As before, officials know the person in custody is a conspirator in a scheme to detonate nuclear devices in each of the ten largest US cities and has accurate information about the whereabouts of those devices that would enable officials to disarm them before they go off. In the modified version, however, officials do not know whether the conspirator will respond to being tortured by disclosing the information. It seems clear that officials would be justified in torturing the conspirator – despite the fact that officials do not know whether the conspirator will break – to save so many lives.

The second, and more worrisome, type involves uncertainty about whether the content produced by someone in response to being tortured is veridical. It is frequently asserted that torture is highly unreliable in producing accurate content because victims will say anything to stop the pain. Since the content produced by torture tends to be inaccurate, officials will not have sufficient reason to think in any given instance that torture will be efficacious in producing information which will prevent an egregious moral violation.

There are a number of different problems that can arise here. Officials might lack adequate reason to think the victim is a participant in some egregious scheme; if the victim is not a participant, then torturing him or her will not yield information that would, other things being equal, legitimate torture – because he or she does not have it. This uncertainty has to do with lacking adequate information that would justify a belief that the victim is culpable and is not really a problem of uncertainty about the efficacy of torture.

Alternatively, officials might have adequate reason to think that the victim is a participant in some act or scheme but not have adequate reason to think that the act or scheme involves an egregious moral violation that would, other things being equal, legitimate torture. This uncertainty has less to do with the efficacy of torture than it does with evaluating the act or scheme under moral standards – and is just the problem that was discussed in the last section.

More to the point, officials might have adequate reason to think that the victim is a participant in an egregious moral scheme that would, other things being equal, legitimate torture, but lack adequate reason to think that the victim has information that would assist officials in preventing the violation. In such cases, officials lack reason to think that torture will produce reliable information, not just because they do not know whether the victim will break, but because they do not know whether the victim has the right kind of information.

Indeed, in many common cases, officials may have some reason to think that culpable participants do not have the right kind of information. It seems reasonable to think, for example, that lower-level prisoners of war (POW) will not have much information about future operations likely to pose a significant threat. While POWs might have been engaged in ongoing operations, one would expect that, in the unstable conditions of battle, plans cannot be made too far in advance. Moreover, it would seem to be prudent for persons in immediate command to disclose as little as possible to soldiers to protect against disclosure in the event they are captured and tortured. For all officers may be presumed to know in ordinary cases, what information lower-level POWs have is not likely to result in saved lives.

This kind of uncertainty does make a difference in our judgments about whether torture is permissible. Suppose officials know that the conspirator in *TBE* is a low-level participant but have good reason to doubt she has any information that would lead to the location of any of the nuclear devices. Here torture would not be a means for producing information the victim is known to have, but would rather be something akin to what lawyers call a "fishing expedition." In such circumstances, officials would have significant doubts about whether the victim has information that would otherwise legitimate torture, but would be engaging in torture on the off chance that she has such information and will disclose it.

These circumstances approach the limits of how much uncertainty is compatible with being justified in torturing someone. The problem here is that when torture is justified as a means of producing information, it is partly because the victim's possession of the information puts him or her in a position to stop the torture by disclosing it. Although the choice to disclose the information is, as we noted earlier, forced, it nonetheless remains a choice that enables the victim to stop the torture at any time. In circumstances where it is not clear that the victim has the information, it is not clear that this important element is satisfied: the victim who does not have the information officials are seeking cannot stop the torture by disclosing it. Since officials would not be justified in torturing someone for information they know he or she does not have, uncertainty about whether the victim has the relevant information militates against thinking that torturing the victim is justified.

There is, however, no bright line here. It is not unreasonable to think that the great harms involved in the *TBE* examples outweigh even significant uncertainty about whether a low-level participant has and would disclose information that would avert those harms. The amount of harm involved in the *TBE* examples, however, is far greater than is involved in the circumstances in which torture has been used as an empirical matter. Though intuitions here tend to be far less sharp, it is not unreasonable to think that the harms involved in ordinary combat situations, in contrast to those involved in the *TBE* examples, do not outweigh significant uncertainty about whether a lower-level POW has information that would otherwise legitimate torture. In any event, the important point for our purposes is that uncertainty about whether the victim has the right kind of information, like uncertainty about whether the relevant act involves an egregious moral violation, can defeat otherwise legitimate reasons for torture – and this poses a significant obstacle to justifying torture in ordinary combat circumstances.

4. OTHER LIMITS ON JUSTIFIED TORTURE

The idea that torture might be justified in any particular instance should not be construed to imply that torture is something that can be taken lightly. Any context in which torture might be justified presents a situation that is highly undesirable because *persons* are being treated in the worst way imaginable. While torture might be justified, the structure of its justification presupposes that it is a necessary evil – the terrible evil involved in torturing a person being outweighed by the terrible evil that would be caused to other innocent persons. A necessary evil is no less an evil for being necessary, and the choice for a necessary evil is no less tragic because the evil is necessary. Regardless of context and justification, torture is a truly tragic choice for any nation or official to have to make.

This means that torture should be administered, when justified, in a spirit that reflects the moral gravity of the situation. This requires officials to distinguish between treatment that is acceptable and treatment that is unacceptable and to resist any temptation to go beyond what is justified in the circumstances.

The line between what is and is not proper in the context of torture is difficult to draw, but we can look to the context of punishment to get a sense for how to draw it. Incarceration of prisoners is justified as long as prison officials are (1) taking steps to ensure that the prisoners' basic needs are being satisfied; (2) not enjoying the spectacle of the prisoners' unhappiness; and (3) not inflicting more discomfort than is necessary to achieve the justifying rationale of punishment.

The same seems to be true of torture. If torture is justified as a means of producing information in a particular situation, then it justified so long as (1) it does not involve treatment that is worse than appears reasonably necessary to produce the information; (2) officials are making sure that the victim is otherwise receiving proper nutrition and medical care; and (3) officials are not taking enjoyment in the ill-treatment of the victim. What is incompatible with respect for human dignity in this context, as in others, is treatment that is not morally justified.[6]

NOTES

1. For example, Amnesty International asserts: "The use of torture is an affront to human dignity that can never be justified. . . . No political or military objective or public emergency – whether it is combating terrorism, a state of war, the threat of war, or internal political instability – can justify torture." See http://www.amnestyusa.org/stoptorture/talking_ponts.html.
2. At the outset, it is worth noting that the argument of this chapter is concerned only with the use of torture in interrogational contexts. Torture could be used for a variety of other purposes.

3. This is not intended to be a consequentialist analysis. It might be that the affront to human dignity takes a certain value without regard to whether it bears at all on human utility or well-being.
4. Affront to human dignity is not, of course, the only evil involved in torture; accordingly, the claim is not that the value of one innocent life outweighs the total evil involved in torturing someone.
5. It is worth noting that this principle is a difficult one to satisfy in the context of contemporary armed conflicts in which torture is most likely to be contemplated by nations like the United States. In most cases, each side to an armed conflict believes that its aggression is morally justified. In some instances, one side of a war (e.g., the United States in World War II) might be justified beyond reasonable doubt in thinking the other side has made a moral mistake, but not in all. Where there is widespread disagreement within a nation about whether its involvement in a war is morally justified, officials are probably not justified *beyond reasonable* doubt in believing that the other side's aggression is morally wrong – at least not if we assume that citizens who oppose the war are generally reasonable people. But this seems to preclude the use of torture in wars, like the Iraq War, the legitimacy of which is contested by a significant percentage of the population in the United States.
6. If the above considerations are somewhat vague, their requirements are sufficiently clear to justify some observations about the treatment of Iraqi prisoners at Abu Ghraib. First, the attempts to humiliate prisoners by forcing them to pose in sexually suggestive ways is wrong because such treatment is not reasonably calculated to achieve any legitimate purpose; humiliation, as noted above, is not likely to produce any information that might otherwise legitimate torture. Second, in many instances, the soldiers appeared to ignore the moral gravity of the situation and took pleasure in the treatment and discomfort of prisoners; such evident cruelty is obviously wrong.

DAVID LUBAN

LIBERALISM, TORTURE, AND THE TICKING BOMB

Torture used to be incompatible with American values. Our Bill of Rights forbids cruel and unusual punishment, and that has come to include all forms of corporal punishment except prison and death by methods purported to be painless. Americans and our government condemn states that torture; we grant asylum or refuge to those who fear it. The Senate ratified the Convention Against Torture, Congress enacted antitorture legislation, and judicial opinions spoke of "the dastardly and totally inhuman act of torture."[1]

Then came September 11. Less than a week later, a feature story reported that a quiz in a university ethics class "gave four choices for the proper U.S. response to the terrorist attacks: A.) execute the perpetrators on sight; B.) bring them back for trial in the U.S.; C.) subject the perpetrators to an international tribunal; or D.) torture and interrogate those involved." Most students chose A and D – execute them on sight and torture them.[2] Six weeks after September 11, the *New York Times* reported that torture had become a topic of conversation "in bars, on commuter trains, and at dinner tables."[3] By mid-November 2001, the Christian Science Monitor found that one in three surveyed Americans favored torturing terror suspects.[4] American abhorrence to torture now appears to have extraordinarily shallow roots.

To an important extent, one's stance on torture runs independent of progressive or conservative ideology. Alan Dershowitz would permit torture, provided it is regulated by a judicial warrant requirement;[5] and liberal senator Charles Schumer has publicly poo-poo-ed the idea "that torture should never, ever be used."[6] He argues that every US senator would back torture to find out where a ticking time bomb is planted. On the other hand, William Safire, a self-described "conservative and card-carrying hard-liner," expresses revulsion at "phony-tough" protorture arguments, and forthrightly labels torture "barbarism."[7] Examples like these illustrate how vital it is to avoid a simple left-right reductionism. For the most part, American conservatives belong no less than progressives to liberal culture, broadly understood. Here, when I speak of "liberalism," I mean it in the broad sense used by political philosophers from John Stuart Mill on – a sense that includes conservatives as well as progressives, so long as they believe in limited government and the importance of human dignity and individual rights.

It is an important fact about us – us modern liberals, that is – that we find scenes such as the Abu Ghraib photographs, to say nothing of worse forms of abuse and torture, almost viscerally revolting (and I am convinced that this is just as true for those who believe that torture may be acceptable as for those who do not). That is unusual, because through most of human history there was no taboo on torture in military and juridical contexts. On the contrary, torture was an accepted practice as a means for terrorizing civilian populations, as a form of criminal punishment, as a method of extracting confessions in legal systems that put a premium on confession as the form proof should take in criminal cases, and – above all – as the prerogative of military victors over their vanquished enemies.

Indeed, Judith Shklar notes a remarkable fact, namely that cruelty did not seem to figure in classical moral thought as an important vice.

[O]ne looks in vain for a Platonic dialogue on cruelty. Aristotle discusses only pathological bestiality, not cruelty. Cruelty is not one of the seven deadly sins. . . . The many manifestations of cupidity seem, to Saint Augustine, more important than cruelty.[8]

It is only in relatively modern times, Shklar thinks, that we have come to "put cruelty first," that is, to regard it as the most vicious of all vices. She thinks that Montaigne and Montesquieu, both of them protoliberals, were the first political philosophers to think this way; and, more generally, she holds that "hating cruelty, and putting it first [among vices], remain a powerful part of the liberal consciousness."[9]

What makes torture, the deliberate infliction of suffering and pain, specially abhorrent to liberals? This may seem like a bizarre question, because the answer seems self-evident: making people suffer is a horrible thing. Pain hurts, and bad pain hurts badly. But let me pose the question in different terms. Realistically, the abuses of detainees at Abu Ghraib, the Afghan Salt Pit, and Guantanamo pale by comparison with the death, maiming, and suffering in collateral damage during the Afghan and Iraq wars. Bombs crush limbs and burn people's faces off; nothing even remotely as horrifying has been reported in American prisoner abuse. Yet, much as we may regret or in some cases denounce the wartime suffering of innocents, we do not seem to regard it with the special abhorrence that we do torture. This seems hypocritical and irrational, almost fetishistic, and it raises the question of what makes torture more illiberal than bombing and killing.

The answer lies in the relationship between torturer and victim. Torture self-consciously aims to turn its victim into someone who is isolated, overwhelmed, terrorized, and humiliated. In other words, torture aims to strip away from its victim all the qualities of human dignity that liberalism prizes. It does this by the deliberate actions of a torturer, who inflicts pain one-on-one, up close and personal, in order to break the spirit of the victim – in other words, to tyrannize and dominate the victim.

Torture, in short, is a microcosm, raised to the highest level of intensity, of the tyrannical political relationships that liberalism hates the most. Liberalism incorporates a vision of engaged, active human beings possessing an inherent dignity regardless of their social station. The victim of torture is in every respect the opposite of this vision. The torture victim is isolated and reduced instead of engaged and enlarged, terrified instead of active, humiliated instead of dignified. And, in the paradigm case of torture, the victor's torment of defeated captives, liberals perceive the living embodiment of their nightmare – tyrannical rulers who take their pleasure from the degradation of those unfortunate enough to be subject to their will.

In other words, liberals rank cruelty first among vices not because liberals are more compassionate than anyone else, but because of the close connection between cruelty and tyranny. The history of torture reinforces this horror, because torture has always been bound up with military conquest, royal revenge, dictatorial terror, forced confessions, and the repression of dissident belief – a veritable catalogue of the evils of absolutist government that liberalism abhors. It should hardly surprise us that liberals wish to ban torture absolutely, a wish that became legislative reality in the Torture Convention's insistence that nothing can justify torture.[10]

But there remains one reason for torture that I have not mentioned, and which alone bears no essential connection with tyranny. This is torture as intelligence gathering, torture to forestall greater evils. The liberal rationale for the state, namely to secure the safety and liberty of its citizens, may make it particularly important to obtain time-sensitive security information by whatever means are necessary. For that reason, it will dawn on reluctant liberals that the interrogator's goal of forestalling greater evils, by torture if that is the only way, is one that liberals share. It seems like a rational motivation, far removed from cruelty and power-lust.

Thus, even though absolute prohibition remains liberalism's primary teaching about torture, and the basic liberal stance is empathy for the torture victim, a more permissive stance remains as an unspoken possibility, the Achilles heel of absolute prohibitions. As long as the intelligence needs of a liberal society are slight, this possibility within liberalism remains dormant, perhaps even unnoticed. But when a catastrophe like 9/11 happens, liberals may cautiously conclude that, in the words of a well-known *Newsweek* article, it is "Time to Think About Torture."[11]

But the pressure of liberalism will compel them to think about it in a highly stylized and artificial way, what I will call the "liberal ideology of torture." The liberal ideology insists that the sole purpose of torture must be intelligence gathering to prevent a catastrophe; that torture is necessary to prevent the catastrophe; that torturing is the exception, not the rule, so that it has nothing to do with state tyranny; that those who inflict the torture are motivated solely by the looming catastrophe, with no tincture of cruelty; and that torture in such circumstances is, in fact, little more than self-defense.

And the liberal ideology will crystalize all of these ideas in a single, mesmerizing example: the ticking time bomb.

Suppose the bomb is planted somewhere in the crowded heart of an American city, and you have custody of the man who planted it. He won't talk. Surely, the hypothetical suggests, we should not be too squeamish to torture the information out of him and save hundreds of lives. Consequences count, and abstract moral prohibitions must yield to the calculus of consequences.

It is a remarkable fact that everyone argues the pros and cons of torture through the ticking time bomb. Senator Schumer and Professor Dershowitz, the Israeli Supreme Court, indeed every journalist devoting a think-piece to the unpleasant question of torture, begins with the ticking time bomb and ends there as well. The Schlesinger Report on Abu Ghraib notes that "[f]or the U.S., most cases for permitting harsh treatment of detainees on moral grounds begin with variants of the 'ticking time bomb' scenario."[12] In the remainder of this chapter, I mean to disarm the ticking time bomb and argue that it is the wrong thing to think about. And, if so, the liberal ideology of torture begins to unravel.

But before beginning these arguments, I want to pause and ask why this jejune example has become the alpha and omega of our thinking about torture. I believe the answer is this. The ticking time bomb is an argumentative move against liberals who support an absolute prohibition of torture. The idea is to force the liberal prohibitionist to admit that yes, even he or she would agree to torture in at least this one situation. Once the prohibitionist admits that, then he or she has conceded that his or her opposition to torture is not based on principle. Now that the prohibitionist has admitted that his or her moral principles can be breached, all that is left is haggling about the price. No longer can the prohibitionist claim the moral high ground; no longer can he or she put the burden of proof on his or her opponent. He or she is down in the mud with them, and the only question left is how much further down he or she will go. Dialectically, getting the prohibitionist to address the ticking time bomb is like getting the vegetarian to eat just one little oyster because it has no nervous system. Once he or she does that – *gotcha!*

The ticking time bomb scenario serves a second rhetorical goal, one that is equally important to the proponent of torture. It makes us see the torturer in a different light, one of the essential points in the liberal ideology of torture because it is the way that liberals can reconcile themselves to torture even while continuing to "put cruelty first." Now, the torturer is not a cruel man or a sadistic man or a coarse, insensitive brutish man. Now, the torturer is a conscientious public servant, heroic the way that New York firefighters were heroic, willing to do desperate things only because the plight is desperate and so many innocent lives are weighing on the suffering servant's conscience. The time bomb clinches the great divorce between torture and cruelty; it placates liberals, who put cruelty first. But, I wish to argue, it placates them with fiction.

I do not mean by this that the time bomb is completely unreal. To take a real-life counterpart: in 1995, an al-Qaeda plot to bomb eleven US airliners was thwarted by information tortured out of a Pakistani suspect by the Philippine police. According to two journalists, "For weeks, agents hit him with a chair and a long piece of wood, forced water into his mouth, and crushed lighted cigarettes into his private parts. His ribs were almost totally broken and his captors were surprised he survived."[13] Grisly, to be sure – but if they had not done it, thousands of innocent travelers might have died horrible deaths.

But look at the example one more time. The Philippine agents were surprised he survived – in other words, they came close to torturing him to death *before* he talked. And they tortured him *for weeks*, during which time they presumably didn't know about the al-Qaeda plot. What if he too didn't know? Or what if there had been no al-Qaeda plot? Then they would have tortured him for weeks, possibly tortured him to death, for nothing. For all they knew at the time, that is exactly what they were doing. You cannot use the argument that preventing the al-Qaeda attack justified the decision to torture, because *at the moment the decision was made* no one knew about the al-Qaeda attack.

The ticking bomb scenario cheats its way around these difficulties by stipulating that the bomb is there, ticking away, and that officials know it and know they have the man who planted it. Those conditions will seldom be met.[14] Let us try some more honest hypotheticals and the questions they raise:

1. The authorities know there may be a bomb plot in the offing, and they have captured a man who may know something about it, but may not. Torture him? How much? For weeks? For months? The chances are considerable that you are torturing a man with nothing to tell you. If he does not talk, does that mean it is time to stop, or time to ramp up the level of torture? How likely does it have to be that he knows something important? 50:50? 30:70? Will one out of a hundred suffice to land him on the water board?
2. Do you really want to make the torture decision by running the numbers? A 1% chance of saving a thousand lives yields ten statistical lives. Does that mean that you can torture up to nine people on a 1% chance of finding crucial information?
3. The authorities think that one out of a group of 50 captives in Guantanamo might know where Osama bin Laden is hiding – but they do not know which captive. Torture them all? That is: torture 49 captives with nothing to tell you on the uncertain chance of capturing Osama?
4. For that matter, would capturing Osama bin Laden demonstrably save a single human life? The Bush administration has downplayed the importance of capturing Osama because US strategy has succeeded in marginalizing him. Maybe capturing him would save lives – but how certain do you have to be? Or doesn't it matter whether torture is intended to save human lives from a specific threat, as long as it furthers some goal in the War on Terror?

This question is especially important once we realize that the interrogation of al-Qaeda suspects will almost never be to find out where the ticking bomb is hidden. We do not know in advance when al-Qaeda has launched an operation. Instead, interrogation is a more general fishing expedition for any intelligence that might be used to help "unwind" the terrorist organization. Now one might reply that al-Qaeda is itself the ticking time bomb, so that unwinding the organization meets the formal conditions of the ticking bomb hypothetical. This is equivalent to asserting that any intelligence which promotes victory in the War on Terror justifies torture, precisely because we understand that the enemy in the War on Terror aims to kill American civilians. Presumably, on this argument Japan would have been justified in torturing American captives in World War II on the chance of finding intelligence that would help them shoot down the *Enola Gay*; and I assume that a ticking bomb hard-liner will not flinch from this conclusion. But at this point, we verge on declaring all military threats and adversaries that menace American civilians to be ticking bombs, whose defeat justifies torture. The limitation of torture to emergency exceptions, implicit in the ticking bomb story, now threatens to unravel, making torture a legitimate instrument of military policy. And then the question becomes inevitable: Why not torture in pursuit of any worthwhile goal?

The point of these examples is that in a world of uncertainty and imperfect knowledge, the ticking bomb scenario should not form the point of reference. The ticking bomb is a picture that bewitches us. The real debate is not between one guilty man's pain and hundreds of innocent lives. It is the debate between the certainty of anguish and the mere possibility of learning something vital and saving lives. And, above all, it is the question about whether a responsible citizen must unblinkingly think the unthinkable, and accept that the morality of torture should be decided purely by toting up expected costs and benefits.[15] Once you accept that only the numbers count, then anything, no matter how gruesome, becomes possible.

I am inclined to think that the path of wisdom instead lies in Holocaust survivor David Rousset's famous caution that normal human beings do *not* know that everything is possible.[16] As Bernard Williams says, "there are certain situations so monstrous that the idea that the processes of moral rationality could yield an answer in them is insane," and "to spend time thinking what one would decide if one were in such a situation is also insane, if not merely frivolous."[17]

There is a second, even more important, error built into the ticking bomb hypothetical. It assumes a single, ad hoc decision about whether to torture, by officials who ordinarily would do no such thing except in a desperate emergency. But in the real world of interrogations, decisions are not made one-off. The real world is a world of policies, guidelines, and directives. It is a world of *practices*, not of ad hoc emergency measures. Any responsible discussion of torture therefore needs to address the practice of torture, not the ticking bomb hypothetical. Somehow, we always manage to talk about the ticking bomb instead of about torture as an organized social practice.

Treating torture as a practice rather than as a desperate improvisation in an emergency means changing the subject from the ticking bomb to other issues – issues like these:

Should we create a professional cadre of trained torturers? For instance, should universities offer undergraduate instruction in torture, as the Georgia-based School of the Americas did in the 1980s? Do we want federal grants for research to devise new and better torture techniques? Patents issued on high-tech torture devices? Companies competing to manufacture them? How about trade conventions in Las Vegas? Should there be a medical subspecialty of torture doctors, who ensure that captives do not die before they talk? Consider the chilling words of Sgt. Ivan Fredericks, one of the Abu Ghraib perpetrators, who recalled a death by interrogation that he witnessed: "They stressed the man out so bad that he passed away."[18] Real pros would not let that happen. Who should teach torture-doctoring in medical school?[19]

The questions amount to this: Do we really want to create a torture culture and the kind of people who inhabit it? The ticking time bomb distracts us from the real issue, which is not about emergencies, but about the normalization of torture.

Perhaps the solution is to keep the practice of torture secret in order to avoid the moral corruption that comes from creating a public culture of torture. But this so-called "solution" does not reject the normalization of torture. It accepts it, but layers on top of it the normalization of state secrecy. The result would be a shadow culture of torturers and those who train and support them, operating outside the public eye and accountable only to other insiders of the torture culture.

Just as importantly: who guarantees that case-hardened torturers, inured to levels of violence and pain that would make ordinary people vomit at the sight, will know where to draw the line on when torture should be used? They never have in the past. They did not in Algeria.[20] They did not in Israel, where in 1999 the Supreme Court backpedaled from an earlier permission to engage in "torture lite" in emergencies because the interrogators were torturing two-thirds of their Palestinian captives.[21] In the Argentinian Dirty War, the tortures began because terrorist cells had a policy of fleeing when one of their members had disappeared for 48 hours.[22] Authorities who captured a militant had just two days to wring the information out of the captive. One scholar who has studied the Dirty War reports that at first many of the officers carrying it out had qualms about what they were doing, until their priests reassured them that they were fighting God's fight. By the end of the Dirty War, the qualms were gone, and hardened young officers were placing bets on who could kidnap the prettiest girl to rape and torture.[23] Escalation is the rule, not the aberration.[24]

Interrogators do not inhabit a world of loving kindness, or of equal concern and respect for all human beings. Interrogating resistant prisoners, even nonviolently and nonabusively, still requires a relationship that in any other context would be morally abhorrent. It requires tricking information out of the subject, and the interrogator does this by setting up elaborate scenarios to disorient the subject and propel him into an alternative reality. The subject must be gotten to believe that his high-value intelligence has already been discovered from someone else, so that there's no point in keeping it secret any longer. He must be fooled into thinking that his friends have betrayed him, or that the interrogator is really his friend. The interrogator disrupts his sense of time and place, disorients him with sessions that never occur at predictable times or intervals, and manipulates his emotions. The very names of interrogation techniques show this: "Emotional Love," "Emotional Hate," "Fear Up Harsh," "Fear Up Mild," "Reduced Fear," "Pride and Ego Up," "Pride and Ego Down," "Futility."[25] The interrogator may set up a scenario to make the subject think he is in the clutches of a much-feared secret police organization from a different country. Every bit of the subject's environment is fair game for manipulation and deception, as the interrogator aims to create the total lie that gets the subject talking.[26]

Let me be clear that I am not objecting to these deceptions. None of them rises to the level of abuse or torture lite, let alone torture heavy, and surely tricking the subject into talking is legitimate if the goals of the interrogation are legitimate. But what I have described is a relationship of totalitarian mind-control more profound than the world of Orwell's *1984*. The interrogator is like Descartes's Evil Deceiver, and the subject lives in a false reality as profound as *The Matrix*. The liberal fiction that interrogation can be done by people who are neither cruel nor tyrannical runs aground on the fact that regardless of the interrogator's character off the job, on the job every fiber of his concentration is devoted to dominating the mind of the subject.[27]

Only one thing prevents mind-control games from crossing the line into abuse and torture, and that is a clear set of bright-line rules, drummed into the interrogator with the intensity of a religious indoctrination. American interrogator Chris Mackey reports that warnings about the dire consequences of violating the Geneva Conventions "were repeated so often that by the end of our time at [training school] the three syllables 'Lea-ven-worth' were ringing in our ears."[28]

But what happens when the line is breached? When, as in Afghanistan, the interrogator gets mixed messages about whether Geneva applies, or hears rumors of ghost detainees, or of high-value captives held for years of interrogation in the top-secret facility known as "Hotel California," located in some nation somewhere? What happens when the interrogator observes around him the move from deception to abuse, from abuse to torture lite, from torture lite to beatings and waterboarding? With the clear lines smudged fuzzy, the tyranny innate in the interrogator's job has nothing to hold it in check.[29] Perhaps someone, somewhere in the chain of command, is a morally pure soul, wringing hands over whether this interrogation qualifies as a ticking bomb case. But the interrogator knows only that the rules of the road have changed and the posted speed limits no longer apply. The liberal myth of the conscience-stricken interrogator overlooks a division of moral labor in which the person with the fastidious conscience and the person doing the interrogation are not the same.

The myth must presume, therefore, that the interrogator operates only under the strictest supervision, in a chain of command where his every move gets vetted and controlled by the superiors who are actually doing the deliberating. The trouble is that this assumption flies in the face of everything that we know about how organizations work. The basic rule in every bureaucratic organization is that operational details and the guilty knowledge that goes with them gets pushed down the chain of command as far as possible.

We saw this phenomenon at Abu Ghraib, where military intelligence officers gave MPs vague directives like "'Loosen this guy up for us.' 'Make sure he has a bad night.' 'Make sure he gets the treatment.'"[30] Strictly speaking, that is not an order to abuse. But what is it? Suppose that the 18-year-old guard interprets "Make sure he has a bad night" to mean, simply, "keep him awake all night." How do you do that without physical abuse?[31] Personnel at Abu Ghraib witnessed far harsher treatment of prisoners by "other governmental agencies" – OGA, a euphemism for the Central Intelligence Agency.[32] They saw OGA spirit away the dead body of an interrogation subject, and allegedly witnessed contract employees and Iraqi police raping prisoners.[33] When that is what you see, abuses like those in the Abu Ghraib photos will not look outrageous. Outrageous compared with what?

This brings me to a point of social psychology. Simply stated, it is this: we judge right and wrong against the baseline of whatever we have come to consider "normal" behavior, and if the norm shifts in the direction of violence, we will come to tolerate and accept violence as a normal response. The psychological mechanisms for this renormalization have been studied for more than half a century, and by now they are well understood. Rather than detour into psychological theory, however, I will illustrate the point with the most salient example – one that seems so obviously applicable to Abu Ghraib that the Schlesinger Commission discussed it at length in an appendix to their report. This is the Stanford Prison Experiment. Male volunteers were divided randomly into two groups, who would simulate the guards and inmates in a mock prison. Within a matter of days, the inmates began acting like actual prison inmates – depressed, enraged, and anxious. And the guards began to abuse the inmates to such an alarming degree that the researchers had to halt the two-week experiment after just seven days. In the words of the experimenters:

> The use of power was self-aggrandizing and self-perpetuating. The guard power, derived initially from an arbitrary label, was intensified whenever there was any perceived threat by the prisoners and this new level subsequently became the baseline from which further hostility and harassment would begin. . . . [T]he absolute level of aggression as well as the more subtle and "creative" forms of aggression manifested, increased in a spiraling fashion.[34]

It took only five days before a guard who prior to the experiment described himself as a pacifist was forcing greasy sausages down the throat of a prisoner who refused to eat; and in less than a week, the guards were placing bags over prisoners' heads, making them strip, and sexually humiliating them in ways reminiscent of Abu Ghraib.[35]

My conclusion is very simple. Abu Ghraib is the fully predictable image of what a torture culture looks like. Abu Ghraib is not a few bad apples. It is the apple tree. And you cannot reasonably expect that interrogators in a torture culture will be the fastidious and well-meaning torturers that the liberal ideology fantasizes.

That is why Alan Dershowitz has argued that judges, not torturers, should oversee the permission to torture, which must be regulated by warrants. The irony is that Jay S. Bybee, who signed the Justice Department's highly permissive torture memo, is now a federal judge. Politicians pick judges, and if the politicians accept torture the judges will as well. Once we create a torture culture, only the naive would suppose that judges will provide a safeguard. Judges do not fight their culture. They reflect it.

For all these reasons, the ticking bomb scenario is an intellectual fraud. In its place, we must address the real questions about torture – questions about uncertainty, questions about the morality of consequences, questions about what it does to a culture to introduce the practice of torture, questions about what torturers are like and whether we really want them walking proudly among us. Once we do so, I suspect that few Americans will be willing to conclude that everything is possible.[36]

NOTES

1. *Filartiga v. Pena-Irala*, 630 F.2d 876, 883 (2nd Cir. 1980).
2. Amy Argetsinger, "At Colleges, Students are Facing a Big Test," *Washington Post*, September 17, 2001, p. B1.

3. Jim Rutenberg, "Torture Seeps into Discussion by News Media," *New York Times* (November 5, 2001), p. C1.
4. Andrew McLaughlin, "How far Americans would go to fight terror," *Christian Science Monitor*, November 14, 2001, p. 1.
5. Alan M. Dershowitz, *Why Terrorism Works* (New Haven, CT: Yale University Press, 2002), pp. 158–161.
6. Senate Judiciary Subcommittee, "U.S. Senator Orrin G. Hatch (R-UT) Holds a Hearing on the Federal Government's Counterterrorism Efforts," FDCH Political Transcripts, June 8, 2004.
7. William Safire, "Seizing Dictatorial Power," *New York Times*, November 15, 2001, p. A31.
8. Judith Shklar, "Putting Cruelty First," in *Ordinary Vices* (Cambridge, MA: Harvard University Press, 1984), p. 7.
9. Shklar, "Putting Cruelty First," p. 43.
10. "No exceptional circumstances whatsoever, whether a state of war or a threat of war, internal political instability or any other public emergency, may be invoked as a justification of torture." Convention Against Torture and Other Forms of Cruel, Inhuman and Degrading Treatment, Article 2 Sect. 2.
11. Jonathan Alter, "Time to Think About Torture," *Newsweek* (November 5, 2001).
12. The Schlesinger Report, reprinted in Karen J. Greenberg and Joshua L. Dratel, eds., *The Torture Papers: The Road to Abu Ghraib* (Cambridge: Cambridge University Press, 2005), p. 974.
13. Marites Danguilan Vitug and Glenda M. Gloria, *Under the Crescent Moon: Rebellion in Mindanao* (Manila: Institute for Popular Democracy, 2000), p. 223, quoted in Doug Struck et al., "Borderless Network Of Terror; Bin Laden Followers Reach Across Globe," *Washington Post*, September 23, 2001, p. A1.
14. See Oren Gross, "Are Torture Warrants Warranted? Pragmatic Absolutism and Official Disobedience," *Minnesota Law Review* 88 (2004): 1501–1503. Gross reminds us, however, that the catastrophic case can actually occur. Ibid., pp. 1503–1504. The ticking bomb case might occur if a government has extremely good intelligence about a terrorist group – good enough to know that it has dispatched operatives to carry out an operation, and good enough to identify and capture someone in the group that knows the details – but not good enough to know the details without getting them from the captive. Israel seems like a setting in which cases like this might arise; and indeed, Mark Bowden reports on just such a case. Mark Bowden, "The Dark Art of Interrogation," *The Atlantic Monthly* (October, 2003), pp. 65–68. Importantly, however, the Israeli interrogator got the information through trickery, not torture. (For that matter, the Philippine police who tortured the al-Qaeda bomber eventually got their information not from the torture but from the threat to turn him over to Israel.)
15. For a powerful version of the consequentialist argument, which acknowledges these consequences and accepts them (at least for dialectical purposes), see Michael Seidman, "Torture's Truth," forthcoming in the *University of Chicago Law Review*.
16. David Rousset, *The Other Kingdom*, trans. Ramon Guthrie (New York: Howard Fertig, Inc., 1982) (1947), p. 168.
17. Bernard Williams, "A Critique of Utilitarianism," in J.J.C. Smart and Bernard Williams, *Utilitarianism: For and Against* (Cambridge: Cambridge University Press, 1973), p. 93. Williams suggests "that the *unthinkable* was itself a moral category. . . ." Ibid., p. 92.

18. Quoted in Seymour M. Hersh, *Chain of Command: The Road from 9/11 to Abu Ghraib* (New York: HarperCollins, 2004), p. 45. The man was later identified as Manadel Al-Jamadi. According to various news accounts, Navy SEALS beat him with rifle muzzles and broke his ribs; he was then turned over to the CIA, who placed him in a stress position known as "Palestinian hanging" or the "Palestinian necklace" – suspended by the arms from a grate, a position that places great stress on internal organs. Al-Jamadi died that night, after which CIA operatives packed his body in ice in a shower stall before smuggling it out. One of the Abu Ghraib scandal perpetrators, Army Specialist Sabrina Harman, was photographed leaning over Al-Jamadi's corpse, grinning and flipping a hearty thumbs-up. The SEAL commander was tried and acquitted. According to Associated Press reports, after his acquittal he said, "I think that what makes this country great is that there is a system in place and it works." Seth Hettena, Associated Press, May 28, 2005, http://www.sfgate.com/ cgi-bin/article.cgi?file=/news/archive/2005/05/27/state/n171730D65.DTL.
19. This is hardly far-fetched. Summarizing extensive studies by researchers, Jean Maria Arrigo notes medical participation in 20–40% of torture cases. One study, a random survey of 4,000 members of the Indian Medical Association (of whom 743 responded), revealed that "58% believed torture interrogation permissible; 71% had come across a case of probable torture; 18% knew of health professionals who had participated in torture; 16% had witnessed torture themselves; and 10% agreed that false medical and autopsy reports were sometimes justified." Jean Maria Arrigo, "A Utilitarian Argument Against Torture Interrogation of Terrorists," *Science and Engineering Ethics* 10 (3) (2004), p. 6. at http://www.atlas.usafa.af. mil/jscope/JSCOPE03/Arrigo03.html. Evidence has emerged of participation of medical personnel in abusive U.S. interrogations. M. Gregg Bloche and Jonathan H. Marks, "When Doctors Go To War," *New England Journal of Medicine* 354 (January 6, 2005), pp. 3–6.
20. This is the conclusion Michael Ignatieff draws from the memoirs of French torturer Paul Aussaresses, *The Battle of the Casbah: Terrorism and Counter-Terrorism in Algeria, 1955–1957* (New York: Enigma Books, 2002), who remains completely unapologetic for torturing and killing numerous Algerian terrorists. Michael Ignatieff, "The Torture Wars," *The New Republic*, April 22, 2002, p. 42.
21. Bowden, "The Dark Art of Interrogation," pp. 74–76.
22. Mark Osiel, *Mass Atrocity, Ordinary Evil, and Hannah Arendt: Criminal Consciousness in Argentina's Dirty War* (New Haven, CT: Yale University Press, 2002), p. 40.
23. Osiel, *Mass Atrocity*, p. 120.
24. This is a principal theme in Ignatieff.
25. These are tabulated in the Schlesinger Report, *The Torture Papers*, pp. 965–67. See also Chris Mackey and Greg Miller, *The Interrogators: Inside the Secret War Against Al Qaeda* (Boston: Little, Brown, 2004), pp. 479–83; see also US Army Field Manual FM 34-52.
26. See the discussion in Bowden, "The Dark Art of Interrogation."
27. Given my earlier argument that liberal revulsion at torture is grounded in its similarity to tyranny, the question arises why I am willing to accept the forms of tyranny involved in tricking information out of detainees. The answer, though theoretically untidy, is straightforward: pain matters, and the pain of torture makes it a more devastating assault on the dignity and personhood of the victim. I thank Steven Lee for calling this question to my attention.
28. Mackey and Miller, *The Interrogators*, p. 31.

29. This point is forcefully made in the Jones/Fay Report on Abu Ghraib, reprinted in *The Torture Papers*. After noting that conflicting directives about stripping prisoners and using dogs were floating around simultaneously, the Report adds, "Furthermore, some military intelligence personnel executing their interrogation duties at Abu Ghraib had previously served as interrogators in other theaters of operation, primarily Afghanistan and GTMO. These prior interrogation experiences complicated understanding at the interrogator level. The extent of 'word of mouth' techniques that were passed to the interrogators in Abu Ghraib by assistance teams from Guantanamo, Fort Huachuca, or amongst themselves due to prior assignments is unclear and likely impossible to definitively determine. The clear thread in the CJTF-7 policy memos and published doctrine is the humane treatment of detainees and the applicability of the Geneva Conventions. Experienced interrogators will confirm that interrogation is an art, not a science, and knowing the limits of authority is crucial. Therefore, the existence of confusing and inconsistent interrogation technique policies contributed to the belief that additional interrogation techniques were condoned in order to gain intelligence." LTG Anthony R. Jones and MG George R. Fay, "Investigation of Intelligence Activities at Abu Ghraib," in *The Torture Papers*, p. 1004.
30. Hersh, *Chain of Command*, p. 30.
31. As a military police captain told Hersh, "when you ask an eighteen-year-old kid to keep someone awake, and he doesn't know how to do it, he's going to get creative." Hersh, *Chain of Command*, p. 34.
32. "Working alongside non-DOD organizations/agencies in detention facilities proved complex and demanding. The perception that non-DOD agencies had different rules regarding interrogation and detention operations was evident. . . . The appointing authority and investigating officers made a specific finding regarding the issue of 'ghost detainees' within Abu Ghraib. It is clear that the interrogation practices of other government agencies led to a loss of accountability at Abu Ghraib." Jones/Fay Report, *The Torture Papers*, p. 990.
33. Hersh, *Chain of Command*, pp. 44–45.
34. Craig Haney et al., "Interpersonal Dynamics of a Simulated Prison," *International Journal of Criminology and Penology* 1 (1973), p. 94, quoted in the Schlesinger Report, *The Torture Papers*, p. 971. See also Philip Zimbardo et al., "The Mind is a Formidable Jailer: A Pirandellian Prison," *New York Times*, April 8, 1973, §6 (Magazine), p. 41; and the remarkable internet slide-show of the experiment, Zimbardo, Stanford Prison Experiment: A Simulation Study of the Psychology of Imprisonment Conducted at Stanford University (1999), at <http://www.prisonexp.org>.
35. See John Schwartz, "Simulated Prison in' 71 Showed a Fine Line Between 'Normal' and 'Monster'," *New York Times*, May 6, 2004, p. A20.
36. This chapter is based on a longer essay with the same title appearing in the *Virginia Law Review* 91 (6) (October 2005), pp. 1425–1461, and it appears here with the permission of that journal.

DEIRDRE GOLASH

TORTURE AND SELF-DEFENSE

It is widely agreed that torture is ordinarily impermissible. But, since the attacks of September 11, 2001, nightmare scenarios involving individuals in possession of weapons of mass destruction[1] have lost their fantastic quality, and senior government officials have been heard to defend the use of torture in some circumstances. The dilemma is classically presented in the case of the ticking time bomb.[2] Suppose that officials have learned that a nuclear bomb is set to go off within a few hours, but do not know its location. They have, however, captured the person who placed the bomb, and know that she will reveal its location if and only if she is tortured. They also know that there is no other way to prevent the deaths of millions that will result from the detonation of the bomb.

One disturbing thing about this kind of example is the idea that officials at the investigative stage could ever know the things we are to assume they know here. How do they know a bomb has been placed, without knowing where? How do they know she is the one who did it, without giving her a full-dress trial? How are they to know what her response to torture will be? For all the reasons that we do not allow police, or even prosecutors, to mete out punishment for crimes they "know" have been committed, we should hesitate to give them the power to decide when they know enough to torture.

Let us assume, however, that they do know all these things, and that the person in captivity is in fact the bomber. It is of course ordinarily wrong to deliberately inflict extreme pain on a fellow human being, or to force her to do what we want. But if we do not do so in this case, millions of lives will be lost, and millions of others not actually killed will also suffer extreme pain. Moreover, it is the bomber himself or herself who is responsible for this threat. These facts are clearly sufficient to justify the use of some force against the perpetrator: because she threatens harm, we may force her to desist. But does this include the use of torture?

Pain is a strong motivator, especially when it is a question of doing something that will result in immediate relief. I shall assume that, while individuals with competing motivations can resist pain for longer than others, there is, even for the most strongly motivated, a point beyond which pain cannot be borne, in the sense that one will do anything in one's power to stop it. In short, my assumption is that torture can produce the desired result. But, I shall argue, this is exactly why we should not use it.

Superficially, torture is of a kind with other forms of violence, seeming to differ from them only in degree. Were this the case, the same arguments that justify other uses of force or infliction of pain would serve to justify torture, provided only that the stakes be sufficiently high. I shall argue that torture, especially where it is directed to breaking the will, is qualitatively different from acceptable forms of coercion and transgresses the limits of permissible punishment or self-defense, regardless of the degree of the bomber's guilt or the magnitude of the evil to be avoided.

The prospect of allowing millions to die in a preventable bombing may seem to provide a compelling case for just about any measures available. But suppose that, while we have not been able to capture the bomber, we have been able to capture her three-year-old child, and we know that if we torture the child, we can get the bomber to provide the information. Yes, of course it is wrong, egregiously so, to torture three-year-old children; but look at all of the lives – including lives of other three-year-olds – that will otherwise be lost. And remember, this is the *only* way that we can save those millions of lives. Or suppose that she will detonate the bombs unless some personal enemy of hers is publicly tortured and humiliated, or unless a hundred virgins are publicly raped by their fathers, or unless the president of the United States is summarily executed. If she directly demands these acts, we may refrain from complying in order not to encourage others to make similar demands. But suppose instead that we simply judge that, in the circumstances, one of these acts will suffice to avert the danger. At such a moment, we are confronted with uncomfortable questions about what we value, and, indeed, about who we are – and who the bomber can force us to become.

If, to save the threatened millions, officials decide in favor of the rape, torture, or killing of innocents, what are we to say? Presumably, no one wants to say that such behavior is justified – to say that it is right. The officials – who may well see themselves as damned if they do and damned if they don't – may be regarded as excusable, but these actions are not right. They are grievously wrong. There is a sense in which the number of people saved is simply irrelevant to the wrongness of doing grave harm to innocents in order to save them. This, I take it, is what we mean when we say that the innocents have a *right* not to be so harmed.

Equally, the millions in danger from the bomb have a right not to be killed; but we may not contravene the important personal rights of some in order to preserve the comparably important rights of (a larger number of) others. To do so is to use people as mere means to social ends – to fail to respect them as persons. It is part of the meaning of rights that their violation cannot be justified by a simple weighing of evils. Sometimes, doing right ourselves means allowing others to do wrong, even wrong of fantastic proportions.

The perception that there are circumstances in which it would be wrong (if excusable) to do what is necessary to save the threatened millions has two important implications for the original ticking bomb example. First, we cannot decide on the moral course of action simply by weighing the consequences. We must accept the possibility that, in doing what is necessary to save millions, we do wrong. Second, if torturing the bomber is justified (as torturing innocents is not), it must be on the basis of her guilt for imperiling the lives of so many others.

The key question, then, is whether the bomber has, through her culpable behavior, forfeited her right not to be tortured. Retributivists would argue that anyone who commits a crime forfeits at least some of her rights: she deserves to be punished in ways that would otherwise violate her rights. If the proposed torture counts as deserved punishment for threatening the lives of millions (and if we do have the right person in custody), then the wrong done in torturing the bomber is reduced to a due-process violation. Separately, aggressors who pose an immediate danger to others forfeit some of their rights on the spot. Those others (or persons acting on their behalf) may do harm to the aggressor in self-defense, including harms that would otherwise violate the aggressor's rights. I shall argue that torturing the bomber for the purpose of breaking her will is neither justified punishment nor justified self-defense.

Some retributivists draw the line of justified punishment short of the death penalty, but others argue that the guilt of a murderer justifies executing him. Assuming that the latter group is correct, does it follow that the much greater guilt of the bomber justifies torturing her? Retributivists argue that punishment must be proportionate to guilt. To sentence a person to a year in prison when the punishment proportional to his crime would be six months is, for retributivists, as wrong as sentencing an innocent man to six months in prison: each serves six months he does not deserve. Disproportionate punishment clearly violates the rights of the offender. But what punishment would be disproportionate to the deaths of millions?

Let us assume for the moment that torture is not disproportionate to the crime. Consider, for example, what we would say in the case of the commandant of a Nazi concentration camp who is responsible for the torture and killing of thousands of persons. One such person, turned over to concentration camp survivors, was repeatedly wheeled into the fires of the crematorium after being severely beaten, then removed and beaten again, until he was burned alive.[3] Few would blame the survivors for their actions, and we cannot say the punishment was disproportionate to the crime. Yet I think we must say that it was not justified retribution, as I shall explain.

Retributive punishment is limited, not just by proportionality, but also by the need for such punishment to remain consonant with the autonomy and dignity of offenders. The main advantage that retributivism has over consequentialist theories is its claim to accord respect to the wrongdoer, leaving him free to retain his own conception of the good even as he is punished according to the prevailing conception.[4] Jeffrie Murphy eloquently explains how torture violates these basic retributive precepts:

[T]orture is addressed exclusively to the sentient or heteronomous – i.e., animal – nature of a person. Sending painful voltage through a man's testicles to which electrodes have been attached, or boiling him in oil, or eviscerating him, or gouging out his eyes – these are not human ways of relating to another person. He could not be expected to understand this while it goes on, have a view about it, enter into discourse about it, or conduct any other human activities during the process – a process whose very point is to reduce him to a terrified, defecating, urinating, screaming animal. . . . We have here a paradigm of not treating a person as a person – and thus an undermining of that very value (autonomous human personhood) on which any conception of justice must rest.[5]

It may seem that torturing people for information is less objectionable than torture designed to inflict a predetermined amount of pain, because the victim is in a position to stop the torture by providing the desired information.[6] This, however, does not make it less terrible, even though it may result in less actual pain being inflicted. The victim's control over the duration of the torture may come at the price of the loss, not only of ordinary human dignity, but also of any vestige of personal integrity. George Orwell describes such a loss in *1984*, when the protagonist, exposed to the source of his one deepest fear, betrays what is most precious to him.[7] He is left with deep self-loathing and the feeling that his life is entirely meaningless. Torture independent of the victim's will may deprive its victim of autonomous human personhood, but torture for purposes of obtaining information may also deprive the victim of her very self – while yet leaving her with the knowledge of that loss. The peculiar horror of this kind of torture is that it can force the victim to give up everything she values. Its evil consists not merely in overriding the will of the victim – as may be done by killing or otherwise defeating her – but in making her the instrument of her own destruction.

It may be objected that, in the ticking bomb example, torture only forces the bomber to do what is right and saves her from committing a terrible wrong. It may seem that in this respect her moral integrity is enhanced, even as her personal integrity is diminished. But the action through which she avoids doing a grave wrong – revealing the information – is in an important sense not *her* action at all. In so acting against her deeply held beliefs, she is merely the puppet of the torturer, so that what she does must reflect on the torturer's character, not on hers. Rather than having kept her moral integrity, she has lost her moral agency.

Suppose that we had the power at any moment to take control of any person's behavior and direct their actions as we would those of a character in a video game. Suppose further that we were able to monitor everyone's intentions, and strictly refrained from using this power except where the subject unquestionably intended to do wrong. In all cases where such intent was detected, however, we would redirect the subject's course of action so that no harm occurred. We would thus vastly reduce the number of wrong actions, and the world would be immeasurably safer. Nevertheless, I submit, this is not a morally better world – as it would be if the erstwhile wrongdoers voluntarily changed their behavior. Instead, the would-be wrongdoers have lost their ability to choose right or wrong, and thus their moral agency. The officials who monitor and direct their behavior have greatly expanded scope for their moral agency – but only at the cost of effectively destroying the agency of others.

In the world as we know it, it is not ordinarily possible to direct the choices of others this completely. But there are ways of influencing those choices through persuasion or coercion. Actions on my part that present you with a choice between something that violates your rights (e.g., being physically harmed) and something you would prefer not to do (e.g., leave the area I have arbitrarily defined as my "turf") are coercive, and become increasingly coercive as the gravity and plausibility of the threatened harm increase. Your choice to comply is increasingly unfree. My actions are wrong because I am making you my instrument, substituting my choices for yours. We call my behavior coercive because it impermissibly reduces your freedom of choice. Faced with such a threat, you do still have a choice in the narrow sense. If you feel especially strongly about the importance of resisting the local mafia, you can choose to accept the threatened harm rather than comply. There are two ways in which I can deprive you of this last shred of choice. In the first, I make your choice irrelevant by physically coercing you – carrying you by main force out of the designated area. Here, I take away your choice, in the sense that I do not allow you to act on it – but there is also a sense in which your choice still stands. Even if I take away all of your future choices by killing you, I have not negated your choice not to comply, as the reverence for martyrs attests. In the second, I literally make you choose to comply, by escalating the harm to the point that, regardless of how strongly you wish to do otherwise, you will in fact so choose. There can be no greater disrespect for an individual as a person – a choosing being – than this literal commandeering of the choice itself.

Torture to gain information, or other forms of compliance, is thus a deeper denial of personhood and autonomy than is torture as punishment. To say that the bomber deserves this kind of treatment is to say that she has, through her actions, forfeited all of the respect due to persons – that she has forfeited her claim to personhood itself. But if any right can be said to be inalienable, the right to retain one's personhood, in the sense of being permitted to make (if not to act on) one's own judgment, must be such a right. To put the point another way, to say that the bomber has forfeited this right is to say that, in virtue of her culpable behavior, she is no longer a person at all.

It may seem that the considerations applicable to punishment are inapposite. In the ticking bomb example, we are not in the position of retrospectively punishing the bomber for her acts, but rather in the position of seeking to prevent the destruction of millions of people. I have argued that neither the balance of evils nor the guilt of the bomber justifies torturing her, but there remains the possibility that the combination of both will do so. Given that it is as a result of her culpable behavior in placing the bomb that we must now choose whether to subject her to torture or to accept the deaths of millions, may we not torture her in self-defense?

The normally applicable limits of justified self-defense are necessity and proportionality. That is, the harm done must both be necessary to prevent the threatened harm, and proportional to it. Thus, if we apprehended the bomber in the act of detonating the bomb, it would be justifiable for us to use coercion – including deadly force – to prevent her from doing so. Indeed, if the only way we can prevent her from reaching the switch involves causing her extreme pain (perhaps we can only stop her by dumping a bucket of hot tar on her head) it is permissible to do so. As Philip Montague has argued, she has forced us to choose between harm to her and harm to innocents, and under such circumstances we are justified in choosing to harm the aggressor.[8] I shall argue, however, that we may not, in pursuit of the same end, inflict extreme pain for the purpose of breaking her will.

As in the case of retributive punishment, the idea that the only limit on measures necessary for self-defense is proportionality has unacceptable implications. This idea is unproblematic when it is a question of deflecting a punch in the nose with a counterpunch, or of shooting at the person who is aiming a loaded gun at me. But suppose that two conspirators have kidnapped an innocent person and are taking turns torturing him by breaking his fingers one by one until he agrees to do whatever they have in mind. Police capture one of the conspirators in the act of mailing a videotape of these proceedings to the victim's family. He refuses to tell where the kidnap victim is being held. Unable to shake his resolve, they, in turn, proceed to break the conspirator's fingers one by one until he yields. Or suppose that there is a new cult, the "Cult of the Virgin," which subjects unwitting new recruits to an initiation ceremony in which all females are systematically raped to assure that the cult's leader will be the only virgin in the group. May you, as an infiltrator who has attained a trusted status, rape the Virgin herself to dissolve the myth and protect the new recruits?

Both examples involve harms to guilty parties that are proportional to the harms we seek to prevent. In Montague's terms, it is their fault that we have to choose between harm to them and comparable harm to innocents. If necessity and proportionality were the only limits on self-defense, these examples would be unproblematic cases of justified self-defense (or defense of third parties). They would be the direct analogs of cases in which the person attacked (or someone acting on her behalf) kills a murderous aggressor.

Our hesitation to approve the defensive measures proposed in these cases suggests that there is another kind of limit on what we may do in defense of innocents – a limit comparable to those we place on retributive punishment. That is, there is some upper bound to what we may do, regardless of proportionality. The two limits are not exactly the same: breaking someone's leg will often be permissible self-defense, but never permissible punishment. But we do not need to be able to specify the exact nature of the boundary to know that our right to force other persons to refrain from harming others must stop short of violating their inalienable rights – even if they propose to violate the inalienable rights of others. To say otherwise is to put the limit of what we may do at the limit of what the most vile among us will do. And if there are any inalienable rights, as I have argued, they must at least prohibit torture for the purpose of breaking the will.

I have said earlier that it would be permissible (if necessary) to inflict an equal amount of pain in order to prevent the bomber from reaching the switch. This may suggest that I am appealing to the distinction between foreseeable and intended consequences captured in the doctrine of double effect, which holds that it is permissible to cause certain kinds of consequences if they are regrettable side effects of permitted action, but not to aim directly at these consequences. But my argument does not turn on this beleaguered distinction.[9] It is not a question of causing the same harm for a different purpose, but rather of causing a different harm: that of the complete usurpation of another's will. It is this harm, and not the infliction of extreme pain as such, that I have argued is absolutely prohibited. In principle, it is prohibited whether intended or merely foreseen, although it is difficult to imagine circumstances where it would count as unintended. As with other grave harms, it is wrong to attempt to inflict this harm as well as to succeed. The infliction of pain in the course of such an attempt is wrong because the attempt itself is wrong, just as the infliction of pain in the course of an attempted kidnapping would be wrong.

Why limit the measures we may use in defending ourselves against aggressors who have no such scruples? Torture inflicted by others is primarily their moral responsibility, not ours; but torture we inflict is our moral responsibility. Torture inflicted by the officials of our society is our collective responsibility, insofar as we have any control over them. When we authorize (or require) them to rape or torture, we all become the kinds of human beings who are willing to rape or torture others. In adopting the tactics of those who have themselves renounced this constraint, we take a significant step toward becoming as depraved as they are. As Sartre put it, each action we take helps to define what it means to be a human being. The measures that we will and will not resort to under threat – and the ways in which we will use or refrain from using our power – tell a great deal about who we are as a society. The bomber seeks to dictate our choices: we can refuse to allow her to do so, by refusing to accede to her demands. We still have that last shred of choice – the choice to accept the threatened harm. As well, we have the option of seeking to avoid the choice she offers by sacrificing the last constraints of human decency. We should decline to do so, even if it means we cannot survive as a society. Some lives are not worth living, as Orwell's story shows, and this is as true of societies as it is of individuals.

How can we prevent terrible things such as torture and mass murder? Each of us has a vision of the way that the world should be, and all of us agree that in that world no terrible things will be done. There are two paths to this world. One path is to try to force others, by any means necessary, to refrain from doing terrible things. The powerful are invariably tempted to this path, but it is ultimately self-defeating where the necessary means involve our doing equally terrible things ourselves. The other path is to declare, for ourselves and for others whose actions we legitimately influence, that *we* will do no terrible things. It is only in this way that we can effectively declare some actions to be beyond the pale of what a human being will do.[10]

NOTES

1. I avoid the term "terrorist" because it is more a badge of stigmatization than a descriptive term. As the Online Etymology Dictionary notes, usage going back as far as the 1956 British action in Cyprus reflects "the tendency of one party's 'terrorist' to be another's 'guerrilla' or 'freedom fighter.'" Douglas Harper, *Online Etymology Dictionary*, 2001. Available at http://www.etymonline.com/index.php?term=terrorism (accessed July 31, 2005).
2. The case for use of torture in such circumstances is made by Ken Himma, "Assessing the Prohibition against Torture," Chap. 14 in this volume.
3. Matthew Brzezinski, "Giving Hitler Hell," *Washington Post Magazine*, July 23, 2005, p. 8.
4. The leading argument for this point is that of Herbert Morris in "Persons and Punishment," *Monist* 52 (1968), pp. 475–501. I have argued elsewhere that both retributive and consequentialist theories fail. See *The Case Against Punishment* (New York: New York University Press, 2005).
5. Jeffrie Murphy, "Cruel and Unusual Punishments," in his *Retribution, Justice and Therapy* (Dordrecht, The Netherlands: Kluwer Academic Publishers, 1979).
6. Henry Shue, in his excellent article "Torture," considers the argument that the prisoner may defend himself by providing the desired information, so that he is not properly regarded as defenseless. *Philosophy and Public Affairs* 7 (1978), pp. 124–143.
7. George Orwell, *1984* (New York: Signet Classic, 1950).
8. Philip Montague, *Punishment as Societal-Defense* (Lanham, MD.: Rowman & Littlefield, 1995).
9. For a critique of the doctrine of double effect, see Warren Quinn, "Actions, Intentions, and Consequences: The Doctrine of Double Effect," *Philosophy and Public Affairs* 18 (1989), pp. 334–351. See also Alec Walen's proposed alternative view in "The Doctrine of Illicit Intention," *Philosophy and Public Affairs* 34 (2006), pp. 39–67.
10. I am indebted to Eric Forste for his helpful comments on an earlier version of this chapter.

SALLY J. SCHOLZ

WAR RAPE'S CHALLENGE TO JUST WAR THEORY

War rape comes in many forms, is perpetrated for many reasons, has multiple victims and multiple culpable perpetrators. This chapter examines war rape, asks whether Just War Theory (JWT) can tackle the specific challenges posed by the reality of sexual violence during wartime, and suggests that it might actually have an important conceptual framework to offer to philosophical analyses of the problem of war rape. I argue that JWT can be used to ferret out the important differences and functions of various forms of war rape while offering a normative theory in support of human rights that might provide individuals who attempt to resist participation in war rape with normative justification for their resistance. However, JWT falls short of meeting all of the challenges posed by war rape due to a lack of emphasis on the nature and harm of war crimes that target individuals on the basis of gender and that use the body as weapon and site of the war crimes or the war itself.

Two broad categories of war rape may be observed though of course variations within these categories abound. The two categories are individual rapes and mass rape. While it may be tempting to describe these as "old" and "new" respectively, history belies such a temporal distinction. Mass rape has been evident since biblical times[1] but only recently has it received the media attention[2] and moral approbation long overdue. So too, individual rapes continue to be overlooked by militaries while they simultaneously degrade individual victims and their communities. Where there is a difference between old and new is in the international laws against war rape. The "old" law held that rape during war was a war crime. The "new" laws, since 1993, recognize not only rape as a war crime, but mass rape as a crime against humanity and genocide.[3]

Following the schematic of JWT, an analysis of war rape must scrutinize the various causes, uses or intentions, and ends of both individual rapes and mass rape. Rapes that occur during conflict situations are blamed on sexual needs, boredom, inevitability, entrenched systems of domination, reactions to the constant threat of violence, among other causal factors. Rape is said to be used as a release of tension, an instrument of torture, and a weapon in combat. I discuss these causes and uses, as well as others, below, but an analysis of war rape would be incomplete without a discussion of its ends or purposes which are conceptually though not necessarily practically distinct from its causes and uses. Rape degrades, demoralizes, and dehumanizes enemy combatants and non-combatants, it splits communities, it becomes an instrument in ethnic cleansing through forced pregnancy, and it is both a means to and a form of genocide. In addition to targeting women because they hold political, cultural, or ideological positions, rape creates a war within a war wherein all women are targeted as women. In short, rape in war has multiple causes, multiple uses, and multiple ends.

In Section 1, I offer a definition and a system of categorization for war rapes that highlights the differences between forms of war rape. As I show, the context of war makes war rape conceptually different from everyday or peacetime rapes, though there may be some compelling links between the two.[4] In Section 2 I use the tripartite distinction mentioned above – cause, use, and purpose – to underscore the particular features of war rape and use the mass rape in Serbia as a demonstrative case. In Section 3, I use Michael Walzer's *Just and Unjust Wars* to examine the relation between human rights and JWT with the aim of addressing the question I posed earlier: can JWT meet the challenges posed by war rape and does JWT have something to offer in this context? Section 4 addresses the weakness of JWT.

For the purposes of this chapter, I wish to bracket the inclusion of rape of an ally or a fellow soldier under the rubric of war rape. Most accounts of war rape include prostitution and rape of allies (citizens or military personnel) and fellow combatants, in part because they emphasize the ideology of rape within the military. I restrict the current account of war rape to enemy combatants or civilians because I think the element of opposition or enmity within these forms of rape alters their nature – makes them categorically different from the rape of a fellow soldier – and because I wish to focus attention on the obligations of JWT.

1. IDENTIFICATION OF WAR RAPE

Section 920, Article 120 "Rape and Carnal Knowledge," of the US Uniform Code of Military Justice defines rape accordingly: "Any person subject to this chapter who commits an act of sexual intercourse, by force and without consent, is guilty of rape and shall be punished by death or such other punishment as a court-martial may direct." Furthermore, "Penetration, however slight, [is] sufficient to complete" the offense of rape.[5] But this is by no means a universally accepted definition of rape.[6]

Many feminists note the male-centric focus of a definition that relies on penetration. So too, "force" and "consent" have proven to be relative concepts difficult to prove and often undermining victim testimony.

The context of war alters perceptions of rape in four distinct ways. War turns rape into an act of a state, nation, ethnic group, or people. "[A]trocities by soldiers against civilians are always considered state acts" during wartime.[7] Second, war provides an excuse for rape's perpetration. In some sense, war changes the universal censure of rape toward something resembling complacent acceptance (though not, of course, justification). Third, rape simultaneously becomes part of the war effort, albeit an unjust part. The context of war alters the cause, intention, and purpose of rape. Finally, while all rapes effectively objectify the victim, an oppositional objectification of the enemy that extends beyond combatants to encompass civilians of all ages and genders is usually in place well in advance of any occurrence of war rape.

Broadly speaking, war rape is the willful, blatant, nonconsensual, sexual violation of the bodily integrity of a person – combatant or noncombatant – from an opposing side during wartime. This definition is necessarily broad in order to encompass the horrific variety of methods used.[8] The definition refrains from indicating a reason or purpose to the rape because rape during war has multiple causes and serves multiple purposes. The rape of a six-year-old girl by three men during the Rwanda mass rape campaign cannot have forced impregnation as its end,[9] but the rape of many of the women of Rwanda did have this aim. So too, this definition is necessarily broad so as to include instances wherein victims are forced to rape each other, that is, when the aggressor orchestrates sex among victims through violence. Forcing a son to rape his mother, as occurred in Haiti[10] – and no doubt elsewhere – surely counts among the atrocities of war rape but does not directly involve the body of the perpetrator. Both son and mother are victims of rape. The Rwanda tribunal defined rape as "'a physical invasion of a sexual nature, committed on a person under circumstances which are coercive'" so as to include "the horrific violations that had been described to them – women penetrated by sticks and bottles as well as penises."[11] Rape is both a form of sexual abuse and distinct from it. Other forms of sexual abuse during wartime may violate bodily integrity via abuse of the genitals (e.g., fastening electrodes to the genitals of a prisoner) but do not constitute rape. As we have seen, penetration distinguishes rape from other forms of sexual abuse in much of the literature, but victims of war rape would more likely use the terminology of forced sex[12] under conditions of duress.

There are two main categories of war rape: individual rapes and mass rape campaigns. Both target females and males of every age. Individual rape, rape of a single person, might be broken down into two different forms: (1) rape by one soldier and (2) rape by multiple soldiers or gang rape. In addition, the rape may be of an enemy civilian, an enemy combatant, or a prisoner of war. Individual rapes are not generally thought of as systematic, at least not in the sense that characterizes mass rapes. On the contrary, individual rapes are relatively isolated events wherein an individual soldier or a small group of soldiers act immorally. Individual rapes fall under the traditional category of war crimes.

The key difference between individual rape and mass rape is that mass rape is systematic. The rapes of mass rape campaigns may be (1) part of a larger war effort, (2) an escalation of violence within a war, and/or (3) the very purpose of the war itself. Most of the recent mass rape campaigns have been sanctioned by the state or ruling party, but this is not a necessary condition to the category of mass rape. Every instance of mass rape is systematic but not every instance constitutes the very purpose of a war effort.

2. CAUSES, USES, AND ENDS OF WAR RAPE

2.1 *Causes of War Rape*

Because war itself is about the intentional infliction of harm on an enemy, rape has often been overlooked, tolerated, or seen as commonplace.[13] But saying war is violent and begets the violence of rape conceals other possible causes that may be embedded in a cultural tradition.

One of the primary feminist accounts of the root cause of rape identifies it as an act of violence, power, and domination rather than an act of sex. As Susan Brownmiller states, rape is "nothing more or less than a conscious process of intimidation by which *all men* keep *all women* in a state of fear."[14] Brownmiller describes an "ideology of rape" that often supports rape as a demonstration of prowess or male bonding especially evident within the military.[15] It is also clear from her analysis of rape in *Against Our Will* that prostitution and pornography, as coerced forms of domination, are covered by the umbrella concept of rape. Catharine MacKinnon, on the other hand, holds that the structure of heterosexual sex within a sexist system is causally responsible. She describes sex and violence as "mutually definitive" and notes the difficulty of distinguishing sexual intercourse and rape "under conditions of male dominance."[16] MacKinnon and Brownmiller famously disagree about whether rape is based in sex or in power, and their positions have been widely criticized for encompassing too much, but their suggestive arguments force us to examine the cultural and gender elements of rape.[17]

War rape may be informed by patriarchal sex-role stereotyping, oppressive race or ethnic relations, other forms of domination, ideological or linguistic disparagement of the body, and countless other cultural factors. Robin May Schott, for instance, specifically argues that cultural and linguistic representations of the body and of maternity bear on our understanding of why war rape happens and how we can prevent it;[18] they also bear on what we understand as rape and how we respond to it. Rape is a crime against the body, but if the violated body is culturally disparaged or viewed as property of another, the interpretation of what counts as rape changes. Rape could become an offense against more than just the victim – her family, community, and culture may consider the violation personal – or rape may be construed as an offense not against a woman (who is often understood as culturally or politically inferior) but an offense against her nearest male kin. How a culture perceives the body, especially the female body, plays a huge role in how rape is understood.

2.2 Uses of War Rape and War Rape as an End in itself

During war, rape becomes a tool, weapon, or strategy. As Schott argues, "a man uses his own body as a weapon of war: his hands, his mouth, his genitals are used to inflict pain, injury, degradation, and often death."[19] MacKinnon also presents evidence that numerous rapes during the Yugoslav conflict were filmed and presented as war propaganda and pornography.[20] Rape directly inflicts harm and indirectly contributes to the destruction of morale among enemy combatants and demoralizes their communities.

In recent years, the international community has witnessed numerous examples of the use of mass rape in the service of war, ethnic cleansing, and genocide. The first to gain international media attention was during 1971 after Bangladesh declared independence. A nine month campaign of mass rape by the Pakistanis began. During that period, it is estimated that three million people were killed, ten million fled to India, and 200,000 to 400,000 women were raped, with 25,000 impregnated.[21] But even before the Pakistanis raped the Bangladeshis, the Japanese raped the women of Nanking. More recently, throughout the mid-1990s, Bosnian Serbs raped non-Serbs; during the genocide in Rwanda, the Hutus raped the Tutsis and other, moderate Hutus; and in 2004 state supported militias began a campaign of rape in the Darfur region of Sudan.

In most of the examples of mass rape, the rapes were condoned (officially or unofficially) in the form of explicit orders to rape (the Rape of

Nanking[22]), vague directives to wipe out a population that might be routinely interpreted as permission to rape (My Lai massacre[23]), personal supervision of mass rape (the case of Jean-Paul Akesyu in Rwanda – the first man tried and convicted of genocide and rape as a crime against humanity[24]), removal of administrative barriers supporting just conduct (Abu Ghraib), or failure to stop mass rape campaigns within one's control (Milosevic in Serbia). For some of the recent mass rape campaigns, there is also documented evidence of rapists attempting to forcibly impregnate women through rape and thereby wipe-out an ethnic group.[25]

Some of these examples demonstrate that mass rape is used in campaigns for "ethnic cleansing," which is "the use of force or intimidation to remove people of a certain ethnic or religious group from an area."[26] Further, cultural dictates in Yugoslavia and Rwanda hold that the child would have the ethnicity of the father, not the mother. Enforced pregnancy from another ethnic group could, it was believed, destroy a culture or ethnicity because no new children would be born with the targeted ethnicity.[27] As Claudia Card explains, "Rape... was used as a weapon of war. Its purposes include intimidating and demoralizing the enemy, forced impregnation, tampering with the identity of the next generation, splintering families, and dispersing entire populations."[28] Coupled with campaigns of massive murders of members of cultural groups, mass rape becomes instrumental in genocidal campaigns. The Rwanda tribunal found that rape was an act of genocide; "a step in the process of destruction of the Tutsi group."[29]

Individual and mass rape during war is a weapon in war; it might be used strategically to demoralize the enemy or only incidentally for the same purpose. Rape is also used as an instrument in torture, ethnic cleansing, and genocide. But rape may not be used solely as a means to some other end; at times, war rape becomes an end in itself. The three cases of torture, prostitution, and some forms of mass rape provide revealing instances of rape used both as a means to some other end and as an end itself.

Consider first rape used in torture. MADRE, an international women's human rights group, has long fought to get rape recognized as an act of torture.[30] Ironically, when men are victims of rape during war, they tend to play down the sexual nature of the crime, referring to it as torture or simply as sexual assault but not rape.[31] Citing personal conversation with Libby Tata Arcel, who worked with rape survivors after the Serbian mass rape campaign and who edited *War Violence, Trauma, and the Coping Process,* Card says "that martial sex crimes by men against men have a long history, but also that they have almost universally been identified by men not as sex crimes, or even as sexual torture, but simply as torture."[32] Rape is used as a means of torture and is itself torture. If we understand torture as the infliction of severe pain, injury, or suffering to the body, whether or not it serves any ulterior purposes such as extracting information or deterring resistance activity, then rape in all its forms during wartime is a form of torture. Of course, rape often is used as one of many tools to extract information or otherwise destroy the will of a person or community in torture situations. But the gratuitous rapes of prisoners of Abu Ghraib serve as a graphic example of how rape might be perpetrated for no other reason than to inflict sexual violence on another human being under one's control.[33]

Card, Brownmiller, and MacKinnon all add forced prostitution to the practices of rape during war. Forced prostitution includes the bordello camps of the Serbs and the Japanese comfort stations.[34] Card argues that the comfort stations were not intended as a weapon of war but as a means to protect "local females in enemy country from uncontrolled war rapes by soldiers," an argument which, in turn, would discourage local peoples from aiding guerilla efforts.[35] She recognizes that forced prostitution was demoralizing for families and communities. Brownmiller sees forced prostitution as merely an extension of the power and domination at work in all rapes. MacKinnon argues that prostitution and rape (and other crimes against women) are: "not primarily abuses of physical force, violence, authority, or economics, although they are that. They are abuses of women; they are abuses of sex."[36] Forced prostitution as war rape is organized and systematic; it targets women for the ostensible purpose of protecting other women but it also serves as an end in itself. Women are forced to serve the sexual needs of men because they are women. Moreover, prostitution illustrates clearly how a war can be bifurcated. Forced prostitution as a war rape practice, as the Serb case illustrates, creates a war within a war.

Finally, as we have already seen, rape is used as a means to genocide or ethnic cleansing, but mass rape has also become an end in itself. In her description of the trial of Akayesu, Elizabeth Neuffer relates how the prosecutor came to realize that "the refugees at the Bureau Communale [the grounds of the local government – Akayesu was burgomaster] were nearly all women, not both sexes, as he had first believed, and that they were there as part of a plan for their rape."[37] This was rape for the sake of rape *as well as* for the sake of genocide. "Witness NN testified to being raped by six different men and then kept locked up by one of them as his sexual slave."[38] MacKinnon argues both that rape is a tool in a genocidal campaign and for "rape as genocide."[39] She challenges us to see the multiple means and ends of rape, saying, "[i]t is as if people cannot think more than one thought at once. The mass rape is either part of a campaign by Serbia against non-Serbia, or an onslaught by combatants against civilians, or an attack by men against women, but never all at the same time."[40] If women's human rights are taken seriously, then rape must be recognized for its multiple purposes – both as a means to genocide and as an end itself. Genocidal rape is "rape unto death, rape as massacre, rape to kill and to make the victims wish they were dead."[41] Effectively, rape creates a war within a war; it is a war in which all women are targeted simply because they are women.[42] This is supported by the fact that many moderate Hutu women were targeted in the Hutu campaign to kill Tutsi and that Serbian women were not immune from rape by Serbian soldiers. The rape-war serves the ends of that other war, but it exists in many ways independently of it; the other war provides a context, means, opportunity, and some would add justification for the rape-war. But the rape-war takes on a life of its own.

In a similar vein, Elizabeth Kelly points out that women and women's bodies have been "constructed as the locus and carriers of culture" and as such, when a state intends the elimination of a cultural group, women become the prime target and the "territory to be conquered." Through forced impregnation, they are also the "vehicles through which the nation/group can be reproduced."[43] Forced pregnancy, in other words, also shifts war rape from being just a weapon of war to also being the purpose of war itself.

2.3 Rape in Former Yugoslavia: A Case Study

Five patterns of rape within Serbian policy were documented by the UN Commission of Experts. The first two patterns demonstrate rape used as a means to some other end – terror and conquest. Rape was used to terrorize the civilian population prior to the onset of major conflict. The Serbs would also use rape in the attack of a town; as part of the strategy of conquest, any remaining population would be divided by sex and age. Some women would then be separated and raped. The third pattern of mass rape demonstrates rape as end in itself insofar as there was no ulterior purpose for the rapes: women were raped at the detention and refugee centers, often multiple times during the night and by multiple people. The infamous "Rape camps" established in various buildings (schools, hospitals, restaurants, etc.) constitute the fourth pattern and demonstrate rape used both as an end in itself – rape for its own sake – and as a means. Many survivors of the rape camps reported that their rapists wanted the women to create Serbian babies. The camps then were both a site of the rape-war and a tool in the program of ethnic cleansing. Finally, in the last pattern, we see quite clearly the creation of a war within a war, a war that has as its ends rape: many women were confined to "bordello" camps where they were forced to "service" the soldiers and then killed.[44]

One victim of the rape campaign in Yugoslavia stated, "The blame [for the mass rapes] can be equally placed on individuals and on the politics in general. I think it was the will of individuals but also the strategy of Serbian politics to perform 'ethnic cleansing' of the non-Serbian population in Croatia"[45] and another described it as "planned in advance and intended to destroy the soul of a nation."[46] Rape was the political strategy – the demoralizing accompaniment – to a war of genocide, but it was also a war against women within the genocidal campaign.

3. JUST WAR THEORY AND WAR RAPE

Rape violates the rights of the victim.[47] This is one reason why rape is so universally abhorred and unquestionably immoral. In his discussion of rape of the Italian women by mercenary Moroccan soldiers in 1943, Michael Walzer specifies that "war convention... rests... on a certain view of noncombatants, which holds that they are men and women with rights and that they cannot be used for some military purpose, even if it is a legitimate purpose."[48] Here, Walzer hits on precisely the traditional and most widely understood conception of war rape as a violation of the *jus in bello* principle of discrimination. The rape of innocent civilians by military personnel clearly and uncontroversially contravenes the principle that "no one can be forced to fight or to risk his life, no one can be threatened with war or warred against, unless through some act of his own he has surrendered or lost his rights."[49] Of course, noncombatant status is not always easily determined, especially in contemporary wars. But that caveat has no effect on whether rape violates the *jus in bello* principles because rape itself, regardless of the status of the victim, violates rights that even combatants do not temporarily forfeit in wartime. The rights to life and liberty are temporarily suspended but the right not to be tortured or enslaved is not, nor is the right to security in one's person. Rape, like torture and slavery, cannot be among one of the possible contingencies that a combatant accepts in taking on the role of state actor in war.

JWT serves another important function: it assists human rights doctrines by providing a normative structure to back up human rights standards. As such, it potentially provides a valuable moral system to which individuals may appeal, especially if others around them fall prey to the collapse of standard morality.[50] Individuals required to examine their consciences in order to scrutinize the practices and purposes of war according to JWT might find the courage not only to resist but to dissent and even challenge egregious instances of moral collapse. If we hope to avoid the atrocity of war rape, we must compel individual actors – who, after all, are the instruments of both individual and mass rape campaigns – to resist and to resist in so vociferous a fashion that massive resistance to an unjust means or end of war, and not massive human rights violations, bear the mark of history.

The responsibility for individual rapes lands primarily on the perpetrator. However, because war rape is different than other forms of rape, others who do not act directly in the rape might also be morally blameworthy. Superior officers who have knowledge of actual or potential rape and do nothing to either stop it or, if the knowledge was after the fact, to punish the soldier, are implicated in the blame for the rape. Soldiers are individuals with consciences, but they are also part of an intricate system that exercises no small degree of control over their actions. Individual war rapes are a failure of conscience on the part of the individual as well as a failure in the system that supports, condones, or ignores immoral behavior. Implicit in this statement is a challenge to two additional factors worthy of attention and blame in war rape, though they in no way excuse or justify it: the military culture (discussed previously) and histories of oppression. Histories of oppression, contexts of colonialism, and similar systems of domination invite the sorts of dehumanization that set the ground work for rape – individual and mass rape.

Prosecution of rape during war has been scant in part because it was perceived as a private matter, a crime against women (a class of crimes that has long been ignored by domestic and international criminal courts), or simply an inevitable part of war. Card uses her "atrocity paradigm" to suggest why rape during war has not been properly prosecuted and punished. The atrocity paradigm would have us look to "the nature of the harm," "what happens to victims," and the "forms of culpability in various perpetrators" to analyze why rape might be tolerated while other war crimes are not. Since we rely on testimony to learn of the nature of the harm and its consequences, and since victims are often killed, silenced by their rapist, their community, or their family, or socially degraded because of their gender, we end up relying on the victor's testimony, according to Card. "The international community's failure to denounce and prosecute war rape by victorious perpetrators makes a certain sense if it takes the victor's point of view and depends on the victor's versions of the facts."[51]

Mass rape that is systematic often creates a war within a war with the sole purpose of rape. In such cases, mass rape campaigns violate both *jus in bello* and *jus ad bellum* principles. This shift in how we conceptualize war rape is very important. Not only does it force a distinction between forms of war rape, it also challenges us to understand both war rape and wars entailing massive rape campaigns quite differently. When rape is the very purpose of aggression, the war itself is unjust and those responsible for organizing, planning, and implementing mass rape campaigns ought to be held morally accountable for violating *jus ad bellum* principles and are legally culpable for "crimes against peace" and/or "crimes against humanity."[52] In addition, the individual perpetrators of rapes that contribute to mass rape ought to be held morally accountable for violating *jus in bello* principles and are legally culpable for war crimes.

Clearly, mass rape complicates the assignment of blame. The case of Rwanda illustrates the problem. Victims raped by their former neighbors, friends, or relatives, put themselves at risk of retribution should they testify against their rapists. This disincentive for the victims to testify meant that perpetrators did not get prosecuted, though at least some of the masterminds to the campaign did. Without careful prosecution and punishment on both levels, individual rape continues to be viewed as a crime that is not "serious enough" for domestic courts, military tribunals, or international war crimes tribunals. Justice to the victims – something that JWT demands – requires that every effort be made to hold those responsible for the mass rape accountable – both those who planned or organized the campaign and those individuals who perpetrated it.

4. LIMITATIONS OF JUST WAR THEORY

In spite of its possibilities, JWT is limited in its ability fully to address the problem of war rape. Four crucial limitations to the applicability of JWT to the problem of war rape include: (1) insufficient attention to the bodily nature of rape during war; (2) inadequate ability to address violations that blur the distinction between *jus ad bellum* and *jus in bello;* (3) lack of measures for individuals to report violations across lines of state; and (4) an apparent inability to address the cultural prescriptions that prohibit (for lack of a better word) reparation to survivors such that they can resume their place in community.

In addition to a violation of rights, rape is a crime against the body and a cultural crime. Rape violently upsets perceptions of the body – cultural or universal. Bodies, not just abstract rights, are harmed, and often it is other bodies doing the harming. In addition, as we have seen, some instances of mass rape rely on a particular understanding of the maternal body as a passive vessel of the rapist's culture. But even as mass rape disrupts and destroys culture, it is through the bodies of rape victims – primarily women's bodies. Schott argues that what is needed in order to prevent rape is more than just a cognitive awareness of the human rights not to be tortured and to security in one's person. "It is crucial," Schott argues, "to incorporate the bodily element of judgment, which places a demand to revise and expand the concept of cognition" such that the rapist acknowledges "wrongdoing in the particularity of his physical transgression."[53] Schott wants to examine the way violence becomes so ubiquitous, commonplace, and acceptable that soldiers who rape are desensitized to atrocity prior to committing the crime. Their bodies have become extensions of their weapons rather than the other way around as is often taught in military training. JWT focuses almost exclusively on rights and thus has a difficult time accommodating attentiveness to the use of the body in violence. In order to do justice to victim accounts and propose adequate responses to war rape, philosophical and legal understandings of war rape must expand to acknowledge the embodied nature of the crime, that is, to recognize that it is with and through the body that victims experience the violation. Prosecution that focuses only on rights violations would overlook the psychological and bodily impact of rape, an impact that has long been recognized for other instances of torture.

The second limitation of JWT pertains to mass rape. Every mass rape may be described as systematic but not every mass rape is a violation of *jus ad bellum*. JWT needs an account of systematic violations that could address those war crimes that blur the distinctions between justice of war and justice in war. Targeting women because they are women – because of real and perceived conceptions of women's bodily nature – creates a gender conflict within the political or ideological conflict. JWT helps to identify this bifurcation of purpose, but it does not easily address it, as is evident when trying to identify culpable persons.

Third, JWT is limited, as is international human rights law, by its focus on states or state actors. Groups within the state and individuals themselves who are raped as part of a conflict must appeal to states that have a vested interest in protecting rapists in part so that they do not come under greater scrutiny regarding their own treatment of women.[54] Some have argued that a human rights approach is more desirable because of the universality of that approach, but it too has been criticized for pertaining to states thereby leaving women little recourse for war crimes committed against them.[55] JWT is challenged to address the actions not just of states and state actors (soldiers), but also to see how military personnel, UN peacekeepers, and others act outside the bounds of states or international institutions and sometimes in concert with unlikely allies. Mass rape campaigns and torture in the name of uncovering so-called stateless terrorists are perhaps the most obvious of these sorts of challenges.

Finally, JWT is culturally inscribed and bounded. Cultural inscriptions affect what counts as rape and how rape affects the victim's communal status. An account of *post bellum* reparations to victims would have to address the cultural prescriptions that often leave a victim of rape ostracized from her community or the children of rape abandoned. I referred to this as an "apparent" inability of JWT because I think that JWT can be adapted to lend some guidance to this extension of the rape tragedy. Rehabilitation, which Brian Orend argues is a *post bellum* principle,[56] should include rehabilitation for the victim, for communities affected by rape, and for families of the survivors and the murdered. The extent of necessary rehabilitation for war rape – individual or mass rape – has yet to be fully explored but is clearly an avenue for further research in this area.

JWT is a useful if limited interpretive tool for addressing the myriad problems of war rape. The conceptual framework of JWT aids in identifying differing forms of war rape thereby contributing to a just accounting for victims and perpetrators. But JWT is limited in its ability to address the use of the body as weapon and site of the war crimes and of the war itself and attend to the array of cultural codes and prescriptions that come into play before, during, and after war rape.

NOTES

1. See, for example, Book of Judges, Chaps. 19–21, discussed in Susan Brownmiller, *Against Our Will* (New York: Simon & Schuster, 1975), p. 21; see also Elizabeth Neuffer, *The Key to my Neighbor's House: Seeking Justice in Bosnia and Rwanda* (New York: Picador, 2001), pp. 272–273. And, of course, Augustine, who is credited as one of the first to articulate principles of JWT, discusses the rape of the Sabine women and draws out the horrific implications not only for the women but also for their home communities and even the perpetrators. His thoughts are brief and far removed from his discussion of just war, but they provide a suggestive historical starting point for a philosophical study of rape and JWT. See Augustine, *The City of God* (New York: The Modern Library, 1950).
2. See especially Brownmiller (*Against our Will*, p. 86) who argues that the 1971 mass rape of the women in Bangladesh by the Pakistanis was the first case to receive international attention in spite of being preceded by Nanking and My Lai, to say nothing of the mass rape in the previous two millennia.
3. Rape and torture were added to the list of "crimes against humanity" for the Yugoslav war crimes tribunal and the Rwanda war crimes tribunal. The Rwanda tribunal also added "forced pregnancy."

4. Elsewhere I discuss some of the links between war rape and peacetime rape. Sally Scholz, "Human Rights, Radical Feminism, and Rape in War," in Jonathan Rowan (ed.), *Human Rights, Religion, and Democracy* (Bowling Green, OH: Philosophy Documentation Center, 2005). See also Brownmiller and Liz Kelly, who argue that war rape is much more closely related to everyday rape (and vice versa) than I would argue. Brownmiller, *Against Our Will*, especially Chap. 3; Liz Kelly, "Wars against Women: Sexual Violence, Sexual Politics and the Militarised State," in Susie Jacobs, Ruth Jacobson, and Jennifer Marchbank (eds), *States of Conflict*, (New York: St. Martins, 2000).
5. US Uniform Code of Military Justice. http://www4.law.cornell.edu/cgi-bin/htm_hl?DB=uscode10&STEMMER=en&WORDS=rape+&COLOUR=Red&STYLE=s&URL=/uscode/10/920.html (accessed September 13, 2004). See also Brownmiller, *Against our Will*, p. 32.
6. For a review of the literature, see Ann Cahill, *Rethinking Rape* (Ithaca, NY: Cornell University Press, 2001), pp. 11–12.
7. Catharine MacKinnnon, "Rape, Genocide, and Women's Human Rights," *Harvard Women's Law Journal* 17 (1994), p. 16.
8. War rapes cannot be defined solely on the basis of involvement of the genitals. Rapists during war have utilized sticks and bottles (Neuffer, *The Key to My Neighbor's House*, p. 291), oral sex, and electric shocks (MacKinnon "Rape, Genocide, and Women's Human Rights," pp. 7, 12), to name just a few.
9. This is the case of Witness J described by Neuffer, *The Key to My Neighbor's House*, p. 279.
10. Laura Flanders, "Haiti: J'Accuse!" in Anne Llewellyn Barstow (ed.), *War's Dirty Secret*, (Cleveland, OH: Pilgrim Press, 2000), p. 161.
11. Neuffer, *The Key to My Neighbor's House*, p. 291; citing the Rwanda tribunal's decision against Jean Paul Akayesu.
12. Tom Shanker, "Sexual Violence," in R. Gutman and D. Rieff (eds.), *Crimes of War* (New York: W. W. Norton, 1999), p. 323.
13. Claudia Card, *The Atrocity Paradigm: A Theory of Evil* (New York: Oxford University Press, 2002), p.120.
14. Brownmiller, *Against our Will*, p. 15; emphasis in original.
15. For more contemporary analyses, see Claudia Card, *The Atrocity Paradigm*, p. 121; and Amy Herdy and Miles Moffeit, "Camoflaging Criminals: Sexual Violence against Women in the Military," *Amnesty Now* (Spring 2004), pp. 22–26. Although males are raped, females are much more likely to be the victims of rape and males are much more likely to be the perpetrators. Nevertheless, there is also ample historical evidence of women raping other women, women raping men and boys, and of men raping other men or boys.
16. Catharine MacKinnon, *Toward a Feminist Theory of the State* (Cambridge, MA: Harvard University Press, 1989), p. 174.
17. While I do not endorse fully their positions regarding rape in general, I do find their accounts of war rape useful for both an analysis of war rape's causes and for an understanding of women's human rights within conflict situations (see Scholz, "Human Rights, Radical Feminism, and Rape in War").
18. Robin May Schott, "Philosophical Reflections on War Rape," in Claudia Card (ed.), *On Feminist Ethics and Politics* (Lawrence, KS: University Press of Kansas, 1999), pp. 195–196.

19. Schott, "Philosophical Reflections on War Rape," p. 188.
20. MacKinnon, "Rape, Genocide, and Women's Human Rights," p. 7.
21. Brownmiller, *Against Our Will*, pp. 80, 84
22. Jackson Nyamuya Maogoto, *War Crimes and Realpolitik* (Boulder, CO: Lynne Rienner Publishers, 2004), p. 87.
23. Brownmiller, *Against our Will*, pp. 103–105.
24. Neuffer, *The Key to my Neighbor's House*, p. 272.
25. See Neuffer, *The Key to my Neighbor's House*, p. 295; MacKinnon, "Rape, Genocide, and Women's Human Rights," p. 13. Both use tribunal records from Rwanda or Serbia.
26. Roger Cohen, "Ethnic Cleansing," in Gutman and Rieff, *Crimes of War*, p. 136.
27. Rape and forced pregnancy are used in the Darfur region of Sudan explicitly to "impregnate women with light skinned babies" (NPR, "Talk of the Nation," July 27, 2004). These testimonies highlight the fact that political policy underpinning the mass rape campaigns was a policy of rape.
28. Card, *The Atrocity Paradigm*, p. 119.
29. Neuffer, *The Key to My Neighbor's House*, p. 291, citing the Rwanda tribunal's decision against Jean Paul Akayesu.
30. Flanders, "J'accuse," p. 160.
31. Shanker, "Sexual Violence," p. 326.
32. Card, *The Atrocity Paradigm*, p. 135. Although beyond the scope of this chapter, it bears mentioning that this is a clear example of how crimes against women are often overlooked because they are "too specific to women to be seen as human" (MacKinnon, "Rape, Genocide, and Women's Human Rights," p. 6) that is, rape of men is torture but rape of women is still struggling to be recognized as torture.
33. See, for example, Seymour Hersh, "Torture at Abu Ghraib," *The New Yorker*, May 10, 2004.
34. Consistent with the definition of war rape, I am considering prostitution by oppositional physical force (not economic coercion).
35. Card, *The Atrocity Paradigm*, p. 119.
36. MacKinnon, *Toward a Feminist Theory of the State*, p. 113.
37. Neuffer, *The Key to My Neighbor's House*, p. 282.
38. Neuffer, *The Key to My Neighbor's House*, p. 290.
39. MacKinnon, "Rape, Genocide, and Women's Human Rights," pp. 8–9.
40. MacKinnon, "Rape, Genocide, and Women's Human Rights," p. 9.
41. MacKinnon, "Rape, Genocide, and Women's Human Rights," pp.11–12.
42. Both MacKinnon and Neuffer present evidence of UN peacekeepers involved in rape as well. This further supports an understanding of mass rape as a war within a war. See also Flanders, "J'Accuse," p. 160.
43. Kelly, "Wars Against Women," p. 50.
44. Todd Salzman, "'Rape Camps,' Forced Impregnation, and Ethnic Cleansing," in *War's Dirty Secret*, ed. by Anne Llewellyn Barstow (Cleveland, OH: Pilgrim Press, 2000), pp. 72–74; see also Catharine MacKinnon 1994, p. 9.
45. Barstow, *War's Dirty Secret*, p. 58.
46. Barstow, *War's Dirty Secret*, p. 62; see also Salzman, "'Rape Camps,'" p. 70.
47. Michael Walzer, *Just and Unjust Wars* (New York: Basic Books, 1977), p. 134.
48. Walzer, *Just and Unjust Wars*, p. 137.
49. Walzer, *Just and Unjust Wars*, p. 135.

50. See Schott, "Philosophical Reflections on War Rape," p. 194, who recognizes the need for such a system.
51. Card, *The Atrocity Paradigm*, p. 121.
52. The war crimes tribunals for Yugoslavia and Rwanda added rape and torture to the list of "crimes against humanity". The Rwanda tribunal also added "forced pregnancy" and in 1997, "rape as a means of genocide" was added to the Rwanda tribunal's case against Jean-Paul Akayesu. The context of war is not a necessary condition for a crime against humanity.
53. Schott, "Philosophical Reflections on War Rape," p. 197.
54. MacKinnon, "Rape, Genocide, and Women's Human Rights," p. 15; and Brownmiller, *Against our Will*, p. 15.
55. See, for example, Carol Gould, *Globalizing Democracy and Human Rights* (Cambridge: Cambridge University Press, 2004), p. 145.
56. Brian Orend, "Justice after War," *Ethics and International Affairs,* 16 (1) (2002), p. 54.

KEN KIPNIS

PRISONS, POW CAMPS, AND INTERROGATION CENTERS: REFLECTIONS ON THE JURIDIC STATUS OF DETAINEES

Our interest is not in trying him and punishing him.
Our interest is in finding out what he knows.
Defense Secretary Donald Rumsfeld[1]

There is a certain conventional wisdom in much contemporary thinking about the ethical standards applicable to the use of torture:

The terrorists of today represent a new species of adversary. They do not wear uniforms or carry arms openly. They may lack a determinate national allegiance. They are strikingly willing – perhaps eager – to sacrifice their own lives. They are concerned to destroy civilian, economic, social and cultural targets rather than military ones. And because the United States has come to possess, by far, the world's most powerful armed force, these vexatious opponents have set aside military models of organization and operation and, instead, sought to exploit largely unsuspected vulnerabilities, deftly sidestepping our most devastating weaponry. In this relatively new type of conflict, knowledge is far more critical than brute firepower. Given such formidable adversaries, the more one can learn about their world views, values, personnel, organizations, locations, intentions, resources and capabilities, the less likely they will prevail. Accordingly, when high-value enemy personnel are taken captive, national defense purposes can arguably be furthered if detainees can either be made to give up what they know or – better – to become double agents, serving thereafter as steady sources of intelligence.

It is against this background that "aggressive interrogation" and torture can emerge as instruments of national defense policy, as tools that promise to expedite the gathering of intelligence. Much of the debate has been framed in these terms.

Less frequently considered are the on-the-ground institutional contexts within which detainees are held for interrogation. The concern in this chapter is narrowly with questions arising at the organizational level. I will try to show that a novel social institution has made an appearance in American political life (albeit not generally in American territory). I will refer to these settings, without originality, as "interrogation centers." It will, I hope, become clear that when one shifts focus to the institutional background, torture falls into place as an element of a larger system of interrelated social practices: perhaps not even the most important element. I will try to show that interrogation centers are neither prisoner of war (POW) camps nor prisons, although these institutions have been misleadingly appealed to in efforts to represent current practice. Both analogs fail as models. Finally I will try to describe some of the salient jurisprudential problems that pervade this emergent social setting and make a few suggestions about how to understand and resolve them.

1. POWS, PRISONERS AND DETAINEES

Camp Delta at Guantanamo Bay and the prison at Abu Ghraib are, at this writing, perhaps the two best-known interrogation centers. The Bagram Collection Point in Afghanistan, where two detainees were reported to have been killed, is also becoming familiar.[2] One would also have to include covert CIA detention facilities in Singapore, Thailand, Pakistan, and other locations around the world.[3] And finally, there are the official "extraordinary renderings" that have recently come under international scrutiny. These are forced transfers of persons detained by American personnel to the custody of countries with fewer reservations about inhumane treatment.[4] The consistent use of overseas venues, arguably beyond the reach of US courts; the implementation of immunity provisions for private contractors and other personnel; the decision not to participate in the International Criminal Court (together with the bilateral agreements intended to insure that United States combatants will not find themselves called before it); and the unprecedented use of secrecy: all of these background conditions erode and diffuse the accountability of the personnel who staff these centers.

There are two important qualifications on what follows. First, the secrecy surrounding both these institutions and the policies and procedures that govern them makes it difficult to obtain a reliable sense of what we are looking at. Any description must be tentative, subject to review as a clearer picture emerges. I have relied heavily on journalists' accounts, particularly Seymour M. Hersh's *Chain of Command*. Second, if aspects of these policies and procedures continue to come to light, if legal complaints are filed and if courts impose corrective measures, then these centers may evolve as judges, elected politicians, military officers, and civilian officials bring current practices into line with emerging juridic standards and oversight procedures. For example, the Supreme Court in *Hamdi* v. *Rumsfeld* determined that a US citizen held in the United States as an enemy combatant could challenge the factual basis for detention before a neutral decision-maker.[5] Although Justice Sandra Day O'Connor opined "that a state of war is not a blank check for the President when it comes to the rights of the Nation's citizens" it is not clear how far judicial and legislative oversight and authority will eventually reach. Accordingly, not only are interrogation centers dimly seen: they may be altering their shape. Indeed it is assumed in what follows that when problems are better understood, they are more likely to be addressed. There is hope for improvement. Of course it is equally possible that both the institutions and the policies governing them will disappear behind a military-bureaucratic curtain. That would be more than a problem for scholars.

While prisons are intended to punish convicts and POW camps are intended to confine those who surrender or are captured on the battlefield, these new institutions appear to be designed to optimize the extraction of information from those designated as "unlawful enemy combatants." This term itself deserves scrutiny, somehow straddling the concepts of convict (unlawful) and POW (enemy combatant), even while falling between the two and failing to be subsumed plainly under either. Detainees are not held pursuant to a juridic determination of guilt, nor do they enjoy internationally recognized legal protections as POWs. What exactly are they? Neither "prisoner" nor "POW" appears to be useful in capturing their status.

Recall that a prison is an institution with the core mission of punishing those who have been juridically convicted of crimes and thereafter sentenced to loss of liberty: imprisonment for some specified period. Convicts are remanded to the custody of wardens whose paramount duties are (1) to provide, during the term of mandated imprisonment, for the basic well-being of inmates (e.g., shelter, meals, and indicated medical care) and (2) to maintain prison security (preventing escape and riot). Since civilly imposed loss of liberty is broadly taken to be a dire consequence, the threat of extended imprisonment is broadly taken to be a weighty reason to forbear the commission of crimes and, if apprehended, a weighty reason to cooperate with the authorities in the hope of receiving a reduced sentence. Note that not all rights are forfeited following conviction. Even those condemned to death have a right to counsel.

A POW camp has a quite different function. Although captured enemy combatants were anciently killed or sold into slavery, there have been moments of impressive moral progress, particularly in the recent past when the Geneva Conventions were internationally acknowledged as governing. In a well-run POW camp, those who have been captured or who have surrendered on the battlefield can be properly confined until hostilities cease. But they are not convicts, being punished following a juridic conviction of wrongdoing. They are there solely because they have been taken prisoner while serving in an opposing army. (The treatment of those committing war crimes is a separate issue.)

There are strong prudential and ethical arguments for the humane treatment of prisoners. When resistance has become militarily futile, an expectation of humane treatment can make surrender a more attractive option, possibly forestalling a fight to the death. There is also a stronger expectation of reciprocal humane treatment when a nation's own soldiers are captured. And humane treatment, however defined, is to be favored just because it is humane. The Geneva Convention of 1949 set out international standards for the treatment of POWs and the organization of POW camps. This was a major milestone in the law of war.

These brief descriptions of the prison and the POW camp are intended to characterize well-governed examples. But any social institution operating without effective oversight and accountability can gradually take up a quite different configuration. For example, some prisons in the South became remunerative sources of cheap forced labor.[6] Holmsburg prison in Pennsylvania became a center for human experimentation, especially in dermatology.[7] Subjected to broad review, these institutional variants have gradually disappeared. In the same way, POW camps can also take on a quite different shape. Like the forced laborers in the South and the incarcerated research subjects in Pennsylvania, POWs can become high-value sources of actionable intelligence.

In marking this transformation, one can use as a baseline the US Defense Department's "Code of Conduct (CoC) Training and Education." Intended for the American enlistee, this is its explanation of the POW's reasonable expectations under the Geneva Conventions:

E2.2.5.1. When questioned, a POW is required . . . and permitted . . . to give name, rank, service number, and date of birth. . . . [T]he enemy has no right to try to force a POW to provide any additional information. However, it is unrealistic to expect a POW to remain confined for years reciting only name, rank, service number, and date of birth. There are many POW camp situations in which certain types of conversation with the enemy are permitted. For example, a POW is allowed, but not required by the CoC, the UCMJ, or the Geneva Conventions, to fill out a Geneva Conventions "capture card," to write letters home, and to communicate with captors on matters of camp administration and health and welfare.[8]

In a parallel discussion, The US Army Field Manual (FM 34–52) describes the reciprocal standards for interrogating captured enemy soldiers. Here is what it says about extracting intelligence:

The use of force, mental torture, threats, insults, or exposure to unpleasant and inhumane treatment of any kind is prohibited by law and is neither authorized nor condoned by the US Government. Experience indicates that the use of force is not necessary to gain the cooperation of sources for interrogation. Therefore, the use of force is a poor technique, as it yields unreliable results, may damage subsequent collection efforts, and can induce the source to say whatever he thinks the interrogator wants to hear. However, the use of force is not to be confused with psychological ploys, verbal trickery, or other nonviolent and noncoercive ruses used by the interrogator in questioning hesitant or uncooperative sources.[9]

Notwithstanding these reasonably clear standards, the use of far harsher treatment has been a feature of war for perhaps as long as there has been war. During the Vietnam era, some American soldiers were reported to have taken small groups of bound Viet Cong aloft in helicopters. They would question one in the presence of the others and if he would not provide information they would throw him to his death. The remaining Viet Cong, having seen "the long step," would, in theory, be more inclined to cooperate. While it is likely that aggressive interrogation has occurred in previous American conflicts, it is plausible that these were aberrations not explicitly permitted by official policies. However, when entire institutions come into view that are organized and staffed to carry out the aggressive interrogation of enemy combatants, something new has appeared.

2. THE INTERROGATION CENTER

Though they may have served other purposes initially, there can be no doubt that intelligence gathering has been the central concern of these centers. In his report on Abu Ghraib, General Taguba noted that a military intelligence brigade was given tactical control of the prison.[10] The earlier practice had been to place such units under the command of the military police. General Geoffrey Miller (the former commander at Guantanamo Bay) was appointed to "Gitmoize" the prisons in Iraq, shifting their focus to interrogation. Miller intended "to turn Abu Ghraib into a center of intelligence for the Bush Administration's global war on terrorism" and envisioned "a system that could drive the rapid exploitation of internees to answer . . . theater and national level counterterrorism requirements."[11] The point was no longer to sequester POWs until hostilities ended. Detainees had become an intelligence resource to be exploited.

While there may be variation in the treatment at different centers and for certain detainees, there are five features that appear to be both common and problematic.

1. The identities of those detained may not be reported to their families, to the Red Cross, or to the press. ("Ghost detainees" – inmates kept off the books – were a presence at Abu Ghraib.) In the most egregious cases, there may be little difference between being detained

and being "disappeared." Communication with those outside the interrogation center may be impossible, including secure communication with attorneys.
2. The specific methods of interrogating prisoners are largely unknown. Those standards that have been leaked, though vague, raise concerns. For example, in attempting to define "physical pain amounting to torture" a Justice Department memo – the Bybee memo – held that it "must be equivalent in intensity to the pain accompanying serious physical injury, such as organ failure, impairment of body function, or even death." Instead of a bright line, we have what appears to be a featureless grey zone.[12] (And, by the way, neither organ failure nor death need be painful.)
3. The duration of detention is not specified temporally (as with a prison sentence) or procedurally (when a war comes to an official end). Indeed it is unclear what could count as victory in a war against "terrorism." If terrorism (as an international problem) is the organized use of violence and intimidation against noncombatants in the pursuit of political aims, then it is evident that quite different political aims can be pursued terroristically. It is therefore probably unrealistic to expect that the use of such means will ever be set aside universally, or – more narrowly – that terrorism could be convincingly renounced by Islamic fundamentalists in the foreseeable future. Of course, when a detainee lacks the ability or willingness to join or rejoin the enemy, and lacks useful information to share with captors, there may be a diminished need to extend detention. But even then, detainees may have information obtained while in captivity – if only about the conditions of detention – that could be useful to the enemy after release.
4. The key structural element in the interrogation center is the subordination of all institutional elements to the intelligence gathering function. The narratives that have emerged from the National Guard military police assigned to Abu Ghraib repeatedly describe their enlistment into the dominant intelligence gathering hierarchy; seeing to it that an inmate "had a bad night" for example. Hersh presents evidence that the photographic records of sexual indignities were to be used to blackmail detainees into service as double agents.[13] Even health care personnel were enlisted, for example, in concealing deaths occurring during the course of interrogation.[14]
5. While prisons and POW camps are subject to various national and international standards of operation, there appear to be few such standards applicable to interrogation centers, and even fewer independent oversight bodies. There are questions about the availability

and independence of healthcare personnel, of religious services, of human contact with other detainees and representatives of international organizations. There are jurisprudential questions about the use of executive authority to designate persons as unlawful enemy combatants, and whether those detained have the power to initiate review processes when and where ongoing hostilities do not rule out such a proceeding.

Drawing from these problematic elements, one can pose five parallel questions regarding the juridic status of unlawful enemy combatants. (1) Should detainees be accorded the right to communicate with others not complicit in their detention? (2) What standards should apply to the aggressive encouragement of disclosure and cooperation? (3) When – if ever – must detainees be released? (4) What structural standards ought to govern interrogation centers? (5) How should these standards be developed and enforced? In a jurisprudential *terra incognita*, the first priority is to get one's bearings. What do these practices suggest and how might they be transformed?

3. THE JURIDIC STATUS OF DETAINEES

The following general provision is set out in the US Department of Defense 2003 orders governing military commissions reviewing the status of detainees.

Sec. 10.6 Non-creation of right. Neither this part nor any Military Commission Instruction issued hereafter, is intended to and does not create any right, benefit, privilege, substantive or procedural, enforceable by any party, against the United States, its departments, agencies, or other entities, its officers or employees, or any other person. Alleged noncompliance with an Instruction does not, of itself, constitute error, give rise to judicial review, or establish a right to relief for the Accused or any other person.[15]

So described, these Commissions operate in a remarkable juridic isolation. As one unnamed military official reportedly quipped: "Guantanamo was the 'legal equivalent of outer space.' "[16]

While detainees' legal status may be novel to modern sensibilities and without parallel in modern jurisprudence, it may be a variant of two older juridic conceptions. With its roots in Norse culture during the age of the Vikings, the concept of the "outlaw" has been around for at least a millennium. Though it has come to refer to the "bad guys" in a generation of low-budget cowboy movies, it originally signified a court-imposed placement of a convicted wrongdoer beyond legal protection. Being "outlawed" was a punishment for the most serious crimes, including, in

Iceland, the crime of harboring an outlaw. In designating evildoers as outlaws – what have been called *hostis humanis generis* or enemies of all mankind – juridic authority effectively can declare open season on them, denying them informal assistance and subsequent access to juridic review.[17]

Notice that, like pirates – also enemies of mankind who could be formally convicted for the crime of piracy – the Norse evildoer had to be tried before being punished. What is remarkable about the "unlawful enemy combatants" of today is the absence of a recognizable juridic process. Instead we see something like the exercise of executive discretion. Recall that the Constitution explicitly prohibits bills of attainder: that is, legislative determinations of personal culpability. It seems that those deemed to be unlawful enemy combatants are being subjected to a comparable executive power.

A second juridic conception, drawn from the past, affords insight. European monarchs traditionally enjoyed the power to imprison those who had fallen seriously out of grace. There are architectural examples of what were called "oubliettes": small prison cells where unfortunates could be forgotten (as the term suggests). Kings could exercise a royal prerogative to impose this "civil death" upon subjects. While those we have detained abroad have not generally been American citizens, their sequestration without recourse is comparable to the exercise of such a power. In its report on American practices in the war on terror, Amnesty International argued that:

> Guantanamo has become the gulag of our times, entrenching the notion that people can be detained without any recourse to the law. . . . If Guantanamo evokes images of Soviet repression, "ghost detainees" . . . bring back the practice of "disappearances" so popular with Latin American dictators in the past.[18]

We would do well to remember that both the Lockean objections to the exercise of unfettered political authority and the American War of Independence stemmed from comparable abuses. The legal requirement of an impartial trial prior to forfeiture of liberty is one of the great remedies for that civil ill. So too have international treaties characteristically ameliorated the treatment of POWs.

It seems not much to insist that if international terrorism is a global problem, the institutions and strategies that are developed to deal with it on a planetary scale should be subject to international standards and oversight. Terrorist organizations acting without state authority fall outside of the traditional rules of war, conceived as a conflict between nation-states. Though it is hard to discern what the rules would ultimately look like, the process for regularizing the treatment of unlawful enemy combatants would have to involve roughly the same broad cooperation that gave rise to the International Criminal Court, including that of the United States. At this writing, the United States government appears to be winging it on its own, making up its own rules (if rules there be) and forgetting much of what we have learned about the linkages between jurisprudence and civil order.

In his *History of the Peloponesian Wars*, Thucydides describes how, following political debate and failed negotiations with the island of Melos, Athens had chosen to crush the Melians. The men were put to death and the women and children sold into slavery. It is common to identify this shockingly unsympathetic outcome, together with the public debate that preceded it, as a watershed moment in the history of Athens: the beginning of its lengthy decline. Writing shortly after the destruction of Melos in 416 B.C., Euripides, in *The Trojan Women*, has the god Poseidon warn:

How are ye blind,
Ye treaders down of cities, ye that cast
Temples to desolation, and lay waste
Tombs, the untrodden sanctuaries where lie
The ancient dead; yourselves so soon to die![19]

To the extent that a state calls its political legitimacy into question, it imperils its stability.

It has not been my purpose to challenge interrogation centers as a necessary tool in the effort to frustrate the purposes of terrorists. For the moment, it seems these settings are here to stay. Americans are taking them for granted much as we once did with Japanese relocation camps. Nor have I been concerned to characterize the American practices of torture. Rather, assuming we are sadly stuck with Abu Ghraib and its siblings, I would urge those of us in social and legal philosophy to start thinking creatively about the jurisprudence that should govern this new and troubling social institution.

NOTES

1. Rumsfeld is speaking of Jose Padilla, an American citizen and "enemy combatant" who was being held in a military brig in South Carolina. CNN, June 11, 2002.
2. Tim Golden. "In U.S. Report, Brutal Details of 2 Afghan Inmates' Deaths," *New York Times*, May 20, 2005, A1.
3. Seymour Hersh, *Chain of command* (New York: HarperCollins, 2004), p. 20.
4. Douglas Jehl and David Johnston, "Rule Change Lets C.I.A. Freely Send Suspects Abroad to Jails," *New York Times,* March 6, 2005.

5. No. 03-6696. Argued April 28, 2004; decided June 28, 2004; 542 US——2004.
6. A. Lichtenstein, *Twice The Work of Free Labor: The Political Economy of Convict Labor in the New South* (London: Verso, 1995).
7. A. M. Hornblum, *Acres of Skin: Human Experiments at Holmesburg Prison: A True Story of Abuse and Exploitation in the Name of Medical Science* (New York: Routledge, 1998).
8. Department of Defense. *Code of Conduct (CoC) Training and Education*. The document is available at <http://www.dtic.mil/whs/directives/corres/html2/i130021x.htm#cr3>.
9. *US Army Field Manual 34-52: Intelligence Interrogation*. The document is available at <http://www.globalsecurity.org/intell/library/policy/army/fm/fm34-52/chapter1.htm>.
10. The "Taguba Report" *On Treatment Of Abu Ghraib Prisoners In Iraq: Article 15–6 Investigation of the 800th Military Police Brigade*. The document is available at <http://news.findlaw.com/hdocs/docs/iraq/tagubarpt.html>.
11. Hersh, *Chain of Command*, p. 11.
12. Dana Priest, "Justice Dept. Memo Says Torture 'May Be Justified.'" *Washington Post*, June 13, 2004. The text of the Department of Justice memo is at:<http://www.washingtonpost.com/wp-srv/nation/documents/dojinterrogationmemo20020801.pdf>
13. Hersh, *Chain of command*, pp. 38–39.
14. S.H. Miles, "Abu Ghraib: Its Legacy for Military Medicine," *Lancet* 364 (2004), pp. 725–729.
15. 32CFR10.6
16. Quoted in "Guantanamo Bay – Camp Delta," at <http://www.globalsecurity.org/military/facility/guantanamo-bay_delta.htm>
17. D. Friedman, "Private Creation and Enforcement of Law: A Historical Case." *Journal of Legal Studies*, 8, pp. 399–415.
18. Amnesty International Report 2005, Speech by Irene Khan at Foreign Press Association, May 25, 2005. At <http://web.amnesty.org/library/index/ENGPOL100142005>.
19. Murray, G. (trans.) *The Trojan Women of Euripides* (New York: Oxford University Press, 1915).

VI. THE IMPACT OF TECHNOLOGY

RICHARD T. DE GEORGE

NON-COMBATANT IMMUNITY IN AN AGE OF HIGH TECH WARFARE

During the past few years the doctrine of *jus ad bellum* has received considerable attention, with much less paid to the doctrine of *jus in bello* (or of right conduct in war). The implications of the doctrine of *jus ad bellum* for peacetime are reasonably well known. Since a country may not justly go to war except in self-defense and only as a last resort, a country is morally required to take the appropriate means of exhausting alternatives to war. Arguably, the doctrine also imposes on nations collectively the obligation to establish mechanisms for averting war.[1] Although *jus in bello* refers to the ethics of the means of conducting a war, and so seems applicable only during wartime, I shall argue that the doctrine has implications for what is both required and allowed for a nation in peacetime. It would be unreasonable for the doctrine to require certain kinds of actions during war and not require taking the necessary means in time of peace so as to be able to carry out one's obligations during war.

I shall deal with three aspects of the portion of *jus in bello* known as the doctrine of noncombatant immunity that have contemporary significance during peacetime. The first has to do with the development of smart bombs. The second concerns directed energy weapons. The third deals with noncombatants and terrorism.

1. SMART BOMBS

What is known in military circles as the Revolution in Military Affairs (RMA)[2] concerns the way that technology is changing the way war is conducted and the implications this has for defense policy. Despite a growing literature and a fairly vigorous debate in some quarters about the future of US military and defense policy, very little attention has been paid to the implications of this revolution for Just War Theory (JWT).

I shall consider here only the development of smart bombs. In the Second Iraq War smart bombs were used in cities such as Baghdad. They had become considerably more accurate than they had been in the first Gulf War. Smart bombs are guided by electronic devices and computers, which are typically used to make weapons more effective. And more effective means that they hit their intended targets with more reliability than noncomputerized weapons. Two happy by-products are that they frequently require less explosive yield and that they can reduce the risk of collateral damage when actually used in war.

This suggests two principles, which I shall call the *Principles of Smart Weapons Development*. The first is the *Principle of Morally Obligatory Smart Weapons Development*. One of the core requirements of *jus in bello* is the immunity of noncombatants or the injunction not to directly harm innocent civilians. Although the doctrine of *jus in bello* covers the activity of nations and armies involved in war, and hence requires that one take care to avoid harming innocent civilians to the extent possible given whatever weapons one has, it has implications that arguably extend outside of war. The weapons one uses in war are often developed when a nation is not at war. It would be unreasonable for the doctrine to require certain kinds of actions during war and not require taking the necessary means in time of peace so as to be able to carry out one's obligations during a war. At least one such obligation, if one develops weapons during peacetime, is to develop bombs and other armaments that will do as little collateral damage as possible to nonmilitary targets. To act otherwise would be to fail to take the doctrine of civilian immunity seriously.

This line of reasoning leads to the unexpected and somewhat counterintuitive result that, if the result of developing smarter and smarter weapons is precise bombing that will allow for less collateral damage than otherwise, the country engaged in such research and development has the moral imperative to develop such technology. Not to do so would be to choose to accept less precise bombs that cause more collateral damage to innocent noncombatants. This violates the injunction not to harm noncombatants if at all possible.

Once a nation possesses smart bombs, moreover, it has the obligation to use them if collateral damage is likely. Since such bombs are more costly than conventional weapons, they are more likely to be developed and produced in countries that are industrially developed and reasonably affluent. Such countries are morally obliged to accept the added cost of using such bombs if innocent lives in an enemy country can be saved. Moreover, it would also seem that any nation that has weapons has the obligation to develop or purchase the most advanced and precise weaponry it can and the moral obligation continually to upgrade its armaments so that in case of emergency it can avoid as much as possible collateral damage to noncombatants.

This is counterintuitive because it sounds like a justification for a continuing arms race. A more intuitively attractive and more popular line of reasoning is that the production of armaments is in itself immoral, as is any arms race, and that therefore the justification does not work. The principle of civilian immunity, it might be argued, requires only that one attempt to the extent possible to minimize civilian casualties. It does not require the development of new weapons. The point is well taken if the development of new armaments means, as it has in the past, the development of more and more destructive weapons. But the argument misses the point and does not apply to smart bombs. First, the requirement to develop smarter bombs that will do less civilian damage applies only to the extent that a country is engaged in the development or procurement of any weapons. If there were a worldwide effective prohibition against any new developments in weapons, there would be no obligation to develop smart bombs. Short of such a prohibition, it would be counterproductive to prohibit the development of bombs that did less collateral damage to civilians than would otherwise be the case. Nor would it help to claim that noncombatant immunity requires simply that we not directly intend the death of civilians, providing there is a proportional reason for allowing such deaths. This line of reasoning is susceptible to Michael Walzer's correction of the principle of double effect to one of double intention, namely that one consider not only the good to be achieved but that one also attempt to reduce the evil to be allowed.[3]

Second, if self-defense is recognized as morally permissible, then absent any enforceable worldwide agreement against armaments and war, developing the means to protect oneself is morally permissible, providing there are external threats that one cannot otherwise control. The principle I am suggesting places limits and restraints on the development of new weapons, and requires that in their development the aim of reducing damage to innocent civilians be an integral part.

One might still argue that since only defensive wars are morally permissible, a country like the United States surely has enough armaments to fight any defensive war that we can imagine. Therefore, there is no justification for its continuing to develop and produce new armaments. The argument, however, misconstrues the nature of a defensive war. Consider World War II. The United States was initially attacked. But the war was not fought on American shores. Fighting a defensive war meant fighting the German and Japanese forces where they were, bombing cities they had occupied and then bombing their military defenses and supplies in their own countries. In the process many civilians were killed. If the United States could have destroyed military targets without killing civilians, it would have had the moral obligation to do so. It thus seems to have the moral obligation to try to achieve that objective, when it undertakes the development of armaments for fighting a defensive war. In the present context this means that if developing more and better weapons for fighting a defensive war is legitimate, then one is obliged to take proper measures to ensure that those weapons will cause as little collateral damage to civilians as possible.

It might further be argued against their production that smart bombs actually make war more acceptable to civilian populations and thus make war more likely. Hence they should not be developed, and it is unethical to contribute to their development. But this argument also suffers from a number of defects. First, it ignores the fact that the existence of smart bombs in no way changes the conditions of *jus ad bellum*. The acceptability or unacceptability to a civilian population of engaging in war is not one of the criteria determining a just war. From an ethical point of view, war remains a last resort and justifiable only as a defense against an aggressor. Second, although it might appear that war would be more acceptable, there is also evidence that aggressors might curtail their aggression more than otherwise, if they knew they would be faced with extremely accurate armaments that would inflict great damage on their military forces with little comparable cost to the enemy. Third, the implication might be drawn that since more accurate weapons tend to make war easier, weapons such as nuclear weapons, which make war harder to accept should be developed rather than smart weapons. Support for this comes from experience with the policy of deterrence during the Cold War. Yet few would accept this argument. Although mutual-total-destruction served as a deterrent to war to some extent, the proliferation of such weapons seems to increase the likelihood of massive destruction, if not through direct intentional defensive first strike, then through accident, miscalculation, or the action of an evil leader. In any event, the implication for smart bomb development is not comparable, since the principle does not justify more destructive bombs, but only bombs that are less destructive with respect to innocent civilians.

The acceptability of the argument in defense of the Principle of Morally Obligatory Smart Weapons Development hinges on the fact that it is severely restricted in its scope. What it justifies is only the development of smart weapons that will do as little damage as possible to innocent noncombatants. It encourages not the development of weapons with greater destructive power, but only the development of weapons, for instance, that are not only better at avoiding collateral damage but that may stun or temporarily immobilize people without doing serious physical damage to them or any damage to nonmilitary property or to a nation's civilian infrastructure. The development of future weapons that will result in less collateral damage to innocent noncombatants, but will also reduce the number of combatant casualties on both sides, is not only morally justifiable but morally mandatory, when and if weapons development is undertaken.

The second principle is the *Principle of Weapons Development Assistance to Others*. If the development of the weapons I just described indeed has the effect of reducing noncombatant casualties, then, providing that they will be used only in wars of self-defense, and providing that they will be used precisely for the purpose of minimizing civilian casualties, nations that develop such technologies have a moral obligation to make that technical information available to others. They are intended to reduce rather than augment damage to noncombatants. So even if such weapons were used against the nation that developed them, if used to reduce collateral damage, the noncombatant population of that nation would be better off than if the aggressor nation used conventional weapons.

But here is the rub. The precise weapons, although arguably better than conventional weapons in reducing collateral damage, are also much more accurate in destroying the targets at which they are aimed. While conventional bombs might cause much collateral damage in an attempt to destroy a specific target, none of them may actually hit the target at all. The smart bombs are much more accurate and the results more certain. Hence countries that develop such weapons are understandably reluctant to make the technology available to others who may in turn use such weapons against them.

We have yet to see what a symmetrical war with respect to smart weapons would look like. In an asymmetrical war, if the nation with smart weapons fights on the soil of another nation, for instance, the first nation has no noncombatant citizens of its own at risk to worry about. But in a situation in which such weapons are in the hands of one's enemies, then the greater accuracy of the weapons means probably more military casualties of one's own. And that is not what any country in a war wishes or what it is ethically required to promote. Hence the obligation to share such weaponry or to make it available to other countries is arguably legitimately restricted to those whom one is fairly sure will not use such weapons except to reduce civilian casualties, and who will not make them available to others who will use them against oneself or others in a war of aggression.[4] Moreover, although smart weapons make it *possible* to reduce collateral damage, it is possible to use them against civilian targets so as to increase civilian casualties with greater accuracy. Hence, although they allow a beneficial use from the point of view of minimizing civilian collateral damage, they also make possible the opposite.

The counter, of course, is that if failure to make such weapons available to one's potential enemies puts a country's own civilian population at greater risk than they would be if the enemy used smart bombs, then the obligation stands. In this case, one is led to consider weighing whether more potential harm is done to one's noncombatant population by giving the enemy smart bomb technology, thereby putting one's armed forces in greater danger, or by keeping smart bombs out of the hands of one's potential enemies and relying on the use of technological advances to counter the enemy's use of conventional, dumb weapons. If the danger of the new weapons being used against civilians to increase harm to them is high, then the obligation to share such weapons does not exist. What is important in the discussion, however, is which strategy better protects a country's noncombatants. The protection of civilians is not to be taken lightly, even if it places military personnel at somewhat greater risk. According to traditional JWT, the immunity of noncombatants is more important than the vulnerability of combatants.

However that weighing is decided, and it seems to be at least an empirical matter, the same kind of argument does not restrict the sharing of weapons (e.g., that temporarily immobilize people rather than kill them) that are not more destructive but that simply produce less collateral damage. Here the principle of assistance to all, including one's enemies, seems to remain applicable.

In reply to those who might say that the principle of noncombatant immunity in JWT applies only to the requirement to minimize civilian casualties to the extent possible, and does not require one to attempt to reduce one's own civilian casualties to the extent possible, the obligation to do so comes from a government's responsibility to protect and defend its citizens from attack and harm.

In a period of asymmetric warfare, if it is unlikely that war will be waged in the traditional sense of invasion of one's territory by an enemy, then the consideration of reducing the number of collateral civilian deaths of one's own does not come into play. In present conditions, the most likely wars do not seem to be between countries of equally developed resources and strength. Moreover, to the extent that the Principle of Morally Obligatory Smart Weapons Development is observed by all parties developing armaments, then the necessity of sharing one's advances in this respect with one's enemy, for the purpose of reducing one's own civilian causalities, carries less weight than the advantage such weapons give on the battlefield.

A more difficult issue is the question of whether in a symmetrical war the use of smart weapons might reduce civilian casualties in the short run, but prolong the war in the long run, producing more casualties overall.

Although theoretically possible, such a scenario is difficult to imagine. More importantly, the implied argument seems to say that the alternative of killing of civilians whose deaths could be avoided by using smart bombs is justifiable if that is a means to shorten a war. That alternative, however, makes the killing of civilians a direct means to an end, or in Kantian terms, uses the civilians as only a means to the end of shortening the war. That scenario is precisely the one that the immunity of civilians doctrine and the double intention version of double effect preclude.

2. DIRECTED ENERGY WEAPONS

The Principle of Morally Obligatory Smart Weapons Development has as its aim the promotion of the immunity of civilians. As a result, it does not, as might be expected, sanction the development of all weapons that minimize direct physical harm.

In early February of 2003, a secret order allowing the development of guidelines governing the use of cyber attacks against foreign computer systems, which had been signed by President Bush in July, became known.[5] It dealt with attacks on computer hardware. On November 27 the *Wall Street Journal*, and on February 20, 2003, the *New York Times*[6] carried articles that brought to public attention the existence of programs for the development of directed-energy weapons, which had been under development not only in the United States but also in Great Britain, China, Russia, and possibly other countries. Yet the articles provoked no public debate and US policy with respect to this case remains secret, if developed. The scenario suggests the *Principle of Public Debate on Weapons of Mass Disruption.*

These high-power microwave weapons produce thousands of volts of energy that destroy electronic devices and melt semi-conductors. They render phones, computers, and anything dependent on electronic components useless, while not harming human beings. They also can penetrate more deeply into concrete than other weapons. The weapons thus can be seen as much more humane than conventional bombs, and would seem to respect the immunity of innocent civilians, for instance, if used in cities. On the battlefield they would destroy control and command functions without killing soldiers – who might be persuaded to surrender. The weapons would thus also be in accord with the *jus in bello* demand of proportionality. The weapons would make possible the reduction of killing and wounding troops. At least they might do so, since in the wrong hands, they could also be used to destroy command and control and so leave enemy troops at the mercy of virtually unopposed bombing, shelling, destruction, and massacre.

Although the weapons do not harm people directly, and might seem to be the kind of weapons whose development I just defended, they raise an ethical issue because they can destroy a country's infrastructure. The more advanced technologically a society is, the more it is dependent on the technology it has developed and uses routinely for all the necessities of life, from providing water and electricity, to communications and transportation. Consider a city like New York. To deprive it of electricity would be to paralyze it. And if all electrical and electronic components were burned out and had to be replaced, the task would be enormous. The damage would include the destruction of the communications systems, the transportation systems, and all the private and business computers. The city would stop functioning except on the most primitive level, and hence the effect on innocent civilians would be devastating.

Now it might be argued that the infrastructure of a society can be destroyed by conventional weapons as well, and that these directed-energy weapons at least do not target or directly harm people. But the directed-energy weapons, if developed and rendered as effective as they might be, damage a wider range of the infrastructure than conventional bombs. Conventional bombs might take out power plants or communications nubs or water supply stations, but do not take out all electronically dependent facilities and instruments, all computers and electronic components, rendering even vehicles unusable. Nuclear weapons, of course, do that and much worse, both to people and property. But directed-energy weapons on a large scale are far from benign, even if benign with respect to direct physical harm to people. To argue that people are not killed or maimed directly, and that therefore the immunity of innocent civilians is respected, is to overstate the case that can be made. On the other hand, that case seems appropriate with respect to battlefield use, if such weapons are used to reduce the loss of life.

The danger of such weapons, of course, is greatest for those nations most dependent on electronics. In the 2003 war in Iraq the technological superiority of the United States was evident. Computer guided missiles and bombs, night vision equipment, the capability of keeping in constant touch with one's troops in all areas of the combat zone, and the ability of those in command to pull all that information together through their computers and to simulate possible responses and scenarios gave war a new command and control dimension that was previously unknown. In Iraq this capability was enjoyed only by the US (and coalition) forces, which were at the same time able, by bombs, jamming radar and other means, to deprive the Iraqi forces of almost all command and control functions. The asymmetry was clear and decisive. What the asymmetry covered over, however, was the vulnerability of the US forces because of their dependence on computers and related technology. In a war against guerilla fighters who use conventional weapons, directed-energy bombs are useless. But they are obviously not useless against an army such as that of the United States that put on such a dazzling show of electronic weapons and command and control facilities in the Iraq war.

Both technologically advanced armies and technologically advanced countries are more vulnerable than those that are less developed. This means that such countries must now invest in hardening their electronics to the extent possible against possible attack by such weapons. It is not clear how a symmetric war in which both sides had more or less equal dependence on computers and electronics, and each side had similar capabilities with respect to directed-energy weapons, would be fought. Traditionally, new weapons that are held by only one side give that side the military advantage. The more equal, often, the bloodier the war is for both sides.

Present directed-energy bombs do not yet have the power, so far as we have been told, to affect whole cities, and their present range is rather small geographically. Nonetheless, if these new bombs can be developed and used over wide areas, they become weapons of mass disruption. They will make modern life, which is dependent on electricity and computers, impossible. They will lead to innumerable civilian deaths from the absence of potable water, from hospitals that are non-functional, from food distribution that becomes impossible, from communications that do not work, and so on – all of which cannot be repaired quickly. As such, weapons of mass disruption rival weapons of mass destruction in their effects. Developing them raises the same ethical issues as the development of the atom bomb. As such they may well deserve similar conventions outlawing them. Fortunately, unlike the situation during World War II with respect to the atom bomb, we are in a position to prevent their development by international agreements. Hence the pressing need for public and informed discussion of a policy not only on the use but on the possible cessation of development of such weapons.

In this as in other cases, the general public must rely on the knowledgeable experts for accurate information on what society is facing, and for bringing the facts to the public for an open discussion of public policy. At the same time, the principle of self-defense arguably imposes on governments the obligation to try to find ways to harden or otherwise protect their computers and systems from destructive attack by others, and it justifies working on such projects. The development of weapons of mass disruption is of such great national and international importance that it should not be treated as a matter only for the military or for government to decide in secret. We can avoid and should not replicate the moral quandaries raised by the atom bomb.

3. NONCOMBATANTS AND TERRORISM

The doctrine of the immunity of civilians takes on a new role in the Information Age. While Sect. 2 involved attacks on hardware, this section raises moral issues about attacks on software. The United States routinely monitors and attempts to infiltrate foreign communications networks, and the sites of the US government are under constant attack.[7] In February 2003 the FBI warned so-called patriotic hackers that hacking remains a criminal act, even if resulting from what might be considered a good motive.[8] Despite the FBI warning, in late March, Al-Jazeera's web sites came under attack, and on March 27 the site's contents were replaced with an American flag.[9] On April 4, Computer Professionals for Social Responsibility (CPSR) called on Internet users to protest the hacking of Al-Jazeera. This leads me to the *Principle of the Moral Unjustifiablity of Private Computer Wars*, including private cyber wars.

For a nation involved in war, denial of service to enemy computers by viruses, worms, or other techniques is comparable to jamming radar and other nonlethal means of warfare and is clearly preferable to more violent means that result in injury and death if they achieve the same purpose, for example, disruption of command and control functions. Clearly, if JWT justifies killing and the destruction of property – military and governmental – in the pursuit of a just war, cyber attacks by nations at war are justified.[10]

Yet even though war and national defense may justify cyber attacks on enemy software by governments and military forces, they do not justify similar actions when done by private individuals. This is the case even though civilians, because of the nature of the Internet and of information technology, may be able to infiltrate enemy computers and systems and damage them in a variety of ways. They may do so from the safety of their office, unlike a patriot in former times who would actually go to the scene of battle. Moreover, although the former patriot might not add much, if anything, to the winning of a battle, the computer warrior may feel that he or she is contributing a great deal to the war effort of his or her country. Yet, both the FBI and CPSR were surely right. Hacking that involves denial of service or that hijacks web sites is both illegal and unethical, even if done from supposedly good motives. Good motives alone do not justify either criminal or unethical behavior. And more is at stake than the patriot hacker realizes.

Individuals cannot justifiably wage their own war and such actions are neither recognized by international law nor by JWT, which requires that war be declared by a competent authority – usually the government of a country.

Private wars are not wars. The so-called patriot hackers who brought down the Al-Jazeera site were not cybersoldiers, and what they did was unethical for many reasons, as well as indicating misplaced concern. Al-Jazeera was not an Iraqi site, but an Arabic Satellite TV Channel based in Qatar. During the Iraq war it broadcast the Arab point of view on the war, much to the displeasure of some Americans. It also has an Arabic and an English-language website, which carry news items. It is the English language website that a hacker disabled for several days. Why he disabled the English-language site is not clear, since that was read by English-language readers, not by Arabic readers. Hence all he did was render unavailable another point of view to people presumably on his own side of the conflict. This violated those readers' right of free access to information. The hacker became the self-appointed censors of his fellow citizens.

The action of the hackers in no way aided the war effort of the "Coalition of the Willing" and in fact hindered it by producing bad publicity and deflecting attention from where it belonged. Most importantly, even if it had helped rather than hindered the war effort, there is no justification for civilians to engage in cyber war, any more than there is justification for civilians to travel to the war zone to throw bombs or shoot soldiers. Such people are not covered by the rules of war, are not soldiers, and are rightly treated as spies, or terrorists, or criminals, depending on what they do.

The private attack would have been unethical even if mounted against Iraqi sites. When individuals and groups engage in acts of what are called cyber war, the acts are not acts of war but are either criminal acts or acts of terrorism. If this were not the case, then there would be no difference between combatants and civilians, and rules of war distinguishing the two would have no meaning. By implication, the civilian cyber-warrior makes all members of a nation combatants – a view that seems to be one adopted by some terrorist groups, but one that (to my knowledge) has not been ethically justified. If it were justified, then any group that could not achieve what it considered its justifiable goals by other means could legitimately declare all the populations of countries that it saw as its oppressors legitimate targets for attack and destruction. But for any group simply to declare that whole populations are combatants does not make them such.

A similar line of argument applies both to those who seek to attack the Internet Service Providers or websites of other nations whose views or policies they dislike and to people, called by some political hacktivists, who attempt to justify at least some intrusions against their own government – for instance in protest against what they consider an unjust war – as acts of legitimate civil disobedience. Because the hactivists do not act openly and publicly and do not wish to accept responsibility for their actions and the consequences thereof,[11] on its face such action falls under criminal trespass rather than under civil disobedience.

Finally, cyber terrorism is simply terrorism[12] by means of the computer and raises no new problems. To the extent that harm is done to innocent people as a result of the attacks, they are unethical. The fact that they are done by computer does not change the results and so does not change the morality of the action. Killing people by changing their medications via computer hacking or by placing misinformation on the screens of air traffic controllers is a means of killing people as surely as doing so directly. Not all cyber attacks by individuals against what they consider an enemy may result in loss of life. But if they do, they are comparable to terrorism via other means, and hence raise no new ethical issues. If the terrorism is state-supported, and if the harm rises to that which constitutes an act of war, then the doctrine of self-defense and the principles of *jus ad bellum* come into play, and the rules of *jus in bello* apply. If it is not state-supported terrorism, then it is not clear that the rules of just war theory apply. Defense of the principle of the immunity of civilians implies a sharp distinction between the notion of a just war and terrorism. Terrorists who target civilians by their actions place themselves out of consideration for justification by JWT.

4. CONCLUSION

The doctrine of the immunity of civilians has important implications for the current RMAs. I have argued not for jettisoning the doctrine as no longer relevant, but for strengthening its role in military planning and armament development. I proposed the two Principles of Smart Weapons Development, the Principle of Public Debate on Weapons of Mass Disruption, and the Principle of the Moral Unjustifiablity of Private Wars to augment the principle of the immunity of noncombatants. In general those with more advanced technology must both use more restraint and are more vulnerable to disruption. In all events, the war against terrorism should not cause the United States to sink to using unethical means of waging war or to losing the openness of the kind of society that its citizens so cherish. And this in turn requires that there be general and public discussion of the policies and moral guidelines governing new technologies and their wartime application under *jus in bello* that American citizens as a nation wish to accept and endorse in the post-September 11 world.[13]

NOTES

1. I shall not discuss here the issue of what constitutes a defensive war, or when a pre-emptive war may be justified as defensive. Nonetheless, it does not seem that a nation must wait to be invaded by an enemy army or to suffer a nuclear attack, if it is possible to avoid an imminent attack. The debate, of course, is when the threat becomes imminent and otherwise unavoidable.
2. An excellent guide to the literature on RMA is available at http://www.comw.org/rma/ (August 25, 2005).
3. Michael Walzer, *Just and Unjust Wars* (New York: Basic Books, 1977), p. 155.
4. Weapons manufacturers may complain that I have overlooked the rights of intellectual property, since armaments are commodities made and sold in a competitive market. Hence the cost of developing the new technology – which is considerable – tends to be not only a military secret but also a trade secret. Whether these are overridden by the earlier obligation to share the technology in order to reduce collateral damage is at least an issue to be considered.
5. Bradley Graham, "Bush Orders Guidelines for Cyber-Warfare: Rules for Attacking Enemy Computers Prepared as U.S. Weighs Iraq Options," *Washington Post*, February 7, 2003, p. 1 (also at <http://www.washingtonpost.com/ac2/wp-dyn/A38110-2003Feb6> (August 25, 2005)).
6. Greg Jaffe, "New Battle Theory Would Be Tested in an Iraq Invasion," *Wall Street Journal*, November 27, 2002, pp. A1, A7; Seth Schiesel, "Taking Aim at an Enemy's Chips," *New York Times*, Thursday, February 20, 2003, pp. E1, E5.
7. Barry C. Collin, "CyberTerrorism: From Virtual Darkness: New Weapons in a Timeless Battle, at <http://www.nici.org/Research/Pubs/98-5.htm> (August 25, 2005), writes: "Recently, the Defense Information Systems Agency ("DISA") reported over a quarter of a million hacks into government systems, with perhaps a third of them being successful."
8. David Pace, Associated Press article, February 12, 2003, at <http://www.computercops.biz/article2125.html> (August 25, 2005).
9. Mick Inghram, "Al-Jazeera web site under attack from pro-war hackers," April 1, 2003, at <http://www.wsws.org/articles/2003/apr2003/jaza01.shtml> (July 15, 2005); Ted Bridis, "Hackers replace Al-Jazeera Web site with American flag," The Associated Press, March 27, 2003.
10. For a somewhat different analysis, see John Arquilla, "Can Information Warfare Ever Be Just?" *Ethics and Information Technology* 1 (1999), pp. 203–212.
11. See, for instance, Mark Manion and Abby Goodrum, "Terrorism and Civil Disobedience: Toward a Hacktivist Ethic," *Computers and Society* 30 (June 2000), pp. 14–19. Most such defenses require changing the conditions justifying civil disobedience and fail to justify the changes.

12. See, FBI Denver Division at <http://denver.fbi.gov/inteterr.htm> (August 25, 2005): "There is no single definition of terrorism. The FBI defines terrorism as, "the unlawful use of force or violence against persons or property to intimidate or coerce a Government, the civilian population, or any segment thereof, in furtherance of political or social objectives." The FBI further describes terrorism as either domestic or international, depending on the origin, base, and objectives of the terrorist organization. See also, Mark M.Pollitt, "CyberTerrorism: Fact or Fancy?" at <http://www.cs.georgetown.edu/~denning/infosec/pollitt.html> (August 25, 2005).
13. This chapter is based on a paper, "Post September 11: Computers, Ethics and War," presented as a keynote address at the Fifth International Conference on Computer Ethics-Philosophical Inquiry: Computer Ethics in the Post-September 11 World, Boston College, June 25–27, 2003. That paper appeared in *Ethics and Information Technology*, 5 (2004), pp. 183–190.

INDEX

Page numbers followed by *n* indicate notes.

A

Abu Ghraib Prison, 227, 238, 248*n*6, 252, 258–259, 262*n*29, 279, 290, 293–294
actus reus, 122
Afghanistan, 139, 144–149, 162*n*29, 163, 180, 191, 257, 290
Against Our Will, 276
aggression, 130, 159, 180, 259, 283, 304–305
Algeria, 256, 261*n*20
al-Harethi, Sinan, 139
Alighieri, Dante, 33
Al-Jazeera, 310–311, 313*n*9
al Qaeda, 105–106, 139–150, 158, 161, 163–164, 179, 191, 194, 196, 210, 253–254
Ambrose, 24
amoralism, 69
Annan, Kofi, 91–92, 94–95, 98, 103*n*2, 103*n*8
Annan Doctrine, 91
antiterrorist morality, 175
Aquinas, Thomas, 6, 25, 27
Argentina, 261*n*22
Argentinian Dirty War, 256
Arguing About War, 84
Aristide, Jean-Baptiste, 91
arms race, 16, 107–108, 110–111, 113, 302–303
Army Field Manual, 292–293
asymmetric warfare, 161, 306

atomic bomb, 66
atrocity paradigm, 282
Augustine, 6, 24–26, 250
aut dedere aut judicare, 206

B

Bagram Collection Point, 290
Bangladesh, 83, 277, 285*n*2
Beirut Airport, 137
belligerent rights, 132, 142, 148–149
Betts, Richard, 126
bin Laden, Osama, 141, 152*n*18, 163, 181, 194, 254*n*3
Bonet, Honoré, 26
Bosnia, 91, 102*n*1, 103*n*1, 277
Boyle, Joseph, 26
Brown, Chris, 126
Brownmiller, Susan, 276, 279, 285*n*2
Brussels Treaty, 28–29
Buchanan, Allen, 131, 202*n*2
Bush, President George W., 59, 121, 137, 140, 142–143, 160–161, 164, 171, 221, 232, 254*n*4, 293, 307

C

captured soldiers, 228
Card, Claudia, 278–279, 282
Central Intelligence Agency, 258
Challenge of Peace, The 25
Childress, James, 34

315

Churchill, Winston, 66–69
Cicero, 24
civilian, *see* noncombatant
Civil War, 28, 95, 98, 102, 174
Clausewitz, Carl von, 28
Coady, Tony, 179
coercion, 268
  preventive, 122–123
Cold War, 9, 84, 93, 105, 111, 304
collateral damage, 6, 11, 16, 41, 79, 175–176, 181–183, 250, 302–306
collective defense, 75
combatants, 6–7, 11, 28, 32, 41–42, 76–79, 163, 182, 281, 306
  enemy, 44–45, 143–148, 229, 274, 277, 291, 296
commonsense morality and terrorist acts, 176–177
communitarianism, *see* community
community, 45, 47, 49, 51, 213
  international, 85, 90, 92, 94–99, 102, 114, 217
  moral, 166–167
  value of, 50
competence de guerre, 28
confederative center, 83
consequentialism, 121, 124–131, 266; *see also* utilitarianism
conspiracy (in law), 113–115, 117, 122
Convention Against Torture, 221, 249
crimes against humanity, 12, 91, 94, 203–205, 209, 211–212, 214, 283
Croatia, 281
Crusades, 25–26, 31
cyber terrorism, 312

D

Dais, Eugene, 8–10, 17, 19, 105
Darfur, 94, 277
Decretists, 25
De George, Richard, 16–17, 301
De Jure Belli Ac Pacis, 222
deontology, 122–125, 129–131

Derrida, Jacques, 33
Dershowitz, Alan, 235, 249, 252, 259
detainees, 290–293, 295–297
deterrence, 35, 125, 128, 189, 304
Dinstein, Yoram, 19, 29, 140
directed energy weapons, 16, 301, 307–310
dirty hands, 51, 53
discrimination, principle of, 4, 6, 10–11, 16, 18, 25–26, 41–44, 114, 162, 164, 180–182, 281
divine law, 6, 24–26, 29
domestic analogy, 9, 122–123
Donvan, John, 64
double effect, principle of, 42–43, 180–182, 270, 303
double intention, 43–44, 182, 303, 307
Due Process Clause, 144
Duquette, David, 6–7, 10, 12, 17–18, 41

E

East Timor, 91–92, 96, 99–100, 103n5
economic sanctions, 80, 87n14, 107, 137
epistemology, 31
equity (in law), 8, 90, 96, 98–102
Erasmus, 33
ethics of war
  alternative, 30–36
  implications for terrorism, 175–182
ethnic cleansing, 7, 15, 80, 82, 85, 92, 99, 274, 277–281
Euripides, 297
European Union, 83–84, 93–94
extradition dilemma, 12, 205–208, 213, 215
extraterritorial jurisdiction, 203

F

failed states, 90–91, 98
fiduciary relationship, 227, 229–231
Finnis, John, 26

first strike, protective right of, 9, 109, 115–118
forced choices and torture, 242–243
forced prostitution, 279
freedom fighters, 171*n*, 174
French Revolution, 28
Fromkin, David, 110

G

Gandhi, Mohandas, 32
Gap, Ri Pyong, 164
Gaudium et Spes, 25
Geneva Conventions, 28–29, 103*n*2, 140, 146, 148, 151*n*14–151*n*15, 221, 232, 233*n*2, 257, 262*n*29, 291–292
  on torture, 21
  view on POWs, 231
genocidal rape, 279–280
genocide, 7–8, 12, 15, 23, 35, 80, 96, 98, 101, 203–205, 209, 211–212, 214, 273–274, 277–281; see also ethnic cleansing
  in Rwanda, 277
globalization, 4–5, 8, 33, 89–93, 101, 212
global pluralism, 84
Gödel's Proof, 53
Golash, Deirdre, 14, 16, 263
Goldstone, Richard, 92
Good Samaritan, 100–102
Gore, Al, 164
Gray, Marcia, 100
Gray v. Romeo, 99
Great Britain, 307
Grisez, Germain, 26
Grotius, Hugo, 6, 13, 25, 27, 228, 231
  on torture of slaves and POWs, 222–225
Grounding for the Metaphysics of Morals, 165
Guantanamo, 140, 144–149, 250, 254, 262*n*29, 290, 295, 296*n*

H

Habermas, Jürgen, 33
hacking, 310, 312
Hague Treaty, 28–29
Haiti, 91, 275
Hamdi v. Rumsfeld, 290
Harris, Arthur, 67–68
Hassan, Ziyad, 149
hate speech, 81
Hebrew Bible/Old Testament, 24
Hegemon Stability Theory, 105
Hersh, Seymour M., 290, 294
Hicks, David Matthew, 148
Himma, Kenneth Einar, 14, 16, 235
Hiroshima, 175
History of the Peloponesian Wars, 297
Hobbesian sovereign, 108
hostis humanis generis, 296
Hubbard, Patrick, 6–7, 59
humanitarian considerations, 224–225
humanitarian intervention, *see* intervention, humanitarian
humanitarian law, 149, 151*n*15, 232
humanitarian obligations and POWs, 229–232
humanity and torture, 221–232
human rights, 5–8, 13, 17, 42–43, 53, 60, 75–85, 89, 91–94, 97–101, 149–150, 163, 178, 200–201, 204, 209, 273–274, 278, 280–282, 284
Hume, David, 54

I

ICJ, *see* International Court of Justice
Idealism, 5, 23, 30–31, 33–34, 41
incapacitation, 158
incarceration, 236
  justification of, of prisoners, 247
independence thesis, 123–124
India, 83, 127, 277
individual rescue (in tort), 8, 90

innocentes, 26
insurgency, 23, 102, 161
International Court of Justice (ICJ), 96
International Covenant on Civil and Political Rights, 144, 221
international crimes, 203–204
International Criminal Court (ICC), 214, 221, 282, 290, 297
international law, 6, 9–10, 13, 18–19, 27–29, 33, 78, 83, 96–97, 100, 107, 113, 116–117, 138, 140–144, 150, 203–207, 211, 215, 216n3, 273, 311
International Monetary Fund, 107
international nonstate terrorism, 10
interrogation centers, 291, 293–295
interrogators, 256–258, 262n29
interventions
    humanitarian, 8, 75–86, 89–102
    preemptive, 158–160
    preventive, 9, 119–131, 158–160
Iraq, 99–101
Iraqi nuclear reactor, 130
Iraq war, 7, 63, 121, 227, 248n5, 250, 301, 309, 311
Israel, 96, 106, 130, 196–197, 202, 256, 260n14

J

Japan, 67, 177, 179, 254
John Paul II, Pope, 34
Johnson, James Turner, 24–25, 27, 34
John XXIII, Pope, 25–26
jus ad bellum (ius ad bellum), 4, 7–9, 15, 17, 30, 41, 108, 114, 119–123, 125, 142, 162, 283–284, 301, 304, 312
jus gentium (ius gentium), 27
jus in bello (ius in bello), 4, 24, 41–55, 110, 114, 123, 142, 162, 190–191, 281, 283, 301–302, 307, 312–313

jus post bellum, 114
Just and Unjust Wars, 27–28, 59–71
just cause, 4, 7, 9, 25, 41, 45–46, 64, 75, 112, 120–124, 129–130, 162, 224
just war, history of, 23–24, 80
    early modern paradigm, 26–28
    implications of, 34–36
    late hellenistic/early medieval paradigm, 24–25
    late modern/contemporary paradigm, 28–30
    medieval paradigm, 25–26
just war theory (JWT), 3–19, 24, 77, 79, 105–118, 121, 160–164, 180–182
    classical statement of, 25
    war rape's challenge to, 273–274, 281–285
JWT, *see* just war theory

K

Kant, Immanuel, 11–12, 33, 165–168, 307
Kantian constraints, 164–168
Karzai, President Hamed, 146
Kellogg–Briand Pact, 28–29
Kelly, Elizabeth, 280
Keohane, Robert, 131
King, Martin Luther, 32
Kinsley, Michael, 164
Kipnis, Ken, 15, 18, 289
Kosovo War, 7

L

Latin America, 91
Law of Peoples, 28
law of war
    detention of enemy combatants, 143–148
    targets in the war on terrorism, 142–143
laws of nations, 6, 29, 222

and POWs' torture, 224
leaders' role-responsibility, 64–66
League of Nations, 28–29
Lee, Steven P., 9–10, 119
Lee, Win-Chiat, 12, 203
legitimacy dilemma, 108, 111–114, 116–117
legitimate authority, 4, 8, 25, 83–84, 208
Levy, Jack, 119
liberalism, 249–259
liberal prohibitionist, 252–253
limited war, 3–4
Lincoln, Abraham, 28
Locke, John, 27, 166
Luban, David, 120, 126, 128, 191–192, 202n2, 249–259
Luther, Martin, 26, 32, 34

M

Machiavelli, 52
MacKinnon, Catharine, 276–277, 279
Macleod, Alistair, 11–12, 18, 187
MADRE, 278
Mandela, Nelson, 32
Martin, Rex, 8–10, 17, 19, 32, 75
mass rape, 15
May, Larry, 13–14, 16, 221
McMahan, Jeff, 124
McVeigh, Timothy, 210
mens rea, 122
microwave weapons, 307
Middle East, 9, 106, 112
militarism, 5, 23, 30–32
military commissions, 147, 294
military necessity, 13, 17–18, 27, 34, 43–44, 125, 221
military violence, 3, 5
Mill, John Stuart, 250
Miller, General Geoffrey, 293
Miller, Richard, 34
moral absolutism, 46
moral commonsense theory, 175–177, 181

moral freedom, 61
Morally Obligatory Smart Weapons Development, Principle of, 302, 304, 306–307
moral realism, 60
moral symmetries, 161
moral universalism, 11, 161–162
Moral Unjustifiablity of Private Computer Wars, Principle of the, 310
Mueller, John, 29
multilateralism, 107
Murnion, William, 5–6, 23
Murphy, Jeffrey, 266
mutual vulnerability of combatants, 76, 78–79

N

Nagel, Thomas, 53
Napoleonic wars, 28
Nathanson, Stephen, 11–12, 171
National Council of Catholic Bishops, 180
nationality, principle of, 203
NATO, 92, 103n1
natural law, 6, 25, 27, 29
Nazis, 64, 77–78, 179
Neuffer, Elizabeth, 279
noncombatant immunity, principle of, 41–45, 54, 173, 175–176, 178–179, 306; *see also jus in bello*
noncombatants, 27–28, 32, 41–43, 45, 51, 54, 75–76, 105, 110, 149, 156, 162, 173, 176, 189, 274, 281, 294, 301–302, 304–306
  terrorism and, 310–312
nonmilitary strategies, for fighting terrorism, 187, 189–201
normative justification, 82
nuclear pacifism, 34
nuclear terrorism, 14
nuclear weapons, 304, 308

O

O'Brien, Connor Cruise, 171
O'Brien, William, 162
O'Connell, Mary Ellen, 124, 127
O'Connor, Justice Sandra Day, 290
OGA, *see* other governmental agencies
ontology, 31
Orwell, George, 63, 257, 266, 270
other governmental agencies (OGA), 258

P

Pacem in Terris, 25
pacifism, 3–5, 18, 23, 30–34, 114
pain, 235–237, 250–251, 263–264, 269–270
Palestinians, 179, 196
patriot hackers, 310–311
Pax Britannica, 105
Peace of Westphalia, 27, 33, 166
Pentagon, 105
perfect terrorism, 9, 106, 110–112
Pinochet, Augusto, 204
pirates, 296
Pisan, Christine de, 26
political realism and terrorist acts, 175–176
POW, *see* prisoners of war
precedent effect, 127–128, 131
precision-guided munitions, 5
preemptive intervention, *see* intervention, preemptive
pretext argument, 127–128
preventive detention, 130–131
preventive first strike, 107, 114, 158–159
preventive intervention, *see* intervention, preventive
preventive military action, 189–191
preventive strikes, 107, 130
prisoners of war (POW), 13, 144–148, 179, 221–232, 290–293
humanitarian considerations for, 224–225
humanitarian obligations and, 229–232
proliferation, 5, 93, 304
proportionality, 4, 9, 43, 46, 114, 121, 124–130, 162–163, 266, 268–269, 307
protective right of first strike, 9, 109, 115–118
Public Debate on Weapons of Mass Disruption, Principle of, 307, 312
punishment
  disproportionate, 265
  legitimizing purposes of, 236
  retributive, 15, 266, 269
  in Western nations, 237

R

Ramsey, Paul, 24, 34
range-limited (unlimited) principles, 209–213
rape, 85, 256, 269; *see also* War rape
  in former Yugoslavia, a case study, 280–281
  genocidal, 279–280
  individual, 273, 276, 278, 282–283
  mass, 15, 273–285
  as weapon in war, 278
rationalist epistemology, 31
Rawls, John, 8, 19, 75–86
  supreme emergency, 75–76
  theory of just war, 75
Realism, 41–55, 59, 61–62, 69, 175–176
  moral, 60, 66, 68
reciprocity, 10, 138, 148–149
Reformation, 26, 31–32
regime change, 101, 109, 115–116, 124, 130
relational sovereignty, 8–9, 89, 92–95

retributive punishment, 15, 266, 269
retributivist theories, 236
Revolution in Military Affairs (RMA), 5, 16, 301
rights of man, 28
Roberts, Adam, 221
Rodin, David, 19, 29
rogue states, 107–108, 121, 129
role-responsibility, 59, 64–66, 69
Roman law, 24, 26
Rousset, David, 255
rules, moral, 41, 51, 53–54
Rwanda, 91, 98, 204, 275, 277–278, 283
Rwanda tribunal, and war rape, 275, 278

S

Safire, William, 249
Saudi Arabia, 106
Schonsheck, Jonathan, 10, 12, 15, 155
School of the Americas, 255
Scholz, Sally, 15–16, 273
Schott, Robin May, 277, 284
Schumer, Charles, 249, 252
security dilemma, 107, 110–113, 116–117
self-defense, 7–8, 15, 24–25, 29, 35, 47, 49, 54, 75–79, 89, 107, 109, 112–114, 120–121, 139, 141–143, 173, 252, 309
and torture, 263–271
self-determination, 99–100
September 11 (9/11), 3, 63, 105–118, 137–142, 149, 171, 179–181, 191, 205–206, 263, 313
Serbia, 92, 274, 278, 280–281
Shklar, Judith, 250
Sidgwick, Henry, 43
simultaneous ostensible justification, 27
sliding scale, 45–46, 64
smart bombs, 16, 301–307

sole world superpower (SWS), 105–106, 109–118
Somalia, 91
sovereigns wars, 27
sovereignty, 5–9, 17–18, 27–28
relational, 89–102
Spain, 27, 106, 204, 206–207, 213, 215, 216n2, 216n7
Stacy, Helen, 8–9, 17, 89
Stanford Prison Experiment, 258–259
starvation, 80, 90, 96–99, 102
status quo ante, 113
stewardship relationships, 229–231
Stimson, Henry, 177
Suarez, Francisco, 25
suicide terrorists, 11, 160–161, 163–168, 169n5–169n6
and criminals, 156–157
and soldiers, 156
undeterrability of, 157
sui generis threat, 155
Summa Theologiae, 25
supreme emergency, 6–7, 11, 13, 17, 34, 41, 45–54, 48n, 75–76, 178–180, 183
SWS, *see* sole world superpower

T

Taliban, 139, 144–149, 156, 161, 163, 191
Teichman, Jenny, 34
Terra Incognita, 11, 15–16, 155–168, 295
territoriality, principle of, 203
terrorism, 10–12, 171–173
commonsense morality and, 176–177
ethics of war, 171–183
Islamic, 9, 156, 161, 197, 294
morally credible criticisms of, 182–183
noncombatants and, 310–312
perfect, 9, 105–118

terrorism (*Continued*)
   political realism and, 175–176
   prevention of, by military *vs.* non-military strategies, 189–191
   sponsor of, 191–192
   universal jurisdiction and, 203–215
   versions of ethics of war and their implications for, 175–182
   Walzer's theory and, 178–180
   war against, 59, 137–150, 187–201
terrorists, 9–11, 113–114, 155–168, 173–174
   acts, features of, 172–173
   and "freedom fighters," 173–174
   thwarting of, 161
Thucydides, 60, 297
ticking (time) bomb example, 13–14, 16, 235
   liberalism, torture and, 249–259
   permissibility of torture in, 237–246
tort law, 8, 96
torture, 13–16, 221–232, 235–247
   absolute immunity against, 236–238
   and confinement, 225–229
   efficacy of, 244–246
   forced choices and culpability, 242–243
   Hugo Grotius view on, of slaves and POWs, 222–225
   justification of permissibility of, 238–246
   liberalism, ticking bomb scenario and, 249–259
   limits on justification of, 246–247
   necessity of evidence in permissibility of, 239–240
   and POWs, 221–225
   and punishment, 237
   self-defense and, 263–271
   of soldiers, 225–229
   in ticking (time) bomb example, 237–238

torturers, 256
traditional just war theory and terrorist acts, 180–182
truck bombing, 137
Truman, Harry, 66–67, 177
Twin Towers, 105

U

Uniform Code of Military Justice, 274
United Nations Security Council, 89, 139
United Nations Security Council (UNSC), 89, 100, 139
United Nations (UN), 8, 83–85, 108, 139, 167, 217
   authorization, 29
   Charter, 89–92, 116
   peacekeepers, 284–285
United States, 9, 101, 206–207, 290
   anti-war protests in, 64
   criminal law of confinement in, 227
   Gross Domestic Product of, 167
   preventive interventions and, 127
   response to suicide terrorist attacks, 164–166
   response to terrorism, 10–11, 110, 138–150
   as sole world superpower, 105
   and torture, 15
universal jurisdiction, 203–215
   philosophical foundation of, 208–215
UNSC, *see* United Nations Security Council
utilitarianism, 48–50
   of extremity, 46

V

Vattel, Emerich de, 27
Vietnam War, 66
Vitoria, Francisco de, 6, 25, 27

W

Wahabism, 161
Waldron, Jeremy, 209
Walzer, Michael, 6–8, 11, 17–19, 41–55, 59–71, 75–86, 178–180
   conception of just warfare, 41
   doctrine of forfeit, 76–77
   Just and Unjust Wars, 47–48
   principle of "double effect," 43
   principle of supreme emergency, 49
   "realistic" model, 67
   theory of just war, 34
Walzer's practical morality, 60, 70
   limits on moral theory in the real world, 64–69
   in terms of western democratic states, 62–64
Walzer's theory and terrorist acts, 178–180
war, 75–86, 105–118, 137–150, 160–164, 175–183, 189, 221–232, 273–285
   against sponsor of terrorism, 191–192
   as legal status, 139–140
   as metaphor, 138–139
   moral reality of, 52, 62, 70
   rejection of reciprocity of, 148–149
   total, 28, 32
war convention, 41–42, 46, 178, 281
war crime, 67–68, 94, 156, 221, 273, 283–284
war ethics, deconstruction of alternative
   analysis of, 30–31
   historical description, 31–34
   implications of, 34–36
   metaethical axes of, 30

war on terrorism, 59, 63, 137, 139–143, 148–149, 150, 160–161, 171, 187–201, 254
   root causes of, 193–200
   functional assessment, 140–141
   positivist assessment, 140
   targets, 142–143
war rape, 15, 273–274
   causes of, 276–277
   identification of, 274–276
   and JWT, 281–285
   Rwanda tribunal and, 275, 278
   uses of, 277–280
war rights, 42, 46, 76
Weapons Development Assistance to Others, Principle of, 305
weapons of mass destruction, 5, 8–9, 23, 32, 101, 105, 121, 156, 161, 263, 309
Weigel, George, 24–25, 34
Westphalian Paradigm of Positive International Law (WPIL), 107–108
Weiner, Allen, 10, 12, 137
Williams, Bernard, 255
World Bank, 84, 93, 107
world hegemon, 105–106, 108–109, 112, 116–117
World Trade Organization, 84
World War I, 44
World War II, 11, 15, 28–29, 67, 75, 77–78, 80, 161, 175, 178, 254, 303, 309
WPIL, *see* Westphalian Paradigm of Positive International Law

Z

Zimbabwe, 97